THE
TIME TEAM
· GUIDE TO ·
THE HISTORY
OF BRITAIN

www.**rbooks**.co.uk

To Katie, Olivia, Elliot and Zoe – the next generation

THE
TIME TEAM
· GUIDE TO ·
THE HISTORY
OF BRITAIN

EVERYTHING YOU NEED TO KNOW
ABOUT BRITAIN'S PAST SINCE
650,000 BC

GENERAL EDITOR:
TIM TAYLOR

Books

CONTENTS

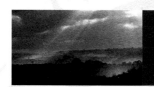

INTRODUCTION

IF YOU ASK a member of the general public to name the important events of British history and prehistory, they respond in a variety of different ways. My parents' generation carries a selection of events in their heads – the Fire of London, the Black Death, the princes in the Tower – often remembered with rhymes such as 'in 1492 Columbus sailed the ocean blue' or recalled as chanted lists of monarchs with their dates. This package comes complete with a series of semi-legendary events that includes kings up trees, boys on burning decks and various characters watching spiders and cakes and heroes laying down cloaks over puddles. If any prehistory is recalled, it is usually characterised by images of primitive 'Stone Age' people occupying caves.

When asked to recall their schooldays, many of the Time Team remembered history being taught as a rather perverse memory test – facts were drilled in with no context or relevance to contemporary life. This left a generation with a knowledge of history based on a sprinkling of random dates and a selection of charming if dubious folk memories. These recalled some of the key elements of our history, disassociated from the main reason for their importance. Henry VIII is renowned for his wives but not the Reformation, while Alfred is inevitably associated with his cakes, but not winning the battle that arguably created the English nation. Charles I is remembered for having climbed up a tree but not much else. Prehistory, if it was taught at all, was seen as a series of invasions and moments when we gratefully received input from the more classical Mediterranean influences.

In many cases, our children's generation has had the benefit of more informed and inspiring teachers, but they tend to have pieces of detailed information about discrete areas without knowing the wider context – the Second World War, Native Americans, the growth of towns in nineteenth-century Britain are taught in great detail, chosen, it would seem, on the whims of the current syllabus designers. There is no sense that one set of historical facts may be more important than another. 'Modern history' is taught because it appears to have a relevance to the present, but it has been at the expense of historical events of the past that had a much wider and more important influence on our lives today.

A sense of proportion in terms of length of time that certain events occupied relative to their perceived importance is also lacking. The Second World War, so dominant in our current interest in history, lasted just six years; the Romans, here for nearly 367 years, are rightly considered to be an important influence – and yet in prehistoric terms compared with events like the Palaeolithic, Mesolithic and Neolithic this is a very short period. For most of our existence as *Homo sapiens*, which makes up 98 per cent of our history and prehistory, we have been engaged in a couple of activities – hunting and gathering – with the dominant technology based on flint. It has been suggested that the hard-wiring in our brain developed from prehistoric times onwards and has mainly been associated with what we call Stone Age technology. The only record of this period we have is supplied by archaeology and it may well have been the perceived difficulty of finding and interpreting this evidence that has encouraged curriculum writers to favour the certainties of more recent events. However, archaeology has made great advances in our understanding of prehistory and so this vitally important area has received more attention in this book than is usually the case.

How we selected the events in this book

When we first set out to select Time Team's list of events we had to ask ourselves the question: 'What makes an event important and influential?' Historically, we've looked for those moments that really did make a difference. Some seem to be more obvious than others.

It's possible to suggest that without Alfred's defeat of Guthrum we might have all ended up Danish, and without Drake's defeat of the Armada we might have become a country dominated by the Spanish. Nelson's victory at Trafalgar arguably saved us from Napoleon, and Churchill's leadership in inspiring the defeat of Germany would also be included from this perspective, but what about the appearance of art and new technologies during the Upper Palaeolithic and the Neolithic Revolution? These were events that lasted tens of thousands of years and have arguably had a greater effect on our species.

Why is it important to recall these events? Why, in our modern world, is the past so important? It seems clear that a knowledge of history and prehistory can give us a sense of comfort when faced with the confusingly swift rate of change that characterises the modern world. It places us in the bigger scheme of things, in contrast to the rather ephemeral moments of our everyday life. We can, if we have the imagination, see ourselves as part of a grand continuum of events.

To a Time Team viewer who asks 'Why is this relevant to me?', the answer is more difficult and complex than a simple reference to the philosophical integrity of the subject. As a starting point we might look at our own experience. We are aware in our lives that it is useful to learn from previous actions. We carry memories of events from the past that can help us make decisions about how we act in the future. Certain activities produce positive outcomes while others bring more negative results. Looking at the past can also give us clues to why we behave like we do, and how we and other people behaved in response to events.

History can be seen as a collective memory of the outcome of various actions by the whole nation, which may help us to not repeat those that have led to trouble in the past. The notion that 'Those who fail to learn the lessons of history are doomed to repeat them' seems a reasonable position, although much of the stuff of history doesn't seem immediately applicable to most people. Large amounts of useless facts about the Corn Laws, obscure battles of Plantagenet kings and tedious streams of legislation from Victorian governments are not obviously relevant.

We are interested in those things that have relevance to us but most of us inhabit a world in which personal issues and transient fashions are more important than the wider political or social context of the present, let alone the past. In general we also lack experience of a wider cultural context, by and large believing that our Western lifestyle is the only way human beings conduct themselves. It might come as a surprise to some people that we haven't always behaved the way we do today and had the same priorities.

What might have happened

To understand some of the big events of the past requires a sense of what our lives would be like if these events hadn't happened. If Britain was still today a Catholic country, our culture would feel different. To experience what this means you need to appreciate the subtle differences that occur in Catholic countries – the power of the local priest, the conservative implications of the Catholic faith which does not sit comfortably with people who have grown up in the Church of England.

To understand what Magna Carta achieved, you have to have lived or had an experience of a place where a king or ruler's power is relatively less restrained. To appreciate the democratic politics of Britain, you need perhaps to have lived under a totalitarian regime like that of the Soviet Union in the recent past. To experience what it feels like to not have civil rights and recourse to the common law, you need to experience a country where the poor man is powerless in the face of the wealthy and powerful. A British 'bobby' may seem a bit threatening but until you've met the gun-toting, baton-wielding version that exists in some parts of the world, you won't know how benign they really are.

It is also true to say that if we don't know how we got to where we are now, with a country that actually has a rather sane balance of freedoms and constraints, we are less likely to be on the alert if people try to take it away from us. We may take our freedoms for granted, historically regarded as a precursor for losing them. If you take the typical British character, it's possible to see that its roots lie in a set of experiences different from other countries and which can be traced in our history. What might be seen as a tendency to enjoy sticking two fingers up to authority – politically, ecclesiastically and legally – is to an extent an expression of our traditional freedoms to do this. Similar actions in other countries would receive a very different response. Our legendary

belligerence and willingness to fight has its historic roots, as perhaps do more subtle traits like our tendency towards politeness.

The danger of forgetting history is that we may not realise that our freedoms, character, language and lifestyle have not occurred by chance. One way of preserving them is to have an understanding of how we arrived at where we are today, which may alert us to attempts by the great and powerful or by other nations to send us in another direction.

It is perhaps no coincidence that Churchill began his vast *History of the English-speaking Peoples* at a time when we were closest to losing the values it celebrates. But for a few airmen and a good dose of luck, we would have been living under a regime very different from what Auden called 'our dear old bag' of a democracy. Sadly you tend to take things for granted until they're threatened. Churchill thought it important to write down what were the key events from his perspective. He followed in the footsteps of the classical Roman writers and Bede, right down to the present-day authors who have attempted to bring some order to the past. Much of the hard work in any such overview is one's choice of what is important and one's confidence in the evidence. We have a great deal more evidence of our prehistoric history than was available to earlier authors and this is reflected in this book. In many ways we are also making personal choices.

How this book works

We all bring our personal prejudices and judgements to this selection and Time Team is no different. Phil provides a cold dose of the prehistoric perspective. He regards most historical events as rather ephemeral compared to the vast time scales and revolutionary events of prehistory. Guy is obviously keen on the importance of the Roman classical influence and Francis makes out a good case for the Bronze Age being critical.

Above: *Some of the key Time Team members looking for evidence of what happened when.*

Mick is an advocate of the medieval influence and the key place of religion, and Stewart brings a post-medieval perspective that focuses on events like the civil war, the industrial revolution and the history of the Empire. Helen finds it hard to think of a period not influenced by the Anglo-Saxons and our other experts are all concerned to make the case for their favourite period. We've asked them to nail their colours to the mast and select the key events and justify them. Why is a particular event important and how do we experience its influence today? We have, where possible, tried to find an archaeological link to the historical events.

Along the way we will also record what we regard as the key technological advances that punctuate the record of the past. People often have a sense of different materials and inventions defining an historic period. Stone, bronze and iron have traditionally been used to label various epochs, but we'll also be looking at how these and more recent technologies influence each period.

On Time Team shoots, one of the most frequent requests is to see Victor's drawing of 'what it looked like', so we've asked him to create a picture to summarise some of the main elements of each period. We hope this will act as an 'aide-mémoire' and we have also included a key object from each period for the same reason. We've restricted ourselves to 100 events in total, and we've short-listed 25 as 'signpost' events, which may be regarded as a good starting point for getting to grips with British prehistory and history.

So with Time Team's help, we hope this will be a definitive, if typically quirky and personally biased view of the key events of the past, placed in chronological order, selected by the team and our regular experts, some of the country's most knowledgeable archaeologists and historians. The story of our past will, we hope, be presented in a way that will make everyone a little more confident of what happened when and why it was important.

TIM TAYLOR

1 PALAEOLITHIC

TIME TEAM HAS excavated at two sites from the Palaeolithic age – Elvedon and Stanton Harcourt – and possibly a third if you count Cooper's Hole at Cheddar where a fairly small fragment of bone could have been dated to the Upper Palaeolithic. At Elvedon Andy Currant, our expert on all things Palaeolithic, described the process of dating events in the Palaeolithic as 'excitingly fluid' – a somewhat ironic reference to the way apparently clear schemes of chronology based on glacial periods or the development of flint technology are regularly undermined by new discoveries.

Twenty years ago, we thought that the oldest human remains in Britain were from Swanscombe (see page 23) and dated to 360,000–400,000 years ago, but finds from Boxgrove (see page 20) in the 1980s put that date back to around 500,000 years

ago, which was where we thought our oldest stone tools could be dated from until hand axes discovered at Happisburgh, Norfolk, turned out to be 650,000 years old. In the same way, we used to think we had a fairly straightforward set of glacial periods until we recently began to examine ice cores and deep sea sediments, which have revealed a much more complex picture.

As Mick Aston points out, finding any evidence from the Palaeolithic is tough: 'We are looking for a landscape that has often been obliterated by later glaciations. Entire river systems, like the one we found at Elvedon, can be diverted and glaciations move vast amounts of the landscape around – often leaving little trace of human presence.' One of the problems of dealing with the Palaeolithic is simply the vast period of time archaeologists have to contend with. So

before you approach the Palaeolithic, and this is crucially important to our story because it's here that you see the appearance of people that are anatomically like us, *Homo sapiens*, you have to take a deep breath and think about time.

The twentieth century with all its technical advances is the finishing point on a timeline on which we can begin to travel backwards. We can use certain great monuments and structures to mark the passage of time – our journey – going perhaps via statues of Victoria, Nelson's battleship, the Globe Theatre, the Tower of London, famous cathedrals and abbeys like Canterbury, the Sutton Hoo ship burial, until we finally find ourselves on Roman roads or looking at Hadrian's Wall and Roman Bath. This is a period of around 2000 years and yet it seems within our grasp, somehow comprehensible and yet in the grand scheme of

prehistory it is the blink of an eye. If our story of the occupation of Britain begins with the hominid bones (an earlier form of our species, from Boxgrove dated to 500,000 years ago), our last little bit of time, 2000 years, is less than half of one per cent – or to put it another way 250,000 blocks of our last 2000 years would fit into the time that divides us from the first human being to set foot in Britain.

Another way of looking at this length of time is to take a year – 365 days. Imagine you are forced to sit quietly in your home and watch it pass! Well, the last 2000 years would only take up a day and a half. The rest is prehistory. When we filmed on an early Palaeolithic site at Elvedon, Phil Harding used the analogy of a journey from Britain's far eastern coastline back to his home in Salisbury. It's only when he approached his own road and could see his house that he would enter the last 2000 years!

Phil is keen to point out that characterising the Palaeolithic as a period dominated by Ice Age hunters living in caves is incorrect and tends to reflect the limited survival of material in the archaeological records. Many of our Palaeolithic ancestors would have lived in small shelters, probably covered in skins. As the climate changed they would have moved to more favourable areas, and there are relatively few areas in Britain that offer large numbers of caves for occupation. I have always enjoyed the thought that on the A30 near Honiton, and at a site close to London's Trafalgar Square, archaeologists have found evidence of hippos who once basked in tropical swamps. As well as hand axes, which Phil will be looking at later, he is keen to emphasise two other pieces of Palaeolithic technology. One is Britain's oldest wooden implement, the famous wooden spear discovered at Clacton-on-Sea, Essex, in 1948, and the other is the wonderful antler hammers which were discovered at Boxgrove – the world's oldest non-stone tools.

At Elvedon we hoped to find evidence of the end of one glacial period, the Anglian, which Phil describes as 'the mother of all glaciations', and the beginning of an interglacial (warmer) period, the Hoxnian, which dated from 427,000 to 364,000 years ago. When the ice melts, it begins the process of life activity itself with micro-organisms creating material that forms the first soils; gradually this becomes populated by algae and eventually the first plants and trees. At Elvedon we found evidence of the next process which sees an increase in small mammals and fish, and it's in the later stages of this process that we get the first signs of flint tools used by hunters in this area.

At Stanton Harcourt we came across evidence of a different interglacial c180,000, where the site was occupied by 'mega-fauna'. We found the tusks and teeth of mammoths and elephants, and

scavenging carnivores like brown bears. The mammoth tusks were over 1.5m (5ft) in length and nearby finds of hand axes indicated that they had probably been butchered on the site. We also found proof of bison which probably roamed the plains of this area in huge herds, before gradually disappearing towards the end of the Palaeolithic.

The Upper Palaeolithic is a crucial episode in our evolution. It is here from 30,000–40,000 years ago that we see the appearance of *Homo sapiens* and an explosion in technology that involves the

production of blades and the appearance of what might be called 'art' – the engravings and carvings, some of which have just been found at Creswell Crags in Derbyshire (see page 30). During our time at Cheddar Gorge, we were able to discuss with Andy Currant the work he had done at Gough's Cave, which included finding evidence of the removal of soft body tissue from skeletons after death. It seems that towards the end of the Palaeolithic more elaborate burial practices emerged, including the deposition of flowers and

bone objects, evidence of which comes from the Paviland Cave site dated to around 26,000 years ago (see page 28).

Previous spread: *The captivatingly wild vista along the gorge at Cresswell Crags. The caves here have only recently given up their ephemeral traces of cave art.*

Above: *Careful and painstaking excavation at Elvedon, an ancient riverside site. Every grain of soil was sieved in the search for evidence from the pre-Hoxnian interglacial period of our development.*

PALAEOLITHIC IN DETAIL

IN WORLD TERMS, the Palaeolithic age begins nearly 3 million years ago, when the first stone tools were created in Africa. In Britain we date it to the period of our first stone tools, between 600,000 and 500,000 years ago. The people who brought these tools into Britain were not anatomically like us, belonging to an earlier form of the human species.

The family tree that leads to today's human species is a complicated, ephemeral structure. The spark that started advanced primates (*Australopithecines* or southern apes) developing larger brains and walking on two legs occurred 4.5 million years ago in Africa. Around 3 million years ago a burst of growth from these small, tough creatures enabled several branches of species to blossom, and for the next million years the African plains became the nursery for more advanced proto-humans to adapt and grow. Then, around 1 million years ago, *Homo erectus*, who came out of Africa, and *Homo heidelbergensis*, whose remains were found at Boxgrove (see page 20), stepped forth and travelled through Europe and Asia on a journey that was to populate many sites across the world.

Climate change

In this era, it's important that we understand the idea of climate change on a prehistoric scale. The Palaeolithic is divided into periods of great cold (glacials) and periods of warming (interglacials). These fluctuations used to be laid out in a regular pattern and given names based on their geological deposits. Our endless search for new evidence has altered our view of the climatic change, but the idea is that we had a climate that varied between extremes of cold and warm. These variations probably occurred over long periods, although the thaws were more rapid than the freezes.

There are two major sources of information on the climate – deep-sea sediment cores and cores from beneath the ice caps. When glaciers formed,

they altered the composition of water in oceans and this can be seen in a change in the chemistry of small creatures called *foraminifera*. During ice ages, a lighter isotope of oxygen, isotope 16, is locked in the ice and less of it can be seen in the remains of the *foraminifera*. During warmer periods it is released and the normal balance of isotope 16 resumes. Over thousands of years these creatures form layers of sediment and by sampling their remains and testing their isotope 16 level, some layers indicate ice ages and others warmer periods. The ice cores show a similar pattern, tracing differing layers that reflect the changes of sea chemistry. This pattern revealed a much subtler, more variable picture of climatic change than the first model, which proposed four main glaciations with five or six interglacials in between, during the Palaeolithic.

Life in the Palaeolithic

The ice ages were not only cold but had the effect of taking up a lot of ocean water. At various times in the prehistoric we were part of mainland Europe and hunters could travel overland from Spain and France to Britain, while at other times we were cut off. The archaeological record shows evidence of people living in both warm and cold periods, and the periods are distinguished by the flora and fauna that existed. To oversimplify, our ancestors would have been living at one stage in a climate like Siberia and pursuing woolly mammoths, and in another living in a climate like equatorial Africa and hunting hippos in swamps.

Above: *An aerial view of the Cresswell Crags gorge shows its interesting topography. It was through this sunken and protected landscape that some of our first artists walked.*

The important thing to remember is that when glaciers were on the advance they forced people out of Britain, although when they were less severe they allowed people to cross over from continental Europe. In the warmer periods, what we now call the English Channel increased in depth to become a permanent feature around 6000 years ago. At various periods the glaciations were so severe that there was probably no occupation of Britain at all. The period from 190,000 to 60,000 is one example. Glaciations also tend to destroy evidence of previous occupation, apart from deep within caves so we cannot be sure of the earlier archaeology.

Aware of the difficulty of interpretation and our distance from this ancient age, we start our journey through time with a handful of sites. With our look at Boxgrove, we get an intriguing glimpse of the earliest hominid remains known in Britain, a community leaving us few clues yet revealing a great skill in toolmaking. The evidence from Swanscombe uncovers people who used a variety of tools to aid survival in an environment shared with straight-tusked elephants and rhinoceros. Cave-dwelling is investigated at Pontnewydd where Neanderthals settled for seasonal hunting, and at Kents Cavern where *Homo sapiens sapiens* faced challenges for their underground safe haven from sabre-tooth tigers.

A developmental landmark is reached when we look at Paviland Cave – the site of an ancient burial revealing not only evidence for care among the prehistoric community but also of a cognitive horizon, humans starting to gain a spiritual system with thought of an afterlife. Finally we investigate the Upper Palaeolithic site at Creswell Crags which has rare evidence for Palaeolithic art in Britain. An etched horse's head on bone and a series of engravings indicate the presence of people who were beginning to think like us.

Understanding the environment

The environment is never far from any Palaeolithic site. It's a fundamental part of understanding the period as a whole. Over vast stretches of time the Palaeolithic period swung between extremes of temperature and weather as successive glaciations gradually ebbed and flowed over the landscape, causing the population to evacuate the country for periods. The moving ice sculpted the landscape, leaving many sites destroyed or buried underneath a modern landscape that no Palaeolithic person would recognise. Ancient marshlands or coastal seasonal settlements now lie in the depths of land-locked, gravel-laden quarries or under thousands of tons of accumulated silts and soils. Yet this ever-moving frontier of Britain was the chosen place for a titanic struggle, a fight for survival which witnessed the development of our species *Homo sapiens sapiens* from early hominids to people who were physically and mentally the same as us. This was a groundbreaking period when our ancestors shared their world with wild and dangerous animals in a country still periodically land-locked with the continent; this was our beginning.

Palaeolithic Chronology

This timeline gives you a quick, at-a-glance guide to what happened when in Britain in the Palaeolithic era, helping you to understand the order of events. We've also included, in orange type, some key events that happened elsewhere in the world.

Happisburg hand axe (see page 31)	**c650,000BP**
Palaeolithic pioneers – first hominid bones (Boxgrove, see page 20)	**c500,000BP**
Anglian glaciation (see page 22)	**c480,000BP**
Swanscombe and the Hoxnian Interglacial (see page 23)	**c400,000BP**
Elvedon and Barnham (flint knapping)	**c400,000BP**
Wolstonian glaciation	**c364,000BP**
Pontnewydd – evidence of Neanderthals in Britain (see page 24)	**c240,000BP**
Humans absent from Britain	**c190,000–60,000BP**
The Ipswichian Interglacial Period	**c126,000BP**
The Devensian Glacial Period	**c70,000BP**
World Event: Humans close to extinction due to 'volcanic winter'	c69,000BP
Homo sapiens sapiens remains at Kents Cavern (see page 26)	**c33,000BP**
World Event: Neanderthal extinction	c30,000BP
Paviland Cave Burial (see page 28)	**c26,000BP**
Late Upper Palaeolithic – Creswell Crags discoveries (see page 30)	**c14,000BP**

World Event: *Humans close to extinction due to 'volcanic winter'* Geological investigation indicates that the human race declined to a point where mere thousands survived in isolated tropical regions following the eruption of Mount Toba in Sumatra 70,000 years ago. The subsequent 'volcanic winter' lasted about six years and preceded 1000 years of the coldest ice age ever recorded. Put into perspective, the tracing of volcanic ash produced by Mount Toba across India suggests that 800 cubic km was displaced, while the eruption of Mount St Helens in 1980 produced only 0.2 cubic km. Cold-sensitive vegetation would have been destroyed, with severe damage to the species that survived. Volcanic eruptions near the Earth's equator cause more substantial cooling – the island of Sumatra lies only 12 degrees north of the equator, hence the devastation.

World Event: *Neanderthal extinction* *Homo sapiens neanderthalensis* or Neanderthal People disappeared during the Palaeolithic Era, around 30,000BC. Neanderthals were capable of primitive speech, were short in stature but a physically powerful species. Their formidable physical structure was a necessity given the harsh Ice Age environment, with their short, stocky bodies ideal for conserving heat. The Neanderthal diet comprised meat and they were probably skilled hunters working together to capture bison, auroch (a relative of contemporary cattle), deer, ox and so on. Neanderthals faced direct competition from early modern human beings (*Homo sapiens*) when they appeared in Europe for the first time approximately 40,000 years ago. The Neanderthals and humans were vying for the same resources and the former eventually lost out. Both species interacted but it is believed that modern humans eventually killed off the Neanderthals.

We are taking the view that dates before the Neolithic period should be BP (before the present). It's only when you get into the Neolithic that the BC dating system has any meaning.

HAND AXE

THE THING THAT makes hand axes so special was that they were made to the same pattern. There's nothing fancy about the design; basically it's a stone that has been flaked on both sides to make a regular shape, but it's that regular shape that makes it special. No two hand axes are exactly the same because every block of raw material is different, and to solve the problem of working the stone into the intended shape you need a well-developed brain. The fact that they are nearly always either tear-drop or oval means that the design was fixed in people's memory.

Everyone who made hand axes had learned from someone else and had remembered how to do it. Every time they made another hand axe, the knapper selected the raw material and visualised where the tool might lie in the stone. They listened to the ring that told them that the stone was good or the hollow rattle of a flawed piece, felt the stone in their hands and used their eyes to watch as the tool progressed. They may either have learned by observation or have used simple language to communicate.

Looking at these pioneering tools, it's possible to see other characteristics, including appreciation of symmetry and pride in workmanship. It's equally possible to observe bad workmanship, which probably left the knapper using the first bad language, but which demonstrates that they could become impatient just as we still do.

Hand axes were essentially butchery tools but must have been used for a million and one other jobs besides, like the Swiss Army Knife of that time. They were frequently made for a specific task, to carve up a carcass, but were abandoned once they had served their purpose; after all they could be easily replaced in 15 to 20 minutes.

Today we rarely find them where they were made or used; most are found in river gravel where they have been swept into the bed of the river from habitation sites on an adjacent bank. They are arguably more beautiful to look at now than when first made because they have often been stained an iron rich colour from minerals in the gravel.

Above: *This Acheulian hand axe represents not only a tool, but also a physical symbol of the cognitive thought that went into creating it.*

PALAEOLITHIC SETTLEMENTS

Victor's Palaeolithic drawing is set in a warmer period and the area has been occupied by *Homo sapiens*. Mega-fauna like elephant and mammoth still exist and they can be seen in the distance. The fundamental tool is the hand axe, but as this illustration is set in the later Palaeolithic, we can also see spears. In the cave a fire has been lit, although exactly when fire was first used is a difficult question to answer. The structure above the cave represents a shelter and emphasises the point that not all Palaeolithic people lived in caves.

The main animal in the foreground is a bear and many caves have revealed evidence of bears, including bones and teeth. At Kents Cavern bear's teeth were found dating from 500,000BP. It is possible that the animal had a ritual significance, but also would have provided rich meat, fur and other food. The wolf or hyena can be regarded as a scavenger. Some roots and tubers would have been gathered, although the diet was predominantly meat. It is likely that the group would have found a water source near the cave.

Hominids at Boxgrove

IN THE DEPTHS of a gravel extraction pit at Boxgrove, near Chichester in West Sussex, we have an archaeological site that belongs to one of the early pre-modern human species, *Homo heidelbergensis*, marking a critical stage in our development.

Here, some 500,000 years ago, our distant ancestors left traces of their daily lives which were sealed by the collapse of a cliff and sands, silts and gravels laid down by glacial action. Like a light in the darkness, Boxgrove leads us back through hundreds of thousands of years to our most distant past in Britain. As well as providing us with remarkable artefacts and environmental evidence, the site has revealed actual *Homo heidelbergensis* remains, examples of only a few known in Britain.

Above: *The cusp of a Homo heidelbergensis tooth discovered at Boxgrove. This example is well worn, indicating a tough diet, while others showed signs of grating against stone tools, possibly indicating the mouth was used like a vice for craftwork.*

A moment in time: the creation of a tool

At Boxgrove a chalk cliff dominates the site. At one time this was a barrier to tidal waters with a sandy beach at its foot. By 500,000BC, during a warmer interglacial stage, soils had collected, creating a flat freshwater grassland environment. The combination of chalk cliff and fresh water provided what we would probably consider a utopian base for our ancestors. The chalk cliff provided a copious supply of flint nodules from which to make tools, while the fresh water acted like a magnet for wildlife.

At some point in time a person knelt on the firm sandy soil and, using a worn antler hammer, knapped out a new ovate hand axe from a pre-selected flint nodule. Each strike would appear almost casual from years of experience, the axe closely examined after each blow and turned and weighed in the hand for feel and symmetry. This event in time wasn't just a person making a tool, it represented an amalgamation of calculated thought, awareness and skill.

The tool-making *Homo heidelbergensis* may have had enough awareness of his environment to choose a place where flint is naturally available close to prey and also developed the skill to cleverly work it, but more than just a purely practical animal, he also had the essence of a conscious mind, the linchpin of our humanity. His very actions gave us clues about how his mind worked. To carry a used antler hammer shows us that a useful tool was appreciated and not discarded once it had served its purpose. Retaining the tool shows us that *Homo heidelbergensis* knew that they would need it again, they had an awareness of a possible future event rather than just instinctively living in the moment like any other animal. The actual creation of a flint tool takes us even further.

If you shop in a supermarket for a cabbage you don't just grab any cabbage – you look at them all, decide which is of the best quality and the correct size for your needs, you may imagine what the cooked result will look like. This same thought process we take for granted as modern humans was happening 500,000 years ago at Boxgrove inside the head of our early ancestors. Before our flint knapper even started work he had to possess forward thought. The selection of a flint nodule was done with a mental picture of what the finished hand axe should be. This ability to imagine beyond his physical environment to a finished artefact yet to be made is a milestone in cognitive thought.

Archaeological evidence

Boxgrove's archaeological evidence is quite extraordinary in its preservation and is most exciting for the Palaeolithic archaeologist. Not only are the scattered spreads of flint flakes, the debris of tool manufacture, preserved *in situ* in manufacturing areas, but butchered animal remains and even *Homo heidelbergensis* remains have been found. Combined with dedicated environmental analysis, this has provided us with enough evidence to build a picture of life for the hominids who once occupied this freshwater grassland during a relatively warm interglacial period some half a million years ago.

Delicate, methodical excavation has reaped great rewards. Preserved in place just moments after being left, caught in time by the collapsing cliff, it's possible to see how the distribution of flakes have landed on the ground around the squatting flint knapper. The clear spaces between the debris betray where he knelt, knees apart, while hammering out a tool. It's even been possible to piece together flint flakes to recreate the original flint nodule, the cavity left within amounting to a negative 'mould' of the finished tool.

The animal remains show that *Homo heidelbergensis* existed on a varied diet ranging from lion and elephant to flounder fish and geese. Cut marks on the bones reveal a system of butchering carcases near the site, but it's the *Homo heidelbergensis* remains that constitute a most fantastic find. Not only do they show us what species occupied the area but they also represent the only known examples of non-cranial remains in the country (cranial remains have been found at Swanscombe and Pontnewydd, see pages 23 and 24).

Homo heidelbergensis teeth have been discovered which display tiny marks caused by grating against flint tools, perhaps a result of using the mouth to strip useful tendon strings from carcases during butchery, a method witnessed in modern ethnographic studies of hunting groups. The star find is a single tibia or shin bone, which has allowed the excavators to build a picture of this archaic hominid resembling a robust individual who stood at around 1.8m (5ft 8in) tall. A remarkable snapshot of the past, the finds of Boxgrove provide us with a fascinating insight to the lives and development of our early ancestors during this earliest phase of Britain's occupation.

PALAEOLITHIC c650,000–10,500BP

Boxgrove c500,000BP

MESOLITHIC

NEOLITHIC

BRONZE AGE

IRON AGE

ROMAN

ANGLO-SAXON

VIKING

NORMAN

MIDDLE AGES

TUDOR

STUART

GEORGIAN

VICTORIAN

MODERN

Anglian Glaciation

AROUND 480,000 YEARS ago the most monumental glaciation that Britain would ever experience started to occur. Following a warmer spell, known as the Cromerian interglacial, the Anglian glaciation gradually spread south as millions of tons of seawater were slowly turned to ice and incorporated into the colossal ice sheet. As the sea levels dropped, Britain once more became attached to the European land mass,

with the ice 'fuelling' the glacier, becoming kilometres thick. Grinding its way south, the ice sheet reached a line stretching roughly from London to Cardiff, making all land above completely inhospitable.

The fringes of the glacier were like huge plains of tundra with grasses and tough sedges breaking through the permafrost in a manner similar to the harsh Siberian landscape of today. Deer and horses, on the very limits of north-western Europe, were drawn to the vegetation and with them, during slightly warmer interstadial periods, were drawn the small bands of hunter-gatherers who relied on the migrating herds as their walking larders. East Anglia has some of the most fruitful deposits which have survived from this episode and it's after this region that the glacier is named.

Though later warmer geological phases would slowly reveal more of the landscape, and glaciers also periodically return to drive people and animals from Britain, the Anglian is the moment of our real beginning here, cold but survivable. A time when the land was shared with straight-tusked elephants, lions and rhinoceroses, and early humans lived precariously and dangerously on the edge of their known environment – the real beginning of what happened when. At no point would the ice again push so far south and as we entered the following Hoxnian interglacial (around 400,000 years ago) Britain truly flourished with an environment that was both inviting and suitable for habitation.

Left: This picture shows the lip of a glacier which fills a valley. The hills on either side have already been carved by previous glacial actions.

Swanscombe and the Hoxnian Interglacial

THE HOXNIAN INTERGLACIAL is the name given to a warm period that lasted from 427,000–364,000 years ago, between two ice ages. It was named after a well-known site in Suffolk, at the village of Hoxne where John Frere, the man often considered the father of British archaeology, made what was to become the greatest discovery of the time: that the Palaeolithic hand axes from Hoxne were earlier than the biblical Noah's Flood. He expressed his thoughts in a note he wrote on 22 June 1797 at the Society of Antiquaries, in London, where he said that the hand axes had been made by people 'who had not the use of metals' and lived in a very remote period 'even beyond that of the present world'. The plaque in the local church commemorating this event incorporates a hand axe specially made by Phil Harding.

The Hoxnian was a warm period, but the climate was probably quite uneven, with warmer and colder spells. In Britain the people of the time belonged to an ancestral form of modern humans, known in the past as 'Upright Man' or *Homo erectus*, as we would term them today, and *Homo heidelbergensis*. These people made tools in two traditions, known as Acheulian (after a site in France) and Clactonian, after the site at Clacton, in Essex. The Acheulian tools are mainly hand axes that were made by removing a series of flakes from a nodule of flint. The Clactonian tools were made from large flakes which were removed from a parent block of flint specifically for the purpose.

The best-known Hoxnian site is in a gravel quarry at Swanscombe in Kent where three fragments of a human skull were found in 1935,

1936 and 1955. The gravels occur in two distinct layers, termed the lower and the middle gravels. The lower gravels contain flint tools belonging to the Clactonian tradition, dating to 420,000–360,000 years ago. Tools from the middle gravels belong to the Acheulian tradition and are also Hoxnian. The three skull fragments were found in the upper parts of the middle gravels. Once considered to be a separate sub-species of human, the generally accepted current view is that this is an early example of a modern human being, but with strong Neanderthal characteristics.

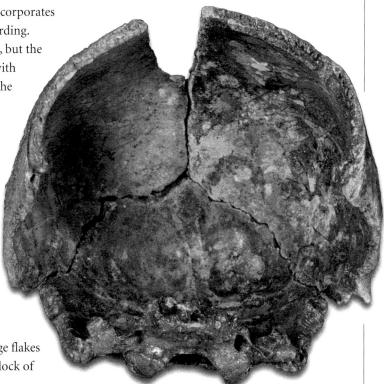

Above: *Three archaic cranial bones which formed the rear section of a skull from one of our early hominid ancestors who once lived in Swanscombe, Kent.*

Hominid Bones at Pontnewydd

EXCAVATIONS AT PONTNEWYDD Cave, in North Wales revealed teeth and lower jaw fragments from two individuals whose bones resembled those of the Neanderthals, a close cousin of modern humans. Although the bones from Pontnewydd have Neanderthal characteristics, their date (around 240,000 years ago) is very early indeed, so they may not in fact be 'pure' Neanderthals. The cave was excavated by Dr Stephen Aldhouse-Green of the National Museum of Wales, in Cardiff.

Aldhouse-Green has examined a number of Welsh caves and has found evidence for the presence of Palaeolithic people in or near them, but so far there is no convincing evidence for large-scale or permanent occupation in them. One reason for this might have been that other animals, such as bears and hyenas, chose the caves for themselves, so they were probably mainly used as lookout spots during hunting, or as overnight stopping-off points. Gnawing on prey bones and other tell-tale signs suggest that at least one site, Priory Farm Cave, above the Pembroke River, was a hyena's den. Research at Pontnewydd and other Welsh caves has shown that large areas of upland Britain could have been occupied during warmer phases of the Lower and Middle Palaeolithic, but all the archaeological evidence has been removed by subsequent glaciers.

Neanderthal people first appear about 230,000 years ago, but they would not have arrived in Britain until about 60,000 years ago, during the final stages of a cold period, and this probably reflects the fact that Britain lay close to the northern limit of their distribution. Pontnewydd Cave is currently the most north-westerly earlier Palaeolithic site in Europe. The countryside would have been very different to that of today. It was largely open and treeless, steppe-like, with huge expanses of grassy plain that extended through Europe and into Asia. In Britain people would mainly have hunted large mammals, such as mammoth, woolly rhinoceros, bear, spotted hyena, wolf and wild horse.

Recently a very exciting discovery at Lynford Quarry, in Norfolk, revealed an ancient river channel where a group of Neanderthal people hunted mammoth. The site has produced flint tools and hand axes of the Middle Palaeolithic

Mousterian tradition. The Mousterian 'culture' is normally closely linked to Neanderthal people. The site at Lynford Quarry is so far unique in Britain. It has revealed many mammoth bones, directly associated with hand axes that were used in the butchery of the carcases. The flint tools are in near-perfect condition and some clearly show evidence of damage when they were used. The flints include 66 hand axes together with flint flakes, but surprisingly not many cores or flake tools. This would suggest that this is a specialised collection of tools that were pre-prepared and were available when the business of butchery began. Very few of the tools show any signs of river or water abrasion, which would suggest that the majority were still *in situ* when found. The condition of the animal bone from the site suggests that while most beasts were probably killed nearby, a number (particularly skulls) were scavenged from further afield.

As for the fate of the Neanderthal race, we know from deposits that they lived side by side with modern humans for some 10,000 years, yet apart from sharing some distant cousin, they were essentially genetically different from modern humans. From this we can draw the conclusion that they didn't interbreed with our species and ultimately died out, possibly from a genetic disease. Unfortunately there is not enough evidence to conclude that they were lost in some kind of primitive genocidal war, though this is obviously a trait modern humans are capable of.

Left: *A stark reminder that archaic humans shared their environment with other fearsome animals. This skull, found in Pontnewydd Cave, belongs to a brown bear.*

Right: *The entrance to Pontnewydd Cave. The fine stone wall belongs to the 1940s and was erected when the site was used as an ammunition store during the Second World War. Today it protects the archaeology.*

Homo sapiens sapiens at Kents Cavern

THE ARRIVAL OF anatomically modern humans, *Homo sapiens* ('he who knows') and our domination as a species is by no means fully understood. The archaeological grounds of contention surround two theories: multi-regional evolution, where different species evolved into modern humans, and the 'out of Africa' theory, where modern humans evolved from a single group some 150,000 years ago and spread across the world, developing regional variations.

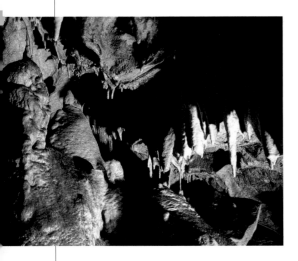

Above: *The cave environment. Safe from the ravages of existing outside, but also prime real estate desired by wild animals and our closest competition – Neanderthals.*

To approach this problem we use three main types of research: archaeology, to study the lives of our ancestors; palaeoanthropology, to examine the anatomy of ancient remains; and recent advances in DNA analysis. Although everyone has their own DNA 'fingerprint', the genetic trail should be traceable back to our ancient past. With only a handful of genetic differences between any two people on the planet it would appear that the 'out of Africa' theory with its common ancestor is the most likely.

Over the gigantic timescale of the Palaeolithic period the emergence of modern humans fills the final moments. As a species we followed in the footsteps of previous groups, journeying out of Africa just some 90,000–100,000 years ago and spreading across the globe to co-exist and compete with the last archaic humans (*Homo neanderthalensis*) in a battle for dominance and resources. The Neanderthals were a tough and clever species who had occupied Europe and Asia for over 100,000 years. It's now believed that Neanderthals and *Homo sapiens* share, at best, a kind of cousin relationship through the ancient family tree back to a common *Homo heidelbergensis* ancestor. It's also interesting to note that both species co-existed in the same environments. The term *Home sapiens neanderthalensis* given to the Neanderthals indicates their close relationship with *Homo sapiens*. In order to distinguish between the two, archaeologists often refer to the more modern form of *Homo sapiens* found at Kents Cavern in Devon as *Homo sapiens sapiens*.

A moment in time: *Homo sapiens* steps forward

The earliest emergence of modern humans in Britain, as recognised at Kents Cavern dating from 31,000BC and a few other sites, was the result of changing climate and environment. During the gradual warming, which signalled the end of the last ice age, *Homo sapiens* slowly spread across Europe in what appears to be seasonal expansion, most likely following herds of animals. The new species looked different and probably walked in a different way too. In contrast to the Neanderthal's stocky build, flat chinless face and elongated head, *Homo sapiens* was taller, less robust and had a rounded, slender face.

The debate continues as to whether the more intellectual and less well-built *Homo sapiens* became dominant through dedicated conflict between the species or through natural events such as a species-specific disease. Whatever the cause, genetics suggests that the vast differences between our DNA and that of Neanderthals mean they became extinct rather than absorbed into the human race through interbreeding. At Kents Cavern evidence has been found for both Neanderthal and *Homo sapiens* material, suggesting that both inhabited the cave at different times. This is an intriguing place which appears to have been witness to the overlapping struggle for survival between these two groups. As ever, it only takes a single fresh discovery to upset a stack of theories based on an ephemeral foundation. One such find is the Lagar Velho Boy, discovered in Portugal. He has the appearance of a modern human but displays some Neanderthal traits, suggesting he could be the result of interbreeding. This remains a highly contentious one-of-a-kind find.

Archaeological evidence

It's at this stage that we see early artwork and ornaments being more widely used as well as increasingly complicated economic systems, such as storage of food for leaner times and long-distance movement of resources such as stone and shells, possibly suggesting trade. Advances are made in the manufacture of tools and the way they are used. As well as hand axes, there is an increased use of blades and hafting, or fixing to a shaft, of the stone tools themselves. Evidence also suggests that spear throwers were first used around this time.

At Kents Cavern a fragment of jaw bone with four teeth has been identified as belonging to an anatomically modern human, *Homo sapiens sapiens* dating to over 30,000BC – evidence of one of the earliest modern humans in northern Europe. Kents Cavern appears to have served as a temporary base, used by this human at a time when Britain was being repopulated following a retreat of the ice sheet. As well as axes, leaf-shaped blades have been discovered which are both practical and pleasing to the eye. Small stubby 'shouldered' scrapers used for preparing animal skins are also common, which typify finds of the Upper Palaeolithic. Bone implements, including an awl for puncturing holes in leather and bone needles, highlight the possible use of tailoring skills with animal skins for clothing and boots, or maybe even temporary structures such as tents.

Little is known about the size of the population at this time. Tools from other sites of the same period look similar, possibly suggesting these were not the products of several pioneering independent groups who traded their artefacts, but belonged to the same community which travelled around the landscape using camps and caves whenever it suited their nomadic lifestyle.

PALAEOLITHIC c650,000–25,000BP

Homo sapiens appears c31,000BP

—— MESOLITHIC

—— NEOLITHIC

—— BRONZE AGE

—— IRON AGE

—— ROMAN

—— ANGLO-SAXON

—— VIKING

—— NORMAN

—— MIDDLE AGES

—— TUDOR

—— STUART

—— GEORGIAN

—— VICTORIAN

—— MODERN

Homo sapiens burial at Paviland Cave

THE SKELETON of the so-called Red Lady of Goat's Hole Cave, at Paviland on the Gower Peninsula of south-west Wales, is a most remarkable find. First uncovered in 1923 by the Victorian excavator, Dean William Buckland of Oxford, it represents an extremely important discovery which was largely misunderstood when it first came to light. Buckland theorised that the Red Lady was a Romano-Briton and a prostitute, and that the bones of extinct animals found around the skeleton were placed there by a biblical flood. He was wrong on all points. Following further examination we now have a much better understanding of the site and its importance. The Red 'Lady' is actually an early *Homo sapiens* man who was placed in a deliberate burial together with bone and shell grave goods. The red colour which dyes many of the bones comes from a deliberate sprinkling of red ochre presumably deposited over the body before the grave was filled.

The most incredible aspect of these remains is the actual act of burial itself. Here we can interpret that a dead person's loved ones placed them in the ground with their possessions and some unknown ceremony. Signs of an act of community, care and thoughts for the remains of the individual and their afterlife; some of the earliest archaeological indications in this country of our humanity. The site has recently been re-examined by archaeologist Dr Stephen Aldhouse-Green who has produced a detailed report. The Paviland body belonged to a man aged 25–30, about 1.74m (5ft 8in) tall and weighing about 73kg (11 stone). His build and weight were somewhat smaller than the average and radiocarbon analysis has shown that he walked the Gower landscape some 27,000 years ago.

The molecular biologist Brian Sykes, writing in Aldhouse-Green's report, describes how DNA extracted from the bones can be related to the

commonest ancestry still existing in Europe. This strongly suggests that the current population of Britain arrived here in the Palaeolithic, rather than spreading to these islands 7000 years ago with the arrival of Neolithic farmers from the European mainland, as previously thought. We know from the 'stable isotope values' of carbon and nitrogen measured during the process of making radio-carbon dates that his diet when the bones were being formed consisted in the most part of fish and seafood. Today the sea is close by Goat's Hole Cave,

but in the Upper Palaeolithic it was about 100km (60 miles) away. Of course fish could have been caught in rivers closer by, but such a fish-rich diet does suggest regular access to the sea, and with it a way of life involving a great deal of travel.

But there is more to the Paviland Cave than just the famous burial. The cave floor also produced numerous flint implements and the by-products of their manufacture, together with charcoal and ash, all of which were found in contexts that must pre-date the famous burial.

Above: The dramatic site of Paviland Cave, a home to many yet also the location of a burial of great significance.

Radiocarbon dates suggest that this earlier occupation only preceded the Red 'Lady' by some 3000 years and there is evidence, too, that the cave had been intermittently occupied both before and after that date. It was also used from time to time after the Red 'Lady' burial. This extended use would suggest that the Goat's Hole Cave was well known to people at the time and was most probably a place of special religious importance.

Earliest Art at Creswell Crags

TO UNDERSTAND WHAT was happening around 14,000 years ago, we must try to imagine life in Late Glacial times. In Britain the people belonged to a culture known as the Creswellian, which produced very distinctive flints that were smaller than those which had been made previously; some were specially suited for the preparation of hides and skins. Warm clothes would have been a priority for these people because at that time Britain was still linked to mainland Europe and the climate was very cold.

The Arctic tundra conditions had gradually been replaced by birch woodland. It would now seem that most Creswellian sites in Britain were occupied around 14,000 years ago, when the climate became briefly warmer. The main wild animals were horse and red deer, but there were also significant populations of mammoth, wild cattle, elk, wolf, fox, arctic fox and brown bear. Many of these are animals that move around. The wild horse and red deer moved through the landscape during the seasons, and the human population who depended on them would have had to be equally mobile if they were to take advantage of the times when their prey was vulnerable to attack, such as during foaling.

It used to be thought that the fine cave art found in Europe at sites like Lascaux, France, was not present in England, but a recent project

Above: What initially looks like a scratched rib fragment actually holds the image of a horse. The mane is incised along the top and the horse faces right.

carried out by specialists familiar with cave art has found clear evidence for art in Church Hole Cave on the Nottinghamshire side of the Creswell Crags of Derbyshire. Their first season of work showed that walls and ceiling of this cave had been decorated with a series of outlined carvings of a bison, a small herbivore, a headless horse and about a dozen fragmentary figures, including the faint painted representation of a horse's head.

The following year their discoveries were even more remarkable. They dispensed with the low-angled, powerful lighting needed to reveal light scratches and re-examined the cave's ceiling with natural or more diffuse light. This new technique revealed a series of low-relief sculptures. The first to be seen was a bird with a long curved beak, possibly an ibis or a flamingo. As work progressed they were able to identify other animals, including a bison, a bear-like animal and a complete red deer stag. Subsequently it was realised that the entire ceiling was covered with figures – so far more than 50 have been identified on the ceiling from a total of 90 in the cave. Thanks to the work of a small team of Spanish and English archaeologists, Church Hole Cave is now by far the richest site in Britain for Palaeolithic cave art.

WHEN ARCHAEOLOGISTS look at early tools, they need to have a clear definition of what constitutes an implement that has been deliberately manufactured. At its simplest level this can be a pebble that has been struck with another object to create an edge. It is not necessarily the case that there will be a simple technological progression from simpler tools to more complex. The technological horizons can be jumped, producing a mixture of simpler technologies existing alongside the more complex.

We asked Phil to give us a simplified guide to Palaeolithic flint technology. It begins with one of his favourite objects: a hand axe. This was the main tool for the majority of the Palaeolithic – the tool used to butcher mammoths and other game. One fascinating aspect of hand axes is the fact that for a long period of time, both in Britain and worldwide, they are remarkably similar in shape and proportions. They fall into two kinds of shape – one ovate and one pointed. It's as though our ancestors throughout the world all came up with a hand-axe shaped tool to meet their needs – a most remarkable uniformity. They do however vary considerably in size. Hand axes are the main tool associated with the site at Boxgrove. From this period we also find flakes and cores. Some of this technology is given the name Clactonian, named after the site of Clacton-on-Sea in Essex where archaeologists also found the wooden spear – the world's oldest wooden object. This find emphasises that many organic objects and tools existed alongside the flint technology.

The next change in technology is given the name Levallois, after the site in France. In this case a large piece of flint is prepared, then a large flake with a flattened surface struck off and the edges knapped. The original prepared flake is called a tortoiseshell flake and the critical aspect of its creation is that it exhibits the quality of predetermination. One piece is being prepared with the awareness that a second piece is going to be created. This also illustrates an element of ongoing development as far as the increased numbers of edges that can be obtained from a piece of flint. In Britain Levallois technology has been found in Bakers Hole, Kent, and from the Lion Tramway Cutting in Essex.

Towards the later part of the Palaeolithic comes the development of blade technology – a blade being a flake that is twice as long as it is wide and which produces the largest amount of 'edge' from a flint core. These slim blades can be broken into small pieces and retouched to produce a wide range of tools.

Above: *This beautiful ovate hand axe displays a wonderful symmetry. Found on a beach in Norfolk, this example is thought to date from over 500,000 years ago.*

2 MESOLITHIC

WHEN MICK ASTON and I talk about the Mesolithic, we often use the shorthand description 'hunting in a warmer climate' to describe its main features. These are key elements but it doesn't really do justice to what is a fascinating and often neglected period of our prehistory.

In 2004 we were lucky enough to record an episode of Time Team on a Mesolithic site at Goldcliff on the Severn Estuary near Bristol. We had a crash course in all aspects of the Mesolithic and were able to see one of the site's star attractions – the footprints of a Mesolithic family preserved in the river silts. Evidence from the site dated to around 6600BP and suggested that it was mainly used during the winter and spring. You can read about this site in detail on page 48.

One big difference you would have noticed if you'd looked around you at the Mesolithic landscape compared to the preceding Palaeolithic would have been the absence of the large mammals such as mammoths and hippos. Sometime at the end of the Palaeolithic there seems to have occurred what archaeologists call the 'death of the mega-fauna'. Whether due to climate change or increased efficiency of hunting methods, or a combination of the two, it seems that huge animals hunted by our Palaeolithic ancestors began to disappear. I like to imagine two hunters discussing the matter and one saying to the other 'We are going to have to run faster!' We know that most Mesolithic sites contain the bones of small animals like deer and horses, often with the signs of butchery in the form of cut marks on the surface of the bone. The warmer climate meant that a new range of plants and trees was able to grow in Britain and new methods of hunting and gathering had to be adopted.

There is some evidence that bows developed at this time – a weapon better suited to smaller swifter prey. When you think of more recent hunter-gatherer communities such as the Inuit in Alaska and the Sami in Finland, there is a relationship with animals which is not yet farming but what Francis Pryor and others call 'close herding'. Wild deer herds are managed in a way that adapts to their seasonal migrations and enables them to be rounded up and selectively culled for food, but they are still essentially wild. Observation of contemporary and recent hunter-gatherer groups can provide a useful insight into the past.

The exploitation of flint changed in the Mesolithic. After the Lower Palaeolithic hand axes and Upper Palaeolithic blades, a new and distinctive form of technology developed which used small knapped pieces of flint called microliths.

These could be used for a variety of purposes, often glued into wooden hafts or spear shafts. There is a continuing trend to getting more and more useful sharp edges out of a single piece of flint. Most major Mesolithic sites have evidence of flint working, and the microlith is one of the key diagnostic signs when looking at a site from this period.

Some of the microliths are tiny. I remember Phil Harding balancing a microlith on his finger at a site in Scotland at Finlaggan and being amazed that he had been able to spot it in the mud. These flints were used in a complex range of tools, which included drills and an early form of sickle. When glued into an arrow head, they also created a deadly barbed point which the animal could not easily loosen.

The Mesolithic hunters also created a range of tools from bone – an incredibly hard substance and capable of being formed into spear tips, digging tools and hammers, as well as the strange object archaeologists call a 'baton de commandement'. This piece of bone with a perforated eye at one end was recreated by Phil in the Cheddar dig in 1999 and, with the help of Andy Currant from the Natural History Museum, very effectively showed that one of its most useful purposes was as an extra lever to help pull in a length of rope, but Phil still favours regarding them as arrow straighteners.

Archaeological records

All this campsite activity can leave relatively little trace in the archaeological record, apart from the areas of flint-working. Archaeologists have made many studies of modern comparable groups and shown that once hunter-gatherers move on, evidence of their campsite quickly disappears.

John Wymer is a mate of Phil's and one of Britain's foremost field archaeologists and a specialist in the Mesolithic. His work at Thatcham has shown how careful archaeologists have to be to detect traces of a Mesolithic campsite and indeed any trace of settlement.

At Mount Sandel in Ireland, we have rare evidence of Mesolithic dwellings. Francis refers to them as 'tent-houses' which are made up of a series of poles – appearing to the archaeologists as a circular set of small postholes with a central hearth in some cases. They are about 5m (15ft) across and would probably have been covered by animal skins.

Star Carr, excavated by the late Sir Graham Clark, was for a long time Britain's top Mesolithic site and his excavation did a superb job in teasing out the detail of life in the period (see page 44). It not only showed areas of habitation but many less obvious aspects of Mesolithic life. Small finds included beads and further personal items. He was also able to show the presence of domesticated dogs, probably used to assist the hunters.

One of the most fascinating objects uncovered was a series of over 20 deer-skull fragments with horns still attached and which had been drilled to provide attachment points. Possibly worn on the head or body of hunters either as a disguise or part of a shamanic ritual, they belong to that mysterious group of archaeological objects that give us an insight into concerns beyond the purely practical.

Hunting and gathering

It's always tempting – particularly for those vegetarians amongst us! – to perhaps believe that our ancestors could have existed on a diet of tubers, roots and fruits gathered from the forest. The archaeological evidence from the Mesolithic contradicts this view. Mesolithic sites show that a lot of butchery went on – carcasses being cut up and bones crushed for the marrow. Isotopic analysis of skeletal remains show that meat was the primary food source. John Wymer makes the point that you would have to eat literally tons of seafood and plant protein in order to get the equivalent volume of food that can be derived from a deer carcass.

In addition, our Mesolithic ancestors were adept at using every element of a carcass – sinew for rope, fat for candle lights, horn for tools, skin for clothes – and on Time Team's visit to Goldcliff, Jackie Wood was able to show how fine bone needles were created from deer antler. It's likely that the Mesolithic in Britain holds even more surprises and many archaeologists regard it as one of the most fascinating areas for future study. It is towards the end of this period that we get the start of communities settling in one place for increasingly long periods of time and managing their resources, which will be an important element in the development of the Neolithic.

Previous page: Dawn spreads over a lush and vibrant countryside. The Mesolithic witnessed an environmental change which heralded a new age.

Right: The tough working environment of archaeologists is taken to extremes as dedicated diggers race against the tide to rescue faint traces of our Mesolithic past at Goldcliff.

MESOLITHIC IN DETAIL

THE MESOLITHIC PERIOD, or middle stone age, marks some important changes in the environment and the way people lived their lives in Britain. From the last glacial maximum (LGM) of the Upper Palaeolithic, which saw the ice sheets finally retreating around 15,000BP–10,000BP, Britain became populated once more by peoples from the warmer southern continent and from this point on, the country has been continuously occupied to the present day.

The Mesolithic is characterised by a general warming which saw the landscape transformed beyond recognition, from an inhospitable tundra with fluctuating periods of extreme cold to a flourishing woodland with temperatures very similar to those of today. With warmer soils and the establishment of mature trees came a change in lifestyle. The larger beasts of the hunt, such as mammoth and rhinoceros, became extinct in Britain while wild pigs, deer and horses began to become abundant and a staple food and resource. The familiar personal tool kits of the Palaeolithic also changed as a result of the requirements of the changing environment. New stone and bone tools developed, based on small blades and points, and hafted axes were made, producing the earliest attempts at carpentry.

This warmer environment also meant that people could live outside of caves (though some were still used), with sites near water being preferred. The ever-melting ice caps raised the sea level until it was no longer possible to walk across plains directly from what today would be London to Copenhagen in Denmark, the rising sea eventually making Britain an island around 8000 years ago.

The hunter-gatherers

The Mesolithic was the domain of the hunter-gatherer peoples – advanced groups who roamed the country in a nomadic fashion with minimal possessions, following migrating animals or taking advantage of seasonal plants. As a result, the evidence of the period is at times fleeting and ephemeral, which means the archaeologist has to be extremely careful and methodical when excavating these sites.

The problem is that little of the Mesolithic hunter-gatherer lifestyle leaves any trace for the archaeologist to find. Imagine a circus coming to town. They bring with them a large tent and a selection of smaller shelters, 50 performers and a ringmaster, plus 30 animals ranging from lions to elephants. In just a day they erect what amounts to a small settlement with everything they need from cooking facilities to toilets, and then every night for a week they create a show that draws hundreds of visitors. When they finally pack up and leave, hardly any archaeological trace is left of the event apart from a few stake-holes in the topsoil of the ground and a handful of discarded rubbish. This seasonal and constantly moving lifestyle epitomises Mesolithic life.

The fact that hunter-gatherer groups didn't use pottery (which is too fragile for regular transporting even if the technology had been known) and relied mostly on organic materials, which are easily lost from the archaeological record, compounds the problems of interpreting this phase in our development. However, the expanding population of Britain means that more archaeological sites from the Mesolithic, though scant of evidence, are known than of the earlier

Palaeolithic period and as a result a better picture of what life was like can be reconstructed.

Mesolithic life

Deadly and highly efficient bow-and-arrow technology became widely used at this time and irreversibly changed the way that hunting was carried out. Instead of luring and herding large animals into ambush-style killing zones, the new forest hunter relied on a more subtle approach akin to the levels of fieldcraft required by a good modern gamekeeper or soldier.

Ethnographic studies, where anthropologists study modern hunter-gatherer groups to see how they survived and related to each other, have shown us that in many ways the hunter-gatherer lives an ideal lifestyle. Extended family groups shared general chores and existed on a varied diet of seasonal plants, fish and meat. Vegetables, fruit, berries, nuts and seeds provided the staple foodstuffs, all collected by women, men and children. Meat would usually only be eaten after successful hunting trips and, without the twentieth-century marvel of the food-preserving fridge, animals were only killed when absolutely necessary. Living purely from the environment in this way, it's been established that many groups foraged and hunted for the day's food in the morning and then spent the afternoon and evening either pottering and doing recreational activities or generally relaxing.

This wonderful lifestyle existed up until some 6000 years ago, when we deliberately started to adopt farming methods and patterns of permanent settlement. Why the change from an almost utopian nomadic way of life to one of hard-labouring farmers? It appears that the Mesolithic was something of an epoch, or period of time when life was stable as the environment flourished. Humans rode the fruitful times and as a result became more successful and demanding. This could be one of the first indicators of an aspect of the human condition which involves us drawing too heavily on our natural resources. The expanding population may have started to tax our environment beyond what it could comfortably supply. An answer was to start to control nature to fit our demands with deliberate planting and harvesting of the plants we wanted and domestication of the animals we needed. However, before we reached this point, we lived as a clever and adventurous people with a freedom which is now lost.

The events and sites explored in this chapter which typify the period, have been chosen to highlight both the environmental and lifestyle changes of the time. We look at the rise in temperature and how that affected the plants, animals and people who lived off the land. We also look at the raising of sea levels, creating our island geography which has ultimately played an important part in many subsequent historical events. We further investigate who the Mesolithic peoples were through a fascinating array of discoveries which have given us fleeting glimpses of the art, society and even spiritual beliefs of these ancient folk.

Right: A barbed antler harpoon which was dragged up in the nets of a fishing vessel over the Leman and Ower Banks in 1938 – a reminder that many sites rest under the sea.

Mesolithic Chronology

This timeline gives you a quick, at-a-glance guide to what happened when in Britain in the Mesolithic era, helping you to understand the order of events. We've also included, in red type, some key events that happened elsewhere in the world.

World Event: 15,000BP Ruins of Tiahuanaco in Bolivian Andes, believed to be world's oldest city	15,000BP
Warming begins after this date (see page 42)	**c10,500BP**
The Flandrian Warm Period	**c8300BP**
Aveline's Hole Cemetery	**8000BP**
Dog domesticated	**8000BP**
Star Carr (see page 44)	**8000BP**
World Event: Kennewick Man	7300BP
Cheddar Man	**7100BP**
Mount Sandel, County Derry (see page 45)	**6500BP**
Goldcliff (see page 48)	**6600BP**
Britain becomes an island for the final time (see page 46)	**6500BP**
Oronsay shell middens (see page 50)	**5500BP**

We are taking the view that dates before the Neolithic period should be BP (before the present). It's only when you get into the Neolithic that the BC dating system has any meaning.

World Event: 15,000BP Ruins of Tiahuanaco in Bolivian Andes

Lying 3,800m (12,500ft) above sea level in the Bolivian Andes are the ruins of Tiahuanaco, believed by many to be the world's oldest city and thought to be the capital of the pre-Inca civilisation known as the Aymara – native South Americans that populated the Lake Titicaca basin in Peru and Bolivia. A Bolivian archaeologist named Arturo Posnansky began a 50-year study of these ruins in the early twentieth century. He considered it the 'Cradle of Civilisation', as he dated its construction to more than 17,000 years ago – long before any civilisation was believed to have existed. This has been regarded as more of a romantic than an orthodox notion but Posnansky used astronomical methodology to align one of the city's temples to show how the Earth oscillates on its axis. A complete cycle in which the Earth adjusts its tilt takes around 41,000 years and Posnansky believed that the alignment of temple ruins indicated a date around 15,000BP. Whether Tiahuanaco are the oldest ruins in the world is not conclusive but investigation continues.

World Event: Kennewick Man

In 1996, two people watching boat races on the Columbia River in Kennewick, Washington stumbled across a skull at the bottom of the river 3m (10ft) from the shore. The Kennewick coroner called in an independent archaeologist, who recovered a large portion of the skeleton, plus a serrated, leaf-shaped projectile partially healed in one of the pelvic bones. Initial study revealed that he was a 40–55 year-old male of a tall, slender build. He had suffered several wounds in addition to the projectile in the pelvis, including six compound-fractured ribs and damage to the left shoulder. The unusual light wear on the teeth belied the eating habits of more recent dwellers in the region indicating dependence on fish as a staple diet. A piece of bone was dated and implied that Kennewick Man died over 9000 years ago. The study was halted when the Native American Graves Protection and Repatriation Act ordered the termination of the project. Native Americans believed Kennewick Man to be an ancestor and campaigned for reburial. The remains were locked away until 2004 when the US Court of Appeal ruled in favour of scientific study.

BARBED SPEARHEAD

THE EARLY HUNTERS of the Mesolithic lived in a world of pine forests, lakes and rivers. They hunted a variety of animals, including red and roe deer, and were also expert fishermen, catching fish with lines and hooks, in traps made from basketry, and with barbed spearheads at the end of long handles.

Some spearheads could be made from small flint blades slotted and glued into bone shafts. Others were made from single pieces of bone (or antler), where the barbs were carved out of the bone. Spearheads made from bone and flint were intended to leave a bleeding wound and were probably used on quarry such as deer or wild horse. Sometimes these bone points were hafted like a harpoon as they allowed the wooden shaft to fall off, leaving the spearhead in the prey. As the beast tried to escape, the spearhead would brush against trees and shrubs and prevent the wound from clotting. The hunters would follow the trail of blood and kill the weakened animal. Smaller bone points could also be mounted as arrowheads; larger examples could be fixed to spears in pairs to make a double-headed fish spear, known as a leister. This fish spear is very effective when used against wriggling fish, such as eel.

Excavations at the famous Mesolithic hunting site on the edges of the now-vanished post-glacial Lake Pickering, at Star Carr in north Yorkshire, revealed about 180 carved bone spearheads. However, the best-known example came from a piece of waterlogged peat, known as 'moorlog'. Most remarkably, the block of moorlog was dredged off the seabed, over the Leman and Ower banks, 40km (25 miles) north-east of the north Norfolk coast in 1931. The moorlog was spotted by a member of the crew of the trawler *Colinda* while working in about 20 fathoms of water. It was very similar to many of the spearheads from Star Carr. It was 218mm (8¾in) long and in mint condition. One side had been deeply scored near the base, presumably to provide better grip for the lashing which secured it to the spear shaft for hunting. The peat in which it was found had formed in freshwater conditions. Recently the *Colinda*'s spearhead has been dated by radiocarbon and it turns out to have been made around 9500BC, somewhat earlier than Star Carr, in the closing years of the Ice Age. The *Colinda*'s spearhead is by no means unique – a number of dryland finds, mainly of Mesolithic and early Neolithic date, have been made at the extreme edge of the North Sea basin, both in England and on the continent. These finds demonstrate that dry ground was available beneath the fringes of the North Sea as recently as the fifth millennium BC.

Above: This flint flake has been enlarged to show the detail in its manufacture. The original is just under 3cm (1in) long and is a classic example of a Mesolithic microlith.

MESOLITHIC CAMP

This is one of our favourite pictures by Victor, based on a Time Team excavation at Goldcliff on the Avon – a site famous for its Mesolithic footprints which are represented by the family at the water's edge.

The climate here is warmer and the glaciations have ended. Deer have been hunted and we can see eel traps being emptied. It's from the Mesolithic that we get our first clear evidence of traps being used to catch fish and it's likely that at sites like this they would have played a major part in the diet. The spears and arrows used to hunt game would have been highly effective and used flint microliths that are so typical of this period.

The dog has possibly become trained to assist in hunting, although not being fully domesticated. In the background are some hunters killing a species of wild cattle, the auroch. A wide range of berries and fruits would have been gathered, including hazelnuts. This was probably not a permanent camp, but might have been a seasonal stopping-off point to exploit the local resources.

Climate Change

BEFORE THE GRADUAL change from the Palaeolithic to Mesolithic period, Britain was populated, and subsequently evacuated, on several occasions over some 500,000 years as the ever-present ice sheets of the northern glaciers ebbed and flowed as global temperatures fluctuated. As the temperature fell, the ice spread south, creating what are called stadial, or cool, inhospitable phases of a glaciation. Eventually, as temperatures rose, the ice retreated northwards and we experienced warmer or interstadial phases.

Above: The Biaowiea National Park in Poland, a remarkable environment which exists today yet displays many elements similar to the environment of a Mesolithic Britain.

During these warm and cold spells, the northern glacier continued its scouring movements as rock, caught under the massive ice sheet up to several kilometres thick, ground down the underlying bedrock, creating valleys, ridges and mounds of debris. Around 17,000 years ago we experienced the last glacial maximum from which the ice retreated and never returned, signalling the end of the Ice Age. Though a few fluctuations in temperature continued, we entered a stage of general warming, an interglacial stage called the Flandrian, which continues to this day.

A moment in time: the return of people

The Loch Lomond interstadial, or last really cold period, lasted for some 900 years and finally subsided around 10,000 years ago. The change from a cold tundra environment to a warm, thriving land with a covering of trees and an influx of other flora and fauna marks the beginning of our current era, a break from our cave-dwelling past. Without this warming, Britain would look similar to Siberia with a harsh landscape. In fact, studies of pollen types held within Mesolithic soils help us reconstruct the prehistoric environment and indicate that the environment of Biaowiea National Park in Poland today is comparable to the ecosystem that developed in Britain as the tundra warmed.

The initial changes in temperature allowed rich grasses and mosses to grow, which acted like a beacon for herds of deer and horses. As the animals migrated across northern Europe into the land-locked body of ground which only later would become our island, they were followed by the roaming groups of hunter-gatherers. These people were not that different from their

Palaeolithic predecessors, but they developed new technologies adapted to the environment, including blades and flint tools known as microliths. Tipped arrows and bows provided a mobile and powerful means of dispatching prey. These initial forays represented the gradual repopulation of our island.

Archaeological and environmental evidence

The archaeological and environmental evidence of this transition from Palaeolithic to Mesolithic is hard to identify. Most of the vast plains of the south east which would have been home to these nomadic people now rest under the North Sea. However, environmental studies have helped us piece together something of what happened on a geological and biological scale, while archaeology from surviving sites has identified some of the changes in material culture and helped interpret how we used to live.

Before Britain was an independent island, hunter-gatherers following herds and travelling great distances across continental Europe shared a common culture, and this allows us to compare fragmentary archaeological finds from Britain with more complete parallels discovered throughout Europe. For example, pine arrow shafts uncovered in Stellmoor, near Hamburg, Germany have helped us understand how Mesolithic arrows may have worked. Ingeniously, the shaft of the arrow is made in two parts. The microlith flint point is held within a section of shaft which is socketed and bound to the end of the main arrow shaft. On impact, the tip can easily break away, allowing the hunter to reuse the shaft if the prey is lost. The prolific manufacture of flint microliths has left us with a significant body of finds. Though their use is not entirely understood, it appears that fixing the small blades to a variety of wooden or antler shafts or handles with an organic glue allowed a range of tools to be made. Their manufacture often displays careful retouching by removing small chips, or pressure flakes, to create fine points.

The value of pollen analysis should also be highlighted as it adds greatly to the evidence for environmental change. The structure of pollen grains incorporates an almost indestructible outer shell with the pollen of each individual plant species bearing a specific shape. Careful examination of pollen types found in Mesolithic soil samples allows archaeologists to see with great accuracy what types of vegetation existed at the time.

Recent work by scientists has compared our ancient pollen and faunal evidence with that of Biaowiea National Park today, to try to identify the animals which would have co-existed with humans. It appears that pine and birch trees, together with mixed deciduous woodland, would have eventually covered over half of the country 7000 years ago, the rest dominated by a mixture of grassland, heaths and fens. Shrews, voles, weasels and mice existed in large numbers, while badgers, foxes and deer were also common. The more dangerous species were brown bears, wild boar and cats such as the lynx.

PALAEOLITHIC

MESOLITHIC c10,500–c5500BP

Climate Change c10,500BP

NEOLITHIC

BRONZE AGE

IRON AGE

ROMAN

ANGLO-SAXON

VIKING

NORMAN

MIDDLE AGES

TUDOR

STUART

GEORGIAN

VICTORIAN

MODERN

Mesolithic Campsite at Star Carr

TODAY THE FIELDS around Star Carr, 8km (5 miles) south of Scarborough, give no hint of the ancient landscape beneath them. The final retreat of the ice sheets at the end of the last Ice Age, around c10,500BC, left Britain a land of arctic tundra connected to mainland Europe. Over the next thousand years the climate warmed and animals and humans began to return. Eventually, pine and birch forests began to colonise Britain and animals such as deer, elk, wild cattle and boar appeared. The hunter-gatherers who had previously followed migrating reindeer herds adopted new hunting strategies in this woodland environment.

The landscape surrounding Star Carr was a mixture of bogs, lakes, scrub and pine woodland on the higher ground. Beside one lake hunter-gatherers established a summer camp. The site of this camp was discovered in 1949 and excavations exposed many hearths and other occupation material. It became the type site for the Mesolithic period and more recent excavations clarified the environmental background. Because the lake eventually turned into a peat bog, the preservation of flint work, animal bone, wood and environmental material was excellent.

To gain access to the water the Mesolithic hunters constructed a brushwood platform, which contains the earliest evidence for woodworking in Britain. Environmental evidence showed that the reeds around the lake had been burnt by these people, who were deliberately altering their environment to attract animals. The main food source was red deer, possibly hunted at the water's edge or in surrounding woodland, supplemented by elk, wild cattle and pig. No fish remains were recovered, suggesting either that fish were not eaten or that their bones had not survived. Over 80 deer carcasses were recovered, including a large quantity of antlers used to make tools.

Above: *One of the antler mantlet 'head dresses' discovered at Star Carr. Hunting camouflage or ritual costume? Probably the latter as the antlers have been closely cropped.*

One of the most interesting finds were several complete sets of antlers still attached to the skulls, one of which had holes drilled through it to mount as a head dress. This may have been used as a disguise during hunting or as a totem during ceremonies to help with the hunt. The flint work includes scrapers for preparing hides or tools, axes for woodworking and tiny microliths (blades of flint used as cutting tools). These microliths are a typical Mesolithic find and were mounted in wood with pine resin to make composite tools, such as arrowheads. The camp was repeatedly occupied over 300 years, as the evidence of many overlapping hearths and windbreaks or tents shows, possibly by the same band of hunter-gatherers.

The camp was only occupied in the spring and summer and at other times the group moved around to exploit different food resources to sustain them during the year. The discovery of a wooden paddle shows that they could row across lakes. The eventual abandonment of the camp can be linked to improving climatic conditions that encouraged woodland growth and probably contributed to the lake turning into a bog. The Mesolithic inhabitants of Star Carr had to adapt to a constantly changing environment, moving to new areas as the landscape changed around them.

Earliest Dwellings at Mount Sandel

THE SITE AT Mount Sandel, Co. Antrim, was excavated by Peter Woodman between 1973–77. The site is positioned close to the River Bann, on a 30m (100ft) high bluff or sandy bank that runs alongside the river. The excavations at Site One showed that the gap that separated the world of the Mesolithic hunter-gatherers and the very first Neolithic farmers was not as wide as was once believed. Meticulous excavations revealed the clearest evidence for tent-like houses formed on hoops of hazel or willow and probably covered with hides, skins, birch bark or light thatch.

The site has been dated by radiocarbon to about 6500BC, which is significantly later than Star Carr, but in certain respects it is quite similar. It is positioned near water in woods of birch and hazel but, unlike Star Carr, Woodman's excavations produced huge quantities of fish bones, of which salmon and sea trout were by far the most common. This provides an important clue to the time of year that the site would have been occupied. Both fish are migratory and enter rivers from the sea, to spawn in summer and autumn. This is the best time to catch them which was probably when the site was occupied. We do not know, however, where the inhabitants went for the rest of the year, although the nearby coast seems probable. Other evidence shows that the diet was not exclusively limited to salmon and sea trout. They also ate eel, pork from wild pig, various birds, including game birds, and hazelnuts.

Mount Sandel is principally famous for its lightweight houses, which are still among the oldest proven domestic structures in the British Isles. There were two types. Six examples of the first type were found, consisting of a roughly circular or oval arrangement of angled stake- or postholes, plus a doorway and often a central hearth. This lightweight house was probably built from curved or hooped poles covered with hides, and the average size was just over 5m (16ft) across, giving a floor area of about 30sq m (36sq yd).

The second type of house was more tent-like and about half the size of the hooped pole structures. It consists of four banana-shaped, shallow ditches or gullies arranged in a rough circle. Presumably these were dug to take the run-off from another type of tent-like structure. As there was no evidence for postholes, we must assume the framework did not require to be securely anchored, being structurally stable and able to shed all but the severest of gales. Maybe it was made from some form of heavy-duty basketry. In this instance the hearth was positioned outside, and opposite, the entranceway.

Both styles of structure are lightweight and entirely appropriate to people whose pattern of life requires regular, probably seasonal, movement through the landscape.

Above: *This reconstruction gives some idea of what Mesolithic dwellings may have looked like.*

Britain Becomes an Island

THE SAME GLOBAL environmental change that caused the general warming and retreat of the glaciers also resulted in a gradual raising of sea levels as glacial melt water flooded into the seas. Whereas once people and animals could walk directly across the plains from what would later be island Britain to the northern reaches of the European continent, a creeping water table slowly swallowed the land bridge under the North Sea and English Channel.

Above: *The coastline of northern Europe c15,000BP, before it changed to something closer to its present position c8500BP.*

Until the later advent of sea-going vessels, Britain remained cut off from the rest of the developing world. As a result, we confronted the challenges of managing our resources and adapted to our landscape in isolation. It's at this point that we start to see independent changes in the tools that we make, evidence of a curtailed nomadic range and an expansion in diet to encompass a greater reliance on fish and shellfish as our growing population adapted to island living. This physical separation not only represents a geological change but also signals the beginning of our own native population: the first Britons.

A moment in time: the last land bridge

The last land bridge linking us with Europe finally submerged around 8500BP. Not only had vast areas of hunting ground been lost, but in those final stages the backward and forward migration of people and animals must have ground to a halt. There must have been a few seasons of final change as the grassland turned to marsh and then the marshland disappeared, until there was just sea. Our climate became wetter, with the temperate conditions helping woodlands develop. The expanding natural larder meant that hunter-gatherers could survive with reduced ranges of movement, or catchment areas. While they still conducted a largely transient lifestyle, it appears that people could spend longer periods at given locations and this semi-permanence resulted in changes in the way people lived.

It's been hypothesised by archaeologists that waterside and coastal sites become more popular as fish and shellfish became a more important part of our diet. Of course, some coastal sites must have existed before we became an island, but their remains now sit at the bottom of the North Sea and at sites like Bouldner Cliff, on the Isle of Wight. This has been attested by fishing trawlers bringing in archaeological evidence with their nets, such as the antler harpoon 'caught' in 1931 off the Norfolk coast.

The tools appearing at this time are rarely found elsewhere in Europe, indicating that we may have lived our lives in a different way. The microlith range expands and the boom in Mesolithic flintwork hints at our expanding population. With family groups enlarging within this fruitful environment and spending more time at seasonal sites within reduced catchment areas, the first tentative signs of regional styles in tool manufacture begin to appear.

Archaeological evidence

The variety of microlith tools shows us that hunting styles were adopted to suit the changing environment. Set into wooden or bone shafts, flints provided sharp tips and barbs to make effective, lightweight spears and arrows, ideal in wooded territory. Axes were also produced which were adapted to create an adze, perfect for working and shaping cut wood into prepared timber – a new carpentry tool suited to the evolving forested landscape.

Sites such as Star Carr, North Yorkshire (see page 44), have also revealed grubbing mattocks, or picks, made from elk antler, shaped into a point and nibbled through with a hole to receive a shaft – a reminder that subsistence also came from digging root vegetables and grubs. Over-hunting would soon see the elk disappear, but deposits at transient sites indicate that a wide variety of animals soon filled their gap at the dinner table, such as red deer, fox and wild pig. Coastal sites such as Morton on Tay in Fife show us that seafood was consumed in massive quantities, as illustrated by large deposits of shells and fire hearths and iron pyrites (used for fire-lighting) betray a command of fire.

A number of intriguing fragments of wood possibly relating to boats and canoes tempt archaeologists to ponder further on questions of waterborne subsistence. The finds of bone and antler harpoon points, carved with a serrated edge, illustrate an artistic ability, while amber and shale beads are also known from several sites, such as Star Carr and Morton. These people had time to create such things and don't appear to have spent their lives continually living in the desperate struggle from hand to mouth.

The hunter-gatherer way of life continued for some 2500 years after we became an island. Compared to the Palaeolithic we have an abundance of evidence, yet the reality is that the lifestyles of the time have left little for us to see. One fact remains – these people worked their environment until it was either too hard pressed to sustain them or they found a sedentary lifestyle more appealing. From this point we see the beginnings of agriculture, pottery production and settlement which provide much archaeological evidence. But this Mesolithic stage, our middle stone age, provides us with our roots as an island and the beginning of our independence as a people.

PALAEOLITHIC

MESOLITHIC c10,500–c5500BP

Britain becomes an island c8500BP

NEOLITHIC

BRONZE AGE

IRON AGE

ROMAN

ANGLO-SAXON

VIKING

NORMAN

MIDDLE AGES

TUDOR

STUART

GEORGIAN

VICTORIAN

MODERN

Mesolithic Camp at Goldcliff

IN THE SUMMER of 2003 we had the unique opportunity to excavate at Goldcliff on the Severn Estuary. Professor Martin Bell from Reading University had been working in this fascinating landscape since directing the Goldcliff Project from 1991. Once a vast marshland, his studies showed how the landscape had been changed after Roman attempts to drain the levels, creating an environment packed with well-preserved archaeology. He invited us to join him with his ongoing investigations and it was a great opportunity for the team.

This was a fascinating site which covered a swathe of the foreshore, all the more exciting because we had to work with the ruthless tide. With just a small window of opportunity when the tide was out in the afternoon, we literally had to take the shore home with us to the incident room for excavation. Working closely with the team from Reading University, a novel method of surveying and removing squares of the ancient Mesolithic estuary shore, in what amounted to cake tins, enabled us to reconstruct areas of the site back on dry land and then carefully excavate them in our own time.

As ever with this distant period of archaeology, the people who sparsely populated the landscape left few clues of their existence. They didn't have permanent structures or use pottery, and their flint tool sets were comprised of minute remodelled chips and retouched flakes called microliths – notoriously easy to overlook. To help us build our picture of a Mesolithic Goldcliff, we conducted a full environmental survey, including an auger survey where soil cores were taken to identify how the landscape had changed over the millennia. Elbow deep in a drum of pumping water, we floated all the soil which came from the shore. This involves breaking down the soil over a

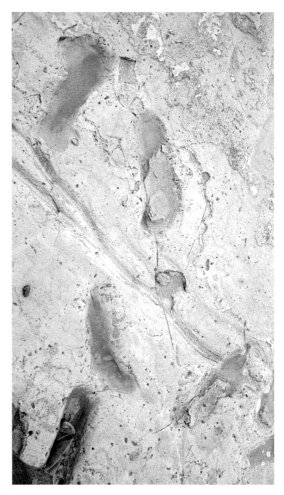

Above: *Captured in time, these footprints belonged to a Mesolithic person who walked the foreshore, or salt marsh as it was then, some 8000 years ago.*

sieving net with water. All the organic material floats to the top, to be collected and analysed. We discovered that the estuary was once much smaller and that the landscape around Goldcliff was akin to a reed swamp or salt marsh.

Goldcliff itself stood out as an island approximately 100m (330ft) across, which would have been covered with a copse-like collection of oak and hazel trees. Environmental evidence in the form of tiny carbonised raspberry and elderberry seeds also suggested that the island was used seasonally in the autumn. The discovery of microliths only added to our confirmation that Goldcliff was once a popular Mesolithic place, but the best was yet to come.

Time Team have found hundreds of buildings and thousands of artefacts over the years, but it's rare for any archaeologist to truly capture a moment in time. We were lucky enough to work with Rachel Scales who has discovered a number of human footprints which have been fossilised in the estuary silts. These Mesolithic 'signatures' belong to long-lost children and adults who walked across the shore to the island some 8000 years ago.

Below: *The foreshore at Goldcliff looks deceptively safe. The shallow silts soon disappear when the tide turns, a deadly change which sees incoming water travelling faster than you can run.*

Coastal Camps at Oronsay

THE SMALL ISLAND of Oronsay lies between the larger Isles of Mull and Jura, off the west coast of Scotland in the Atlantic Ocean. Around 7000BC the first hunter-gatherers visited the Scottish Isles, probably traversing the ocean in skin boats similar to coracles. Eventually, the rising sea levels caused by the retreat of the ice sheets stabilised as the continental shelf rose up. The coastal inundation that had severed Britain from mainland Europe began to slow down and around 5500BC the Isle of Oronsay started to assume its modern form. On the mainland deciduous mixed oak forest blanketed much of the landscape, a very different landscape to the more open environments of the earlier Mesolithic. This dense forest offered far fewer opportunities for hunting the large animals that earlier Mesolithic groups had been accustomed to and survival strategies had to change to cope with this new landscape.

Across Britain the evidence suggests a move away from the forests, to the more open uplands and especially to the coastal fringe, where shell middens mark the presence of hunter-gatherers. On Oronsay, five large shell middens have been found, consisting of hundreds of thousands of shells spread over tens of metres, often several metres deep. They were first excavated in the 1880s by Grieve and Bishop, who identified their human origins, and later in the 1940s Mobius identified the flint tools found as part of a unique Mesolithic culture typical of Western Scotland called 'Obanian'. Recent research excavations by Cambridge University have used environmental techniques to refine the dating and characterise the landscape in which they were created.

As with other coastal camps of the later Mesolithic, the Oronsay hunter-gatherers were subsisting on fishing, fowling and gathering vegetation from the shoreline. Occasionally there is evidence for the hunting of small deer or pigs, but on the whole their diet had changed to a marine-based economy.

The individual midden sites at Oronsay can be shown to have been seasonally occupied, usually for two or three months at a time, apparently in rotation. This is because the fish bones recovered have been studied and the ear bones, or 'otoliths', can be dated to different seasons, which shows when each camp was being occupied. It seems that either one or possibly several groups from the mainland were sailing out to the island and using it as a base for deep sea fishing expeditions all year round. The different locations on the coast indicate that they were chosen either for the shelter they offered from the prevailing winds or because specific migratory routes of fish shoals were being exploited.

Within one of the middens, known as Cnoc Coig, a circular setting of stakes was found – probably the remains of a tent or shelter with a central hearth that had been re-used many times. Within the layers of shells many other hearths and occupation surfaces were found, mixed with flint work, bone tools and personal items such as pierced cowry shells. Analysis of these living surfaces showed that alongside the habitation sites there were areas given over for the preparation and smoking of fish and the fabrication of bone and stone tools.

These coastal sites were occupied for a relatively short period, possibly less than one hundred years, before they became isolated inland on raised beaches as the island continued to rise up out of the ocean. These constantly changing environmental conditions probably contributed to the abandonment of the island as the Mesolithic fishermen moved on to the surrounding islands in search of new fishing grounds.

IN THE MESOLITHIC we see the technologies of the Upper Palaeolithic adapted to cope with life in a warmer environment where very large quarry, such as reindeer and mammoth, were replaced by smaller beasts such as deer and wild horse. The main change in flint technology was the introduction and widespread use of the so-called 'microlith'. Microliths were thumb- or fingernail-sized pieces of narrow, parallel-sided flint blades used to form components of composite tools and weapons. They were produced in a variety of rectangular or triangular shapes and were slotted into bone or antler spearheads to form barbed cutting edges. They could also be mounted on arrow shafts to form either a sharp point or a broad cutting edge, to leave a bleeding wound.

The first bows are found in the Mesolithic, although their origins possibly lie in the final years of the Palaeolithic. The bow had a revolutionary effect on the hunting of smaller, more mobile prey. Fishing became very important in the Mesolithic and this required vital technological advances, including the development of dug-out canoes, known as logboats, and paddles. With the introduction of boats woodworking becomes more sophisticated. The first axes (the earlier Palaeolithic hand axes were not used for felling trees) were made from flaked flint and given a cutting edge with a single sharp blow across the blade. Mesolithic technologies involved the joining together of different elements of a composite tool or weapon, and the watertight joining of wood to wood, as found in certain types of logboat where a board is fitted across the vessel to form the stern.

The period also witnessed a flourishing of 'soft' technologies, the evidence for which only survives in waterlogged sites: new types of ropes and twines were developed, and the working of raw hide in both thongs and sheets (used to roof lightweight houses) improved. Pine resin was used for glues, and birch bark for watertight containers. The Mesolithic also sees the introduction of basketry, often used to make fish or eel traps.

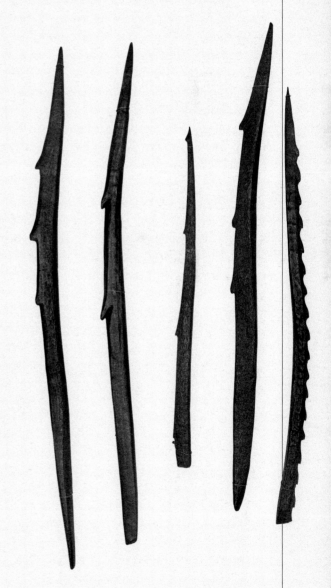

Above: *Reindeer antler points with incised and notched barbs. Over twenty of these were discovered at Star Carr.*

3 NEOLITHIC

PHIL IS ALWAYS DELIGHTED when we are on a Neolithic site, regarding it as 'the last period uncontaminated by metal working'! His connection with the Neolithic period as an archaeologist goes back to the time he dug at Grimes Graves, one of Britain's most important prehistoric flint mines.

In 2005 Time Team carried out its own excavations on a Neolithic site at Blackpatch in Sussex. We were there to look for evidence of a settlement that had been located near to a series of mines. On the final day we found what appeared to be a site where flint had been ritually deposited within the centre of a henge-like monument. Neolithic sites like mines are often looked at in isolation and as Time Team's Neolithic specialists Miles Russell and Francis Pryor pointed out, finding other evidence of

activity was important. It also illustrated that archaeology can sometimes reflect a way of looking at the world that is very different to our own. The people who had mined flint at Blackpatch had decided to bury flint in small shafts and hollows in the surrounding area. This may have been symbolically a way of replacing back into the earth what they were taking out in the mines. We also found pottery and bones deliberately placed in the earth possibly as an offering, a fascinating insight into the Neolithic culture. It is important to note that the advances in agriculture that we associate with the Neolithic were also accompanied by the appearance of henges, the exploitation of flint by the digging of mines, and the creation of causewayed enclosures. Thankfully for archaeologists on our digs, we also get the appearance of pottery.

Francis Pryor has had a great deal of experience digging Neolithic sites and it was his work at Etton (a causewayed enclosure site in Peterborough) that encouraged us to excavate a similar site nearby at Northborough in 2005. Here we were able to find the evidence for segmented ditches and causeways. Discoveries of Mildenhall pottery and flint dated the site to around 3500BC. There was also clear evidence of cattle being present on the site. The interior of the enclosure contained high levels of phosphate and we found both cattle bones and bones from aurochs – a relative of modern cattle. The difference in weight between the two species provides interesting evidence of the effect of domestication, which in general decreases the size of animals compared with those that live in the wild.

It is relatively rare to find evidence of field systems that date to the Neolithic in Britain. Jacqui Wood, who created a small Neolithic camp for us at Blackpatch, pointed out that recent research on bones from the early Neolithic point to a diet where plant foods played a relatively insignificant part in the diet.

Whenever we discuss the Neolithic period, Mick is always keen to emphasise that the old idea that the farming life allows more leisure time than the hunter-gatherer's existence is not sustainable. 'From ethnographic studies it's clear that hunter-gatherers have bursts of activity followed by long periods of inactivity. The idea that many of the new developments in the Neolithic came about because our ancestors suddenly had more time on their hands is misplaced.'

Another interesting idea that has recently caused some archaeologists to review their theories about the Neolithic has come from studies on the effect of Dutch Elm Disease. Jacqui Wood has pointed out that some of the clearance of woods that occurred in the Neolithic may have been caused by disease. There is a dramatic drop of pollen in the records obtained from deep peat deposits, and it now seems possible that this helped the process of forest clearance to create land for farming.

The main implement used for forest clearance was the polished flint axe, and at Blackpatch Phil was able to show that the extra time and effort required to produce a polished stone axe was well worth it (see page 59). The strengthened edge improved the tool's performance and, having watched Phil fell a tree using this kind of axe, it's obvious that they were an efficient implement. The way these axes were obtained raises some interesting questions about early trade.

The sources of the stone in Cornwall, Wales, the Lake District and Phil's favourite site at Tievebulliagh, Co. Antrim in Northern Ireland, as well as the flint mines like Grimes Graves, produced axes that are then found a considerable distance from their source. It's unclear if this represents people trading axes by carrying them to distant markets, or by buyers journeying to where they were being mined.

Neolithic settlements

Evidence of settlement in the Neolithic is relatively rare outside those locations where local circumstances led to homes being built in stone. One of Time Team's favourite sites is at Skara Brae on the Orkney mainland where you can look into a 'sitting room' of stone built in the Neolithic

around 3000BC (see page 62). What is startling about Skara Brae is the familiar appearance of this Neolithic home – there is a hearth, beds, cupboards and even a dressing table built of stone.

As Francis Pryor says, 'Our Neolithic ancestors were beginning to create a world with which we can have some connection, and at its head was the slow development of farming and the improvement of plant species and animal breeds that allowed this to happen'. It is this that makes the Neolithic such a fascinating period.

Previous spread: *The monument of Newgrange, the largest Neolithic passage tomb in Europe, dominates the surrounding landscape.*

Above: *Beaker pottery, with its classic bowl shape and extended collar, stands apart from the rougher wares of prehistory.*

Right: *One man in his element – Phil Harding in a Time Team trench, examining prehistoric archaeological finds.*

NEOLITHIC IN DETAIL

THE NEOLITHIC, or New Stone Age, takes us on an exciting journey, one that sees us adapt our environment and our lives into a new way of living. The period takes us through the struggle to create the first sustainable permanent settlements, the drama of the construction of fantastic earthwork monuments which dominated the landscapes (many still do today) and even the dawn of mass-production economics. After hundreds of thousands of years the hunter-gatherer lifestyle finally begins to be eclipsed by the adoption of agriculture which introduces the farmstead, the small self-sufficient settlement of structures, fields and livestock, and the first examples of one of the archaeologist's favourite dating finds – pottery.

The period as a whole is generally broken into three sub-periods: Early (4000–3300BC), Middle (3300–2900BC) and Later (2900–2200BC), each with their own stages of development and cultural change. The Early Neolithic sees the initial forays into the domestication of plants and animals and acts as a transition from the Mesolithic period. The Middle and Later Neolithic take us through the development of farming, monument building and a variety of pottery styles into a more mature lifestyle increasingly based on fixed settlement.

Our knowledge of the closing phase of the Mesolithic period, around 6500 years ago, is limited by a lack of evidence. The archaeological evidence of late transient occupation sites is almost non-existent, but as Francis Pryor points out, this lack of evidence doesn't mean nothing was happening, just that the way of living has left little archaeological trace. By contrast, the change to farming brings us a wealth of evidence in the form of artefacts (such as querns and sickles), postholes, rubbish pits and other remains. This sudden appearance of evidence once led archaeologists to believe that we had been on the receiving end of an invasion of farmers. Now, however, it's generally accepted that the concept and methods of farming were adopted by existing hunter-gatherer groups, and in all likelihood trade and small-scale immigration were responsible for

the appearance of non-native species of plants and the introduction of new breeds of animals, such as sheep. This was a gradual change which saw the native Mesolithic people slowly adopting a different lifestyle, a phenomenon which replaced hunter-gathering as a lifestyle and spread until settled farming became the normal way of life.

A new way of life

The adoption of a settled agricultural life invariably brings with it changes in society. Without movement to pastures new, a given landscape needs to be worked in order to provide enough resources for people to survive. We can imagine this as a group effort with each individual taking their part in the greater goal of producing enough food and materials to sustain the community. This inevitably leads to changes in the way a society operates and interacts, as groups need to balance their subsistence needs and resulting efforts under some kind of direction, hinting at the evolution of politics.

The Neolithic period also brings to light the first communal construction projects with the advent of large-scale earthworks of banks and ditches arranged to create intriguing monuments such as causewayed enclosures – rings of banks and ditches broken by multiple earthen bridges, or causeways. This defining of space for an unknown purpose has puzzled many archaeologists. The enclosures often appear in regional groups or as part of a landscape associated with other monuments or works which suggest a ritual landscape. They can have defined areas within and some contain unusual deposits, such as human remains or domestic items deliberately placed in the ground at extraordinary angles or in positions opposite to how they would be used in everyday life. These intriguing sites provide the physical evidence of an ancient belief system, or a spiritual awareness that was imagined by Neolithic peoples, which we shall probably never fully appreciate.

Religious activity

At this time the first burial mounds, or long barrows, appeared. These landmarks clearly signal a heritage and ownership of the landscape which is generations old. This is accompanied by further evidence of a ritual practice which involves human remains being used in ceremonial ways. The bones appear to have been periodically removed and replaced, in what has been interpreted as a form of ancestor worship, or some religion in which ancestors' remains played a central part.

The Later Neolithic brings the advent of circular ditch earthworks broken with just one or two entrances, known as henge monuments. Generally accepted as sites of ritual activity, henges are also considered as non-defensive because they are constructed with their banks on the outside of the ditch circle (in contrast to having the bank on the inside like a traditional defence, presenting an attacker with a ditch to traverse first). Of course there is every likelihood that henges are defensive but not in the traditional sense of a fort designed to protect people on the inside from attackers on the outside. Perhaps they were constructed in such a way as to protect the outside world from whatever was going on inside; a reverse protective

enclosure built in the safest way known at the time to harness whatever forces were believed to be assembled.

New technologies

The extent, quality and volume of archaeological evidence that the Neolithic gives us simply isn't matched by earlier periods. The material culture shows us how new technologies and tool types were cleverly exploited to get the most from their land.

Permanence of settlement made the use of pottery practical for the first time. The early forms of pottery vessels are well made with heavy coarse fillers, such as flint chippings, kneaded into the clay before modelling to assist the transfer of heat and provide even firing of the pot. Many examples also contain organic fillers such as grasses, while grain impressions in pottery tell us about the types of crops grown. The brittle nature of pottery makes it useless once broken and it's easily discarded – a bonus for the archaeologist as fragments of fired pottery can survive for thousands of years. The varying styles of pottery vessels are well known and datable, so the emergence of this prolific resource, of what amounts to a liberal scattering of 'time signatures', is welcomed with open arms when trying to date a prehistoric site.

Flint remains the basic material for making tools, but the Neolithic knapper emerges as a master of their craft. Delicate pressure flaking methods are used to create knives and fine points, while some wonderful leaf-shaped arrow heads and polished axes represent masterworks of the craft, the distribution of non-local flint across some parts of the country hinting at trade over long distances. In many ways the Neolithic period set the foundation for how we live today; in essence it marks the beginnings of settled society.

Neolithic Chronology

This timeline gives you a quick, at-a-glance guide to what happened when in Britain in the Neolithic era, helping you to understand the order of events. We've also included, in red type, some key events that happened elsewhere in the world.

Neolithic Revolution – farming and domestication of animals. Eventual settlement Skara Brae (see page 62)	**c4000BC**
World event: Utah Villages	
Langdale axe factories (see page 64)	**c4000BC**
West Kennet long barrow (see page 65)	**c3800BC**
Hambledon Hill (causewayed enclosure) (see page 66)	**c3700BC**
Virulent strain of Dutch Elm disease wiped out thousands of elm trees (similar to events in twentieth century)	**c3200BC**
Passage graves – Newgrange (see page 67)	**c3200BC**
First phase of Stonehenge (see page 70)	**c3000BC**
Wooden henge – Stanton Drew	**c3000BC**
Avebury (see page 68)	**c3000BC**
First metal tools – the oldest bows found in England date from this period, eg Mere Heath Bow	**c2500BC**
World event: Egyptian Sphinx	c2500BC

World event: *Utah Villages*

In 2004 archaeologists revealed an excellently preserved window into ancient life in a remote canyon near East Carbon City in Utah. Hundreds of sites boasting stone pit houses, granaries and an abundance of artefacts were handed over for study by a ranch owner on whose land the remains stood. The rancher had kept this archaeological treasure a secret for over 50 years because he wanted it to remain untouched and free from looters. Deciding to cash in on the land to fund his retirement, Waldo Wilcox presented American archaeology with a unique opportunity to study the Fremont culture, a group of hunter-gatherers and farmers that existed in Utah up to 4500 years ago. The well-preserved villages revealed hundreds of rock art panels in various colours, some depicting human figures amongst animals. Arrowheads and pottery shards lay strewn across the site whilst some of the granaries were still full of grass seed and corn. Many of the sites have yet to be documented with the remains of settlements of the ancestors of Native American Indians spanning 19km (12 miles) along and up the sides of the canyon.

World event: *Egyptian Sphinx*

One of the most majestic and best-known monuments is The Great Sphinx at Giza in Egypt. Originally sculptured from a limestone outcrop, the Sphinx is 74m (240ft) long and stands at a height of 20m (65ft) with its construction dating back to the Third Millennium BC (a few years within the region of 2500BC). For most of its history, the Sphinx has been mostly covered in sand and has suffered from erosion with many attempts having been made to restore the figure over the years. It is probable that the builder was King Khafre, who also built the second largest of the three pyramids on the Giza plateau on the outskirts of Cairo. The body of the Sphinx shows a lion at rest whilst the head is probably based on the visage of King Khafre himself and it appears to be guarding the path to the three pyramids. Many Egyptian deities had animal attributes and the lion represented a place of entry and exit. The Great Sphinx influenced the production of further sphinxes with smaller models being buried with the dead to act as guardians and guides in the spirit world.

POLISHED AXE

WHEN THE FIRST Neolithic farmers started to colonise the landscape, they faced something of a dilemma – how to clear the natural woodland. To some extent this was not a large problem; the Mesolithic inhabitants had created clearings in the woodland on a regular basis by chopping down trees and by burning off the natural vegetation. But the Neolithic farmers needed more substantial timber to create ceremonial monuments, burial chambers and houses. It's possible that they avoided the task of felling trees and relied on wind-blown specimens or undermined the root systems, but they still required efficient axes to prepare the timber.

They had inherited the first proper hafted woodworking axe, the 'tranchet' (pronounced tronchay) axe, from the Mesolithic people. This axe, made by 'chopping off' the end of an elongated, often triangular-sectioned block of flint, had a sharp, efficient edge, but the blade was fragile and not strong enough to remain sharp for long periods of time. So the Neolithic people developed an axe blade that was ground and polished to create an edge that was more durable.

The polished Neolithic axe is not a good friend of the flint knapper; the process of grinding the surface removes all traces of the skilled flaking process that precedes the grinding, yet the act of grinding creates an object that is beautiful to look at, an object of value and highly efficient as a woodworking tool, but at a cost. It takes, on average, between 15 and 20 hours of hard labour on an abrasive sandstone block, lubricated with water, to achieve this. Sometimes only the blade was polished but more often the entire axe was transformed, even though large parts of it would have remained unseen, inside the handle.

Once completed, the axe was slotted snugly into a hole carved in the end of the handle, itself a time-consuming task. A polished axe is nowhere near as efficient as a steel axe but was efficient for its time. It was used with short, downward blows that strike the tree at an acute angle, removing chips that split down the grain of the timber and create a pencil-like point at the base of the tree.

Axes were made all over Britain, some at specialist flint mine sites, the most famous being near Worthing on the South Downs of Sussex, while others were made from rocks other than flint, mainly from volcanic outcrops in Cornwall, North Wales and the Lake District. Some of these rocks could be flaked like flint but others had to be slowly pecked into shape. It is possible to identify the source of many of these axes, which were traded across Britain and were undoubtedly highly prized. Apart from woodworking, it is likely that they were used to signify wealth, exchanged for goods, as marriage dowries, ceremonial objects or as goodwill gestures between neighbouring tribes.

Above: *Though practical to use, this large polished axe dating to around 4000BC would have also represented an icon of status.*

NEOLITHIC LIFE

The main activity here is the mining of flint. This picture was created by Victor to illustrate the excavations we carried out at Blackpatch in 2005. Much of the flint from this site would have been converted into polished stone axes and these played a critical role in clearing the forests to create the sort of glade you see here. The Neolithic sees the beginning of agriculture and you can see a group of animals that have been gathered by the people.

The mining area is shown as a cut-away drawing. The two small galleries you can see would have been a lot lower down in order to reach the flint seams and, as shown by the man mining on the right, there would have only been crawling space in which to work. One of the main tools for mining was an antler pick.

Agriculture and Settlement

ONE OF THE MOST intriguing developments of the Neolithic is our step towards the domestication of crops and animals. The implications of large-scale farming and animal husbandry as seen in the Neolithic take us on a journey of settlement, economy and society which, once embarked upon, was never reversed.

Above: *The inside of a Neolithic house on Skara Brae, Stromness. The use of stone to make shelves, hearths and partitioned sleeping areas has ensured their survival.*

The theory that our hunter-gatherer population became too large for the land to support without farming has been questioned, with some archaeologists suggesting that Early Neolithic farmers were still relatively mobile. The fact remains, however, that a more sedentary trend was set when people began to manipulate nature's resources to suit their own needs.

The key is not to imagine the move to farming and settlement as the result of hunter-gatherers competing over a diminishing natural larder, but to think of it as a change in viewpoint where it was easier to make nature work for you rather than to tag alongside it. The hard work of clearing forest with flint axes and fire constituted an investment in the land which would be difficult to walk away from. It's equally hard to imagine the hunter readily abandoning spears and arrows in favour of the farmer's grubbing pick, so we should visualise a dual subsistence – a combination of farming, hunting and gathering.

The earliest Neolithic structures usually appear as single rectangular buildings, their postholes indicating a timber frame, while later settlements remain small affairs of family-unit farmsteads. The indications are that we settled into small groups spread across the country, yet the sense of wider community and relations between groups is provided by communal monuments and the shared belief systems this implies.

A moment in time: a farmstead at work

A typical scene of a Neolithic farmstead focused on a small, rectangular timber house built on a low stone foundation with a turf-covered roof. Sited within a sheltered area of a valley, the rich soils around the settlement would have been planted with emmer and einkorn wheat, cut with a short hand-scythe, while a few cattle and sheep wandered among grassland and trees. Smoke from the house roof would have betrayed the presence of a hearth within, and outside areas of activity of the compound would have been bounded by a wicker fence. An animal skin, stretched taut within a wooden frame, dried in the sun next to a rubbish pit which steamed under the heat. In front of the house a woman butchered the carcase of a small pig while under a lean-to byre, an old man rocked back and forth as he polished a stone axe against a sandstone slab. In front of the open-sided shelter, newly-made round-bottomed pots dried, awaiting an open fire kiln session.

This picture encapsulates the essence of the Neolithic home. The crops and animals inhabit areas which have been largely cleared of trees. This hard and laborious work has been undertaken by the family using hafted flint axes and controlled fires and the salvaged timber has been used to help construct the house. The animals are tended and protected by herding, while the crops are carefully nurtured to provide the best return.

Archaeological evidence

The archaeological evidence for Early Neolithic farming is limited compared to later periods, but it is much more varied than for earlier ones. It consists of hollows, pits and postholes connected by beam slots, or wall trenches as indications of buildings, such as at Fengate, Cambridgeshire, and collections of flint tools, pottery vessels and grain-processing quern stones from sites such as Windmill Hill in Wiltshire. Evidence for livestock husbandry takes the form of numerous animal remains of cattle, sheep and pigs commonly found at most sites, while analysis of the remains, such as those of cattle found at Hambledon Hill in Dorset (see page 66), indicate that the majority were female. This suggests that cattle were used as dairy herds as well as for meat.

The evidence for agriculture itself is preserved in spectacular style thanks to Later Neolithic peoples building burial mounds, thus inadvertently sealing the Early Neolithic ground surface beneath. At South Street, near Avebury, Wiltshire, the excavation of a barrow revealed hundreds of scores carved through the subsoil by an Early Neolithic plough. Evidence for cereal crops is gained not only from grain impressions preserved in pottery, but also from sites such as Aston on Trent in Derbyshire, where large storage pits dug into bedrock containing carbonised grains of emmer wheat were discovered.

The pottery from this phase tends to be constructed out of coils of clay and follows a standard bowl-shaped, round-bottomed form ideal for nestling in the embers of a fire. Repeated incised lines or notched rims, as well as being attractive, would have served to make the vessels more manageable when hot. Quantities of fire-cracked flint are also common finds. These feature a crazed surface and are known as pot-boilers – once heated in the fire, hot flints could be tossed into a pottery bowl to bring water to the boil.

PALAEOLITHIC

MESOLITHIC

NEOLITHIC c4000–2500BC

Agriculture and settlement c4000BC

BRONZE AGE

IRON AGE

ROMAN

ANGLO-SAXON

VIKING

NORMAN

MIDDLE AGES

TUDOR

STUART

GEORGIAN

VICTORIAN

MODERN AGE

The Langdale Axe Factories

CERTAIN FINE-GRAINED volcanic rocks were as highly prized as flint when it came to the manufacture of polished stone axes in the early Neolithic period. A programme of geological analyses which has allowed certain of these axes to be traced to their source has revealed a number of open-air stone axe 'factories', most of which are situated in western Britain. Perhaps the best known of these is at Langdale on the precipitous sides of the Pike o'Stickle, a near vertical cliff, high in the Lake District. The stone quarried at Langdale is unusual. It is very finely grained and when polished is distinctively greenish-grey in colour.

Most remarkably, the known distribution of Langdale greenstone axes does not concentrate around the quarry area. Instead, most are found on the other side of Britain in the region around the Humber and down through Lincolnshire to the Wash. Outside their main easterly focus of distribution, greenstone axes are known throughout the Midlands and East Anglia, western Wales and as far south as the Solent. This distribution tends to suggest that they were most prized on the eastern side of Britain and it is quite possible that they were traded further south from there. Very often greenstone axes or archers' wristguards are found in graves, or other ritual contexts, which suggests that in many instances their use was ceremonial rather than purely practical. Many axes also appear unused, which supports this view.

Archaeologists are paying increasing attention to what has been described as 'the archaeology of natural places' because it is apparent that certain spots were treated with greater respect than others during the Neolithic. The source near Preseli in south-west Wales that provided the celebrated bluestones for Stonehenge (see page 86) is a case in point. It is spectacular, high above the surrounding countryside atop a high cliff.

Above: *Pike o'Stickle, a towering summit of the Langdale Pikes which dominate the Lake District. This region of Cumbria was famed for its axe 'factories'.*

The Pike o'Stickle quarries are similar, but even more remote and difficult to reach.

The 'factory' at Langdale is on or close by a cliff and despite the fact that identical greenstone occurs in places much easier to reach nearby, the high cliff was the spot selected for the 'factory', which covered an area of some 20 hectares. The 'factory' produced axe rough-outs which were then polished off-site. There is some evidence that the quarry workers were not full-time specialists but came to work at the 'factory' from at least two separate settlements in the region. Their location high in the mountains would suggest that the places themselves were almost as important as the rock they contained. This further implies that the 'trade' in axes across Britain was not trade in the modern sense of the term. The axes themselves were special because they came from a special place. Most probably they were exchanged between influential people in different communities, perhaps as a way of acknowledging each other's prestige and importance.

Long Barrows at West Kennet

ONE OF THE major changes that marked the Neolithic from the Mesolithic in Britain was the appearance of major communal tombs, known as long barrows. These tombs were new to Britain and it has been suggested that their wedge-shaped plan was intended to echo the form of long rectangular houses which appear in mainland Europe from the early fourth millennium BC.

The mounds of long barrows were built from earth obtained from side ditches or quarries that flanked the mound. The wider end of the mound was the 'business end' where funeral ceremonies took place, often in a special forecourt. The end of the mound acted as a backdrop to the forecourt. In stone-built long barrows this backdrop or façade was a vertical wall, usually made from large stones, or megaliths. In timber long barrows, the forecourt façade was built from large posts, set edge-to-edge. At the centre of the façade was a doorway, sometimes partially concealed, leading into the interior of the tomb, which was usually partitioned into chambers, sometimes reached from a central passage. These chambers contained the bones of the dead.

The West Kennet long barrow lies within the extraordinary 'ritual landscape' that includes the great henge of Avebury and Silbury Hill, ancient Europe's largest man-made structure. West Kennet was built sometime after 3800BC during the earlier Neolithic and was in use at the same time as the nearby causewayed enclosure on Windmill Hill. It was excavated in 1955-6 to reveal a large façade built from massive stones. Behind the façade, a short entrance led into a central stone-built passage which gave access to five chambers, two on each side and a slightly larger one at its western end. Gaps between the huge stones were filled by drystone walling. The excavations revealed the remains of 46 individuals, but after examination it

became clear that only one of them was complete. The rest had been mixed together. In one instance a skeleton was only complete to the waist. Another was missing its skull. Research has also shown that others had been poorly recombined, mixing together the bones of different individuals. There is also evidence to suggest that the chambers were used to house different people – the majority of bodies in the main western chamber were adult males, while those in the south-east were younger and of both sexes. So West Kennet was not a 'tomb', as we understand it today, because the bones were not left to rest in peace. Skulls and long bones were removed and taken elsewhere – maybe to places like Windmill Hill where they would have been venerated as symbols of the ancestors.

The long barrow remained in regular use until about 3400BC, but it was not finally 'signed off' until sometime around 3000BC when the tomb and chambers were filled with soil or rubble and a second massive façade of sarsen boulders was erected to seal the entranceway permanently.

Above: *The massive stones which cover the entrance to West Kennet long barrow don't actually seal the internal chambers. You can still enter the monument today.*

Causewayed Enclosures

HAMBLEDON HILL IN Dorset is a fine example of a Neolithic causewayed enclosure. These sites, which flourished in the earlier part of the Neolithic, between 3700–3300BC, are among the earliest field monuments constructed in Britain. They acquired their name because of the strange-looking ditches which surround them. These ditches were dug in short lengths, separated by gaps known as causeways. When viewed from the air, the ditches and causeways seem to resemble strings of sausages. At Hambledon the causewayed enclosure is located on top of a steep and very prominent hill.

Causewayed enclosures (or 'camps' as they were then known) were first identified as a specific class of monument in the 1920s, following excavations at Windmill Hill, near Avebury in Wiltshire, by Alexander Keiller. The first account of causewayed camps was published by the distinguished Sussex archaeologist, Cecil Curwen, in 1930. His report mapped eight enclosures, seven of which were located on chalk downland. The one exception was found during gravel extractions at Abingdon in the Vale of the White Horse, in Berkshire. Apart from Abingdon and the most northerly one in Bedfordshire, all the others were on downland in Wessex and Sussex. After the Second World War the map was transformed by aerial photography, and today we know of 119 causewayed enclosures, the vast majority of which are found south of a line drawn from the Wash to the Severn Estuary. Many of these new sites are located on flat land or in low-lying river valleys. Recent work has also revealed a thin scatter of either certain or possible examples in Scotland, Anglesey, Ireland and the English Midlands.

Hambledon Hill is in fact crowned by a complex of causewayed enclosures that show an elaborate sequence of development. The hilltop

at Hambledon is fairly flat and rather sinuous in plan. The original, and main, enclosure was constructed at the centre of the hill. Somewhat later various outworks were added and these included another much smaller enclosure, known as the Stepleton enclosure, which was in turn constructed as part of an earthwork known as the Hanford-Stepleton outwork. The presence of a Neolithic long barrow just outside the main enclosure (but subsequently perhaps taken into the complex by the presumed western outwork) suggests that the hilltop was a special place.

It has proved difficult to be precise about the role of causewayed enclosures in Neolithic society. It used to be thought that they were sites of seasonal camps or short-lived settlements. Recent excavation has shown increasing evidence for ritual behaviour. At Hambledon, Roger Mercer's excavations revealed human skulls that had been placed upright on the floor of the ditches, close by the causeways. Similar finds, including fragments of skulls and round-based pottery imitations of skulls, have been found at the Cambridgeshire site at Etton in the Welland Valley.

Taken together, the evidence indicates a variety of roles. The sites were often located at possible boundary points between different peoples and landscapes. There is also much evidence for feasting and for funerary rites. Some sites include settlement debris which would suggest that people were living there; some were also probably used as neutral places for markets and ceremonial gift exchange. Many aspects of life seen in causewayed enclosures are also to be found in a more formal form in the henges that follow them. One of the latest examples of a possible causewayed enclosure is the first phase of the ditch that surrounds Stonehenge, which was dug shortly after 3000BC.

Megalithic Art at Newgrange

THE MOST REMARKABLE tombs of the Irish Neolithic are undoubtedly passage graves, and the most extraordinary of these are to be found in the great Bend of the Boyne, or *Brú na Bóinne*. It is such a fabulous site that we had to include it, even though it is not in Britain. The three major passage graves of *Brú na Bóinne* are at Newgrange, Knowth and Dowth. Newgrange and Knowth were excavated in the second half of the twentieth century and only Dowth remains uninvestigated in modern times, although it was mutilated by 'diggings' in the early nineteenth century. All three are surrounded by smaller passage graves and other monuments. Many archaeologists doubt whether the white wall that surrounds the mound was ever as high as it is today.

Newgrange sits at the very centre of the great bend in the Boyne, with Knowth and Dowth atop rising ground to the east and west. It would appear that the Bend in the Boyne had been largely cleared of forest cover by 3200BC when the great tombs were built and people in the area, whose round-houses have been found, earned their living through a mixture of livestock and arable farming.

To date, Knowth and Newgrange have revealed over 200 examples of Megalithic art – mainly geometric designs pecked in light relief on the surface of many of their stones. Newgrange was laid out and constructed around 3200BC. It was a long-lived tomb and probably continued to be regularly visited throughout the life of the ritual landscape around it (possibly as late as 2000BC). The huge mound is roughly circular and conceals a single passage grave which penetrates one third of the way into the barrow. Below the modern white revetment is a continuous kerb of 97 kerbstones, many of which have been decorated. In front of the passage, in the forecourt, is the entrance stone which is decorated with the finest example of Megalithic art in Ireland.

Deep within the mound, the end of the passage opens into the burial chamber, a hall-like open space whose corbelled roof soars 6m (20ft) above the floor of the main burial chamber. Three side-chambers open from the main chamber, one notably smaller than the other two. A similar lop-sided arrangement of chambers and a soaring corbelled vault is found at the end of the eastern passage at Knowth. Each side-chamber contained a large, decorated stone 'basin' which played an important role in the funerary rites. The entrance was sealed by a huge blocking stone in the Later Neolithic period and it remained closed until 1699.

Excavations revealed many fragments of human bone in the chamber floors, around three stone 'basins'. The most remarkable discovery was a small rectangular window-like opening, known as the 'roof box', which was carefully constructed above the lintel of the passage entranceway, facing south-east, towards the midwinter sunrise, allowing a shaft of sunlight to enter the tomb on that day.

Above: *Wonderful geometric spirals and swirls cover this stone at Newgrange. Their meaning may be forgotten, but the artwork still has great impact.*

The Construction of Avebury

AVEBURY IN WILTSHIRE is the second largest henge monument in Britain. Henges are only found in Britain and Ireland and consist of a circular ditch with a bank outside. This arrangement shows they were not defensive and were probably built as the sites of ceremonial rituals which were carried out within the area enclosed by the ditch and bank. Henges are entered by one or two entrances, which are opposite each other. Occasionally, at huge henge sites like Avebury, Mount Pleasant and Durrington Walls, there are four entrances which are usually more or less on the cardinal points of the compass.

Avebury, and Stonehenge a few miles south, are today both recognised as World Heritage Sites. Between them lie the military ranges of Salisbury Plain Training Area which contain some of the best preserved archaeological sites in Europe. Both Avebury and Stonehenge are famous not just for their huge stones but for the so-called 'ritual landscapes' in which they sit. These landscapes consist of other, smaller, henges, shrines and processional ways, plus a variety of barrows and burial sites. They are extremely important because they allow archaeologists to make intelligent guesses on the way that Neolithic and Bronze Age people regarded the worlds of the living and of the dead. They also allow us to chart the way that religion and ceremony changed through time. To judge from Avebury and Stonehenge, Britain in the late fourth and early third millennia BC possessed an extremely rich and diverse ceremonial tradition.

Avebury has been the subject of constant study and academic speculation, from the 1660s and continuing to the present day – when some of the earlier observations, once believed to have been too speculative, were subsequently confirmed as accurate. Avebury is possibly the finest and most complex henge site in Britain and was constructed in an area that had been of continuous religious significance since shortly after 4000BC. Like many other large ceremonial centres of Neolithic Britain, Avebury appears to have been under more or less continuous construction (between c3000–2200BC). If anything, the pace of change increased towards the latter part of this period.

Unlike Stonehenge which has one processional way, known as the Avenue, Avebury seems to have

Right: The sheer scale of the henge earthworks at Avebury can really be appreciated from the air. Dissected by modern roads, the standing stones here are considered equally as impressive as those at Stonehenge.

been approached by two, the Beckhampton Avenue to the west and the West Kennet Avenue to the east. Avebury itself consists of a huge ditch and bank with at least three circles of stones: a large ring of big stones around the inner lip of the enclosing ditch and two smaller rings towards the centre of the enclosure. There are two timber palisaded enclosures towards the River Kennet, to the west of Avebury, and other linked ritual sites include the Longstones Enclosure and the Sanctuary timber and stone circle on the west and east avenues, respectively. Silbury Hill, the largest ancient man-made mound in Europe (and beneath the grassy surface a complex site) was probably constructed in the latter part of the Avebury sequence.

The circle at Avebury is composed of massive boulders of sarsen quartzite sandstone, sourced on the nearby Marlborough Downs. They were not worked into shape like the stones at Stonehenge, and at first glance the circle appears less impressive than its neighbour. However, the stones at Avebury were carefully selected for their natural shape, and the circle consists of alternating column- and diamond-shaped stones. It is thought that these alternating shapes represent male and female aspects within the monument.

The First Stage of Stonehenge

TWO DISCOVERIES IN the past 40 years have produced evidence that the site where Stonehenge was later to be constructed had been sacred or special for a very long time. There are hints of such longevity elsewhere in Britain, but nowhere else are they as clear as here.

The evidence comes in the form of four mysterious pits which were found during the construction of the visitors' car park across the road that passes close to the stones. The first three were in a row and were found when the car park was built in 1966. The fourth was found about 100m (330ft) to the east when new visitor facilities were constructed in 1988. The pits had been dug to contain large pine posts of about 600–800mm (24–32in) in diameter and it is impossible to suggest that they served any practical purpose. Ritual or religion seems the only explanation. But what makes these post pits remarkable is their radiocarbon dates which range between 8500–7650BC, placing them firmly in the Mesolithic. The radiocarbon dates are supported by pollen analyses carried out on samples taken from the pits. These show an early post-glacial environment of open mixed pine and hazel woodland. This explains why the posts are made from pine, not oak.

We can only guess at what these huge posts signified, but we cannot deny their existence, nor their date. Most particularly we cannot deny their location. The long gap of some 4000 years between the car park posts and the earliest, non-stone phase of Stonehenge could probably be filled if the area around the stones was subject to large-scale, open-area excavation, but that is unlikely to happen because Stonehenge is both a World Heritage Site and also protected by British law. We do know, however, that the earliest ritual monuments and long barrows in the surrounding landscape were constructed around 4000BC, which narrows the gap by another millennium.

The use of the site where the stones now stand began around 3000BC with the digging of the large circular ditch and bank around the outside of the monument. This ditch was dug in 28 segments, which recalls the construction of causewayed enclosures, although they are not separated by distinct causeways. The outer ditch had two entranceways, of which the one that faced north-east was to remain the most important throughout the life of the site. Around the inside of the ditch was a bank but there was also a smaller one, known as a counterscarp bank, around the outside. A series of 56 postholes was dug around the inside of the internal bank. These are known as the Aubrey Holes; they are evenly spaced and do not leave gaps at either of the two entrances.

The second pre-stone phase lasted between about 2900–2400BC, in the Late Neolithic and Early Bronze Age. This phase sees a change in emphasis away from a monument whose roots lie firmly within the Neolithic, towards something very different, which involved rituals to do with individual people. A series of timber structures were built, including an elaborate blocking of the main entranceway with a setting of four posts just outside it.

A series of cremations was placed in some 24 of the 34 Aubrey Holes that have actually been excavated. Over 200 cremations are known from twentieth-century excavations of Stonehenge, which make it the largest cremation cemetery of the period in Britain. The cremations were placed in small pits in the ground throughout the early and mid third millennium BC. So the practice began in Late Neolithic times and continued into the earlier phases of the stone monument, which began in the centuries after about 2500BC.

THE MOST IMPORTANT new development in Neolithic technology in Britain was brought about by the control of fire. We think people learned to make and light fires in the Palaeolithic, both because there is evidence for hearths and charcoal and because it would be impossible to live in an Ice Age world without heat. But an open fire is uncontrolled heat. If one wants to make pottery, for example, the heat must be raised and it must also be sustained and this requires technology. The first pottery to be made in Britain dates to the Neolithic and was probably fired in open domestic hearths. At some point it is possible that a form of controlled fire, known as a clamp, was used. There are different ways of making clamps but the general principles remain the same. The dry but unfired pots were heaped up around the fuel and the whole thing was covered with a layer of turf or soil to retain the heat. No bellows were employed, but the clamp did need to have a good source of air, which could either be an opening in the outer covering, or a scoop dug towards the centre.

The Neolithic period sees the introduction of farming – itself a sort of technology – but it was a way of life that gave rise to many technological developments. During the Neolithic houses became larger and more substantial, with post-built walls and heavy, wind-resistant roofs, covered with thatch of reed or straw. Although it seems likely that many trees were cleared by pigs, who would scuffle around the roots, and by sheep, who prefer the bark and sweet sap of young trees to grass, many were also cut down with axes. Neolithic axes were made by flaking and polishing flint or fine-grained stone with an abrasive mixture of sand and water on a shaped stone, known by its French name of polissoir. It is slow work, and it can take two days to make a large polished axe, whereas Mesolithic tranchet axes could be made in under an hour. We have done experiments at Time Team where Phil used a polished axe and Francis a tranchet axe. Phil's was much more effective, but we wondered whether the better axe was really worth the extra effort it took to make. Maybe the beautiful look of a well-made polished axe was very important to Neolithic people.

Neolithic farmers needed to plough their fields and garden plots, and the first ploughs were known as ards. Even the simplest of ards has to be well-made because the forces needed to drag something through the soil are considerable. The source of power could have been an ox or two oxen, but it is just as likely that the first ploughs were pulled by people. The part of the ard which cuts into the soil is known as the share and it was usually made from a wedge-shaped stone, although wooden shares are also known. Ards are not true ploughs because they don't turn the soil over as they pass through it. This is why they are sometimes known as scratch ploughs and are most effective when they are used in two directions, a form of working known as cross-ploughing.

Below: A stone-edged area, possibly for storage or sleeping, from a Neolithic house on Skara Brae, Stromness. Most prehistoric houses were furnished with wooden items which rarely survive the processes of decay.

4 BRONZE AGE

FOR SOME MEMBERS of Time Team and its experts, the Bronze Age was the most exciting period in British history. It lasted for some 1700 years, from about 2500BC, and it began quite slowly, emerging from the previous Neolithic period. The first bronze objects, mainly flat axes and daggers, appeared around 2500BC and were used by people who still lived a Neolithic lifestyle. The Bronze Age really got going as a distinctly new period in the two or three centuries before 2000BC, then it gathered momentum and the people of Bronze Age Britain created some of the most extraordinary sites in Britain, including one of the best-known archaeological sites anywhere in the world, Stonehenge.

The period gets its name from the fact that the first metal in widespread use was a mixture of 90 per cent copper and 10 per cent tin, known as bronze. Tin was found in streams in Cornwall and copper was mined in open-cast or surface workings and in massive, deep underground mines, at places like Great Orme in North Wales (see page 84). The alloy bronze is significantly harder than pure copper.

This was the period when human beings learned how to create and control the high temperatures needed to smelt and melt metal. Smelting is the process where metal is removed from the original ore, so when bronze implements became old or damaged they could be melted down to form new ones. Lead was added to the bronze later in this period. This made the molten metal easier to pour into moulds but did not affect its hardness, but if too much was added, as happened towards the end of the period, the quality of the metal deteriorated.

Time Team filmed the making of a bronze axe, at Flag Fen which gave us a chance to talk to Francis Pryor about one of his favourite periods.

The Bronze Age has been described as the period when the Neolithic Revolution actually happened. It used to be believed that the introduction of farming in the Neolithic also brought with it settled lifestyles. People became more sedentary because they had to settle down and guard their crops and animals. Recent research makes it clear that while permanent settlements, complete with large timber houses, were constructed in the Neolithic in Ireland and much of Scotland, this did not happen in England and Wales until the Bronze Age. Neolithic field systems are extremely rare, even in Ireland, where people started to live settled lives from around 4000BC. On mainland Britain the earliest fields and farms become fixed in the landscape from about 2000BC. By the middle of the Bronze Age, say from 1500BC, they are becoming relatively commonplace. By the end of the Bronze Age, large areas of lowland Britain are covered with fields and farms.

The appearance of fields and farms over the British landscape was what was supposed to have happened in the so-called Neolithic Revolution, which was a trendy concept in the 1950s and 60s. We know now that the parcelling-up and permanent partitioning of the rural landscape mostly happened in the Bronze Age, which was the period when the landscape of Britain took on a form that would be familiar to us today. Huge areas of forest were cleared of trees and the great open plains of the Neolithic, covered with grass and bushes, were replaced by fields and paddocks separated from each other by drystone walls, hedges and ditches. Some of the best preserved Bronze Age fields are the stone-walled Reeves of Dartmoor, in Devon.

The changes that began in the Neolithic really gather pace in the Bronze Age. There are many reasons for this. The population was growing and as settled communities came into existence, so roads and trackways improved. Communications didn't just improve on land. We find evidence for the earliest proper sea-going vessels which were beautifully made from oak planks sewn together and sealed with moss and clay.

Boats of the earlier Bronze Age have been found at Ferriby on the Humber and near Dover harbour, on the south coast. It is estimated that the Dover boat was capable of crossing the Channel. It could have coped with choppy conditions, but would have sunk in a storm. As if to prove this, we also know of Bronze Age shipwrecks discovered on the south coast, where all that survives is a scatter of bronze tools on the seabed.

Francis Pryor, Time Team's Bronze Age expert, believes the most spectacular sites of the period in Britain are the great temples and shrines, such as the Ring of Brodgar, in Orkney (see page 82) and Stonehenge (see page 86). The Neolithic was famous for its great tombs, which become less spectacular in the Bronze Age. But while the tombs may have become less showy, the burials within them did not. Gold and other treasure have been found in some of the barrows surrounding Stonehenge. One grave, discovered in 2002 not far from Stonehenge, has been nick-named 'the Amesbury Archer' (see page 83). This man was buried around 2300BC with about a hundred items, including 16 flint arrowheads, copper knives, gold hair ornaments and five complete pots, known as Beakers.

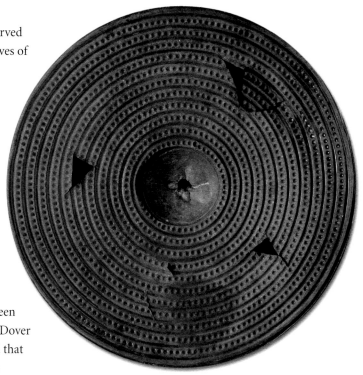

It has been suggested that Beaker pottery, which is well fired and covered with decoration on the outside, came to Britain along with the earliest bronze. Maybe it was made by the same people who also fashioned the metalwork. We still cannot tell for certain, but it is quite an attractive idea. It's also possible that a person of high status, such as the Amesbury Archer, could have been involved with the construction of the stone monument at Stonehenge. Stonehenge began life at the end of the Neolithic period as a shrine or temple made from earth and wood. The composition of his tooth enamel tells us that the Amesbury Archer began his life in central Europe, proving that people were far more mobile in the Bronze Age than we once believed.

Previous spread: *An atmospheric picture of Avebury henge monument in winter.*

Above: *A bronze shield discovered in the River Thames. The ability to manufacture sheet metal illustrates a leap in technological knowledge which must have appeared magical to those without the know-how.*

The ceremonies that attended the building and rebuilding of the great religious sites of the Bronze Age drew thousands of people together. These gatherings were part of their purpose, which was to provide somewhere for different communities to gather. These sites began to be used less regularly towards the end of the Bronze Age, and Francis connects this with the transition to activities in sites like Flag Fen, on the outskirts of Peterborough, where Time Team excavated in 2000.

From the Middle Bronze Age we see the great stone monuments abandoned, and people turned their religious attentions to rivers, bogs and fens where new ceremonies took place, which involved the offering of bronze swords and other valuable items to the waters. Flag Fen is one of the earliest and best preserved of these sites. Rites involving water continued throughout the Iron Age and into Roman times.

We have found some bronze objects on Time Team digs and it is often remarkable how well they have survived in the ground. The period does represent our first contact with metal-based technology and the search for the raw materials clearly stimulated a wide range of contacts which heralded our ancestors opening up to the continent. It seems likely that new elements of culture were effectively imported along with trade goods and the archaeology on Beaker sites represents one of the most fascinating areas for archaeologists to study.

Below: *Phil carefully records a Bronze Age cremation burial, discovered in a barrow at Carsington, by drawing a scale plan.*

BRONZE AGE IN DETAIL

THE BRONZE AGE is so called because it heralds the appearance of bronze, copper and gold artefacts, but the period also represents the gradual change in society from the Neolithic hunter-gatherers-turned-farmers into a truly established permanently settled way of life. The initial soundings from the Neolithic became fully accepted and, as a result, our forays into farming became the way that most people lived.

As a period the Bronze Age has been categorised and subdivided at many levels by archaeologists, but to simplify the situation in this book we're going to stick to Early (2600–1400BC) and Later (1400–700BC). The two phases represent the birth of a new technology and the transition that accompanies it, leading into a consolidated and more organised structure of society which ultimately takes us into the Iron Age.

The Early Bronze Age

The Early Bronze Age is the domain of the Beaker Folk; a cultural group that appear around the beginning of the period and continue until around 1400BC. The Beaker style refers to a fine decorated pottery vessel akin to a waisted bowl with a long extended collar. These pots appear to be associated to a large extent with our early metalworking communities and have led some archaeologists to suggest that we suffered an invasion of peoples. The tendency to attribute new cultural styles to physical invasions has its roots in our imperial past as antiquarians and pioneering archaeologists tried to interpret their discoveries from the perspective of the world they understood. Today, archaeologists favour the concept of an invasion of ideas, where existing peoples adopt cultures and fashions of others they come into contact with, such as the American cultural invasion which has happened in our own country in more recent years and placed burger bars in our high streets and baseball caps on our heads.

Whatever caused the spark, the Early Bronze Age started us on a consolidating path from the re-use of Neolithic monuments, such as West Kennet long barrow, Wiltshire, to the further development of flint technology, which sees stone knives and arrow heads taking on a truly artistic quality. This period of consolidation also involved the erection of stone monuments, rich individual burials, the development of regional styles of pottery and, of course, wonderful bronze tools and weapons.

Evidence for Early Bronze Age structures, such as that discovered inadvertently preserved under the Saxon period Sutton Hoo burial mound in East Anglia (see page 145), point towards a varying style of house shape. The rectangular house of the Neolithic is replaced by a circular house with a central hearth. The circle is increasingly adopted as the period moves on in both burial mounds and in the construction of ceremonial monuments, explored later in this chapter. Archaeologists such as Mike Parker Pearson have drawn some interesting relationships between house and burial mound, pointing out that the round barrow with its central burial has a particular similarity to the prehistoric roundhouse and hearth.

The Later Bronze Age

As we move into the Later Bronze Age, we witness a wider use of cremation as a means of disposing of the dead, the ashes often placed in bucket-shaped, so-called Deverel-Rimbury vessels and buried as 'satellite' deposits around the edge of existing burial mounds, or in some cases within their own barrow cemeteries. In many ways the Later Bronze Age takes us into a new, slightly darker era, almost as if the honeymoon of trying out farming and settlement was over and the serious business of forging ahead with some competitive edge had began.

From around 1400BC the number of bronze artefacts in the archaeological record takes on something of a spurt. We start to see new styles of axes such as palstaves and socketed axes, both types exhibiting design features to aid secure hafting, and beautiful long spearheads together with attractive torc bracelets and necklaces. We also see the advent of the sword with leaf-shaped blades up to 50cm (20in) long. Of course the sword is quite a useless weapon for hunting with. It's an implement specially designed for fighting, so here we see some of the first direct evidence of warfare in Britain. The production of such a large metal item as a sword also highlights the quality of casting and metalworking skills attained at this time. Made in a single pouring of molten bronze into a stone mould, the actual method of turning a pile of ore into what must have been an incredibly expensive and high-status weapon must have appeared almost magical; the real 'pulling a sword from the stone'.

Around 1000BC we see another change as the climate appears to turn wetter and colder. Some of our earliest evidence for wheeled animal-drawn vehicles comes to light in ritual deposits at sites such as Heathery Burn in County Durham. Not only does the appearance of carts indicate changes in the economy of the time, but the fact that animals were being used to power transport represents a great leap forward.

By the closing stages of the Bronze Age we again go through a transitional phase as a new technology is embraced with the advent of the Iron Age, but in many ways evidence for the embryonic beginnings of social hierarchycan be seen here, in the Bronze Age. Field systems, such as the Dartmoor Reeves (see page 90), show us that land was divided up with carefully maintained boundaries, while large-scale open area excavations, such as those at Black Patch in East Sussex, have shown us how farmsteads had grown into clusters of four or five roundhouses, each displaying boundary walls and featuring numerous fence lines. The Bronze Age brought land division and status symbol items to the fore and with it came indications of competition and war.

Finally, one can't talk about the Later Bronze Age without mentioning Flag Fen (see page 88), a fantastic waterlogged landscape which has been studied and excavated for years by Francis Pryor and his wife, Maisie Taylor. In this chapter we'll investigate their findings and also delve into the extraordinary world of ritual deposits and water.

Above: A classic palstave copper-alloy axe dated to around 1500BC. The moulded ridges would have aided the hafting of the blade into a handle.

Bronze Age Chronology

This timeline gives you a quick, at-a-glance guide to what happened when in Britain in the Bronze Age era, helping you to understand the order of events. We've also included, in green type, some key events that happened elsewhere in the world.

Ring of Brodgar	**c2500BC**
Completion of Stonehenge (see page 86)	**c2500–1600BC**
Beaker influence and the Amesbury Archer (see page 83)	**c2300BC**
Bronze technology and gold working well established in Britain	**c2200BC**
Copper exploitation, including the mines at Great Orme (see page 84)	**c2000BC**
Flint production at Grimes Grave	**c2000BC**
Flag Fen (see page 88)	**c1300BC**
Penard Phase – European styles increasingly influencing British bronze metalwork	**c1200BC**
Field systems – Dartmoor Reeves, Thames Fields (see page 90)	**c1200BC**
World event: 1341–1337BC – Tutankhamun	1341–1337BC
Ewart Park Phase – commonest type of material found today, eg broken tools and casting scrap	**c900BC**
World event: 776BC – The First Ancient Olympic Games	776BC

World event: 1341–1337BC – Tutankhamun
Due to the discovery of King Nebkheperura Tutankhamun's tomb in the Valley of the Kings by British archaeologists Lord Carnarvon and Howard Carter in 1922, he remains the most famous of all the Pharaohs of Ancient Egypt, ruling around 1333–1323BC. Also known as Amenhotep IV, Tutankhamun was about 11 years old at the time of his accession. Lord Carnarvon provided the financial backing for Carter's excavations and was rewarded with the discovery of the legendary tomb. Carter found that the tomb had been robbed of many of its antiquities but the burial chamber itself had remained untouched. The most astonishing and impressive discovery was of the solid gold inner coffin where the king is depicted as Osiris holding the traditional symbols of kingship – the crook and the flail. Statues of deities and jewellery were also found but the most iconic discovery is the solid gold funerary mask. The mask is a phenomenal example of ancient goldsmith workmanship displaying incredible attention to detail and is inlaid with coloured glass and stones.

World event: 776BC – The First Ancient Olympic Games
The Olympic Games were held in Ancient Greece every four years from 776BC at Olympia until their abolition in AD393 by the Christian Byzantine emperor, Theodosius the First. A 200-yard sprint called the Stade was the sole event for the first 13 Olympic Games. All free Greek-speaking men could compete but women were forbidden even to attend. A second event, a 400-yard foot race or diaulos was added in the fourteenth games and a third variable length foot race (dolichos) included in the fifteenth. Further events such as boxing and the pentathlon were later added and the athletes represented city-states from the entire Greek world. The origins of the Ancient Olympic Games are steeped in religion and were held as part of a festival in honour of Zeus. It is remarkable that the Ancient Olympics were held for over 1000 years. It took another 1500 years for the inauguration of the Modern Olympics in 1896, appropriately hosted by Athens. Barring the intervention of two World Wars, the Olympics have been held every four years since then.

BASAL-LOOPED SOCKETED SPEARHEAD

THE FINEST examples of Bronze Age metalwork were sometimes made for display. This was first clearly demonstrated by Professor John Coles in 1962 when he subjected a replica of a thin Late Bronze Age shield, made from sheet bronze, to a simulated assault with a bronze sword. The shield buckled almost immediately, but wood and leather shields, which are known to have existed at the time, stood up to the experimental attack.

Some of the larger spearheads of the Late Bronze Age were also undoubtedly made for decorative rather than practical purposes. A few examples have been embellished with inlaid gold bands around the socket. The spearhead shown here comes from the River Thames. It was discovered in 1953 near Oakley Court and currently resides in the collections of Reading Museum. This unusual and beautiful form dates to around 900BC, or the Late Bronze Age. It's a variant of what are known as basal-looped spearheads – a design which incorporates perforations or lugs which are thought to be intended for either assisting in the setting of the blade on the end of a shaft (for example by lashing with a thong through the holes), or for a less functional use, such as attaching talismans or trinkets.

The origins of the basal-looped design harp back to the Middle Bronze Age where the lugs and holes featured in spearheads of that time are obviously intended for securing the weapon, but by the time we reach examples such as the Oakley Court spearhead the holes appear more decorative and artistic in their style. Three perforations appear on each side at the base of the leaf-shaped blade. A fourth hole on each side is extended in a wonderful display of artistic flare to create a pair of needle-like slots. These sit either side of the socket, which has an unusual hexagonal profile. This outstanding piece of craftsmanship is further enhanced by the sheer size of the weapon. At 43cm (17in) long, it represents the final goal of a mammoth trail of preparation and effort to produce a work of art.

As for their use, these iconic Late Bronze Age objects have long been debated by archaeologists. Some suggest that they are too long and heavy to be used as proper spears, but perhaps they were hafted on short shafts in a similar fashion to the later Roman cavalry short lances? However, the fact that over 50 per cent of the known examples were found in water courses does suggest they were used more as a symbolic device, either as a token of status or particularly for some religious purpose where water played a relevant part.

Left: This beautiful copper-alloy spearhead was discovered in the Thames. The leaf-shaped design is both aesthetically pleasing to the eye and ideal for creating a well-balanced weapon.

B

BRONZE AGE SETTLEMENT

The Bronze Age settlement shown here could have been one of many around the edge of Flag Fen. In the background one can see an excarnation platform created at the water's edge for the dead. The man's spear may have had a bronze tip and we can see the increasing link between animals and the family occupying the roundhouse. We have traces of fabric, mainly provided as a reference from Danish sites, that have enabled us to imagine the people's clothing and the pottery the woman carries would have often been of fine quality.

Around the edge of the roof-line can be seen the remains of a gully that would have been formed by rainwater – something we often find in excavations – and the house itself would have left a range of different sized postholes. Around the edge of the settlement small-scale metalworking may have taken place, including casting axes or making bronze tools. The family would still have some flint tools such as arrowheads in their tool kits.

On the Bronze Age sites we have excavated there has often been a close relationship between the people and local sources of water and it's possible to imagine that this family would have at some stage deposited bronze objects into the lakes or streams in their area.

The Ring of Brodgar

THE RING OF Brodgar (or Brogar) is a henge which consists of a magnificent stone circle set within a ditch and bank. It forms part of an important 'ritual landscape' that was first constructed on the mainland of Orkney in the later Neolithic period and continued to be built and developed into the Early Bronze Age. This landscape is of international importance because it has escaped being damaged by modern farming practices and survives to the present day very much as when it was in regular use during the later fourth and third millennia BC. Apart from the Ring of Brodgar, the other main sites of the ritual landscape on this island include another stone circle, the Stones of Stennes, with the recently discovered settlement of Barnhouse nearby, and the great chambered tomb of Maes Howe. These are linked together by sight-lines and by rows of standing stones. These were not randomly constructed single sites, but each was clearly built to be a new element of a much larger group, each part of which would have been the subject of special processions and ceremonies.

The Ring of Brodgar is the grandest of the Orkney stone circles. Assuming it was completed (which we should not necessarily assume), the Ring of Brodgar would originally have included 60 stones, forming a ring 103.7m (113 yards) in diameter. Although not quite as tall as the Stones of Stennes, those of Brodgar are still huge: the tallest today being some 4.2m (13ft 8in) high. The surrounding ditch is still massive, measuring 10m (27ft) wide at the surface, but when first constructed it must have been magnificent, especially when filled with water, as it would have been for most of the time. The ditch is broached by two undug entranceways to the north-west and south-east. The construction of the ditch was a vast engineering feat, which involved the removal of no less than 4700 cubic metres (3950 cubic yards) of rock. It has always been assumed that the stones of the great circle were quarried from this ditch, but that may not, in fact, have been the case.

Recent research on the stones used in the construction of the Ring of Brodgar suggests that large stones were deliberately dragged to the site from quarries several miles away. It is likely that these quarries were themselves ritually important and would have been sacred sites in their own right. The new research suggests that the different sources of stone used both at the Ring of Brodgar and the Stones of Stennes represent the contribution of different communities to the construction of the stone circles. There is also evidence to suggest that these circles need not have been 'completed' in the sense that we understand today, because their construction was, at one and the same time, their use. It would be a great mistake to think that they were built, like a church, to be sanctified and then used as a building for worship.

Above: The Ring of Brodgar, like its sister site the Stones of Stennes, is a massive henge monument representing thousands of hours of labour to construct.

Beaker Culture and The Amesbury Archer

THE AREA AROUND Stonehenge has been the subject of scrutiny for over 300 years, but some of the most exciting and unusual finds have been made in the twenty-first century. A huge amount of interest was stirred in 2002 when the body of a man was found on the outskirts of the town of Amesbury, some 5km (3 miles) south-east of Stonehenge. Today the Amesbury Archer, as he is now generally known, is seen to be just one high-status burial that can be dated to the time when the great stones of Stonehenge were being erected.

If Stonehenge was erected as a project that was led by the contemporary elite in the region, the Amesbury Archer could have been such a person. If, that is, it was a top-down rather than a community-inspired project (which is the interpretation we tend to favour). The burial dated to around 2400–2200BC and unusually also contained over a hundred items from the dawn of the Bronze Age, including copper knives, gold hair ornaments and five complete so-called Beaker pots. These were highly decorated and finely made drinking vessels of a most distinctive type known from sites right across Europe. Some believe that these unusual vessels were made by an elite group of people who helped to spread the technology of early metalworking. It's a reasonable idea, but it probably only tells part of the Beaker story.

Analysis of the Amesbury Archer's teeth shows that the composition of his enamel has the distinctive chemical 'signature' characteristic of central Europe. Another nearby grave, with almost the same radiocarbon date, contained similar gold ornaments and the man here had a distinctive skeletal feature, which suggested that he was related to the Amesbury Archer. Yet another grave, found nearby at Boscombe Down, contained the remains of a man and three children, one of whom had been cremated. The bones of a teenager and two men in their twenties also lay at his feet. It appears that the bones from this grave showed certain similarities to the original two men and the human-bone specialist examining them believes they could all be related. The artefacts found in

Above: *The remarkable armoury of the Amesbury Archer included these beautiful tanged and barbed arrowheads, each the result of patient and extremely skilled craftwork.*

the Boscombe Down burial are similar in style to those found with the Amesbury Archer. Does this remarkable group of burials and bodies suggest that the constructors of the final stages of Stonehenge were outsiders, migrants from abroad, or is it all just coincidence? Only time will tell.

Copper and Tin Exploitation

THE EARLIEST KNOWN use of metal woodworking tools in the British Isles has been traced to the Corlea track at Kenagh, central Ireland. Parts of the track were constructed as early as 2250BC from oak in the form of split planks on a birch framework, held in place by wooden pegs. It demonstrates highly competent carpentry using bronze tools to form cut marks, sockets and joints.

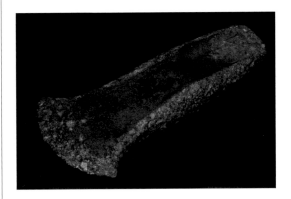

Above: Copper-alloy axe heads such as this basic 'stage VI' style example discovered in Cilgwrrwg, Wales, were increasingly adopted during the Early Bronze Age and eventually became more fashionable than flint tools.

Apart from exquisite flint knives and some intricate fine arrowheads, it appears that in the later Bronze Age the majority of general flint tools, such as scrapers and domestic blades, become increasingly utilitarian. This has led many archaeologists to suggest that flint tools were being replaced by superior metal ones. Bronze is stronger and holds its cutting edge more efficiently when used. It's also a prized resource and an indicator of status as it's expensive and time-consuming to produce.

The exploitation of copper and tin (and later lead) to make a bronze alloy takes us beyond the obvious advantages of a better material from which to make tools, into new realms of industry, power and currency. With the advent of bronze, the Neolithic polished stone axe is replaced by metal tools and artefacts as symbols of success and power.

A moment in time: the first miner

Some 3860 years ago, a Bronze Age person ventured into a fissure within the limestone rock of Great Orme, Llandudno, probably drawn by surface traces of green malachite (a mineral source of copper). Deep underground the veins of copper ore became even more striking and green against an edge of dark brown crumbling limestone. Drawing an antler pick from his belt, he started chipping at the ore, scraping the crumbs of mineral from its rocky grip.

This tentative prospecting led to an expansive working of the copper veins throughout the Bronze Age. Over the next 1200 years the mines were extended by miners using digging and fire to crack the rock to become the most substantial Bronze Age copper mines known in Northern Europe.

At the same time as the mining was taking place underground, the ore was being roasted and smelted in small furnaces on the surface. Unlike later iron working, which requires extremely high temperatures and a huge investment in effort for a result, bronze working is a simpler affair. We can imagine the furnace itself as a small clay-lined, bowl-shaped depression in the ground with an additional collar rising just above the surface. A small fire of charcoal is boosted by small hand-powered bag bellows which vent into the bowl of the furnace, keeping the charcoal a white-orange colour while grains of roasted ore are dropped in to melt and form a cake in the base of the bowl.

This cake, or block of copper, could then be traded to a smith who, using a similar furnace, would use the raw material in a sophisticated casting technique called *cire perdue* or 'lost wax'. This involves forming the shape of the object to be cast, such as a knife, with wax, then surrounding it with wet clay to make a mould. The mould is then heated in the edge of the furnace to harden the clay while the wax pours out, leaving a negative cavity of the knife shape. The bronze alloy of copper and tin is then fired to a temperature of over 1,150°C within a clay crucible to become a liquid, which is then poured into the mould. When cooled, the mould is broken to reveal the cast tool.

Archaeological evidence

Archaeologist and mining engineer Tony Hammond has spent over ten years excavating the tunnels and shafts of Great Orme. With a team of cavers and diggers he has discovered nearly 7km (4 ½ miles) of tunnels and estimates that over 140,000 tons of spoil were removed and dumped on the surface, indicating a great volume of copper ore extracted. This industry suggests a group of dedicated miners who worked a valuable and powerful resource. Unfortunately no trace of their settlement has yet been found, but evidence does exist for the smelting stage in the bronze-working process. Artefactual evidence from Great Orme includes an astonishing number of tools, including 33,000 bone tools and nearly 2,500 stone hammers, clearly showing the importance and continued success of the site.

The search continues (so far unsuccessful) to find evidence of Bronze Age tin mining in Britain, but as tin is available from streams in Cornwall it's assumed that those resources must have been tapped. We also know that resources were imported from Europe where trace element analysis has shown that copper from Alpine regions found its way here, most likely through trade.

In time the development of bronze working allowed the production of sheet metal and bigger and better castings. Bronze also appears to have developed as a form of currency as evidenced by volumes of unusable 'axe' shaped tokens. The ability to afford a bronze sword certainly suggests wealth but the willingness to discard that sword in a ritual watery deposit also suggests great power, and it's in ritual deposits, not domestic settings, that the majority of bronze artefacts are found. The concept of bronze and bronze artefacts representing more than their physical appearance to the people who used them is also substantiated by the discovery of 'model' artefacts, or unusable copies of swords and axes still made from bronze but used purely for ritual deposits, such as those found at Flag Fen (see page 88).

PALAEOLITHIC

MESOLITHIC

NEOLITHIC

BRONZE AGE c2500–c500BC

The exploitation of copper and tin c2250BC

IRON AGE

ROMAN

ANGLO-SAXON

VIKING

NORMAN

MIDDLE AGES

TUDOR

STUART

GEORGIAN

VICTORIAN

MODERN

The Final Phase of Stonehenge

THE IMPRESSIVE AND substantial site of Stonehenge on Salisbury Plain in Wiltshire is one of the most recognised archaeological sites in the world. Its formidable trilithon structures, consisting of two colossal upright sarsen stones capped by an equally immense lintel, are something of a prehistoric icon.

It sits within a landscape brimming with prehistoric ritual archaeology, including barrows, substantial earthworks, the remains of timber circles, curious linear works that stretch for great distances. Further away are other ritual landscapes, such as that around Avebury and Silbury Hill.

Though little is understood about how Stonehenge was used, the fact that it exists represents a number of aspects of prehistoric social and economic life. It has been estimated that as an engineering project it would have taken 30 million man-hours to complete over its 1500 years of building and remodelling. For this to happen, the societies of the time had to evolve into a network capable of supporting a project on such a scale. When work on Stonehenge began around 3000BC, the people around Salisbury Plain had started to develop into chiefdoms – linked groups larger than tribes which, by using a hierarchical system, managed to centralise their power for a common cause or belief. This central control enabled the majority to subsist while simultaneously supporting labour groups and specialists in areas such as crafts or religious duties.

Above: *Stonehenge seen from the air provides one of the best angles from which to appreciate the plan of the monument and is a view that many will recognise. Of course, this is a benefit the original designers certainly lacked.*

A moment in time: the Sarsen phase

About 4000 years ago Stonehenge, having already been a centre of ceremony for some 1000 years, underwent a dramatic change. For an unknown reason the people who controlled the monument removed the Blue Stones and redesigned it to create a monument quite unlike anything else. Surveys by archaeologists estimate that 1000 people would have been needed to move each massive sarsen stone from its natural home on the Marlborough Downs 30km (20 miles) to Stonehenge in the south. Using twisted vegetable fibre or leather ropes, each colossal stone was bound and dragged over timber rollers in a mammoth effort of brute force and dedication.

Not only is the design put together with the greatest accuracy in construction, but the alignments and associations of the stones appear to have been vital too. Much has been written about Stonehenge's alignment with the summer solstice, where the rising sun can be seen captured within the stones in direct line of sight from the avenue and entrance. We do not understand the precise significance of this, but a marking of the seasons would have been important to the agricultural society using the monument.

The vast cost in labour required to upend the stones and drop them into their 'posthole' sockets, let alone the efforts needed to set the lintels in place, displays great engineering skill. It's unknown at which point in the year the main construction took place, but the labour force must have been released from normal farming duties at some point. Perhaps the use of such a large workforce in a communal project was a way of keeping dispersed communities together.

Archaeological evidence

Studies of the artefacts discovered at the site have provided evidence for phases of development. These suggest that Stonehenge began at around 3000BC as a large basic henge monument with no stones. A bank and ditch enclosure encompassed a circle some 87m (285ft) across, while within the perimeter 56 Aubrey holes (named after the seventeenth-century antiquarian) are equally spaced, each measuring roughly 1m (3ft) wide and deep. Possibly holding timber posts, the Aubrey holes were back filled around 2500BC, some with cremated human remains.

Some 400 years after the first construction, the Blue Stones, quarried from the Preseli Mountains of South Wales, nearly 390km (240 miles) away, were introduced. A huge investment in logistics and labour, the 82 stones, weighing nearly 4 tonnes each, were hauled on sledges over timber rollers and then probably rafted along the south coast of Wales to the River Avon, to be further transported by water to Amesbury a few miles from the henge. When finally dragged to the site they were set in a double horseshoe pattern. It's also at this time that the initial stages of the avenue were constructed by the entrance, along with the placing of heel stones associated with the summer equinox.

The most exciting stage occurred around 2000BC when the sarsen stones weighing up to 25 tonnes each were brought to the site, probably by dragging over rollers, from the Marlborough Downs. In a considerable remodelling, the blue stones were removed. The sarsen stones were laboriously shaped with stone hammers to create uniform monoliths, while carpentry-style mortice and tenon joints were nibbled out of the stones to hold the spectacular lintels in place. Once set in the ground, the towering 7m-high (22ft) sarsens created a continuous circle in the centre of the henge around five massive trilithons.

Finally, around 1600BC the Blue Stones were reinstated around the sarsens in a horseshoe shape. Surprisingly, considering the abundance of evidence for hundreds (or even thousands) of people at work, there is hardly any evidence for settlements, only adding to the impression of an eerie ritual landscape.

PALAEOLITHIC

MESOLITHIC

NEOLITHIC

BRONZE AGE c2500–c500BC

Stonehenge c2000–c1600BC

IRON AGE

ROMAN

ANGLO-SAXON

VIKING

NORMAN

MIDDLE AGES

TUDOR

STUART

GEORGIAN

VICTORIAN

MODERN

Late Bronze Age Settlement at Flag Fen

FLAG FEN IS a waterlogged Later Bronze Age site found on the eastern side of Peterborough. It was first occupied around 1300BC and ceased to be maintained after 900BC. It is important for two reasons.

First and perhaps foremost, it is remarkably well preserved through being waterlogged for some 3000 years. The peaty soils in which such sites are preserved are very often so acidic that all bone is dissolved, but at Flag Fen bone survives, as does a huge variety of organic material, including timber, leaves, pollen and seeds. The wood found there is one of the richest sources of information on Bronze Age woodworking and carpentry. By examining samples of peat it has been possible to reconstruct the environment of the Later Bronze Age and the effect that ancient communities had on their surroundings.

The second reason why Flag Fen is so important reflects its position within the landscape. Very often wetland sites, such as trackways, are discovered out in the middle of huge bogs or marshes and it then becomes extremely hard to relate them in any way to what was happening on the dry land – where people actually lived. Flag Fen sits within a large bay-like depression, in which peats began to form from about 2000BC. The dry landscape surrounding the bay on two sides has been the subject of large-scale and detailed excavation since the early 1970s and includes the well-known multi-period site of Fengate. It has proved possible to link what was happening out in the wet parts of Flag Fen with the drier land at Fengate.

The picture that results is possibly unique in Britain and it shows a succession of landscapes and settlements, complete with burials and ceremonial monuments, that starts around 3500BC and extends well into the Roman period. In late Roman times water levels rise sharply and settlement moves further inland, to ground that is today buried beneath the city of Peterborough.

Flag Fen consists of a causeway, or post-alignment, built from five rows of large posts and many tens of thousands of planks, branches and brushwood which were laid on the wet ground within and around the posts to form a slightly raised walkway. This causeway crosses a kilometre-

wide (⅔ mile) band of wet ground between the fen-edge landscape of Fengate, to the west, and Northey, to the east. Northey itself forms a part of a much larger Fenland 'island', or drier area, which today includes the market town of Whittlesey. In amongst the timbers of the causeway archaeologists found hundreds of bronze items, including swords, daggers, spearheads and jewellery which had been consigned to the waters as offerings, possibly to the shades of the ancestors. Flag Fen is remarkable because it allows us to examine the details of Bronze Age rituals.

Below: *A reconstructed example of a typical Bronze Age roundhouse at Flag Fen. The carpentry skills required to make such a building were certainly comprehensive and are little different from those used in construction today.*

Field Boundaries and the Dartmoor Reeves

THE DARTMOOR REEVES are an extensive system of field banks on the hillsides of the moor that have been known about since the Victorian period. During the 1970s, fieldwork by Andrew Fleming and other archaeologists began to reveal how ancient these land boundaries actually were. The work of environmental archaeologists showed that the moor had originally been a mixed landscape of woodland and open grassland that was gradually colonised throughout the Neolithic and Early Bronze Age. Towards the end of this period communities were permanently occupying these uplands, creating large enclosures, as at Shaugh Moor, and farming small irregular fields. The spread of settlements on the moor appears to be linked to growing numbers of animals being kept and a change from seasonal to permanent occupation of the uplands.

By the Middle Bronze Age (c1500BC), this increasingly settled landscape was divided up by a system of field banks that traverse the moor, often for many kilometres. These reeve boundaries were part of a planned system of land division, with major reeves running between river valleys and smaller reeves running at right angles across the landscape. The large blocks of land created were then sub-divided into small fields and paddocks that were farmed by the communities that lived in settlements scattered amongst the fields. These large field systems are called co-axial systems due to the way they run across the landscape, often ignoring the underlying land forms, whilst maintaining their rectilinear layout. This form of communal land division marks the transition in prehistoric society from the creation of ceremonial monuments towards the direct control of the landscape itself.

The very success of this system of co-operative land use was ultimately its undoing, as by the Late Bronze Age (c1000BC) the pollen record shows the spread of heathland and a decline in agriculture. It seems that a combination of over-exploitation and climatic deterioration was turning the upland pastures into moorland. Similar climatic changes can be traced elsewhere, as in the Somerset Levels, where Late Bronze Age trackways were overwhelmed by floodwaters and abandoned. This was a slow process, probably not complete until the Iron Age, but it marks the beginnings of the retreat from the uplands and the replacement of permanent farming communities with seasonal pastoralists. Today, visitors to Dartmoor assume that the moor is a natural phenomenon, but actually it is the result of prehistoric society's attempts to impose itself on the landscape.

Left: The dramatic landscape of Dartmoor was once filled with farming communities who exploited the landscape to their advantage. Their reeves, or Bronze Age field boundaries, still exist today.

BRONZE AGE ADVANCES

TECHNOLOGY

IN EUROPE the very first metal is copper, but in Britain the use of copper and bronze seems to happen at about the same time. Gold, a softer metal that requires less heat to work effectively, also appears in the early Bronze Age. The processes of smelting (the production of metal from an ore) and melting requires the use of a true furnace as copper needs to be heated above 1300°C to melt and retain it in a pourable liquid form, for casting. No complete fired clay furnaces have been found in Britain, but their form is known from elsewhere. The most common remains are the fired clay nozzles that protruded into the furnace from the bellows. Some sites have produced thick-walled, teacup-sized, fired clay crucibles that were used to pour metal into the moulds, made from stone, clay or even bronze. The advantage of bronze over pure copper is that it has a lower melting point, is easier to pour into a mould, and is harder when cold.

The improved control of heat is reflected in certain, but not all, types of Bronze Age pottery. The finely-fired and highly-decorated style known as Beaker is often associated with Early Bronze Age metalwork in graves, such as the Amesbury Archer. Although the period is most famous for metal, the Bronze Age also saw improvements in masonry, as witnessed by the great dressed stones of Stonehenge. The spinning of wool began in the Neolithic, but the first true looms appear in the early Bronze Age, around 2000BC. The earliest wheels and wheel-ruts in Britain date to the Middle Bronze Age (after 1500BC), but it seems probable that wheels may have been introduced sometime in the Neolithic.

One aspect of Bronze Age technology that has received much recent attention is boat-building. The earliest plank-built boats were made just

Above: *This group of socketed axe heads and gouges represent both a fine selection of carpentry tools and an example of how the bronzesmith's art had advanced by the Later Bronze Age.*

before 2000BC. The boards were sewn together with ties made from flexible pieces of yew and the gaps were sealed with packed moss. The best preserved Bronze Age boat was found in Dover, dating to about 1600BC. It would have been capable of carrying large cargoes across the Channel in winds approaching gale force.

5   IRON AGE

THE IRON AGE is the name given for the period when we begin to see a range of changes in our development that go well beyond the simple acquisition of new technology. Like the other prehistoric periods, the actual starting point represents a period of transition. The Iron Age didn't simply start at the point where we began using iron and where many features of the earlier Bronze Age continue. The Iron Age is usually regarded as beginning around the eighth century BC and continuing until first century AD.

One of the most visible signs of the period in the landscape are hillforts, and there is a general belief that along with an increase in population, there was an increasing competition for resources. The hillforts may have played their role in defining territories, and certainly Francis Pryor considers this to be the case: 'Whatever their

position in the Iron Age landscape, sites like Maiden Castle (see page 102) were clearly intended to frighten and impress. So far there is no good evidence to suggest hillforts were the sites of large-scale pitched battles or extended sieges. Most of the evidence for warfare indicates that fighting was on a small scale, maybe involving raiding or perhaps cattle rustling. Such attacks would probably have happened in the autumn, when crops had been safely harvested.'

It has been estimated that there are some 3000–4000 hillforts in Britain, and Time Team's dig at Gear in Cornwall in 2001 showed how intensively used the interior can be.

There is some evidence for deterioration of the climate around 900BC. This comes mainly from the pollen record where there are signs of an increase in plants and trees that can survive

in colder and wetter conditions. It's possible that this change added to the pressure on resources and caused groups of people to wish to defend their own territories.

There was also an emphasis on powerful leaders – what might be called the rise of the chieftains – and certainly burials of this period contain evidence of individuals with great power and prestige, buried with high-status goods, including beautiful objects like iron swords decorated with what we now call 'Celtic' design.

The earliest Iron Age objects discovered in Britain tend to be copies of implements formerly made in bronze. A sickle and sword were found as part of the Llyn Fawr hoard in Glamorgan and these have been dated to the early Iron Age. Iron ore from areas like the Forest of Dean provided the raw material, and by the third century BC

large amounts of the metal were being traded around the country in the form of ingots and currency bars.

There is something of a paradox about iron production itself. The technology was originally developed by the Hittites who lived in an area now occupied by Syria and Turkey around 3000–2000BC. Although the technology is more complex and requires a higher temperature than smelting copper, iron is in theory more widely available as a material. I say in theory because every time we have looked for so-called 'bog iron' (small nodules of iron that occur on the surface of swampy areas), it has been incredibly difficult to find.

The critical difference between a bronze axe and an iron axe is the sharpness and durability of the edge. I asked Maisie Taylor for her definitive view of this difference and she was quite clear. 'You can cut green timber easily with a bronze axe, but once it becomes hard and seasoned it will round off the blade.' She points to the evidence of a log boat found in the Fens that was initially built using bronze axes and adzes, but when it was later modified iron axes had to be used.

Bronze and copper objects were still made alongside the new material, but we begin to find large quantities deposited as hoards towards the middle of the Iron Age and an emphasis on the high-quality, artistic pieces that often served a ritual purpose. One of the most beautiful objects from the Iron Age is the torc – a neck ring often made from gold. Classical representations of Iron Age people show this ornament and they represent the skill and artistic refinement developing in Britain at this time.

The business of depositing objects in rivers and pools continued into the Iron Age and it's from such material, particularly from the Thames, that we see one of the most distinctive elements of this age – the designs we call 'Celtic'. Beautiful shields, helmets and mirrors with the distinctive swirling designs have been found but it's important to understand the limitations of the term 'Celtic'.

Francis Pryor is keen to put the record straight. 'The Iron Age is seen by many people as the Age of the Celts. The Celts are usually portrayed as rather wild and warlike people, much given to brawling among themselves. The trouble with this view is that it assumes that there was indeed a tribe who styled themselves Celts. So far as we know, no such tribe has ever existed in Britain. It used to be believed, too, that the Celts

migrated to Britain in the early Iron Age, around 500BC, from central Europe. We now know that no such migration ever happened. Even so, the word Celtic is a useful way to describe decoration found on many of the better Iron Age metal objects and on some of the finer pottery. At its best, Celtic art is very good indeed and is considered by many as Britain's first, and possibly its most important, contribution to European decorative art.'

The connection with Europe, enhanced by trade, introduced new ideas, including the use of money. The Iron Age is the period when we begin to see coins. There is evidence that before this, iron bars were used for trade, but the earliest coins in Britain appear at this time, often naming an Iron Age ruler and copying a continental model.

Iron Age settlements

In the north of Britain a distinctive building known as a broch is one of the main features of the Iron Age and, like hillforts, they seem to be partly defensive and partly a statement of status intended to impress both friends and enemies. Time Team excavated a broch in 2005 and you can find more details on page 104. Francis points out that these are the largest upstanding buildings in pre-Roman Britain.

Towards the end of the Iron Age, after around 250BC, there seems to be a coming together of Iron Age settlements into features that are not quite towns or urban developments, but the first step towards regional centres. Colchester and St Albans are examples and are perhaps the earliest towns we have in Britain. Archaeologists refer to these as 'oppida' and they were the centre of a tribal society.

The Roman influence

This was a society with a politico-religious elite – the Druids – and we know that the Romans made a particular point of attacking the power base of the Druids, culminating in a massacre on Ynys Môn (the island of Anglesey) in AD59. Parts of Iron Age Britain would become a centre of resistance to the Romans, but many of the tribes, especially in the east, had grown used to coming into contact with the powerful empire across the Channel, and begun to find the Roman way of life attractive. Historically we consider the Iron Age to end with the Roman invasion, but a large proportion of the population would continue with the old ways and the term Romano-British is the best way of describing them.

Previous spread: The striking and huge earthwork defences of Maiden Castle in Dorset – an Iron Age stronghold and scene of siege fighting during the Roman invasion.

Opposite: A beautiful polished bronze mirror of Iron Age date, the back of which is finely decorated with typical swirls and geometric shapes popular in the period.

Below: The busy scene of Time Team excavations at Applecross in Scotland. The rubble spills betray where walls once stood in a rich site littered with Iron Age archaeological features.

IRON AGE IN DETAIL

A SLOW AND steady embracing of a new iron-working technology during the eighth century BC signalled the beginning of the Iron Age. This is our first period where, with the written accounts of Julius Caesar and later classical authors, we encounter the historical record. After thousands of years of prehistory interpreted using archaeology alone, we get our first written eyewitness accounts of what Britain looked like and how the Britons lived towards the later stages of the period.

Though undoubtedly a huge advantage for the archaeologist, it's also worth bearing in mind that history is just another tool in the archaeologist's arsenal. History is most commonly written by the winners, the intellectuals and often by the biased. Though based on facts and real events, history is commonly recorded as one side, or version, of a story. Politics of the day can influence the writer and it's not unknown for history to be re-written.

It's with these cautionary thoughts in mind that the archaeologist can start to use history and carefully add flesh to the bones of archaeological evidence. While this tentative partnership of disciplines can sometimes lead to conflict, for example when the archaeology doesn't fit with the historical record, it can also serve to infuse our understanding of the past with colour, characters and excitement. In the case of the Iron Age, we earn the names of regional groups and their leaders, gain an understanding of their lifestyles and religions, and also become immersed in the politics, economics, structures and stories of the day.

The origins of the Iron Age

As with earlier periods, there was no single historic event which led us into the Iron Age; rather Bronze Age peoples discovered the production techniques of working iron. Both iron and bronze technologies were used at the same time for a long period, but for the sake of simplicity archaeologists have broken the period into three separate phases which are distinguished by their different types of material culture.

The Early Iron Age (700–300BC) marks the transition from the Bronze Age, a time when defended sites become more popular and hilltop settlements are more widely used. This, combined with an apparent greater use of swords, has led to a generally accepted theory that life at this time included a certain amount of unrest. The Middle Iron Age (300–100BC) is typified by regional types of pottery and the first use of coinage in Britain. Iron use becomes more widespread and the social environment appears to have settled down as many hillforts are abandoned.

Our impression of life at this time is greatly enhanced by the records of Roman writers and it's from these sources, and the distribution of artefacts, that we can see truly established tribal groups who, at times, even feature on the international stage, though continental links and influences may well have been established before they were recorded by history. The AD43 cut-off date for the Iron Age may seem rather abrupt, but it signifies the year of the Roman invasion of Britain, a subject we shall explore later.

Iron Age settlements

Julius Caesar tells us, in his work *The Conquest of Gaul*, that Britain in the Later Iron Age was a land divided like a patchwork into some 25 different tribal groups, each ruled by separate chieftain kings. The society of the time was built on this territorial leadership as each individual tribe existed with their own laws, traditions and regional styles of artefacts. The tribes were inward looking; there was no sense of a greater nation. Most people lived in timber-built roundhouses in a range of settlements from small farms to larger collectives, which appear more like villages. The hillfort evolved into one of the largest forms of settlement with examples such as Maiden Castle in Dorset becoming elaborate and bustling tribal centres (see page 102).

Though settlements are widespread, the locations of artefact production sites remain relatively unknown. We only have the results of their labours – iron weapons and tools – as evidence that industrial workshops must have existed in most areas. The economy continued to be based on mixed agriculture, and Iron Age farmers understood their livelihood well enough to rotate their crops to preserve the fertility of the soil. Peas and beans were grown together with wheat and barley, while pigs, cattle and sheep were the main animal stock. Cottage industry thrived as weaving was a common pastime, evidenced by a proliferation of loom weights discovered by archaeologists on many settlement sites.

If we were to take the classical sources at face value, we'd see the Later Iron Age peoples as little more than savage barbarians, but this is a terminology that the empire used to define unromanised people. The reality appears to be one of a somewhat complex society. Some of the tribes based in the far north and west remain a mystery. They didn't produce any pottery or coinage and at present remain archaeologically silent. The most advanced settlements appear in the lowland south and east. Here we see tribal groups who aspire to a more accomplished culture. They produced coins based on European designs which promote their leaders and tribal identities in a similar fashion to Roman issues. Wheel-thrown pottery of a high standard is commonly used, suggesting specialist manufacturers, and the discovery of prestige items, such as fine polished metal hand mirrors and items of artwork decorated in a continental Belgic style, suggests international trade and tribal connections. The political activity of some of the most powerful tribes and their leaders was well documented by the Roman writers and from their accounts we can see that far from being primitive and barbarian, some of the Iron Age 'aristocracy' led lives of an equally high standard as their European counterparts.

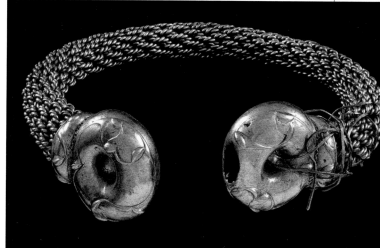

Above: *A most beautiful silver torc necklace, one of nine gold and silver examples buried at Snettisham around 75BC. A mark of status, the torc also illustrated the technological prowess of the 'barbarian' peoples.*

Iron Age Chronology

This timeline gives you a quick, at-a-glance guide to what happened when in Britain in the Iron Age era, helping you to understand the order of events. We've also included, in brown type, some key events that happened elsewhere in the world.

Iron Age hillforts/Maiden Castle (see page 102) — **c700BC**

Construction of Old Sarum begins — **c500BC**

Scottish Brochs (see page 104) — **c400BC**

Llyn Cerrig Bach hoard (see page 105) — **c500BC–100AD**

World event: Alexander the Great — 356-32BC

Gallic trade and Pythias' first reference to Britain (see page 106) — **c330BC**

Metal coinage comes into use — **c150BC**

Iron Age settlement, eg Colchester (see page 109) — **150BC**

Carn Euny, Cornwall Iron Age village featuring a 'fogou' — **c100BC**

Caesar's failed invasion of Britain (see page 110) — **55BC**

World event: Murder of Julius Caesar — 44BC

Claudius' invasion of Britain — **AD43**

World event: Alexander the Great

Alexander III of Macedon was born to Philip II and his wife Olympias, in the Greek kingdom of Macedonia in 356BC. More famously known as Alexander the Great, he was educated by Greek philosopher Aristotle and inherited his father's turbulent kingdom in 336BC. Alexander is credited with single-handedly altering the ancient world through his military campaigns, leading his powerful Macedonian army to victory over the Greeks in 336BC before turning his attention to the Persians in response to their attempts to invade Greece. His military tactical genius defeated the Persians and he assumed control of Asia Minor, Egypt and Syria. By the age of 25 Alexander held the titles of King of Macedonia, leader of the Greeks, Pharaoh of Egypt, Overlord of Asia Minor and King of Persia. The subsequent eight years saw Alexander establish an empire that spanned over two million square miles across three continents, stretching from Greece to India. However, Alexander's empire was rapidly torn asunder amidst power struggles by his successors after his death in 323BC, at the age of 32.

World event: Murder of Julius Caesar

Born in 100BC, Julius Caesar was a successful politician and military commander and expanded the Roman Empire significantly. He progressed through the Roman senate to the prominent post of Pontifex Maximus, albeit through bribery and blackmail. Caesar served as governor of Further Spain (Roman territories that included Portugal and parts of Spain). He returned to Rome in 60BC, allying himself with Pompey and Crassus to achieve election to the senate. The pact was known as the First Triumvirate and Caesar forced through legislation to suit his allies. Caesar appointed himself governor of Gaul in 58BC and led campaigns to Britain in 55 and 54BC. However, events turned sour for Caesar. He was unable to pay his debts, the Triumvirate expired after the death of Crassus in 53BC and he embarked on a civil war against Pompey's republicans, which led him to Egypt and the liaison with Cleopatra. Having defeated the republicans over various territories, Caesar declared himself dictator for life and undisputed master of Rome. This autocratic rule angered his enemies, who organised a conspiracy led by Marcus Brutus and Cassius. On 15 March 44BC the conspirators stabbed Caesar to death in the senate.

THE KIRKBURN SWORD

THE KIRKBURN SWORD represents a most beautiful and dedicated piece of craftsmanship. Discovered at Kirkburn in 1987 during excavations on burials, which included the famous Wetwang-style chariot internments, or 'bicycle burials' as Mick calls them, after their typical plan of a corpse laid over two chariot wheels, the Kirkburn sword was actually found in a smaller less formal burial of an older man.

This is one of the finest examples of an Iron Age sword discovered anywhere in the world. At 70cm (28in) in length, it's what would be classed as a long sword, a type which the Roman writer Tacitus later tells us was feared by the Roman legionaries. Dating to around 300BC, the Kirkburn sword would have been created by a metalsmith who had a wide range of skills at his disposal. The composition of the sword is extraordinarily complicated with over 30 parts, including the iron blade with bronze, horn and enamel inlays, brought together to create an extremely high-status work of art.

The individual who bore this sword was obviously important, yet it wasn't only a symbol of power. One of the adjacent burials featured an individual wearing a very early example of chain mail, so they may also have been a fighting group. The advent of swords in the Bronze Age is often credited as a sign of

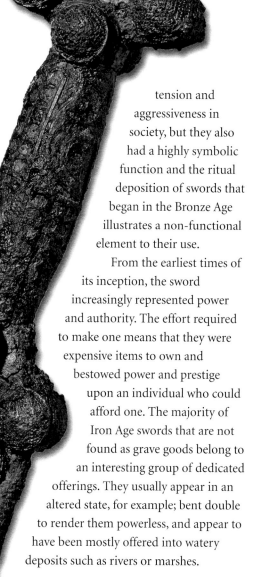

tension and aggressiveness in society, but they also had a highly symbolic function and the ritual deposition of swords that began in the Bronze Age illustrates a non-functional element to their use.

From the earliest times of its inception, the sword increasingly represented power and authority. The effort required to make one means that they were expensive items to own and bestowed power and prestige upon an individual who could afford one. The majority of Iron Age swords that are not found as grave goods belong to an interesting group of dedicated offerings. They usually appear in an altered state, for example; bent double to render them powerless, and appear to have been mostly offered into watery deposits such as rivers or marshes.

Left: The hilt and grip of the Kirkburn sword, a remarkable example of craftsmanship which involved the smith compositing over 30 different parts to make a weapon of great value.

IRON AGE FORT

The Iron Age settlement shown here is based on some of the houses found at Gear. We have added more ramparts to represent a typical small Iron Age fort.

The men here carry swords and the blades are made of iron. Their clothes and shields carry elements of what we now call 'Celtic' designs. The man carrying the spear has the kind of spiky hair that the Romans recorded as having been distinctive of Iron Age Britons.

In the background are Iron Age cattle which played an important role both in the agriculture and also the social status of their owner.

Around the huts would have been large numbers of pits which are common on Iron Age sites. Some were used for storage of grain but often seemed to have some ritual significance. It's likely that within the huts there would have been frames for weaving cloth.

This village has access to imports of wine and oil from continental sources, showing increasing trade at this time. It's possible that this family and the settlement they stand outside would have been more conscious of external threats and the need to defend their territory than in previous times.

The Age of Hillforts

FROM THE SIXTH to the fourth centuries BC there was a boom in the construction of fortified sites on hilltops and escarpments. Though much of the population still lived in small settlements or farmsteads in agricultural lowlands, some of these sites also appear to gain defences. A renewed enthusiasm for boundary marking, by digging bank and ditch earthworks, hints at the importance of defining areas of ownership, and it's from these protective measures that some archaeologists have interpreted the Early Iron Age as a period of general unrest.

The image that springs to mind is one of people living in fear as warriors roamed the land. The reality is probably less dramatic. The large-scale earthworks of sites such as Maiden Castle in Dorset and Danebury in Hampshire represented a statement of power and status and probably served as a deterrent. The lack of archaeological evidence for large tribal battles also takes our attention away from comparisons with set-piece conflicts. Alternatively, just because evidence has not been found doesn't mean that fighting didn't take place. The physical remains of the massive earthworks and the fact that they were built are the main clues we have and it's from these we must try to build our picture of the past.

Above: *A great view of one of the many rampart ditch sections of Maiden Castle in Dorset. Attackers would have to surmount these banks, and an additional timber palisade which has long since been lost, if they were to attempt to infiltrate the interior of the site.*

A moment in time: Maiden Castle ramparts

The ramparts of Maiden Castle are awe inspiring, yet what we see today are only the remains. The original defensive works were topped by a timber palisade, while the ditches would have featured sharper profiles. This power centre of the Durotriges people was a formidable fortress, but it didn't survive the Roman invasion. Originally it was a site of importance for prehistoric peoples, clearly seen by the remains of a Neolithic causewayed enclosure and barrow. Some time before 500BC a set of ramparts was added to enclose storage pits for grain – a stronghold for the wealth produced by the Durotriges. Then, about 150BC, when many other hillforts had declined, a development programme took place.

During this later phase, roundhouses fill the interior, creating one of the largest settlements in the country, but it's the works on the ramparts which captivate us, constructions so vast they remain over 2000 years later. Hundreds of workers toiled with picks, shovels, wicker baskets and timbers as thousands of tonnes of soil and chalk rubble were excavated in a monumental effort to construct colossal glacis ramparts. These ramparts are so called because the outside face of the bank acts as a direct continuation of the internal slope of the ditch, creating an almost insurmountable defensive incline. Earthworks at the main gate are of an unsurpassed quality, designed to make a maze of corridors through which any offensive force must run the gauntlet. The very act of creating this final stage of Maiden Castle represents a great engineering feat. Maiden Castle was an icon in an age of power display, when regional tribes flexed their muscles like the superpowers of today.

The historical and archaeological story

With some 47 acres enclosed by 2.5km (1.6 miles) of ramparts made from massive earthwork banks and ditches, Maiden Castle stands as a remarkable symbol of Iron Age engineering and design. The historical record, under the writer Suetonius, tells us that the Roman general Vespasian 'fought thirty battles, subjugated two warlike tribes and captured more than twenty oppida', and it has been suggested that Maiden Castle was one of these sites.

A store of thousands of pebbles used for slings was discovered within the fort during excavation, but the most intriguing evidence for conflict at Maiden Castle is the burial of the dead. Human remains have been found which show battle scars inflicted by Roman weapons. Skulls display the telltale square holes punctured by ballista bolts and one burial even contained the projectile in situ, wedged into the spine. However, recent re-assessment of the material has downplayed the 'war cemetery' theory, regarding it as a not untypical Iron Age cemetery.

The phenomenon of hillforts in Britain is varied and Maiden Castle can be seen as rather special. Fortified hilltop sites tend to fall in central and southern Britain with addition hillfort 'zones' in the north and Scotland. Their purpose and periods of use appear to be quite diverse. Some early hillforts, such as Breiddin in Powys, evolved out of Bronze Age structures while some regions, such as East Anglia, only constructed hillforts towards the Later Iron Age. Some examples, like Crickley Hill in Gloucestershire, are small and contain evidence for occupation, while other larger sites have no trace of roundhouses and appear to be just defended enclosures. This has led to many theories about hillforts, from safe havens only occupied during times of trouble to first indications of urban living. Some suggest that hillforts are not suitable for permanent occupation as they do not have a water supply, but walking long distances to fetch water is common practice in many developing-world communities. Whatever the reality, this phenomenon of major earthwork construction provides us with some of the most impressive Iron Age sites.

PALAEOLITHIC

MESOLITHIC

NEOLITHIC

BRONZE AGE

IRON AGE c700BC–AD43

The Age of Hillforts c700BC

ROMAN

ANGLO-SAXON

VIKING

NORMAN

MIDDLE AGES

TUDOR

STUART

GEORGIAN

VICTORIAN

MODERN

Fortified Houses – Scottish Brochs

BROCHS ARE THE best-known form of prehistoric defended tower house, found in the Western Isles, Orkney and Shetland, and on neighbouring parts of the Scottish mainland. They were massive, circular, windowless stone towers, built using an unmortared drystone technique. The best preserved of them, the Broch of Mousa, in the Shetlands, and originally one of a pair, still stands 13.3m (44ft) high, making it the tallest prehistoric building in Britain. Their main characteristic was a carefully constructed and very strong hollow wall, inside which ran stairs. The interior of the tower was most probably roofed and the wooden supports for an upper floor, or floors, were lodged on an internal ledge, known as a scarcement. Each floor was reached by a narrow entranceway through the inner 'skin' of the wall from the internal staircase. The cavity within the wall contained small cell-like compartments and galleries at each floor level and there was always a

substantial 'guard chamber' close to the front door, at ground level. This was the only entrance and it led into a corridor which passed straight through the wall into the interior.

It used to be thought that brochs were places of refuge, but there is now sufficient information from excavated sites, such as Dun Vulan on South Uist in the Western Isles, to suggest that these were places of permanent domestic habitation. This suggestion finds support from the discovery at Scalloway Broch, on Shetland, of huge quantities of burned grain. The excavators of Dun Vulan believe that brochs were never built to deter serious or sustained attack; instead they see them as monumental houses, rather than small forts. Their defences were simply too weak: the rough walls could readily be climbed by determined attackers, the roof was unprotected from such assault, and the entranceway arrangement lacked any form of outer protection, so the door could easily have been rammed. External visibility is essential to any fortification and brochs lacked windows to the outside. It was also impossible to access the top of the wall from the interior of the building, thereby denying the defenders an important tactical advantage.

Traditionally it was believed that brochs were in use between 100BC and AD100, but recent radiocarbon dating from the broch at Scatness, in Shetland, suggests that the first true brochs were built from 400–200BC and they continued to be occupied throughout the Scottish Late Iron Age (AD300–900). It was also once believed that brochs were introduced to Scotland by folk from outside the region, but this is no longer generally accepted. Instead, they are now thought to have developed from an existing tradition of thick-walled round buildings, which were being constructed in the north-west of Scotland from at least 800BC.

Above: The solid foundation remains of many brochs can be seen throughout Scotland. They are testament to the great towers which once stood upon them as strongholds in times of trouble.

The Llyn Cerrig Bach Hoard

FROM LLYN CERRIG BACH on Anglesey comes probably the best-known example of an Iron Age votive offering in the British Isles. The offerings, mostly of metalwork, were first discovered in a partially silted-up lake, during the construction of a new airfield in 1942 and 1943. The site became famous not just for the remarkable finds it produced, but for the illustrated report and catalogue written by Sir Cyril Fox who was then Director of the National Museum of Wales. In his report, published in 1946, Fox makes some important remarks about the definition and description of British Celtic Art.

The discoveries at Llyn Cerrig Bach were made in wartime and included a number of human bones not reported at the time – probably for reasons of morale or censorship. Fox was inclined to place the deposition of the metalwork in the very late Iron Age, as part of Druidic rites, because we know that the Roman army, under Suetonius Paulinus, defeated an army of Britons fighting under Druidic leadership or inspiration, shortly before AD60. This bloody battle took place on Anglesey and it was the Romans' intention to defeat the Druids, whom they regarded as a threat. Today we would date the artefacts recovered from the lake to a rather longer period of time than Fox, ranging from the Early Iron Age, around 500BC, to sometime after AD100. This range of material would suggest that Llyn Cerrig Bach was not the site of a one-off Druidic ceremony but was a long-lived ritual pool where votive offerings were made over many years and on several occasions. Other sites of this tradition, which has its roots in the Bronze Age, are known elsewhere in Britain.

The best-known finds were two sets of neck-rings for five slaves. They are beautifully made and well thought-out: the chain between each prisoner is passed through the fastening loops, allowing

Above: *One of the bronze decorative and ceremonial plaques that belonged to a hoard discovered at Llyn Cerrig Bach, Llanfairyneubwll.*

individuals to be added to, or removed from, the gang, without disrupting the others. Sadly these unpleasant objects are not unique, as others are known from the territory of the Catuvellauni, the most powerful Iron Age tribal kingdom based in south-eastern Britain, where the slave trade seems to have been based. We cannot say what the social effects of this trade were, but they were probably severe. The market was provided by the Roman Empire and tribes living around the periphery were willing to export people, presumably captives taken in local disputes, for the slave trade.

Other items from the lake include swords, parts of harnesses, and pieces taken from carts and their wheels. Spearheads and a decorated shield were also found, plus part of a bronze trumpet and two large fragments from bronze cauldrons. These can be seen in the National Museum of Wales, in Cardiff.

Cross-Channel Trade

IT IS LIKELY that the presence of minerals such as tin provided the impetus for the first traders to come to Britain. The Dover boat discovered in 1992 was capable of crossing the Channel and carrying up to three tons of goods. Dating from the Bronze Age, it was probably one of a number of craft that could make the journey. Tin is a vital ingredient in making bronze but it is relatively rare. The only two sources in Western Europe are south-west Britain and Spain. The Romans knew that there was lead, silver and gold in Britain and one of their earliest names for Britain, *Cassiterides*, translates as the 'Tin Islands'.

In the Later Iron Age period, trade would be stimulated by the import of wine and olive oil from the Roman Empire, and on archaeological sites, including Gear Farm where Time Team excavated in 2002, we find amphorae (the main containers for imported materials) dating from the Iron Age, so it is clear that a considerable trade was already underway. Early documents refer to 'Ictis' – an island off Cornwall, probably St Michael's Mount – where local traders brought tin out over a causeway to be traded. As early as 600BC British tin was being transported to the Mediterranean and Irish gold was well known to early traders.

The first recorded exploration of the British Isles took place probably sometime around 330BC. The explorer was a man named Pythias, who came from the Greek colony at Massalia (modern Marseilles). His journey has been reconstructed by Professor Barry Cunliffe from passages quoted from the account, *On the Ocean*, Pythias wrote on his return. The original work no longer survives but it has been quoted by no less than 18 ancient authors, all of whom mention Pythias by name. Cunliffe believes that he was both a keen and an accurate observer who made significant scientific observations on his travels. For example, he made measurements of the changing day-length as he travelled north and of the height of the sun from which it was possible to calculate latitude. He even noted there was no star over the true north pole.

Barry Cunliffe believes that Pythias did not sail from Massalia, as some have suggested, but journeyed overland and boarded a local ship at the mouth of the River Gironde in the Bay of Biscay, making his remarkable journey in a series of short legs, each in a local vessel. From the Gironde he went to western Brittany, when he embarked for Britain, which he refers to as the Prettanic Isles. He probably took a local vessel bound for the tin-producing areas of Cornwall and he writes about a promontory called *Belerion* (probably Land's End). Pythias reckoned the round trip from the Gironde to Cornwall was a voyage of some ten days. He also refers to two triangular promontories in Britain as *Kantion* (Kent) and *Orkas* (Orkney). He travelled up the western side of Britain and noted the presence of Ireland. He may have gone as far north as Shetland, but then returned along the east coast. When he reached the English Channel he seems to have turned eastwards and travelled along the North Sea coast, perhaps as far as the River Elbe, where he noted the occurrence of amber on beaches.

As he makes reference to tin and amber, it seems likely that Pythias was exploring potential trade routes for Greece, whose supply of these commodities had been cut off by growing hostility between Greece and Carthage in the fifth century BC. The Carthaginians, based in modern Tunisia, controlled the Straits of Gibraltar and could have prevented Greek access to the Atlantic. This may explain why Pythias probably chose to travel overland to the Gironde at the start of his journey.

Right: The dramatic shoreline of Hengistbury Head. Little changed from prehistory, was this a site of early international trade?

CELTIC ART, which probably began in western and central Europe sometime around 500BC, has been called Britain and Ireland's only major contribution to world art. It evolved through a number of styles, which were originally quite restrained, but developed remarkable fluidity in the three centuries BC. It probably reached its artistic peak at about this time in Britain, where native craftsmen produced objects of extreme beauty, many of which were placed in rivers as deliberate offerings. A remarkable early flowering of Celtic Art has been discovered in the Arras cemeteries of east Yorkshire, starting in the fourth century BC. This northern tradition produced the remarkable Kirkburn sword (see page 99), whose scabbard is richly decorated with Celtic Art designs.

In southern Britain, Celtic Art came to an end following the Roman Conquest of AD43, but it continued to thrive in Ireland, northern and western Britain, in areas outside the direct sphere of Roman influence. It also continued in a modified form in southern Scandinavia during Roman times. Following the fall of the western Roman Empire, Celtic Art played an important role in influencing and revitalising the emerging art styles of the Anglo-Saxons, the Vikings and the western British and Irish.

The term 'Celtic Art' is probably incorrect, as much doubt has been thrown on the existence of an ethnically distinct group of people known as the Celts (see page 94). It should perhaps be known as Iron Age Art, but that is unlikely to catch on so it will probably continue to be known as Celtic Art.

The art is characterised by stylisation and the imaginative portrayal of prancing horses and moving animals. There is a strong sense of balance, but not of symmetry, giving an impression of motion. It is also characterised by blurring the distinction between naturalistic and abstract. In the past this has been seen as primitive. Thus the depiction of royal heads or prancing horses on early Celtic coinage is more about portraying royalty and movement than showing accurate representations of either. Similarly, concentration on eyes, sometimes portrayed as bulging, possibly reflects the belief that the eyes are the key to a person's character and thus require emphasis. Like Picasso and other twentieth-century artists, their Celtic forebears were concerned with expression and symbolism, more than representation pure and simple. They were interested in drawing animals and people from more than one direction at a time.

Those who created the finer examples of Celtic Art were superb craftsmen particularly adept at using compasses to mark out complex swirls and trumpet-like designs that seem anything but mechanically drawn. Sometimes these abstract shapes would gradually transform themselves into the faces of humans and animals. Some designs are caricatures that leave little doubt that the artists in question possessed a lively sense of humour.

Above: One of the most amazing finds in British archaeology, the Battersea Shield is a ceremonial item of armour which dates from around 350BC. Decorated with enamel beads, the shield is too thin to have been used practically.

Colchester and the First Towns

ALTHOUGH COLCHESTER, or *Camulodunum*, was Roman Britain's first town, and became an important early Roman garrison, it actually dates back to the Iron Age. The earliest Romano-British towns, like Colchester, were often placed near the sites of pre-Roman markets. The century and a half prior to the Roman Conquest of AD43 sees the first appearance of named British rulers. The most famous of these was Cunobelin, king of the Catuvellauni, who ruled his newly created kingdom from a large capital, which later became the site of Roman Colchester. His domain consisted of a confederation of tribes comprising most of East Anglia to the south of Norfolk, plus Kent and parts of southern England. His reign lasted over 30 years, which was very much longer than any of his contemporaries. He died sometime around AD40.

Today Late Iron Age remains around Colchester include some very impressive earthwork defences, substantial settlements and a number of important burials. One beneath a large mound known as the Lexden Tumulus is possibly that of a tribal king called Addedomaros who was buried in a planked wooden chamber around 15–10BC. His body was surrounded by fabulously valuable grave goods, including several large amphorae of wine imported from the Mediterranean.

It has been claimed that Colchester is Britain's earliest town, but of course that depends on what is meant by the word 'town'. Most people would see a town as a place where a large number of people lived and where certain things were either done for them, or were made easier to do. In the past, and perhaps today in certain places, country people lived in a more self-sufficient way: they drew their water from their own wells or springs, they disposed of their own rubbish and they saw to it that their drains emptied out at a sufficient distance from their houses to prevent smells and the spread of disease. In true towns people clubbed together, either to collect taxes that could be used to pay others to look after their water, rubbish and sewage, or to organise the work amongst themselves. The point is that town life requires some form of local government. 'Life in towns' is rather different to 'town life'. The term 'life in towns' suggests that people lived close by each other, but in an essentially rural way. In other words, individual households were essentially self-sufficient, and organised their own water, refuse and sewage, but probably not always very efficiently.

In the later years of the Iron Age, certain places in south-eastern Britain, like the regions around Colchester in Essex and St Albans, Welwyn and Baldock in Hertfordshire, began to take on some of the characteristics of towns. Settlements were closely packed together along well-defined roads, and defences sprung up in key areas, while cemeteries were marked off from housing.

Markets, too, were probably an important part of these large Iron Age settlements. There were also quite substantial farms and fields within the settled areas, but there is no suggestion of a common water supply, nor of regular rubbish collection, nor of any form of local government.

So were these towns, as we would understand the word today, or were they a series of rural settlements that had become densely packed together, simply because people wanted to live in that particular area – usually, just as today, for economic reasons to do with work, jobs and money? The simple answer is that we just do not know.

The Invasions of Julius Caesar

THE ROMAN EMPEROR Julius Caesar made two visits to Britain in 55 and 54BC. These two expeditions were essentially to gather intelligence and should be seen as a part of his campaigns in Gaul (France), which began in 58BC and ended in 51BC. The effects of his military operations in Gaul on Britain were to prove quite severe. In particular the long-established trade, conducted by a Gallic tribe known as the Veneti, between ports in Brittany and Dorset, first Poole Harbour and then Hengistbury, was disrupted when his army attacked Brittany in 57BC.

The general trade routes were probably very old, dating back at least as far as the time of Pythias the Greek (see page 106), but the quantities and range of goods moved began to increase after 100BC, with the first large-scale importation to Britain of wine in distinctive fired-clay vessels known as amphorae. The trade links were greatly enlarged after the fall of southern Gaul.

Exports from Britain included raw materials (metals, grain, hides) and, most importantly, slaves. Imports were mainly luxury goods: large quantities of wine, jewellery and other fine objects. Trade with Britain was not resumed until after Caesar's two visits when it shifted decisively away from the Brittany/Solent route, north-eastwards towards the Gallic tribe known as the Belgae who had close links with Kent and other powerful British tribes, such as the Catuvellauni around the Thames estuary.

Caesar's first expedition to Britain in 55BC involved 98 transport ships carrying two legions (each of some 10,000 men), plus cavalry and many accompanying warships. The landing was resisted and there were numerous subsequent skirmishes with the British. Eventually Caesar retreated back to Gaul, taking many hostages with him. Although to all appearances victorious, he had not had his own way entirely.

The following year he did things on a much larger scale. This time there were 800 ships transporting five legions and 2,000 cavalry. This huge force met stiff resistance under the leadership of Cassivellaunus, leader of the Catuvellauni, a tribe centred on Verulamium and parts of what is today called 'Mid-Anglia' (Hertfordshire and areas around). Caesar had a hard fight through Kent. He crossed the Thames into the Catuvellaunian heartland and eventually British morale broke down and Cassivellaunus sued for peace. Caesar returned victorious, again with many hostages, but he had met fierce opposition and was most probably relieved to have left Britain with his military honour intact.

The political history of relations between Britain and Roman Gaul in the 100 years after the second visit of Caesar is complicated in the extreme. There were numerous issues of coinage which provide us with very useful sources of information, showing that contacts with the continent grew stronger as Roman rule provided much-needed stability for Gaul. At this time, too, the Roman Army was busy conquering parts of Germany so Britain was not invaded for many decades. The result was a period of prosperity and a measure of stability. Early in the first century AD, the remarkable king of the Catuvellauni, Cunobelin, came to power and ruled for over 30 years, during which time he was able to exert some degree of authority over the constantly feuding British tribal kingdoms. He died sometime around AD40 and instability returned. Doubtless the instability that followed Cunobelin was a significant factor behind the Roman decision to invade Britain, some three years later, in AD43.

THE CONTROL OF heat and fire continued to improve throughout the Iron Age. Most of the advances were in the field of metalworking, and pottery still seems to have been fired either in open hearths or in simple clamps (see page 71). It is not until the Later Iron Age, after about 150BC, that the hardness of pottery suddenly improves, which would suggest that the first kilns were being made. Simple kilns can produce temperatures of around 1000–1200°C, enough to produce very hard pottery. Also at this time we find the first evidence for the use of the potter's wheel, which was probably little more than a simple turntable.

The first iron tools found in Britain around 750BC are copies of bronze tools, so it seems likely that they were made locally from the outset. Both iron and bronze continued to be used together until the start of the fourth century BC, when iron became the dominant metal for tools and weapons. Iron ores occur widely in Britain and although it sometimes only requires temperatures of 800°C to smelt iron from iron ore, it needs temperatures of 1000–1100°C to work the metal. The 'raw' iron produced by smelting needs to be heated above, or close to, its melting point (1540°C) to remove impurities. The main problem that confronted early ironsmiths was not just reaching high temperatures, but retaining them long enough to fashion the metal and controlling the air supply, which needs to be carefully regulated.

Unlike bronze which is poured, iron is worked by repeatedly heating and hammering against an anvil, a process known as smithing. Iron is much harder than bronze and retains a cutting edge far longer. In the Iron Age most common tools took on recognisable forms: axes were made with a hole for the haft and knives with a pointed tang for the handle. The heavier shaft-hole axes of Iron Age type are much more effective than bronze axes. Later in the Iron Age, some swords seem to have been made from a form of carbon steel which can be made by heating iron to high temperatures in close contact with charcoal.

Waterlogged sites have revealed evidence for fine Iron Age fabrics and for expert carpentry. The period also saw the manufacture of the first spoked wheels and of carts and chariots with an early form of sprung suspension. The introduction of linked horses' bits also gave riders much better control of their mounts. During the Bronze Age and Neolithic wheat and barley were ground to flour using so-called 'saddle querns' that were worked by rubbing two stones backwards and forwards. In the Iron Age these were replaced by the more efficient rotary quern where the upper of two flat, circular stones was rotated by a long handle.

Above: *The heavily corroded blade of an Iron Age sword dating to around 100BC. Unfortunately the nature of iron means that it quickly decays, resulting in many lost examples through time.*

6 ROMAN

TIME TEAM HAS dug at over 20 Roman sites, including Hadrian's Wall, Arbeia Roman fort, large villa sites such as Dinnington with its wonderful mosaics, Tockenham and Turkdean, where we discovered a sunken Roman bath. We have searched for remnants of Roman roads, temples and forts and have been lucky enough to find many beautiful objects, including rings and high-status pottery. We discovered two rare Roman inscriptions at Greenwich and Ancaster, which was probably one of our most fascinating digs, revealing a Roman coffin buried according to Christian rites and yet containing a plaque dedicated to the pagan god Viridius.

When we look back on these digs and consider the difference between the Roman period and what went before, contrasting images come to mind. The softer, more organic nature of Iron Age round-houses that we have found and reconstructed is different from the hard-edged classically styled stonework that we've seen on villa sites; while the dark peat floors inside the roundhouses in which we've found bone tools and pottery are in marked contrast to the mosaic pavements and concrete floors found on Roman sites. The technological advances that accompanied the Roman invasion have been emphasised by our reconstructions.

One favourite example was the building of a Roman hypocaust which, on the final day, featured Mick and Phil warming their sock-clad feet on heated terracotta floor tiles. Watching their clear delight at the heat, which around AD200 would have probably been accompanied by the luxury of a warm bath afterwards, made you realise the difference such comforts would have made to wealthy Iron Age families during a British winter.

One of the key finds on villa sites we dig are hypocaust tiles. These specialised items provide evidence of Roman underfloor heating and their existence emphasises the control and organisation of labour needed to keep them in operation. These heated rooms were often decorated with mosaics. They are not only utilitarian but full of artistic, decorative touches that involved the employment of skilled artisans whose sole occupation was the laying down of such floors for the wealthy Romans. These and other luxury artefacts make any archaeologist conscious of the tremendous increase in consumer goods that came in the wake of the Roman Conquest. Time Team always feels relieved to dig Roman sites because we are more likely to find artefacts than in the earlier periods.

I asked a number of Time Team's experts about the key excavations that have informed our knowledge of Roman Britain. Guy de la Bédoyère, somewhat mischievously, offered the following thought: 'Once you've got the historical documents and sorted the dates out, the next most important contribution to our understanding of the Romans in Britain comes from the inscriptions and coins.'

His point is that much of what we know about this period has stayed fairly constant since the early part of the twentieth century. The excavation of a new villa site or bit of road merely adds what he calls 'a bit of set dressing'. In search of another view, I talked to Tony Wilmott and Richard Reece, two of Time Team's regular experts. Tony pointed out that more recent excavations have given us new insight into types of settlement that had previously been neglected. He cited the work on fort sites like Inchtuthil, created to house temporary detachments of troops. Richard Reece pointed out the way more recent work on town sites like Verulamium, near St Albans, had shown its continuity from what was originally an Iron Age centre, through the first-century Roman development and its reconstruction after the Boudican revolt, and then its later history well into the fourth century.

A number of our experts referred to Barry Cunliffe's work at Bath as having added greatly to our understanding of religion in Roman Britain and in particular how local Celtic gods were incorporated into the Roman system. At Lullingstone, Hinton St Mary and Water Newton, evidence of a thriving Christian culture helped to illustrate aspects of Roman life that are normally less obvious in excavations.

Of course, the Roman presence was not just about home comforts and imported luxury items – there was military power. We have often worked with the re-enactment group, the Ermine Street Guard and seeing them in action makes you realise that the Roman army's planning and technological advances were on a different scale to the Iron Age. There is a precision and regularity to the projection of power. Forts, villas, cities are constructed to a precise set of plans, at least in principal and these are systematically laid out in instruction manuals which emphasise that here is a power that depends on the literacy of large numbers of its citizens.

The oral tradition of the Iron Age was replaced by a culture that communicated through documents and books. The Celtic bard with his harp, if such a person ever existed, was superseded by historians and philosophers, such as Tacitus and Dio Cassius who recorded the events of history to provide lessons for the empire's citizens. Caesar himself felt it important to record the lessons he'd learnt during the wars with the Gauls. It was the Romans who first brought schools and a system of education to Britain. They were able to force through these cultural and political changes because they had supreme military force.

Britain's place in the Empire

Rome was perhaps the first European superpower and Britain was initially on its fringes. Existing on the edge of a large and expanding empire must have felt to the Iron Age Britons, like those small countries close to superpowers like China, America and Russia feel today. Aware of their vast economic power and military strength, the choice is to engage with them economically and perhaps be eventually absorbed or to hold out and risk an eventual invasion.

When considering the Roman contribution to British history, it is useful to make a distinction between those technological advances which brought a degree of civilised comfort – control of water supplies, heating for houses, architectural advances, many of which decayed rapidly after the Romans left – and those that had a more permanent effect.

After the invasion

In terms of historical epochs, compared to the prehistoric periods, 360 years is not a vast amount of time. However, the Romans occupied Britain for a period longer than that which today separates us from Civil War, and their influence was critical, particularly in imposing a unified political and geophysical state that created a whole out of what had been dispersed and often warring chiefdoms.

The roads that linked the new entity were critical to controlling the country and they had a permanent influence on the rest of Britain's history. So too did the creation of London as the capital. The Thames had previously been a tribal boundary and many other towns, including Colchester, could claim to be more important. The Romans made London the key city, and the Thames and the roads radiating out from London became the hub of Roman Britain. Over 9660km (6000 miles) of roads were constructed by the Roman legionaries who were both soldiers and construction labour.

After the successful Claudian invasion of AD43, the Romans set about establishing working relationships with those chiefs who accepted their role and using legions to crush those that didn't. Heavy-handed treatment and a total failure to win 'hearts and minds' led in some cases to revolt. Boudica's rebellion was the most dangerous (see page 124).

According to Tacitus, over 70,000 people died but Roman discipline and military skill enabled them to defeat a force that vastly outnumbered them. Roman reprisals were without mercy, but it seems it taught the Romans an important lesson and a fairer treatment of local disputes resulted. In fact Guy points out that the Romans 'wrote up' the story of Boudica, as a lesson to local commanders and out of a desire to criticise the ineffectual Emperor Nero.

The Roman legacy

With a more settled period came the chance to create many of the monuments we consider as examples of Roman civilisation – sacred sites like Aquae Sulis at Bath, completed around the end of the first century AD, city centres with amphitheatres, market places and temples and in the countryside,

opulent villas which could almost qualify as palaces, like Fishbourne. Architecture is one of the great influences from this period and there was a conscious attempt by Roman rulers to express themselves through iconography – symbols of power. The temple of Claudius in Colchester was among the first buildings in Britain erected to impose and impress Roman power on its viewers.

For Guy, this is part of a package which brings order, stability and predictability: 'A roundhouse is an organically flexible concept, but a set of columns in a particular Roman style created a regularity which was appealing. One thing we are all terrified of is the unpredictability of the natural environment. A power structure that communicates a sense of some sort of control is impressive. Because we are so used to that idea of order, I think we can scarcely imagine what the transition from the Iron Age world would have been like.'

Previous spread: The magnificent remains of the Roman baths at Bath, Avon.

Above: Phil Harding carefully excavates a stone-lined Roman burial. Roman burial practice varied from cremation to burial, with and without deposited grave goods, throughout the period.

ROMAN IN DETAIL

FROM THE MOMENT that Roman legionaries, encumbered with equipment, climbed down from their boats and waded through the waves to the British shore, nothing would be the same again. The Roman invasion of Britain in AD43 is one of the most significant events in our history; it led to a fundamental change in the structure of the country and an advance into a new civilised world. It was a period when we first saw evidence of Christianity in this country.

As we have seen in previous chapters, prior to the invasion people lived under a system of tribal government with the country divided into domains controlled by a variety of monarchs. If we could climb into the Time Team helicopter and fly over the Later Iron Age landscape – a largely agricultural way of life – farmsteads and occasionally fortified hilltop settlements would be a familiar sight across the country. We'd see small fields of crops, smoke trails rising from small gatherings of roundhouses and scarce traces of prehistoric trackways. In many ways, our view from the air would be little different had we flown 1500 years before over a Bronze Age Britain. This isn't to say that Later Iron Age life was a static affair of long summer days spent tending cattle and family in a kind of primitive utopia. The royal hierarchies were certainly powerful, influential and, at times, involved on the world stage, but technologically and governmentally the average Iron Age Briton would have had little grasp of the scale of changes waiting to come over the horizon.

With the invasion of AD43, Britain lost its independence and became a province of the Roman empire (Britannia). During the history of our island's 357-year occupation, the Roman lifestyle was both despised and craved, enforced and willingly adopted. The Romanisation of Britain left a permanent and, at times, exotic mark on our past. To a certain degree everyone was either Romanised or in the shadow of the imposing Roman empire. Those living within the boundaries of the frontier were obliged to live under the Roman authority and all that entailed, from following Roman laws to paying taxes, while people existing outside the frontiers still lived close to and were influenced by the economic and military influence of the all-powerful empire.

The Roman way of life

One of the great successes of the Roman method of conquest was the encouragement of native peoples to adopt the Roman way of life. Before the invasion a small number of large settlements already existed, mostly within the hillforts built on high ground and escarpments and while these served as tribal centres, they were on the whole hardly what we would call towns. Most of the population existed in small rural farmsteads and, in an effort to build some formal structure into their newly adopted society, the Roman administration embarked on a system of creating towns – places which set examples to the natives of civilised living and centres of regional control. To be Roman was to adopt a new way of living. The ultimate prize was to become a Roman citizen, but for those unable to reach those heights, emulation remained as an acceptable alternative.

The towns were places to be Roman. They contained temples dedicated to Roman gods (often united with native deities), forums and markets selling exotic goods from across the empire, and public baths in which to exercise and socialise. The urban centres even echoed with a different language – Latin, the language of government.

Roman government

There was no common feeling of a united nation holding the tribes of Britain as a collective before the Romans arrived. This changed when the invaders introduced our first ever centralised government. The province was commanded by a governor who was a direct representative of the emperor. Like our modern-day Prime Minister, the governor served a term of three or five years but he was not elected. He was chosen personally by the emperor for the post.

While a system of government controlled the populace, a continual feature of the province, as a frontier zone, was the ever-present military. The Roman army, certainly of the first century, was of a very high standard and the disciplined, organised force was almost unbeatable. For the conquered Britons, the army represented not only the occupying force but also an opportunity. The Roman army actively recruited native peoples into its auxiliary units. In one form this served to build the army, but in another it absorbed local men of fighting age and sent them safely away to different parts of the empire, thus keeping rebellion at bay. For instance, the auxiliary troops serving in Britain were often from as far away as Syria and Spain. For the recruit, the army offered regular pay, specialist training, quality food, shelter and clothing, opportunities and most revered of all, citizenship, which was awarded after 25 years of service.

Roman influence

Over the length of the occupation many people took to the Roman way of urban living, but towns also required the support of resources. The ever-expanding road network allowed the farmsteads in the countryside to fuel the towns and, as a result, some of the more successful farmers developed their smallholdings into impressive villa estates.

Though these often became lucrative businesses, for the majority of native Britons living in the countryside the small family farm continued and for most only some of the trappings of Roman civilisation are likely to have been absorbed.

For all the different influences the Roman period represented, from government and civilisation to the introduction of new technologies and urban living, the whole of Britain was never fully conquered. Some consider this a sign that the ancient Briton was too tough a nut to fully crack. Severus, for example, found Scotland almost impossible to control, but it might also have been that ultimately Rome just didn't consider the further reaches of great enough importance.

Though we may have only been on the fringe of greatness, and often low on the emperor's list of priorities, the fact that we did, for a time, come under the influence of Rome, and were part of an empire which reached from here to Syria and from Germany to North Africa, provides us with a fascinating and culturally stimulating port of call in our journey through time.

Above: *A fourth-century mosaic discovered in a villa at Hinton St Mary, Dorset. The 'P-X' featured behind the central figure is a Chi-ro, an early sign symbolising Christian faith.*

This timeline gives you a quick, at-a-glance guide to what happened when in Britain in the Roman era, helping you to understand the order of events. We've also included, in red type, some key events that happened elsewhere in the world.

World event: Jesus Christ is born	c5BC
Roman invasion of Britain (see page 122)	AD43
Foundation of Colchester	AD49
Caractacus (Caradog) is captured in Wales and taken to Rome	AD51
Revolt and suppression of Queen Boudica of the Iceni tribe (see page 124)	AD60–61
Conquest of Wales and the North completed	AD70–84
World event: Mt Vesuvius erupts and buries Pompeii and Herculaneum	AD79
Northern frontiers:Hadrian's Wall and Antonine Wall (AD143) are built (see page 125)	AD122
London as capital – London's city wall completed	C AD200
Emperor Septimus Severus arrives and invades Caledonia (Scotland)	AD208
St Alban martyred for sheltering Christians	C AD210
Constantine recognises Christianity as legal religion (see page 126)	AD312
Roman golden age of villas in Cotswolds (see page 127)	AD340–380
Picts, Scots overrun Hadrian's Wall and ravage northern Britain	AD367
Christianity the official religion of the Roman Empire	AD391
Saxon raids on Britain increase	C AD408
Rome unable to defend Britain (see page 128)	AD441
World event: Attila the Hun	AD453
Time of legendary Arthur (see page 130)	C AD500

World event: Mount Vesuvius erupts

The morning of 24 August AD79 caught Pompeii unprepared for the catastrophe of the next 24 hours. Vesuvius had lain dormant for a long time but the magnitude of the eruption buried the town and most of its population. Roman culture held a fascination in predicting the future and detecting portents to foretell the 'wrath of the gods'. The irony of this is revealed in preserved and detailed letters offering eyewitness accounts. Seismic activity and plumes of ash emanated from Vesuvius in the days before the eruption but were largely ignored due to the belief that the volcano was inactive. However, as volcanologists know today, long periods of inactivity increase the force of the eruption. Pompeii responded in panic as clouds of ash and pumice descended. Instead of fleeing, many decided to weather the storm under shelter, but later that night pyroclastic surges (an avalanche of hot ash, pumice, rock fragments and volcanic gas) meant instant death. The emissions buried Pompeii and preserved an archaeologist's dream as the buildings provided a valuable insight into Roman life. Artefacts and wall paintings have been discovered, whilst parts of the uncovered town have been reconstructed.

World event: Attila the Hun

One of the most feared and barbaric rulers ever, Attila ruled the Huns between AD433 and 453. Of Mongol ancestry, Attila originally shared the throne with his brother, Bleda, but killed him in AD445 to become sole ruler. Attila ravaged much of the European continent, causing devastation and bloodshed. He attacked the Balkan city of Naissus with horrific cruelty (AD441–442) and secured a firm position on the Roman-occupied side of the Danube. By AD447 Attila had cut a swathe between the Black and Mediterranean seas and managed to defeat the Byzantine Emperor, Theodosius II, who pleaded for peace and offered an annual tribute. When Theodosius died in AD450, his successor rescinded payments to Attila, who reacted furiously. 'The Scourge of God' mobilised a huge army and vented his wrath on the West. Attila invaded the Rhine with a force numbering hundreds of thousands and left a trail of death and destruction through Germanic territories and Gaul. An alliance between Romans and Visigoths halted Attila's advance and he turned to Italy, but was dissuaded from pillaging Rome by Pope Leo the First. Attila died in AD453 after a night of drinking to celebrate his marriage.

ROMAN COINS

THE ROMANS INTRODUCED a money-based economy into Britain and their coins changed the way goods were exchanged. They also provided a way of emphasising Roman power and control and symbolised the stability of a state that could support such a system. Richard Reece, Time Team's Roman coins expert, refers to the relatively small numbers that were in circulation, but with the legions being paid in coin, smaller denominations soon filtered down to the rest of the citizens. The system was based on payment to soldiers and higher officials in gold, but then these coins were returned to the state in the form of taxes. Enough bronze coinage had to be in circulation to ensure that the gold coins could be returned.

The coins shown here illustrates the use of the financial system to advertise victories and conquests. On the reverse is a picture of a triumphal arch with Claudius triumphing over his enemies. We see an early version of the country's name written as 'de britann'. The head of Claudius sculptured in classical style makes it clear who is the man in charge.

For archaeologists, coin finds can be crucial in identifying and dating sites. We often discover them as stray finds but when found in a distinct stratigraphic layer in the context of an excavation, they can be a useful tool for dating the site.

Many Roman coins were minted in Gaul, but the main source was Rome. This was a complex operation involving the transport of raw materials and the safe carriage of the finished coins. Forgery was rife and we have often found clever forgeries where copper has been tinned to give a silver appearance. As the empire declined so did the source of coins and by around AD430 Britain had virtually ceased to be a money-based economy. After AD400 there are fewer coins and it is interesting to note that they become increasingly worn through use.

Above: *Bronze sestertius of the Emperor Claudius dating to the time of the invasion.*

ROMAN ROADS

This reconstruction reveals the benefits of Roman civilisation. The central feature is the road which provides easy transport for troops and commerce. The legionary cavalry soldier, accompanied by a foot soldier, is of high status and would have a cohort of legionnaires not far behind him. In the distance you can see the classical design of a villa which represents the beginning of an architecture that was new to Iron Age Britain.

A small settlement takes advantage of the passing traffic. A woman is selling food and drink and you can see the amphora containing oil and wine – examples of imports introduced by Roman merchants. The buildings are roofed in tile and some have painted plaster. However, despite these innovations, you can also see

Romano-British carrying on with their lives, emphasising that not every aspect of British life was romanised. The soldiers pay in coin – most likely small denomination bronze-copper alloy coins, received as change after paying taxes with silver or gold coins received as wages. The soldier on his knees in the foreground has lost the gold coin that represents a month's wages – it will be this coin that will be found 1800 years later.

The road is the Fosse Way – still a major route today. As in Roman times, it links up with a system with London as its hub.

The Roman Invasion of Britain

PRIOR TO INVASION, ever present across the sea, lay the fringes of the Roman empire, a sprawling superpower commanding provinces from North Africa to the Rhine and Syria to Spain. Rome was aware of Britain following the expeditions of Julius Caesar some 100 years before, but civil war in the Roman republic left Britain out of the limelight. This didn't stop some of the Roman emperors, such as Augustus, attempting to intervene in British Iron Age matters. Roman writers such as Strabo tell us that Britain posed little threat to Rome in these intervening years and so it's safe to assume that there was scant appetite for an occupation, but a series of events was underway both in Britain and within the new Roman empire which were to make invasion impossible to avoid.

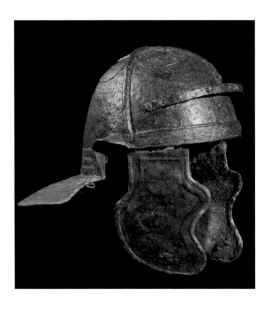

Above: *A Roman military helmet made from bronze, dating from between the first and third century* AD.

In Britain the treaties agreed during Julius Caesar's expeditions were generations old. The growing economy of the south-east made some tribes extremely powerful, including the Catuvellaunians, a tribe stretching from Northamptonshire and Cambridgeshire to Buckinghamshire and Essex. Aggressive expansion by the Catuvellauni seems to have been tolerated by Rome, but closely monitored. When the Catuvellaunian king, Cunobelin, died his sons, Togodummnus and Caractacus, embarked on a further phase of expansion which sent messengers and princes from neighbouring tribes, including Verica, King of Atrebates, to Rome to ask for help.

In AD41 Claudius was named emperor following the untimely death of Caligula. Considered by many to be unsuitable for the post, he needed the kudos of a victory to gain the support of the people and senate of Rome. The catalyst came in the form of Verica with his perfectly timed request for help.

A moment in time: the invasion

For his invasion to work Claudius needed a capable and well-respected commander. He chose Aulus Plautius, the governor of a Danube province with battle-hardened experience from fighting in the region. Gathering at Boulogne, Plautius brought the IX Hispana Legion and drew three more from the Rhine area: the II Augusta, XIV Gemina and the XX Valeria. It has been estimated that the initial invasion force would have numbered some 40,000 men. The author Dio tells us that some difficulty was experienced in getting the army to embark across the sea because the island was outside the known world, but following a rousing speech by an emissary of Claudius the invasion was underway. With this snippet of history it's interesting to note that Claudius was not with his troops and commander as they massed on the Channel coast.

The voyage of Dio's 'three divisions' was not without drama as rough seas and lightning all added to the ordeal. Yet when they did land, the vista of thousands of highly trained, well-equipped soldiers must have been a sight to behold, a scene the likes of which had only been experienced on a far smaller scale some 100 years before with Caesar's invasion, vaguely remembered in folk songs and tales.

The actual landing site remains unknown. Whether Dio's three divisions landed at three separate locations, or were staggered in their timing to land as waves at a single point, is open to interpretation, but there is doubt that wherever they landed – maybe Kent or even Sussex – they had a huge impact.

The archaeological evidence

The opposition to the invasion was nowhere to be seen, either caught unaware of the timing of the invasion, or more likely reserving commitment until the scale and location of the invading force was fully appreciated. The native Britons held out in the countryside while the Romans secured their beachhead. As the Romans advanced north and west they encountered the massed warriors of the Britons and closed battle twice in desperate pitched fighting, finally pausing after a battle on the Thames. It's at this point that the whole invasion was put on hold. Aulus Plautius waited for his emperor Claudius, who arrived with an entourage of guards and politicians, and even elephants, to observe the taking of Colchester and receive the submission of kings. After 16 days, Claudius returned to Rome to bask in the glory of his success, leaving Plautius to continue his campaign as governor of the new province, Britannia.

As Britain was a province under military influence, the archaeology of the Roman army is substantial and well documented. However, evidence for the initial invasion is relatively scant. Most of the known temporary camps and early forts belong to the consolidating phases of conquest which followed in later years. We have no evidence of coastal defences built to counter the Roman invasion threat. This could partly be credited to a distinct lack of central command and shared objectives of the defending Britons. The lack of a unified preparedness, combined with the transient nature of an invading army on the march, makes defining the archaeology of invasion difficult.

Intriguing evidence takes the form of a coin hoard discovered in 1957 at Bredgar in Kent. This selection of 37 gold coins represented about four years' savings of a legionary and dates to the year of the invasion. Perhaps they were buried by a soldier before a battle, hoping to reclaim them at a later date.

PALAEOLITHIC

MESOLITHIC

NEOLITHIC

BRONZE AGE

IRON AGE

ROMAN AD43–c AD410

Roman Invasion
of Britain AD43

ANGLO-SAXON

VIKING

NORMAN

MIDDLE AGES

TUDOR

STUART

GEORGIAN

VICTORIAN

MODERN

Boudica's Revolt

THE STORY OF the Boudican revolt contains all of the aspects of a good thriller – tragedy, despair, intrigue, revenge and a dramatic ending, but it's the sum of all these parts that makes this revolt such an important event. The potent image of a warrior queen defying an invader, a snowballing revolution against injustice, the British people united in resistance to the last – all these themes have been seized upon in more recent times with Boudica (pronounced Boo-dikka) fitting the Victorian and Georgian requirements for a British hero (it was the Victorians who corrupted her name to Boadicea (Bo-de-see-ah).

The Roman writers Tacitus and Dio both leave us an historical record of the Boudican Revolt of AD60–61, when the Iceni tribe (covering modern-day Norfolk and Suffolk) rebelled after the savage treatment of their queen. Archaeological evidence in the form of a deep burnt layer of stratigraphy shows that Colchester, London and Verulamium, near St Albans, suffered devastating fires and destruction during the first century, and one of the most amazing Roman finds of all time is connected with these events – a large bronze hollow-eyed statue head of emperor Claudius. Archaeologists like to think that it may have once belonged to a dominating edifice in the temple precinct at Colchester and was looted by Boudica's forces.

In AD60, 17 years after the invasion, during the early years of Roman administration the native tribes of the occupied territories struggled to maintain their identities while dutifully adhering to Roman rule. On his deathbed, King Prasutagus of the Iceni tribe tried to arrange for half his wealth and territories to be left to the Roman emperor Nero in the hope of guaranteeing his family partial rule. However, the Romans saw the retention of half the estate as an insult, so they seized all and had Boudica, his widow, publicly

Above: *Boudica, symbol of British rebellion. She may have ultimately failed in her revolution against the Roman oppressors, but she left her mark on our national identity.*

flogged and her daughters raped. This lit the fuse of British rebellion and by AD61 the undercurrents of native fear and anger reached boiling point.

With a large part of the Roman army in Wales subduing the Druid cult based on Anglesey, the first unprotected town to fall was Colchester, the Roman model of civilised living. Boudica led her forces on a violent campaign against all Romans and collaborators. Even a counter-attacking rescue by an infantry detachment of the IX Legion Hispana was destroyed. Buoyed by their success, the British gathered more forces and laid London and St Albans to ruin.

On a tide of victory Boudica took her army north-west to meet the might of Rome marching back from Anglesey. They collided somewhere in the Midlands, where the highly trained and disciplined Romans crushed the rebellion and destroyed the British hopes of independence. Her future bleak, Boudica took her own life with poison.

Building Hadrian's Wall

THE HISTORY OF Roman Britain is told by Roman historians, in particular Tacitus, whose biography of Roman military leader Agricola refers to the army garrisoning the south-west highlands of Scotland after defeating the Caledonians at the battle of Mons Graupius in AD84. Agricola's recall and events on the Rhine frontier meant the advance was halted and a gradual retreat to lowland Scotland began. Most of this later period has to be pieced together from excavations and inscriptions as no histories survive.

The main concentration of Roman forts at this time was between Carlisle and Corbridge along a valley road known as the Stanegate, connecting two coastal roads leading north into Scotland. Beyond these, some advance forts were maintained, especially at Dalswinton and Newstead to supervise border tribes. This new border had probably been in existence for a decade when renewed hostilities saw the outpost forts burnt and the Stanegate forts over-run, probably between AD100–105. Reconstruction of the Stanegate frontier was undertaken with fortlets and towers constructed between the forts, but the outpost forts were abandoned and the new frontier now stretched from Kirkbride to Newcastle.

Even this frontier was not stable as further inscriptions indicate more disturbances before the accession of Hadrian in AD117, who began a policy of re-enforcing Rome's frontiers. Hadrian's arrival in Britain in AD122 heralded the creation of one of the most evocative of these new frontiers, Hadrian's Wall. Planned, we believe, to be 10 Roman feet thick (about 3m/9ft 6in) and 20 Roman feet high and stretching from Bowness to Newcastle, the wall ran north of the Stanegate on high ground with a large outer ditch and a series of castles.

This grandiose design was undoubtedly Hadrian's, but it was built by the British legions (2nd Augusta, 6th Victrix and 20th Valeria as stone inscriptions on the wall attest), directed by the governor A. Plautius Nepos. Flaws in the original plan became apparent, such as the lack of suitable stone in the western sector which led to its completion in turf and the narrowing of the stone wall to speed up progress. The forts were also moved up to the wall and in all 16 forts were built, probably garrisoned by 10,000 cavalry and infantry troops. Forts were also constructed along the vulnerable western coast of the Solway Firth and the old outpost forts were re-occupied.

Construction was still underway when Hadrian died in AD138. The new emperor Antoninius Pius decided to abandon it and re-occupy Scotland. In the words of a contemporary '…he conquered the Britons through his governor, Lollius Urbicus and after driving back the barbarians, built another wall of turf'. This campaign took place in AD140–143 and the Antonine Wall was started soon after, running between the Clyde and Forth isthmuses. The new turf wall was up to 4.3m (14ft) wide and 2.7m (9ft) high, with an outer ditch up to 12m (40ft) wide and 3.6m (12ft) deep. Twenty earthen forts were placed along the wall, with fortlets in-between.

This frontier lasted until a rebellion in AD154 in the demilitarised territory of the Brigantes, south of Hadrian's Wall. The events of the next decade are confused, but it seems the Antonine Wall was abandoned and troops moved back to Hadrian's Wall to quell disturbances. The Antonine Wall was re-occupied between AD158–163, but a new governor, Calpurnius Agricola, arrived by AD163 with a new policy and the turf wall was abandoned. The new Hadrianic frontier saw the final completion of the stone wall, demonstrating that the Roman government had finally accepted that without more troops, Scotland could not be held. Thus Hadrian's Wall marked the northern limit of the empire.

The Introduction of Christianity

KEY EVENT AD306

IN THE YEAR AD306 the city of Eboracum (York), was the provincial capital of Northern Britain and military base of the emperor Constantius who had been campaigning against the Scots, accompanied by his son Constantine. However, on 25 June, Constantius died in the city. The assembled troops immediately heralded his son as emperor and the reign of one of the most influential of the Roman emperors began. Constantine had been born in AD273 at Nis in Serbia where his father was a junior army officer and his mother Helena is thought to have been an innkeeper's daughter. When he became emperor he had a distinguished military career behind him, but his succession was not assured, despite his bloodline.

He was a usurper as Severus had been chosen to succeed Constantius and the declaration at York brought about civil war in the empire. There was also another usurper in Rome, named Maxentius, and Severus marched against Maxentius, but his

army deserted him so he was forced to surrender. In AD312 Constantine moved against Maxentius and their armies met just outside Rome on the Milvian Plain. Constantine was victorious and in the same year he declared religious toleration of Christianity throughout the empire. Only two years later three British bishops, one from York, attended the Council of Arles, showing the speed at which the new religion had spread and it's likely that it had existed underground before this date.

Tradition says that Constantine was converted to Christianity by a vision just before the battle, but he was not baptised until just before his death. His approach to Christianity was pragmatic and his prevailing characteristic was one of conservatism, so his adoption of Christianity did not lead to a radical re-ordering of society. Constantine had been brought up in a time when military expertise was seen as an essential attribute for an emperor, but he had to control an empire where the greatest problems involved an economy in crisis.

Constantine ruled with an iron hand, but he gradually built up prosperity to a remarkable level. By entrusting some government functions to the Christian clergy, he actually made the church an agency of the imperial government. When he died in AD337 he had been given the title of 'Constantine the Great'. His support for Christianity was instrumental in it becoming the religion of Western Europe. In AD627 King Edwin of Northumbria built a church on the ruins of the Roman principia there. That church was the first minster and the forerunner of the cathedral that symbolises York today.

Left: *The old city walls of York, known to the Romans as Eboracum, once visited by Constantine who later embraced Christianity.*

The Golden Age of Roman Villas

BY THE BEGINNING of the fourth century, Britain had been Roman for more than 250 years. The Romans had introduced metalled roads, towns, a centralised system of law and order, everyday coinage, and innovations in land and water management. And in art and religion, a unique blend of Roman and Celtic styles and traditions had created what we call Romano-British culture.

Increasing barbarian threats in the third century destabilised the Roman world and helped provoke civil war. In Britain the system of towns, which served as the economic and political foundation of the Roman way of life, were in decline. The rich and influential members of society increasingly invested their time and money in country villas in the best agricultural land. During the fourth century some of these villas developed into virtual palaces.

Far more than just farms, the great villas in the Cotswolds and the south-west, such as Chedworth, Woodchester and Dinnington, became showcases for wealth. From them powerful men controlled local politics and the economy, and emphasised their importance by spending lavishly on mosaics, painted wall-plaster, silver tableware and other luxuries.

We don't know who the owners of these villas were, but the descendants of the tribal aristocrats who sided with the Romans during the conquest period are the most likely. Originally they had ruled their districts through the towns the Romans founded. Now they did so from their villas, showing off how Roman they had become by using themes from Roman myth and religion to decorate their houses and possessions.

These great villa owners set the pace for their age. Hundreds of less well-off families around Britain set out to imitate them, like the owners

Above: A mosaic fragment from Chedworth villa in Gloucestershire. Partying was a central part of villa life for Romanised Britons and this floor depicts scenes of debauchery.

of the modest villa at Sparsholt in Hampshire who could only afford one mosaic.

Villa economies relied on urban and foreign markets to sell produce and earn the profits that paid for building, running and decorating the villas. In the late fourth century Britain fell victim to barbarian invasions and a series of military opportunists who took troops away to fight in mainland Europe. Many villas show signs of decay or abandonment dating from this time. When Roman government ceased in Britain by 410, the system fell apart for ever. Over the next century all the remaining villas fell into ruin, even if the land surrounding them was still farmed. The gold and silver wealth mostly disappeared into the melting pot, but some hoards have survived, like the treasures from Mildenhall and Hoxne.

The Roman Withdrawal

THE END OF Roman Britain was a gradual process, influenced by internal events and happenings outside the province. Though Britain displays the archaeological remains of many great examples of Roman civilisation and architecture, in the context of the empire, our province was very much on the fringes, a position further complicated by administrative changes which occurred in the fourth century as a result of wars directly threatening Rome. During this time imperial efforts concentrated on the homeland, yet in the provinces we see a confusing contradiction where many towns and villas show periods of prosperity. While most areas doggedly continued and remained successful, under the steadily crumbling administration, the veneer of civilisation started to decay with almost imperceptible cracks.

Above: *A detail of Trajan's Column in Rome, a triumphal monument which contains great detail of Roman military equipment and structures.*

The emperor Diocletian reorganised the empire in AD293. Britain became one of twelve dioceses and was further divided into four provinces. A major restructure of the army followed and it was now commanded by a new elite of Comes (counts) and Dux (dukes). The outlying barbarian forces of the Scots from Ireland and the Picts from Scotland became unsettled, so much so that in AD343 the emperor Constans himself was forced to come to Britain to stabilise the turbulent situation. Saxon raiding at this time made the fortification of the south and eastern coast a priority and the establishment of the Saxon shore forts created a network of strong points from which to deter bands of Saxon raiders. Around AD350 the beginning of a trend, which was to continually sap Britain of its resources and security, started with the first big withdrawal of troops taking place as the usurper Magnentius made his claim for the imperial throne.

A moment in time: the barbarian conspiracy

The year AD367 brought more turmoil with what Roman writer Ammianus Marcellinus referred to as the 'barbarian conspiracy'. By the beginning of the fourth century the emperor Diocletian, and subsequently Constantine, had introduced reforms which settled the borders of the empire. But following

Constantine's death in AD337, a series of events unfolded which would bring the empire almost to its knees. The empire was inherited from Constantine by his sons, uninspiringly named Constantine II, Constans and Constantius II. Their infighting led to attempts by usurpers, such as Magnentius, to take the empire for themselves. Under this atmosphere of disorder (and constant troop withdrawals) the unromanised peoples saw their chance for revolt, and the barbarian conspiracy is a typical example of the unrest of the time.

The conspiracy happened three years after emperor Valentinian came to power, but it was the preceding authority which created the conditions for it to happen. According to Ammianus, as Valentinian set about returning security to the empire, news arrived that Britain was on the verge of ruin. The Scots were attacking in bands from the west, while Picts surged from the north. At sea and on the south-east coast Saxons and Franks raided by ship. The Roman general of the northern forts, Fullofaudes, was captured, while in the south Nectaridus, the count of the coast, was killed in combat. A rescue was orchestrated by the Roman count Theodosius who, with several units of troops, restored order through a series of clear-up actions and a programme of returning stolen property. Many of the fortified towns of the province gained extra defences.

The historical and archaeological story

While the barbarian conspiracy may have been something of a highpoint of civil unrest, by the late 380s fighting still continued, nibbling away at the façade of Roman civilisation, and the environment produced another British usurper, Magnus Maximus. Roman writer Zosimus tells us that Maximus withdrew even more troops to the continent for his battles against emperor Gratian. By the turn of the fifth century things had turned so bad for the empire that Rome itself was under direct threat from the warring Visigoths. The downfall and decay in Britain was now irreversible. By AD410 emperor Honorius decreed that 'Britannia must fend for herself'. This final political declaration signalled the end of the province as far as Rome was concerned.

Archaeology has found that the use of coinage quickly declined. Wealth held more currency in the metal of the gold and silver coinage rather than in the actual tokens, and a boom in burying hordes of valuables, such as those found at Hoxne and Mildenhall on the Norfolk and Suffolk borders, betrays an increased threat to the livelihood of well-to-do Romano-Britons.

Though some towns such as Cirencester fell into decay, others such as Silchester may have continued to be successful into the fifth century. With no central government and with the turmoil of continuing raids from abroad, Britain fragmented into a dispersed array of independent settlements and kingdoms. The influx of migrating peoples from northern Europe which ensued caused the next cultural development to unfold; the Saxon Age was upon us.

PALAEOLITHIC

MESOLITHIC

NEOLITHIC

BRONZE AGE

IRON AGE

ROMAN AD43–410

Roman
Withdrawal AD410

ANGLO-SAXON

VIKING

NORMAN

MIDDLE AGES

TUDOR

STUART

GEORGIAN

VICTORIAN

MODERN

The Arthurian Legend

TIME TEAM WENT in pursuit of the Arthurian legend in a special programme which showed how wide-ranging the story has become. Medieval storytellers, references in the lives of British saints and folk legends encouraged the belief that such a figure existed. Around AD600 a source fairly close to the likely time of Arthur's existence wrote in a Welsh poem titled *The Gododdin* that a local warrior who had not come up to scratch was 'no Arthur', implying that this was a reference familiar to his readers. The whole legend was given another potential twist by the discovery of a slate with a few letters claiming to spell 'ARTOgNOV' appearing at Tintagel. Most archaeologists, including Time Team, are sceptical but willing to believe there may have been a leader or two or three leaders whose exploits in holding back the invading tide of Anglo-Saxon pagans passed into our folk traditions.

Arthur became a convenient symbol for later kings to use to legitimise their reign, and much of the romantic elaboration such as knights and round tables was added by Geoffrey of Monmouth's interpretation in the 1130s, which appealed to Henry II and, even later, Henry VIII. Arthur also became a symbol of the struggle against invading forces. It seems that the period after the Romans had left was the main source of the legend, with people living in the 'Dark Ages' looking back nostalgically to a period of stable Roman life and Arthur provided a focus for their inspirations.

A ninth-century monk named Nennius recorded a number of Arthur's battles, including his greatest victory at 'Mount Badon', possibly close to Swindon, where he defeated an army of Saxons. Many historians and archaeologists have attempted to locate Arthur's castle – referred to in the legends of 'Camelot'. In the sixteenth century John Leland referred to local legends that claimed South Cadbury was restored by Arthur, but from what we know of chiefs in the post-Roman period, it was highly likely that Arthur would have been at the head of a highly mobile group of cavalry and unlikely to have tied himself to one location. In the twelfth century the monks at Glastonbury, possibly in need of funds, claimed to have found Arthur's body and that of Guinevere, thus generating an ongoing and lucrative link with Glastonbury.

The legend is well spread, including many references in the folk lore of Brittany, and it continues to appeal. It's interesting to note that a recent film portrays Arthur as a Romano-British leader trying to preserve some Roman values, including Christianity, in a post-Roman world, and leading a band of scruffy warriors based in temporary camps against a range of invaders. This is nearer to the truth than the romantic knights, round table and Camelot image.

Left: Tintagel, Cornwall. Wrapped deeply in Arthurian legend, the dramatic coastline features a medieval castle and wonderful clear waters and caverns below.

THE FIRST ROADS in Britain were built by the Roman legions, which had their own surveyors, engineers and the equipment they needed for this type of construction work. The availability of local materials dictated the details of road construction, but the basic principles were always the same. The road took the form of an embankment, raised above the level of the surrounding land, with drainage ditches on either side. It would be built up in a series of layers, comprising a foundation of large rocks, followed by smaller stones, gravel and sand laid down in successive layers and rammed into place.

A cobbled surface was commonplace in towns or areas of heavy use, but usually it would be gravel. The embankment was cambered for drainage, often 10m (33ft)or more wide; it was rarely less than 3m (9½ft) wide to allow room for two-wheeled vehicles to pass. As elsewhere, Roman roads in Britain were built as straight as possible. The Roman surveyors had no need to worry about who owned the land along the route-way because as conquerors they could choose the most direct route. Nevertheless, they by-passed mountains, marshes and forest, where they posed particular obstacles, and they would seek out suitable crossing points at rivers.

Although their primary purpose in the early days of the conquest was to speed the movement of troops, roads subsequently became even more important as communication routes between different parts of the empire. They enabled important information to be passed between Rome and the provincial governors of the areas under their control. In Britain, the Roman economy was agricultural, based around villa estates, which produced surplus food to provide supplies for the army and the urban populations. The roads also made possible the movement of pottery and other goods, whose production became commonplace in Britain in the third and fourth centuries AD.

Well-known Roman roads include Watling Street, which ran from London to Chester and the Fosse Way, which crossed England from Exeter in the south-west to Lincoln in the north-east. The latter followed a route in use since prehistoric times and around AD47 it marked the first

Above: *One of the finest examples of a surviving Roman road in Britain, Blackstone Edge, on Rishworth Moor near Manchester, is remarkably well preserved with rain gullies and close-fitting cobbles still intact.*

boundary of the new Roman province. Roman roads later became a liability because invading barbarians could travel along them as quickly as the Roman armies. The Salisbury–Badbury road was deliberately blocked by the Bokerley Dyke during a crisis in the fourth century. The roads went into decline after the Roman departure and not until the advent of railways in the nineteenth century did Britain again enjoy such an efficient communications network.

7 ANGLO-SAXON

TIME TEAM'S SEARCH for Anglo-Saxon remains, particularly of the early part of the period, has often been a frustrating business. We have been on many sites where, at the end of day three, we are left with the tricky job of interpreting a set of brown stains of varying shades, which someone has tentatively suggested might be beam slots. As Phil Harding says, the archaeological evidence seems to indicate that 'the Anglo-Saxons died but never lived' because a lot of what we know about this period comes from burials which are relatively rich compared with the settlement sites. This is mainly because early Anglo-Saxon buildings were built from wood and often leave only faint traces in the ground. In addition, Anglo-Saxon pottery is fairly poor stuff, being fired at low temperatures, which makes it decay quickly in the soil.

When searching for Anglo-Saxon buildings, Phil points to a site he worked on where the only way of interpreting the range of marks in the ground was by excavating a large area and then getting far enough above the site to see a pattern which, in the case of Petersfield in Hampshire, revealed large rectangular buildings indicated by the alignment of postholes.

One of Time Team's first digs uncovered early Anglo-Saxon burials at Winterbourne Gunner in Wiltshire. We can all remember the thrill of finding Time Team's first brooch, and the excitement of seeing it after conservation. Thankfully the Anglo-Saxons initially had a rich tradition of grave-goods which means that there is often a wide range of objects to find. This sort of information, combined with the rare sites where we have evidence preserved of settlement like West Stow (see page 144), has

c410–c790

helped to build up our understanding of the people who can be said to have founded the English nation. We also have one of Britain's most spectacular sites – Sutton Hoo – which represents the richness of the late part of the early Anglo-Saxon period. Time Team has involved Helen Geake on most of the Anglo-Saxon sites we have visited so we asked for her overview of the period.

For someone like Helen, who sees the start of the Anglo-Saxon period as the real beginning of our society today, it's easier to think of things that the Anglo-Saxons *didn't* do for us! Almost all the foundations of modern Britain, and particularly England, date from the Anglo-Saxon period. Before the Anglo-Saxons, we were in another world – the classical world of slaves, empire and central control, more familiar from films than from real life. From the Anglo-Saxon

period onwards, we can see a world that is recognisably our own.

Firstly, and most fundamentally, our language is basically Anglo-Saxon. We have a few words and a bit of grammar from the Vikings, and a few more words came in with the use of French as a court language in the medieval period. Likewise, lots of our long words are from Latin or Greek, and arrived in the eighteenth and nineteenth centuries, but all the basic vocabulary and grammar that we use to make ourselves understood every day comes straight from the language of the Anglo-Saxons. This language, despite its difficulties and peculiarities, has proved so flexible that it is now the most widely spoken language in the world.

Another really important thing that the Anglo-Saxons did for us was to give us our sense of local identity. Most of our English counties and towns bear Anglo-Saxon names, and one could just as well say '*ic eom from Ægelesburg – ic eom an Buccingahamscir mann*' then, as 'I'm from Aylesbury – I'm a Buckinghamshire man' today. Local and national identities developed over the Anglo-Saxon period, starting with individual kingdoms, such as Kent, Wessex, East Anglia or Northumbria. Some of our counties are much older, but most of the shires date from the late Anglo-Saxon period – the ninth to eleventh centuries AD.

The AD system of counting years is very useful. It's hard to imagine being without it, but in the Anglo-Saxon period there were lots of different and much more clumsy ways to express a date. People often picked a noteworthy event – such as the number of years after the current king, queen or pope had begun ruling – but these depended on you knowing when that in turn had happened! Often two or three different systems had to be quoted before writers could be sure that their readers would understand which year they were talking about. Although the Anno Domini system was originally invented by an obscure Russian monk called Dionysus Exiguus, it wasn't used much until it was made popular all over the Christian world by the Anglo-Saxon historian Bede. For archaeologists and historians, dating is clearly crucial, and every time we use a date, we are continuing something started by Bede.

We can thank Bede for another revolutionary concept – the idea of England itself. He wrote one of his most popular books, *The Ecclesiastical History of the English People*, in 731 – well before there was any such place as England. It has been argued that the impact of Bede's book was such that the various peoples of England began to think of themselves as a single entity, and so were ready to join together at a later date. It is interesting that the English use this particular word, derived from 'Angle' – as Bede did – to describe themselves, whereas their neighbours tend to use the word 'Saxon', as in *Sassenach* or *Sais*. By the end of the Anglo-Saxon period, the English had become dominant in much of the British Isles. The other peoples living here – the Welsh, the Cornish, the Cumbrians, the Scots, the Manx, the Irish – had also crystallised into distinct ethnic entities, perhaps as a reaction to the threat of the English.

Many of the things that we owe to the Anglo-Saxons are more ideas than tangible things. It is often said that the British like heroic defeats almost more than mighty victories, and most people point to the Battle of Hastings as the first example of this. But there is an even more remarkable example; the Battle of Maldon. This took place between the men of Essex and a Viking war band in the year 991. The Vikings were trapped on an island, and could only move towards the Anglo-Saxon army one by one across a narrow causeway. The Essex men could pick them off easily using spears or archers, and were obviously going to win the battle. Then the Vikings appealed to what was to become the British sense of fair play – they suggested that the Anglo-Saxons let them all come across the causeway and have a proper pitched battle on the other side. Quite incredibly, the leader of the Essex men, the ealdorman Byrhtnoth, agreed – and of course the battle was lost. But a great poem was composed, and we remember the heroic failure to this day.

The arts and culture of the Anglo-Saxons are perhaps one of the most remarkable legacies that they have left behind. The epic poem *Beowulf* could be described as the Homer of the northern world; it bears comparison with the great epics such as the *Iliad*, the *Odyssey* or the *Epic of Gilgamesh*. The surviving Old English poems include tragic poetry that can still move us to tears, love poetry, and of course the famous riddles – some of which are very rude! Reading these puts us very close to the Anglo-Saxons; we feel the same emotions and delights that they did.

Anyone who has seen the Early Medieval galleries at the British Museum will know that

Anglo-Saxon craftsmanship at the time of Sutton Hoo was absolutely the best in the world. The goldsmithing, gem-cutting, glassworking and sword-forging is of almost miraculous quality to us today, when many of the techniques of the seventh century have been lost. Much scientific endeavour (and many Time Team experiments!) have gone into understanding how these incredible objects could have been produced, but there are still many mysteries. Were the craftsmen who made the fine gold filigree (and drew the later manuscript illuminations) short-sighted, to let them see such tiny work? Or were their working lives over very early, when their eyesight began to deteriorate? We may have lost the skills, but the objects themselves remain to awe us. The level of artistic achievement is simply stunning, and often imitated in modern designs when, irritatingly, the complex interlace patterns are usually called 'Celtic'.

Today we are rightly proud of our long traditions of public life, such as parliamentary democracy and trial by jury. The roots of these traditions go far back into the Anglo-Saxon period, and one of the best examples is the Witan. This was the council that advised the later Anglo-Saxon kings, and it grew out of assemblies of bishops and nobles held in all the early kingdoms of Anglo-Saxon England. By the tenth century, the Witan had gained an even more important role – they actually *elected* the kings. Normally these kings would be from the royal family, but they didn't have to be. Harold Godwinsson, famous as the King Harold defeated by William at the Battle of Hastings, came from a family of obscure origins. The election of Harold Godwinsson as king was an extraordinary event, which perhaps did not have any lasting significance. But the principle that the king must govern with advice, and must not be an absolute ruler, laid the way for the constitutional monarchy that we have today.

Previous spread: *Reconstructed timber houses at West Stow in Suffolk, the site of a classic Anglo-Saxon settlement.*

Above: *Time Team excavating the remains of an Anglo-Saxon settlement.*

ANGLO-SAXON IN DETAIL

THE VACUUM LEFT by the Roman withdrawal was more than simply the lack of a central administration. The Romans, as great writers and record-keepers, provided us with a commentary on life in Britain during their time and as they left, so too did the written record. This left a literary hiatus for over 100 years until monastic writers slowly come into play. This gap in our history, commonly known as the Dark Ages, is what archaeology strives to fill.

The evidence suggests that, far from an overnight fall into anarchy, a splintering of administration took place. Some towns remained successful, almost like independent town states, while others fell into decay. In truth, the general collapse of Britannia was a drawn-out affair starting as early as the fourth century as the dramas suffered by Rome caused numerous repercussions throughout the empire, ultimately resulting in the emperor Honorius stating in 410 that Britannia must fend for herself (the official end of Roman Britain). The confusion caused by contrasting archaeological signs of decay and success throws the post-Roman period off kilter. But by careful examination of the evidence we can see that, though under change, Britain was not a cultural wasteland.

The sudden decline in coinage use and the apparent collapse of the pottery manufacturing industries, combined with a trend towards abandoning Roman buildings and living in timber structures, which do not survive archaeologically, creates a complicated archaeological phase in which sites can be difficult to identify. However, the material finds that do appear from this period include outstanding examples of high-quality jewellery (see page 151) and fasteners such as belt buckles, and extremely well-crafted weapons which were interred in graves at sites such as the early Anglo-Saxon cemetery at Mucking in Essex. These show us that far from being a Dark Age, the period shines with examples of exceptional Germanic art.

The record-keepers

The historical record for the Anglo-Saxon period, particularly the early phase, is patchy at best. The record-keepers and pioneering academics of the time were monks. A native British monk called Brother Gildas was busy putting the world to rights and recording his impression of a barbarous Britain as early as the mid 540s with his suitably entitled work, *The Ruin of Britain*, while the Venerable Bede, who hailed from the monastery of Jarrow in Northumbria wrote his *Ecclesiastical History of the English People* much later in 731, at a time when Anglo-Saxon culture was much more absorbed into society.

Another compilation of documents called *The Anglo-Saxon Chronicle* appears later in the period and acts as a chronological record of English events. This, together with some poems and artworks, amounts to nearly all the references we can call on. Only the combined use of archaeology and history of the period helps us piece together the past.

The Saxon connection

Contact with Saxon raiders is recorded as early as the third century. Groups of seaborne warriors hailing from powerful Germanic tribes harried the coastline of Britain, increasing their efforts as the province appeared weakened by successive Roman troop withdrawals. The initial reaction was to construct a line of coastal fortifications, known as the Forts of the Saxon Shore, and to a degree these proved successful in checking large-scale attacks.

It may be the case that the first introduction of settlers takes the form of Saxon Germanic mercenaries brought into Britain by the Roman administration to replace Roman troops withdrawn at various times during the closing stages of Roman rule. In a time of Saxon raiders this may seem strange, but bands of freelance warriors for hire became an aspect of security increasingly relied upon during the fourth and fifth centuries by an administration short on resources. Though a time of general unrest (and events such as the Barbarian Conspiracy of 367 only add to the appearance of a widespread invasion), it appears that the reality was one of gradual immigration and settlement led first by the mercenaries and then more so with a gathering pace as their families came to join them and other groups followed suit. The traditional view of a single Saxon invasion is now disputed by many archaeologists who prefer to interpret the evidence of an increased Saxon cultural presence as a gradual influx of settlers over a period of time.

The rich culture of the Saxons, Angles and Jutes, all hailing from northern Germany, became a fundamental part of Britain. By the seventh century powerful kingdoms were established with their own complex judicial systems, governing bodies, warrior class and kings. While these proud domains built a society which included the widespread conversion of the population to Christianity, bolstered by extensive sponsorship of monasteries, a centralised single king remained elusive. The powerful Mercian royal family, which controlled much of the midlands, held great influence and appeared to be the first candidates to unite the nation, but the influx of Vikings from the late eighth and ninth centuries sent Britain into turmoil and drove much of the Anglo-Saxon world to the brink of destruction. The house of

Wessex emerged from a country in the depths of despair as the most triumphant kingdom under the leadership of King Alfred the Great. With a succession of alliances and diplomacy, Alfred did much to unite the land under a common English identity, while Scotland and Wales came under their own rulers. Lessons learned from a capable Anglo-Saxon administration became an integral part of our society, and many aspects of Anglo-Saxon law and organisation continued into the Middle Ages.

Above: *Much of Anglo-Saxon archaeology relies on studying burials, and from the pagan period they often contain grave-goods.*

Anglo-Saxon Chronology

This timeline gives you a quick, at-a-glance guide to what happened when in Britain in the Anglo-Saxon era, helping you to understand the order of events. We've also included, in blue type, some key events that happened elsewhere in the world.

Angles and Jutes settle (see page 142)	**c400**
West Stow settlement (see page 144)	**c450**
Ethelbert, later over-king, becomes King of Kent	**560**
World event: Muhammad, founder of the Islamic religion, born in Mecca (died 632)	**570**
St Augustine brings Christianity to Kent (see page 146)	**c597**
World event: Tang Dynasty reaches a high point in Chinese civilisation	**618–907**
Burials at Sutton Hoo (see page 145)	**c625**
Synod of Whitby	**664**
Venerable Bede (see page 148), Christian learning at Jarrow	**673–735**
Synod of Hertford and Battle of Trent, marking the beginnings of the rise of Mercia	**679**
Ethelbald becomes King of Mercia	**716**
Bede completes his Ecclesiastical History	**731**
Death of Ethelbald – Offa becomes King of Mercia	**757**
Offa's Dyke constructed (see page 150)	**c783**

Note: The Saxon period continued in parallel with the Viking. We are taking 790 as a convenient point for the end of early and middle Saxon periods.

World event: Birth of Muhammad

The Islamic religion was founded on the Arabian Peninsula by the Prophet Muhammad in the early 600s. Born c570 in Mecca, he was the last in a long line of Judeo-Christian prophets and altered the basis of his faith after receiving his first revelation in 610. Muslims believe the archangel Gabriel revealed the word of God to Muhammad and he interpreted his revelations in the Qu'ran. Muhammad's preaching of a social-religious order was built upon an allegiance to one deity, Allah. The Qu'ran provides the framework for a just and equal society based on guidelines for appropriate behaviour. The leaders of Mecca did not welcome this new faith and in 622 forced Muhammad to settle in the northern oasis town of Medina. This was the year of emigration (hijra) and it marks the beginning of the Muslim calendar. In Medina, Muhammad attracted more followers and, within a few years, returned to Mecca, which had now embraced the Muslim religion. The Prophet died in 632 but his followers spread the message of Islam to the Mediterranean lands and to Iran. The Arabs subsequently conquered Syria, Palestine, Egypt, Iraq and Iran. From here the Islamic faith developed religiously, politically and culturally.

World event: Tang Dynasty reaches a high point in Chinese civilisation

Historians regard the Tang Dynasty as possibly the greatest of China's dynasties. The Tang Dynasty was founded by Li Yuan and ruled from 618 to 907, during which time Chinese authority extended into central Asia, Tibet, Korea and Annam. It became the world's largest empire of its time. The Tang period saw the formation of a centralised administrative system for ruling its territories whilst contact with India and the Middle East brought an era of great creativity. Buddhism became a permanent aspect of Chinese culture, the development of block printing instigated a golden age in Chinese literature and art, and scientific advances introduced gunpowder. The Tang Dynasty even introduced the only female ruler in Chinese history when Empress Wu Zetian reigned in her own right. The dynasty reached its peak between 712 and 756 under the reign of Emperor Tang Xuan Zong but the prosperity that took years to develop was all but destroyed by the An Lushan rebellion in 755. Over the subsequent 150 years, regional military governors grew in power and eventually ended the Tang Dynasty when the last emperor was deposed.

SUTTON HOO HELMET

THE SUTTON HOO helmet is unique and part of one of the greatest archaeological treasures ever found in this country. It was discovered within the largest burial mound at Sutton Hoo (see page 145), along with a cache of armour, weapons and other luxurious goods which formed the regalia and grave-goods of the dead king. The burial was probably contained within a wooden chamber, which archaeologists believe collapsed onto it at some point. This appears to have shattered the helmet rather than crushed it, meaning it was recovered in many scattered fragments. Reconstructing its original appearance from the remaining pieces has been a painstaking process over many years.

The helmet is made of sheet iron, covered in tinned bronze stamped with relief designs and gilded bronze decorations. As well as being a fully functional protective piece of armour, the helmet's rich decoration and high-quality craftsmanship make it something akin to a crown – the mark of an exceptional warrior and king.

What makes the helmet so striking is the facemask – a separate guard piece, complete with eyebrows, eyesockets and cast bronze nose with breathing holes. Garnets and silver wire decorate the eyebrows, which end in gilded bronze boars' heads. A similar set of gilded bronze dragons' heads on the forehead link up with eyebrows and nose piece to give the front of the helmet the appearance of a flying dragon with outstretched wings.

The main body of the helmet, the cheeks and neck guards are decorated with panels carrying designs of animals and heroic images. Some feature dancing warriors and horse riders, others elaborate interlaced zoomorphic patterns. The designs on the helmet, like the ship burial itself,

are rare in Britain but have strong parallels in Scandinavia, particularly Sweden. Archaeologists have speculated whether Scandinavian craftsmen were involved in the decoration of the helmet, or whether it strongly reflects close ties and shared heritage between the kings of East Anglia and Sweden in the seventh century.

Even today, the Sutton Hoo helmet is a work of remarkable beauty, giving a powerful insight into the wealth and sophistication of the kings of East Anglia. Its extraordinary craftsmanship creates a vivid picture of a warrior-king of great influence and long-distance connections in this crucial period of English history.

Above: The early seventh-century Sutton Hoo helmet is a remarkable find. Discovered in the famous burial mound of a Saxon king, it's made of iron and then finely decorated with tin-plated bronze, silver wire and garnets.

ANGLO-SAXON BURIAL

One of the earliest excavations of a cemetery completed by Time Team was on a set of sixth-century Anglo-Saxon burials, and this drawing reflects some of the evidence we found during the excavation. At this time, Saxons were pagans and we see various grave-goods being buried, including swords, spears, shields and personal jewellery. One of the people buried would have had a brooch, probably made from gilded copper with a distinctive Saxon design of rings and dots.

The settlement in the background shows a typical large Anglo-Saxon dwelling, although possibly the crossed wooden structure at the front of the roof relates more to continental examples than those we have been able to find in Britain.

When we reconstructed an Anglo-Saxon burial for the Bawsey programme, we placed the shield over the face of the re-enactor in the position you can see here. This was based on the fact that in excavations the shield bosses tend to be found in approximately this location.

Early Anglo-Saxon Settlement

THE MASS MIGRATION of people is difficult to understand. Many of us hold a mental image of columns of refugees trudging their way across Europe during the Second World War, as the extreme situations they found themselves in caused them either to seek safer havens voluntarily or, under even darker circumstances, to undertake enforced evacuations.

Above: *A timber planked Saxon house from the reconstructed settlement at West Stow, Suffolk. A typical example of a post-Roman dwelling.*

Undoubtedly it takes a lot to make people leave their homes in large numbers. The underlying reason is usually survival. It appears that European unrest as the Roman empire collapsed, a dreadful deterioration of their home climate, and the knowledge that a better place existed all conspired to cause the Anglo-Saxon migrations.

Through a combination of archaeology and scraps of history, we can see that the Anglo-Saxon migration is a clearer event to chart than some prehistoric cultural changes. New groups from northern Europe did settle here in large numbers from the fifth century, but this was a drawn-out affair over a few centuries. Added complications include the fact that some fighting occurred between native peoples and Anglo-Saxons, while others appear to have willingly adopted the culture of the incomers. More murky waters also exist where the native Britons themselves were not far removed from their new Anglo-Saxon neighbours, adding difficulty to the identification of early sites. Essentially the Anglo-Saxons who filled the Roman vacuum continued with our native Iron Age, almost as if Roman occupation was an interruption.

A moment in time: a new home

A fascinating element of the Anglo-Saxon occupation of Britain is the fact that most Roman buildings appear to have been disregarded as places to live, with villas and townhouses falling into decay. A minority of buildings is known to have been reused, but this often takes a form which appears completely mindless to the preservation or appreciation of what had gone before. The Anglo-Saxons built new structures in timber and so while many of the towns continued to exist, the evidence that archaeology finds usually consists of Roman rubble with barely a trace of Anglo-Saxon life because the timber structures simply don't survive. It's also worth considering the fact that for all the Anglo-Saxons knew, the Romans could return at any time to reclaim their province. Perhaps the reluctance to occupy abandoned property has its roots in early settlers exercising caution in an uncertain time. The pattern of building new timber homes in traditional Germanic style also reflects the Anglo-Saxons bringing their culture with them.

A typical early Anglo-Saxon house was the Grubenhaus, or sunken-floored building. Grubenhausen served as multipurpose buildings for both living and industrial activity. They tend to consist of a timber pitched roof suspended over an excavated living space. A characteristic scene would involve groupings of Grubenhausen creating small village settlements, such as at West Heslerton, North Yorkshire, which also included larger structures based on postholes. With areas of the settlement divided up for different social and economic activities, this early homestead for migrating Anglo-Saxons thrived until it was abandoned some 500 years later following Viking raiding and conquest.

The historical and archaeological story

Gildas, in his pugnacious style, tells us that the Saxons 'first of all fixed their dreadful claws on the east side of the island. Hence the sprig of iniquity, the root of bitterness, the virulent plant that we so well deserved, sprouted in our soil with savage shoots and tendrils.' This colourful description depicts the Anglo-Saxon influx akin to a disease as the monk tries to come to terms with the pre-Christian past; a time when his native Britain was settled by barbarian pagans, but archaeologically the evidence indicates a cultured and skilful people making Britain their new home after leaving an inhospitable homeland.

As an Anglo-Saxon, the Venerable Bede is more at ease with migration. He tells us that Saxons were successfully absorbed into British culture on a regional basis depending on where the groups settled. He says that 'from the Jutes descend the people of Kent and the Isle of Wight', that from the Saxons 'came the east, south and west Saxons' essentially covering the south and south-west, and that from the 'Angles are descended the Middle Angles (East Anglia), the Mercians (covering the Midlands), and all those of Northumbrian stock.'

Sites of the initial Anglo-Saxon activity are few but those that are known, such as Ancaster, Lindsey, West Stow and Dorchester-on-Thames, produce artefacts which have strong stylistic links with northern Europe. A settlement at Mucking, Essex, appears to have originated as a mercenary camp, where freelance warriors were based for the protection of London, later developing into a more permanent village, probably as a result of soldiers' kin coming to Britain to join them. A cemetery discovered at Wasperton, Warwickshire, holds evidence of the actual native adoption of Anglo-Saxon culture. The site, which covers the transitional period between Roman occupation and the immediate period afterwards, revealed individuals buried wearing Roman footwear but accompanied by early Anglo-Saxon personal items.

PALAEOLITHIC

MESOLITHIC

NEOLITHIC

BRONZE AGE

IRON AGE

ROMAN

ANGLO-SAXON c410–c790

Early Anglo-Saxon Settlement c400–500

VIKING

NORMAN

MIDDLE AGES

TUDOR

STUART

GEORGIAN

VICTORIAN

MODERN

The Settlement at West Stow

THE MOMENT OF building the first settlement at West Stow represents a huge break from the past. West Stow sits in the middle of the Lark Valley in west Suffolk, and all around would have been the Roman landscape. The nearby town of Icklingham might still have been occupied, but its stone ruins would certainly have been visible to the carpenters and thatchers putting up the small wooden buildings a few miles away at West Stow.

West Stow represents an entirely new way of living – the English way, not the Roman way. The English way was to turn away from the cumbersome Roman state (with all its expensive benefits, such as civic buildings, bath-houses, roads and the army) and towards a down-sized, more personal relationship with your family, your neighbours and your local leader.

The decision to abandon the Roman way of life and adopt Anglo-Saxon culture would have been huge and irrevocable. Once Roman administration had gone, it could not be brought back. It is hard to imagine what was going through the minds of those people who began to build the houses at West Stow – did they realise what they were doing?

We still don't know whether the first inhabitants of West Stow were incomers who had come across the North Sea by ship, or whether they moved out of local Romano-British stone houses into these more convenient and easy-to-heat wooden houses. Although there was a cemetery associated with the settlement, it was excavated in the nineteenth century and no bones survive, so we cannot carry out DNA or isotope analysis to find out where the people grew up or from whom they were descended. But the buildings, and the burials, seem to start around AD450 already looking remarkably sophisticated. It doesn't look as if one Romano-Brit turned to another and said, 'I can't get any slaves to bleach my toga. Shall we change into trousers, and try building a house with this axe I got from an Anglian trader?'

There's no evidence that the West Stow people made any mistakes as they learnt how to dress, build and bury their dead in the Anglo-Saxon manner. Any shaky transitions and failed experiments seem to have been lost in the darkest age of all, between when we can prove that Roman life was still carrying on (in the first decade of the fifth century AD) and when we are certain that Anglo-Saxon culture had begun (around the middle of the fifth century). What went on in these few decades is still the biggest mystery in British archaeology, and sites like West Stow are crucial in working out the answer.

Above: Interior of one of the reconstructed Saxon houses at West Stow. Note the wattle and daub walls and the 'sand-box' hearth which suspends the fire over the wooden floor.

The Sutton Hoo Burials

THE FUNERALS AT Sutton Hoo were extraordinary events, like no others in Anglo-Saxon England. Sutton Hoo is the only group that we know of elite Anglo-Saxon burials, under mounds, with no burials of everyday people around them.

The first funerals to inaugurate the site as a place of 'separated' burial were giant cremations, accompanied by animal sacrifice and exotic grave-goods. The two ship-burials came perhaps a few decades later, and may well have taken place together, maybe even on the same day; these funerals must have been truly epic, with hundreds of men dragging immense ships up a steep hill from the river. The poem *Beowulf* describes similar events, designed to live on in the memory for ever, but these were thought to be merely the result of the poet's imagination until the excavation of Mound 1, the intact ship-burial, in 1939.

When one stands on the reconstructed Mound 2 at Sutton Hoo, with a mind full of the great treasures and mysterious rituals, the first question that comes to mind is – what was it all for? And the answer must be that it was to create kingship.

There's no real evidence for the existence of kings in Anglo-Saxon England before the last years of the sixth century AD. The earliest burials at Sutton Hoo coincide with this moment. We don't know exactly how the new kings came to power, but their burials certainly seem to have been important. Of course, every time a king dies the kingdom is vulnerable, so putting on a lavish display of riches and confidence is a sensible tactic. But other than this there seems to have been little consensus about just how a king should have been buried. At Prittlewell in Essex we see the king buried among his band of heroic warriors. At Sutton Hoo, the kings were buried away from the common folk and in a ship. And in Kent, the contemporary kings were buried in a church, apparently without any grave-goods at all.

The funerals at Sutton Hoo were of crucial importance in establishing Anglo-Saxon kingship. The extraordinary craftsmanship apparent in the ships and in the grave-goods shows us the wealth and sophistication of the kings of the East Angles, and the range of imported objects tells of their distant contacts. The remarkable rituals evident from the animal bones and sand-bodies shows that pageantry and theatre were as potent in king-making as riches. But eventually the power of kings was going to depend on a holy alliance with the Church, who preferred the wealth and ritual to be channelled through them. The magnificence of Sutton Hoo, buried beneath the ground, was eventually forgotten, and replaced by the great cathedrals still to be seen today.

Above: *The beautiful and intricate gold belt buckle of the Saxon king of Sutton Hoo. Made by a master of their craft, the thick buckle conceals a series of latches and slots to work the locking mechanism.*

Early Christianity and St Augustine

DURING THE LATE third century a new Christian movement was formed and spread out from the Egyptian deserts. The first monasteries were established and developed over subsequent years and by the fourth century both communities and hermits had spread across the Middle East and into western Europe. The conversion of some western Europeans led to the birth of Celtic monasticism and it's through this path that monasteries and Christianity initially become more established in Britain, though not without conflict with existing pagan beliefs.

Above: *The nunnery at Iona. Orders established here from the sixth century made the island a cultural centre of Christianity.*

Monasteries and Christianity became intertwined with Anglo-Saxon society and most were sponsored by kings as a guarantee of safe passage to heaven. However, the early monasticism establishing itself here was almost completely destroyed in the later Anglo-Saxon period by the Vikings.

A moment in time: St Augustine's mission

From the accounts of Gildas, we know Ireland was converted to Christianity during the fifth century by St Patrick who came from Britain, while St Columba in turn came from Ireland and founded his monastery on Iona in 563 from which monks travelled out to convert the pagan Anglo-Saxons of the north and west. The fifth and sixth centuries were pioneering eras for the establishment of Christianity in Britain, and while many monasteries and churches were founded in the name of Celtic Christianity across the landscape, the influence of Rome, or the rule of Roman monasticism, continued to grow abroad.

In 597 Pope Gregory I sent a mission led by Augustine from Rome to convert the Anglo-Saxons to the Roman church. Augustine and his group landed at Thanet in Kent and were cautiously received by the king of Kent, Ethelbert, who himself was a pagan. Fortunately for Augustine, Ethelbert's wife, Bertha, was already a Christian. After careful contemplation the Saxon king converted and was baptised that year. From this point on Augustine was given use of an old church at Canterbury for his mission where he became the first Archbishop of Canterbury. Over the next 80 years the Celtic and Roman monks slowly but surely converted ever-growing numbers of Saxons until, by the middle seventh century, the religion was truly widespread. However, there was a cultural clash between Celtic and Roman Christianity would soon call for an administrative overhaul across the Church.

The historical and archaeological story

The essential difference between the Celtic and Roman factions of Christianity was one of allegiance to their respective cultural religious practices. The Christian year rotates around the feast of Easter which, because it is directly related to the Jewish Passover, has always been a moveable feast linked to the phases of the moon. The Celtic Christians had been isolated from Rome and had fallen behind with changes in the method of calculating Easter, leading to the two different factions celebrating the feast at different times.

The answer was to hold a meeting so both sides could agree on the formal timetable of seasonal events. King Oswy of Northumbria called a grand synod at Whitby in 663 and here the Celtic faction in Northumbria agreed to accept the Roman timetable, and other Roman practices such as the Petrine tonsure, or bald crown hairstyle, in a general conversion to Roman rule. Over the next century the Roman church gained power as Celtic monasticism lost popularity.

The key to the success of Christianity was how the religion was marketed to the population. In an age where many people worshipped different gods for different causes or protections, here was an all-powerful single force which could save everyone, from influential kings to destitute peasants. Speed of conversion was of the essence as people were told that they were already damned yet the antidote was waiting for them if they converted and followed the rule of the Church. With a respectful nod towards the kind nursing of the ill, educating of the people and spiritual comfort that the Church brought to many Anglo-Saxons, the skill of this early historic marketing cannot be denied.

Archaeologically, many early monastic sites are hard to identify as they often contain little trace of their original purpose and don't follow the set plans we see in later monasteries. Churches can also be difficult to determine because existing buildings could easily be dedicated, rather than new structures specifically built. Most of the recognised Anglo-Saxon church remains have only survived because they have been retained or incorporated into later developments, such as the crypt at Ripon, the architectural features preserved at Earls Barton, and the foundations of Jarrow and Monkwearmouth. A church can also be identified by the burials around it. Seventh-century burial practices are very varied, but in churchyards nearly all burials are neatly aligned east-west and have no grave-goods. Away from the churches, seventh-century burials have provided some of the most remarkable archaeological discoveries in Britain, and Anglo-Saxon burials in general highlight the varied social and economic background of those who lived in this fascinating age.

— PALAEOLITHIC

— MESOLITHIC

— NEOLITHIC

— BRONZE AGE

— IRON AGE

— ROMAN

ANGLO-SAXON c410–c790

Early Christianity and St Augustine 597–c700

— VIKING

— NORMAN

— MIDDLE AGES

— TUDOR

— STUART

— GEORGIAN

— VICTORIAN

— MODERN

Bede and the First History of Britain

BEDE WAS a world-famous historian and the author of the first history of England. Born around 673, he entered his local monastery at Monkwearmouth in County Durham at the age of seven, and three years later moved to the newly founded monastery at nearby Jarrow, where he spent the rest of his life as a monk and priest.

He was a man of enormous scholarship and learning, and we know of many different books which he wrote during his lifetime. Bede said of himself 'It has always been my delight to learn or to teach or to write', and he was the author of many hymns and commentaries, as well as studying astronomy, history, chronology, natural phenomena and poetry. Even on his deathbed in 731, his students reported that he was still dictating translations of religious works to them.

However, it is his historical works which ensured his fame, particularly *The Ecclesiastical History of the English People*, written shortly before his death. It tells the story of national events, saints, abbots and key political figures, and is the first history of England as we understand it. The only substantial historical work prior to this was a text called *Concerning the Ruin of Britain*, written by Gildas, believed to be a Welsh monk living in the sixth century. In it he bemoans the Saxon invasions of Britain and the inability of the British to resist them. Gildas' work is not regarded as history, being more of a diatribe about the state of the country than an objective account.

Like Gildas, Bede had a motive in writing his history; his purpose was to celebrate God, and it is largely a description of how the Anglo-Saxons were converted to Christianity, from the arrival of St Augustine in the late sixth century up until his own lifetime. However, unlike Gildas, Bede was aware of himself as a conscientious historian, carefully explaining his use of ancient documents and traditions to create a reliable story of his subject matter.

The Ecclesiastical History contains a wealth of detail about the history of religious and secular life in Anglo-Saxon England. In fact, much of what we know about monasteries, and life generally, in this period comes from Bede. Through his work, the northern English monasteries of this period, before the Viking attacks, became regarded in later times as a 'golden age' of religious life. The abbey at Jarrow was one of a number of great pioneering monasteries founded in the Anglo-Saxon kingdom of Northumbria in the seventh and eighth centuries, which fused together Roman and Celtic ideas, producing new religious and artistic achievements. These institutions weren't laid out around a cloister like later medieval monasteries, but Bede's home would still have been a substantial establishment with several stone churches surrounded by extensive timber cells, domestic halls and workshops for the monks. Today the parish church at Jarrow is located where the monastic churches were, but the rest of the monastery Bede was familiar with has vanished. Instead, its biggest legacy is Bede's work.

The Ecclesiastical History became famous across Europe within decades of its publication, and was regarded as an outstanding work. It had huge influence on the development of the English language and scholarship throughout Europe in the Middle Ages. It was, for example, the first work to popularise the use of the *anno domini* system of chronology we use today. More fundamentally, it played a vital role in creating the idea of England as one Christian nation, and was a milestone in historical writing as we understand it.

Right: *A section of illuminated manuscript dating to the eighth century and belonging to the Venerable Bede, the first historian of England.*

OFFA'S DYKE IS a series of massive linear earthworks which run roughly along the boundary between England and Wales. It is one of Britain's most impressive archaeological monuments, its scale and engineering truly exceptional for an era of few archaeological remains or historical records.

At the end of the ninth century, King Alfred's biographer Asser states that 'a certain king called Offa … had a great dyke built between Wales and Mercia, from sea to sea'. It is the first mention of the earthwork, and the origin of its attribution to Offa, one of the great leaders of eighth-century Europe. He ruled Mercia, an independent Anglo-Saxon kingdom centred on the English Midlands. There are few historical records to flesh out his reign, but he was clearly powerful here and abroad, having links with both Charlemagne and the Papacy. Through a combination of political alliances (his daughters wed the kings of Wessex and Northumbria) and military campaigns, he extended his control over much of England.

The earthwork is hard to date conclusively, and archaeologists believe that what exists today as Offa's Dyke may incorporate several different episodes of construction. The main surviving section runs almost continuously for over 110km (70 miles) from Kington in Herefordshire northwards towards Wrexham. It consists of an earthen bank, originally covered with turf, with a ditch on the Welsh side, and together they probably measured about 8m (26ft) from top to bottom, and over 20m (65ft) wide. It has commanding views across the Welsh countryside, and it is probably this stretch which was constructed at Offa's command in the late eighth century, as part of his territorial dealings with the Welsh.

Right: The ancient boundary – Offa's Dyke was constructed along the border of England and Wales on the orders of King Offa. This section is near Knighton, Wales.

Beyond this, there are other sections of earthworks running along a similar course north and south, which are traditionally considered to form part of Offa's Dyke as well. However, it seems likely that Asser's description of 'from sea to sea' was an exaggeration, and new fieldwork suggests that these earthworks are part of other campaigns to define the English-Welsh border. For example, Wat's Dyke, to the north of Wrexham, may be as early as the sixth century, and it is possible that some sections date as late as the Norman Conquest.

The biggest question has always been whether the dyke was a defensive military frontier, designed to keep the Welsh 'out' or a symbolic boundary between the two territories. Traditionally, it has always been seen as the latter, because its extremely patchy length 'from sea to sea' would have been impossible to defend militarily. However, new studies suggest that the main section may have been intended by Offa as a serious defensive boundary against the inhabitants of Powys.

Offa's Dyke remains something of a mystery, but this does nothing to undermine its impact. Each of the earthworks that it comprises were huge undertakings. To build a boundary on such a scale required enormous labour, resources and political control over the local population, which only strong leaders like Offa could have achieved.

Nowhere is the technical prowess of Anglo-Saxon craftsmen revealed more than in their metalwork. They developed a series of innovations in the decorative and practical working of iron, gold and other metals that provide a unique contribution to the archaeological record. From unknown sources they imported the skills of pattern-welding, a method of forging some of the highest-quality blades ever produced. The sword-blade from the famous ship-burial at Sutton Hoo, for example, was made from eight bundles of seven fine iron rods, each either twist-forged with alternating twists or left untwisted, all hammered together, back to back.

This lengthy and difficult process enabled Anglo-Saxon weapon-smiths to produce the perfect blade for combat. As well as imparting great tensile strength to the blade, pattern-welding gave it a distinctive and attractive rippled interlace appearance when polished, as replicas have shown.

In the example discovered at Sutton Hoo, it is appropriate that the magnificent blade had been fitted with a hilt, scabbard, and harness adorned with gold filigree and gold and garnet cloisonné. The Old English word for cloisonné was sinc, where the gems appeared 'sunk' or enclosed in honeycomb-like structures of gold. Examination of the gold cloisonné from the sword and elsewhere in the Sutton Hoo ship-burial has revealed other aspects of the technical and creative ingenuity of Anglo-Saxon craftsmen. Innovative details involved such high precision cutting of inlays and preparation of gold settings at so small a scale that it seems impossible that it could have been done without the use of some sort of magnifying glass. The famous Alfred jewel, shown here, combines many of these techniques in a piece that may have been the personal possession of Alfred himself.

Above: *The beautiful gold, rock crystal and enamel Alfred Jewel. Dating to around 880, this masterpiece is believed to be the handle of a pointer used for reading by King Alfred.*

Anglo-Saxon woodwrights were also highly skilled, particularly at the building of great halls and ships, although the evidence is understandably often far less well preserved than the metalwork. Within the world of the great hall, recent work on musical instruments has also allowed us to appreciate the technical refinements in the making of the harp or lyre. The finest example so far discovered comes from Sutton Hoo (see page 145), and the most recent discovery is from the East Saxon royal burial at Prittlewell, near Southend.

8 VIKING/LATE ANGLO-SAXON

VICTOR'S RECONSTRUCTION drawings first caught my eye when I saw his portrayal of the Viking attack on Lindisfarne in a history book. The monks are seen fleeing from the attack, pursued by the Vikings who, with axes swinging, seem to be enjoying their assault on the defenceless occupiers of the Holy Isle. However much our modern revisionist view seeks to replace the idea of invasion with a slow 'transition of cultures' view, it seems that the Vikings were, in the early period of their contact with Britain around 790–860, a bunch of armed raiders who were bent on destruction. The stimulus that created the Viking desire to spread out from their homelands and create havoc has always been something of a mystery. Pressure on land and resources, the development of a ship technology that enabled them to cross the

oceans, an aggressive warlike culture – all may have been involved.

Helen Geake, Time Team's Anglo-Saxon expert, points to another Viking piece of technology that she regards as having a vital influence on their military prowess – the lowly stirrup. This was invented for war and has led, it can be argued, inexorably to warfare in the modern era. It had been introduced by the Chinese in the fourth century AD, but its popularity in Europe was due to the influence of the Vikings. Being able to place your feet firmly in stirrups meant that it was much easier to control your horse, and much harder to get knocked off. This meant for the first time that it was possible to fight effectively from horseback.

It's been argued that the effectiveness of the cavalryman with stirrups led to a greater need for

military service from the rich, who could afford to breed and train the horses, and less need for the ordinary folk to muster on foot to defend themselves. So the invention of the stirrup led to the creation of a fighting elite who were rewarded by land grants – and the entire medieval feudal system. Without stirrups, it could be argued, warfare might have never become so popular among the rich and powerful, and our world would be very different today.

As the Vikings settled, they brought a range of influences that included a new way of making decisions and governing. Helen regards this as our first experience of a kind of democratic government. They believed in democracy, and invented the first parliament. This was known as the 'Thing', meaning 'assembly', and the name survives in Iceland's Althing ('whole assembly')

and the Isle of Man's Tynwald ('assembly field'). Both the Althing and the Tynwald claim to be the oldest parliament in the world, and both date from Viking times.

In Britain the Vikings have had the advantage, at least as far as the popular imagination is concerned, of being represented by the wonderful museum called the Jorvik Centre in York. It's in such a place that we get a sense of the way the late Viking period became after settlement, when the raiding culture was replaced by those who created homesteads and became part of the British story.

Two contacts with the Vikings stand out in terms of Time Team programmes. One relates to our excavation of a small boat burial on the Shetland island of Fetlar and the other is the general awareness that one has of the effect of what the Scottish call the Norse presence in the

north of Britain. It may come as a surprise to many people that a large amount of Scotland was once ruled by Norway, and that you can still see today the influence of the Vikings on the place names throughout the Northern and Western Isles. Some of the earliest Viking settlements were in this area, and the islands were just part of an empire that reached out across the European continent. Some of the first Viking ships were capable of covering vast distances along Europe's rivers and of making long-distance journeys including, some believe, making the initial discovery of America. In Britain Viking sites often reveal evidence of this contact through, for example, Arabic coins and metalwork from the Middle East.

Although the Vikings kept few written records, their travelling exploits were recorded by Anglo-Saxon chronicles and Helen points to three texts that give us a particular insight into the Viking world. 'Perhaps the two most remarkable accounts of Viking life come from opposite ends of the world – the tales of Ohthere and Wulfstan, told at the court of the English King Alfred, and

Previous spread: The Viking settlement of Jarlshof on the Shetland Islands – a familiar sight to those who barrel into Sumburgh airport, banking around the lighthouse before landing.

Above: The Cuerdale Hoard – over 8500 silver objects crammed into a lead-lined Viking chest. Discovered in Lancashire, this is one of the greatest treasure hordes in British archaeology.

the account of Ibn Fadlan, a native of Baghdad. Ohthere and Wulfstan were Norwegians who were explorers and traders, and who had joined the court of Alfred after travelling very widely. Ohthere's story is of travel around the Kola Peninsula into the White Sea, more than 480km (300 miles) north of the Arctic Circle. He tells of whaling, hunting for walrus ivory and trading with the Lapps and the Finns, and gives a detailed description of the country. Wulfstan tells us of river journeys deep into eastern Europe, and of the customs of the Estonians. All of this is written down in Alfred's own words, as an addition to the king's translation of Orosius's geographical description of the known world.

Ibn Fadlan was on a diplomatic mission from Baghdad to Bulgar, on the River Volga, between Moscow and the Ural mountains. He wrote about the burial of a Rus chief who died while travelling down the Volga soon after 920; it is the best written source we have for pagan Viking burials. Archaeologists always have to remind themselves how little of the ritual associated with funerals survives in the ground, and Ibn Fadlan, who talks of ritual sex, human and animal sacrifice, alcohol and final conflagration, emphasises this.

Helen is keen to remind us when we discuss this period that it is also the time of the late Saxons. In one of our earliest Time Team programmes, we excavated the site at Wedmore, Somerset, near to the abbey built to celebrate Alfred's victory over the Vikings in the south west.

Below: *Excavating a fascinating burial site where Time Team found a number of burials complete with sets of beautifully decorated containers.*

THE VIKINGS IN DETAIL

THE VIKING INFLUENCE on Britain runs parallel to the later Anglo-Saxon period. As Anglo-Saxon Britain developed into a variety of powerful independent kingdoms, often warring with each other, their kings precariously holding power through delicate alliances and campaigns of feuding, an equally strong force was gathering across the North Sea. The Vikings were a clever, inventive, artistic and, at times, ruthless race of people mainly from Denmark, Norway and Sweden.

The Viking raids

From the late ninth century onwards bands of warriors known as 'Northmen', raided, invaded and settled, becoming an influential part of our society for over 200 years and incorporated thereafter. The name Viking comes from a Norse descriptive word for going on an expedition in a quest for honour and reward, as in to go 'a-viking', and the name has become synonymous with terror, plunder and destruction. Yet the Vikings were not the mindless ogres as often depicted in legend and, in more recent times, by Hollywood. True, they were fighters of great renown and lived by a code of honour and status backed up by a culture of individual strength and combat prowess, but they also betray the most remarkable talents in seamanship, economics, crafts and art.

The Vikings raided the British Isles with skilled surprise attacks. Bands of warriors would arrive by sea and then either attack isolated coastal settlements or venture inland as war parties foraging for loot. Many of the status-enhancing expeditions were focused on the poorly defended monasteries which held valuable items as well as people who could be taken as slaves or held for ransom, and it's the ecclesiastical writers of the time who were the first to portray the Vikings as mindless savages.

Writers in the nineteenth century created the romanticised image of the massive Viking topped by his two-horned helmet, yet no helmet of this type from this period has ever been found by archaeologists. In reality, certainly by the later part of the ninth century when the Vikings had established settlements in the highlands and on the east coast, their reputation would have been more justified as extremely successful traders with a network of sea routes and connections spread widely across the northern hemisphere. With their established trading routes the Vikings were connected with, and ultimately influenced, many other peoples. Their exceptional navigational skills allowed them to trade as far as Uzbekistan in Russia and the Red Sea, and there is evidence that they settled across the Atlantic in Newfoundland.

Viking influence

The common perception is one of the Anglo-Saxons comfortably at home in Britain by the eighth century, having filled the power vacuum left by the withdrawal of the Roman administration, while the Vikings arrive and pick on us like some unstoppable playground bully, forcing regional kings to pay them off with huge deposits of gold and silver (Danegeld) as protection money. In truth, the concept of paying tribute was well established in the ancient world and the comfortable status quo of Anglo-Saxon kingdoms is something of a misconception. The influence of the Vikings, apart from war, is ultimately more subtle. Anglo-Saxon kings held their positions through a careful juggling act of diplomacy and allegiances. While the often precarious nature of regional control caused the ebb and flow of the political map, the Vikings were essentially just another element, though potent, of the unrest of the time, skimming booty and profit off the top of the pile.

As far as warriors, weapons and technologies of the time were concerned, both Anglo-Saxons and Vikings were remarkably similar. The difference appears in their cultures. The Vikings, particularly in the early stages, were focused on raiding and gathering wealth, while the Anglo-Saxons were dedicated to building and protecting their own dominions.

By the mid to late 800s a change started to occur. An increase in Viking settlement in Britain followed what appears to have been an increasing pressure to leave their homeland, caused by an ever-expanding society and the resulting demands on home-grown resources. Late Anglo-Saxon Britain had become an organised society with established laws, revitalised towns and more robust kingdoms. Into this emerging nation came not bands of Viking warriors, but a Viking army, claiming lands from East Anglia to Northumbria, a region which became known as the Danelaw. The Viking settlement of the ninth century has left its mark on our cultural identity. Major changes in Anglo-Saxon society occurred because of the Viking presence, such as the building of fortified towns, and Viking influences in artistic style seeped through into the Anglo-Saxon culture, while place names and elements of Viking language continue to be used by us today.

Settlements such as York (Jorvik), captured by the Vikings in 866, show us that a thriving Viking society developed urban living. Excavations in the 1970s and 80s discovered a wealth of preserved material, including streets of workshops and houses with small cellars, all part of a trading and economic hub of the north-east, while the industrial capacity of the settlers resulted in mass production of pottery and large-scale manufacture of metal items. But this growing emphasis on making Britain their home also meant that the Vikings became more permanently embroiled in the politics of the day and an integral part of the national power struggles of the late ninth and early tenth centuries.

The West Saxon king Alfred benefited from the Viking invasion because it reduced the power of his rivals. He also achieved great victory with the submission and baptism of the Viking leader Guthrum in the late ninth century, but the Viking presence caused no end of trouble for his successors. Campaigning from both sides during the opening stages of the tenth century caused great unrest. Though the Danes were actively involved in the power struggles of the time, a second faction – the Norwegians, or Norse – added further turmoil with their own conquests mounted from Ireland. For some 50 years the control of the nation was held by the House of Wessex by the tiniest thread amidst a constant battering of uprisings and contests. The end of the tenth century witnessed renewed attacks on Britain from a new Danish army and by 1016 a weakened English royal family gave way to Cnut, a Danish king of all England.

Above: *The Mammen Axe from Denmark – a fascinating example of 'zoomorphic' art displaying intertwined beasts, a typical Viking style.*

Viking Chronology

This timeline gives you a quick, at-a-glance guide to what happened when in Britain in the Viking era, helping you to understand the order of events. We've also included, in blue type, some key events that happened elsewhere in the world.

Vikings raids begin and attack on Lindisfarne (see page 162)	**789–793**
Death of Offa	**796**
Vikings, under the leadership of Turgeis, found Dublin (see page 164)	**841**
Alfred the Great becomes King of Wessex (see page 166)	**871**
Mercia falls to the Danes	**874**
Alfred defeats the Danes	**878**
Death of Alfred – Edward the Elder becomes King of Wessex	**899**
World event: Islamic Muslims begin to invade India	900
World event: Inca Empire commences, ending in 1532 with Spanish conquest (lasting approx 500 years)	900
Irish regain Dublin from the Vikings and rule for 15 years	**902**
Danelaw divisions (see page 168)	**991**
Coronation of Cnut as King of England (see page 169)	**1016**
Viking/Norse kingdoms in Scotland (see page 170)	**1020**
Edward the Confessor rules England supported by the Danes	**1042**
Christian Crusades when Pope Alexander II granted indulgences to the knights who had fought the Moorish invaders in Spain	**1060**

World event: Islamic Muslims invade India
In the early eleventh century Muslims launched a series of invasions on the Hindu regions of India, allegedly and other precious artefacts found in Hindu temples, with many places of worship being destroyed. Muslim incursions into India were not continuous but the impact of the Islamic faith permeated the lower classes of Indian society, although some converts did belong to the ruling classes. The imposition of the Islamic faith upon the Indian people affected many aspects of their culture. Language, dress, cuisine, architecture and design, together with social values and customs, all adopted a Muslim influence. The Hindus suffered greatly with the Muslim invasions, which lasted for several centuries. It is estimated that the Hindu population lost many millions of followers at the hands of the Muslims between 1000 and 1525. Evidently, these events dramatically altered the demographics of India and some Indian historians believe this period conceals perhaps the biggest instances of genocide in world history.

World event: Inca Empire commences
The Inca Empire commenced between 900 and 1000, existing for some 500 years. This Ancient Peruvian culture of South American native Indians ruled an empire stretching from Ecuador to Chile. The empire had a political system governed by priests, with an economy based on agriculture. There was a hierarchical system with the land-owning emperor at the top and the farmers, peasants and servants at the bottom. The Incas dominated the Andean region by force and conquered peoples were relocated and assimilated into their culture. It is believed the Inca Empire grew to around 13 million people. Religion dominated society, with many gods worshipped. The chief deity was the sun god, as the Incas believed their emperors were descended from him. The remains of Inca architecture are testament to their amazing feats of engineering and they were adept at working with stone, building massive forts, roads, tunnels, bridges and aqueducts. The Inca civilisation came to an untimely end when the Spanish invaded.

VIKING PROW

FOR THE DWELLERS of Britain's coastline, the sight of Viking ships approaching across the sea must have filled them with fear.

The distinctive carved ends of the ships were superb examples of Viking woodworking skills. Carved out of oak, they often took the form of geometric shapes or beasts from the Viking sagas. The most elaborately decorated examples yet found were on the Oseberg ship excavated in 1905 in a burial mound in southern Norway. Recent tree ring dating shows the burial took place in 834. It is likely that the carved sterns were created both to lift the spirits of those who sailed the ships but also as a testament to the wealth and status of the owner who, in many cases, would eventually be buried in the ship.

The intricate details found on many of the figurehead carvings are evidence of the fine range of tools, mainly iron, that were available to Viking shipwrights. We also know that they had developed steel, which would have sharper edges for carving than iron. Archaeologists have found tools such as chisels, augers, adzes and axes on many Viking sites.

In many cases, the finest examples of figureheads would have been made separately and could be removed from the main body of the ship.

Much of the evidence for Viking ship technology comes from excavations carried out at sites in Norway and Denmark. In Britain, no evidence of the larger Viking boats has yet been found, although fragments recovered from bed of the River Thames suggest that ships of this size once visited London.

Above: *This animal figurehead has a frightening appearance with huge jaws and prominent teeth. It was probably intended to be protective, to ward off evil forces encountered at sea.*

VIKINGS ATTACK LINDISFARNE

The attack on Lindisfarne, in 793, was a critical moment in making the whole nation aware of the Viking threat. This was one of the first attacks on monasteries in Northumbria. The monks represented easy prey and the wealth that some of the churches and abbeys had accumulated made them an attractive target. The Vikings' navigational skills and the quality of their ships made any part of Britain's coast vulnerable, and as the raids increased they began to over-winter on the British mainland.

We know from finds in the Viking homelands that Christian plunder was taken on a regular basis. The monks here are probably from an order founded by Columba, and would have regarded Iona as their inspiration. The attackers carry the typical axes and shields of Viking raiders and the landscape in the background shows one of the distinctive features of the island. Surprisingly, the Lindisfarne Gospels and the relics of St Cuthbert survived this attack.

Viking Raiders

THE ANGLO-SAXON Chronicle gives us our first reference to Viking raiders in the records of the year 789: 'In these days came first three ships of Norwegians from Hörthaland and then the reeve [a representative of the king of Wessex] rode thither and tried to compel them to go to the royal manor, for he did not know what they were: and then they slew him.'

Above: *A poignant gravestone from the island of Lindisfarne, which depicts a line of Viking warriors with axes held aloft. The Vikings destroyed the monastic settlement in 793.*

Though this initial contact was with a small band of warriors, it signalled the start of a frightening series of attacks which went on for well over 200 years and would culminate in a massive proportion of eastern Britain being absorbed into the greater Viking kingdoms.

The Vikings came from a culture steeped in the prowess of combat experience and bolstered by the tradition of family loyalties and the giving of prestige gifts as signs of allegiance and trust. This culture, combined with an apparent need for adventure and bravado in the unknown foreign lands as a symbol of achievement, led to the first raids which so terrified the Anglo-Saxon population. The most lucrative targets were the Anglo-Saxon monasteries. By the ninth century, monasteries had become integral parts of society. They held great power and influence and were extremely wealthy. For the Vikings they represented easy pickings – communities who could barely defend themselves and who lived in isolated places, often near the coast.

A moment in time: Lindisfarne

The monastery of Lindisfarne was built from timber and set as a collection of monks' cells, and possibly two churches, on the isolated and windswept Holy Island off the Northumbrian coast. The remoteness of the monastery was emphasised as each day the rising tide cut the island off from the mainland. Monks from Iona settled here at the request of King Oswald of Northumbria, and as the monastery grew so did its influence and importance. The position of the monastery, sponsored by the king, led to great wealth being held by the church. The bishops gave advice and counsel to the king, whose palace was at nearby Bamburgh, and were an integral part of the politics of the day, but life within the monastery itself was one of hard work and simple living. St Cuthbert, who Bede described as a miracle worker who saved ships from the stormy sea, lived here and even made a home on one of Holy Island's islets, now called St Cuthbert's Island. Here the old monk existed in great solitude with his small vegetable plot and herb garden, following a basic and humble life.

Though St Cuthbert died over a hundred years before the first Viking raid, we can imagine his fellow monks living the same simple lifestyle when Viking longships appeared in 793. The Anglo-Saxon chronicler, Symeon of Durham, paints a colourful picture of what followed in his work, *Historia Regum Anglorum et Dacorum*: 'And they came to the church of Lindisfarne, laid everything to waste with grievous plundering, trampled the holy places with polluted steps, dug up the altars and seized all the treasures of the holy church. They killed some of the brothers, took some away with them in fetters, many they drove out, naked and loaded with insults, some they drowned in the sea.' We can only imagine the horror with which news of the raid must have been received by the people of Northumbria. Alas, it was only the beginning.

The historical and archaeological story

As Mick Aston points out in his book *Monasteries in the Landscape,* many monastic sites existed before the Vikings, but they are hard to identify because early Christian sites don't tend to follow exact plans and layouts as witnessed in later centuries. The historical record, and an abundance of archaeological material, tells us that Northumbria was a centre for Christianity in the seventh century. Lindisfarne was founded in 635 by St Aidan who came from St Columba's monastery on Iona, off the west coast of Scotland. Monks from Lindisfarne established monasteries over much of the north-east, including Jarrow, founded in 682 by Benedict Biscop. The power and influence of the monasteries didn't escape the Vikings' notice and all three major houses suffered raids in successive years (Lindisfarne 793, Jarrow 794 and Iona 795).

The result of these and other violent raids sent shockwaves through the Anglo-Saxon world. The monastery was an important and integral part of Saxon life and greatly respected. The continued persecution of the Church by pagan Vikings led to what Mick refers to as 'monasticism virtually being extinguished in Britain'. Only later, with the slow and gradual conversion of a different generation of Scandinavians, and the all-powerful influence of the Normans, did the status and power of the monasteries return. As for Lindisfarne, a body of Benedictine monks from Durham built a second monastery on Holy Island during the reformation period following the Norman Conquest. The visible remains on the island today belong to that period, where for nearly 500 years the monastery enjoyed successful growth, despite its geographic position making it a focus of troubles as ongoing feuds between England and Scotland unfolded. The monastery was finally dissolved by Henry VIII in 1536.

PALAEOLITHIC

MESOLITHIC

NEOLITHIC

BRONZE AGE

IRON AGE

ROMAN

ANGLO-SAXON

VIKING c790–1066

Viking Raiders c790

NORMAN

MIDDLE AGES

TUDOR

STUART

GEORGIAN

VICTORIAN

MODERN

Dublin becomes Viking

THE VIKINGS HAD a fundamental impact on Ireland in the ninth century. In particular, Dublin is in origin a Viking settlement, one of the most important of the Viking world. As with the rest of the British Isles, Ireland had become a target for Viking raiders in the late eighth century. The Irish coast and offshore islands were home to many ancient, wealthy monasteries which provided attractive plundering grounds and contemporary Irish chronicles, such as the *Annals of Ulster*, record repeated looting and violent attacks.

In the 830s, the character of the Viking raids on Ireland changed. The small 'hit-and-run' attacks on individual institutions were replaced by much larger fleets of as many as 60 ships, which inflicted much greater devastation, fighting battles over a wide area and taking captives as well as looting. To achieve this, it seems likely they were no longer making exploratory journeys from Scandinavia each summer, but raiding from bases around the Irish Sea. Certainly in 841, the *Annals of Ulster* record the establishment of a major Viking *longphort* or fortress on the mouth of the River Liffey near Dublin. With a permanent settlement to protect their ships, the raiders could overwinter in Dublin and operate throughout the year.

Ninth-century Ireland was home to many feuding kings and chieftains, and the new Viking settlers rapidly became part of the shifting political landscape. The settlement at Dublin became Viking, its leaders forming alliances with, or fighting against, the Irish kings, and even other Vikings; in 851, the Irish Vikings fought off a large fleet of incoming Danish raiders. In the ensuing decades, several Viking families fought over the lordship of Dublin. The greatest character we know about was Amlaib, a formidable leader who launched major attacks on Scotland, expanding Viking domination there, and plundered heavily in Armagh, killing or capturing over 1000 people. The heavy toll on Irish settlements, combined with internal feuding, made Dublin vulnerable, and in 902, the native kings of Brega and Leinster joined forces to drive the Vikings out of Ireland. As chronicles from the period relate, 'they abandoned a good number of their ships, and escaped half-dead after they had been wounded and broken'. However, Dublin had become a permanent feature in the Irish landscape, and within a few years, it was back under Viking control. The powerful Viking dynasties of Dublin were the most influential in the British Isles in the tenth century. In the aftermath of the death of the English King Athelstan in 939, it was a Dublin Viking, another Amlaib, who became King of York and effectively ruler of half of England.

There are few historical records relating to the Viking kingdom of Dublin, but remarkable archaeological excavations in the city from the 1960s to the 1980s have provided a detailed insight into life there in the tenth and eleventh centuries. It was a walled settlement, laid out with a network of wood- and stone-paved streets, substantial houses and regular fenced plots. The incredible range of preserved artefacts demonstrates clearly that Dublin wasn't just a political entity, but one of the great ports of trade and economic powers of the Viking world as well. Thriving industries produced many goods, both for export and the domestic market – everything from amber and jet jewellery and high-quality textiles to antler combs and shoes. Many imported luxury commodities from all over Europe and Asia have also been found here, including coins, ceramics, glass, even soapstone and ivory.

Right: *Excavations in Dublin in 1968 reveal Viking timber walkways dating to the earliest days of the settlement, a stronghold of the Viking presence in ninth-century Ireland.*

Vikings Defeated by Alfred

BY THE LATE ninth century, after nearly 100 years of Viking raiding and conquest, Britain was at the mercy of the pagan warriors. No longer returning year after year on seasonal campaigns, the Vikings were now beginning to settle and becoming a permanent feature on the landscape, controlling vast stretches of the north and east – the Danelaw. The Anglo-Saxon kingdoms were on their back heel and the continued raiding and more dedicated campaigns of the Vikings had taken the Anglo-Saxon royal houses to the brink of destruction. Some, such as the kingdoms of East Anglia and Northumbria, were simply annihilated. One king, Alfred, the King of Wessex, remained as the most influential with a powerbase in the west country, but even he was forced to pay huge tributes of silver and gold to the Vikings to keep them at bay.

In the year 878 a new army appeared, led by the Danish king, Guthrum, no longer content with their annual bribe. Their ruthless campaign forged deep into Wessex and Alfred was given no choice but to seek refuge in the Somerset marshes, an inhospitable landscape which held a small haven of high ground, Athelney. From this lonely and remote base Alfred, the clever king renowned for his intellect, took stock of his desperate situation and in a truly remarkable tale of heroism and leadership, mustered an army to save his land from the depths of despair.

Above: The White Horse of Westbury in Wiltshire. Was it originally carved to mark the battle of Edington in 878? Archaeology has yet to prove the link.

A moment in time: the battle of Edington

At Athelney Alfred built a stronghold, a fortress in the marshes from which groups of Saxon warriors could venture out as raiding parties, harrying the Vikings with hit-and-run guerrilla tactics which turned the depths of Somerset into a deadly no-go area for the domineering Danes. As the strength and confidence of Alfred's forces grew, he set about building an alliance with the backing of outlying settlements co-ordinated by a series of clandestine meetings. Slowly his resistance movement gathered momentum until in May 878 he had built an army capable of fighting the Vikings in a pitched battle.

The Anglo-Saxon Chronicle tells us, 'Then, in the seventh week after Easter, he rode to Brixton by the eastern side of Selwood and there came out to meet him all the people of Somersetshire, and Wiltshire, and Hampshire and they rejoiced to see him.' Gathering the extra men, Alfred made for Edington in Wiltshire where he met the Viking foe head-on. In a tough and bloody battle the Vikings were broken and routed and the Danish king Guthrum was forced to surrender. In a remarkable act of submission, the pagan Viking king was baptised 'with thirty of his worthiest men'.

In the aftermath of the Viking defeat, the Danes withdrew to a weakened Danelaw, while Alfred went on to pursue a programme of stronghold building across the south-west. His fortified sites, known as burhs, effectively became defended towns – places of refuge commonly used by rural communities in times of trouble. Not only did Alfred build his string of bases, but also the force to protect them. After Edington, Alfred created a standing army and by careful diplomatic handling, ruled successfully as the leading light in Anglo-Saxon Britain until his death in 899.

The historical and archaeological story

Alfred's *burhs*, commonly traced in place names ending in 'borough', were a great success. Alfred took care with his early attempts at town planning and the more substantial burghal towns contained churches and, equally as important, markets which became hubs of the local economy. Though the Vikings continued to cause unrest with later campaigns under new power-hungry leaders, the kingdom of Wessex remained secure with its system of defensive sites.

Alfred spent the last years of his life dedicated to consolidating his kingdom with great diplomacy and the introduction of just laws for his subjects. He also devoted great efforts to education and learning. He personally translated Latin works into the common language of Anglo-Saxon, Old English, and it's through his labours in conserving these ancient texts that we have such a rich historical resource preserved today.

In many respects Alfred was England's last hope in a desperate hour of need. If he had not survived the initial Viking attacks on Wessex, our country today could be quite a different place. His last stand and the subsequent reorganisation of his domain set a precedent which subsequent kings would try to follow, eventually resulting in the conquest of the Danelaw. His remarkable life earned him the title 'The Great' and to this day he remains an iconic national figure. Alfred's chaplain Asser, later a bishop of Sherborne, wrote a biography of the king which includes the story of the burnt cakes: Alfred, having taken shelter in a family's home, is told to mind the cakes (probably simple, flat bread or oat cakes). Out of tiredness or distraction, he allows them to burn and is told off by the mother. A charming story that perhaps hints at the closeness of Alfred to the people.

PALAEOLITHIC

MESOLITHIC

NEOLITHIC

BRONZE AGE

IRON AGE

ROMAN

ANGLO-SAXON

VIKING c790–1066

Vikings defeated
by Alfred 878

NORMAN

MIDDLE AGES

TUDOR

STUART

GEORGIAN

VICTORIAN

MODERN

York and the Danelaw

IN THE 870s the *Anglo-Saxon Chronicle* records a change in the activities of the Viking raiders. Different Viking armies were campaigning throughout the English kingdoms and are often described as conquering them, presumably extracting tribute and prisoners and exerting some political control. But in 876 they also 'shared out the land of the Northumbrians, and started to plough and support themselves', shortly afterwards doing the same in Mercia and East Anglia. It was the beginning of Viking settlement in England.

These areas of north and east England became known as the 'Danelaw', a Viking territory distinct from the rest of the country under Anglo-Saxon control. A treaty between Alfred and the Danish leader Guthrum recognised the two separate regions and defined a boundary, which ran approximately from the Thames estuary to the Wirral. However, exactly how the Danelaw differed in character from the rest of the country, and how 'Viking' its inhabitants were in the ninth and tenth centuries, is hotly debated. Traditionally, historians imagined settlers arriving in the Danelaw from Scandinavia, primarily Denmark, but today it is seen more as a term signalling political overlordship than large-scale migration. Perhaps it was largely just the campaigning armies themselves who settled, integrating with the existing local population.

Evidence for life in the Danelaw is sketchy. Most famously, place name analysis appears to suggest a strong Viking influence. Plotting place names with a Scandinavian element, such as those ending in 'by' (eg Grimsby) or 'thorpe', on a map shows a high concentration in the north-east of the country, and almost none south of Alfred's Thames estuary/Wirral boundary. However, in archaeological terms, the Viking presence is much harder to recognise, with very few examples of sites with distinctly Scandinavian artefacts and culture. Later historical sources, such as the Domesday Book and royal law codes, do suggest that the Danelaw enjoyed slightly different legal and agricultural practices to the rest of the country. But whatever it meant for the people living within it, it was a key political frontier for both Viking leaders and the Saxon kings.

The most significant settlement within the Danelaw was York. The history of the city illustrates how complex the politics of this period was. York was already an important Anglian town when it was captured by the Vikings in 866. Throughout the following hundred years, it became the centre of an influential kingdom, with many rivals for its leadership – not only the displaced Anglo-Saxon kings, but different Viking leaders as well. York was in a key strategic position, and the politics of the city were tied to power struggles in Viking Ireland, Scotland and Scandinavia, as well as England. The displaced Viking kings of Dublin based themselves at York in the ninth century, and it has been suggested that the Cuerdale Hoard (a famous collection of Viking silver found on the river route between the two cities) was possibly a war chest, intended to aid the effort to regain control of Dublin.

The gorily named Norwegian Erik Bloodaxe was the last Viking king of York. He was finally expelled from York by the Northumbrians in 954, and the English monarchy regained control of the city. Nonetheless, York retained its strongly Scandinavian character, and thanks to its Viking heritage remained a major economic centre in the centuries that followed – by Domesday, it was the second largest city in England. As with Dublin, incredible archaeological discoveries from the city have revealed a thriving town, producing goods for trade over a wide hinterland, and receiving many items from the local area and across Scandinavia.

Cnut: The First Viking King

CNUT (or Canute, as we used to call him) was the first Viking truly to become King of England. It was his actions, and those of his father Sven Forkbeard, which established a Viking claim to the English throne, a significant factor behind the Battle of Hastings and the Norman Conquest. Sven Forkbeard was a Danish Viking who led a raiding army against England in 991. It was a new wave of fearsome attacks more akin to invasions than raiding parties. Sven's huge fleet of ships presented a major threat, and after a humiliating defeat at the Battle of Maldon, the English king Aethelred paid heavily to avert similar threats. However, this defensive strategy failed to put an end to Viking attacks, and large armies returned many times, extorting huge sums in tribute from southern Britain. Finally in 1013, Sven landed once more at Sandwich in Kent, this time with conquest, rather than tribute, in mind. Aethelred was driven into exile and Sven seized the English crown. He may not have lived long to enjoy his success, dying just over a month later, but he had ensured a Danish claim to the English throne.

Eleventh-century England was an attractive target – a wealthy kingdom, with a booming economy, new towns, and large quantities of the silver coin prized in the Viking world. After Sven's death, the throne had reverted to Aethelred, but Sven's son Cnut launched a new invasion in 1015. He campaigned across the West Country and North of England before taking London, finally being crowned King of England in November 1016, on the death of Aethelred's son Edmund.

Cnut is remembered as one of our greatest leaders, and he was certainly a king with an effective propaganda machine. He was revered as a devout Christian by ecclesiastical chroniclers, and is remembered for his failed attempt to hold back the sea at Southampton. This was, so legend has it, to show sycophantic advisors that he was wise enough to know the limits of his power. Cnut was a successful statesman in many respects. He unified many existing Anglo-Saxon legal practices, and laid the foundations of a territorial system of governance based on four great earldoms, which would survive for centuries. He became King of Denmark on the death of his brother, and after a successful attack, was also briefly King of Norway.

Cnut died at Shaftesbury in 1035 and was buried in Winchester in the Old Minster. His tomb was exhumed when the Minster was demolished, and a Tudor chest containing his bones can still be seen in the presbytery of Winchester Cathedral. Cnut's dynasty was shortlived, and his sons only ruled England for another seven years, before Edward the Confessor, son of Aethelred, regained the throne. However, Cnut's legacy was an enduring Viking claim to the throne, which resurfaced with profound consequences in 1066.

Right: *The formidable stone and earthwork fortress of Fyrkat, Denmark, home to the Viking king Cnut before his invasion of England.*

Viking Scotland

THE VIKINGS HAD a profound effect on northern Scotland, creating a powerful kingdom which became an important player in the politics of the rest of Britain and Ireland. However, compared to the chronicles of England and Ireland, there are few historical records for Scotland in this period and thus little information about their arrival. It seems likely that the northern and western coasts of Scotland suffered similar raids to England and Ireland. We certainly know of attacks on the island monasteries of Iona and Skye in the late eighth century, and, of course, Lindisfarne, historically part of Bernicia in the Anglo-Saxon kingdom of Northumbria.

For the Norwegian Vikings, northern Scotland offered a valuable stepping stone in the North Atlantic from their homeland to the rest of the British Isles and Europe. Environmentally, it also offered a landscape and climate they were more familiar with than other parts of Europe. Thus in the early ninth century, they appear to have started settling many of the islands and parts of the coastline. Mapping Scandinavian place names reveals clusters of Viking settlements along the north and west coast of mainland Scotland, particularly Caithness in the extreme north, and dense occupation on Shetland, Orkney and the Inner and Outer Hebrides.

Historians have long argued over whether the Viking settlement in northern Scotland was a peaceful integration or violent takeover. The local population were Picts, a sophisticated tribe with an artistic tradition. Archaeology suggests that in some areas, such as Orkney, Pictish settlement may have been in decline by the ninth century, meaning little direct contact between natives and incomers. Elsewhere, at Jarlshof, a large Viking settlement on the southern tip of Shetland, archaeologists have discovered a settlement occupied almost continuously from the Bronze Age to the Middle Ages, suggesting that its Viking occupants were just one part of a very long tradition of fishing and farming on the island. In contrast, recent excavations at Portmahomack on the Tarbat peninsula on Moray Firth suggest a possibly more violent scenario. A long-lived Pictish settlement here appears to have been abruptly replaced with Viking longhouses in the eighth or ninth century.

Whatever happened in individual settlements, it is clear that a powerful Viking aristocracy had emerged in northern Scotland by the mid-ninth century, particularly on Orkney and Shetland. They had strong dynastic links with the developing Viking kingdom of Dublin, and between them, they launched many attacks on the Picts and other areas of the Britain, extracting tribute or prisoners and exerting political pressure. In 839, historical sources suggest that the Vikings of northern Scotland wiped out the Pictish royal family altogether.

The Viking presence in northern Scotland survived longer than in any other part of Britain. Many settlers became Christian and absorbed some Pictish culture, but the region retained a strong Scandinavian identity. Distinctive Viking boat burials have been found on the islands. The most famous one at Scar, on Sanday, contained a man, woman and child and a wealth of Viking artefacts, including trading weights and a whalebone plaque carved with dragons' heads. Many of the islands and some coastal areas remained as semi-independent Viking earldoms into the Middle Ages, although under complex Norwegian and sometimes Scottish overlordship. Norway didn't give up its Scottish possessions until the thirteenth century, even then retaining Orkney and Shetland. These remained part of the Norwegian-Danish kingdoms until the fifteenth century, when they were granted to Scotland as a royal wedding dowry.

VIKING SHIP TECHNOLOGY

ONE OF THE MAIN contributions the Vikings made to the advance of technology, apart from their ships, was the way they increased production of many everyday items to an almost industrial scale, such as the pottery, combs, small iron articles and jewellery that turn up on typical Viking sites like York, where Time Team excavated in 1999. There is a vast increase in pottery that may have been an expansion of existing local industries, stimulated by Viking traders.

The Vikings used large amounts of wood and bone and were skilled at working both materials which only survive where waterlogged deposits preserve organic remains. At Coppergate in York, there are bowls and antler combs, plus the tools to produce them. The blacksmith was so revered by the Vikings that they were celebrated in their mythology, and finds have included knives that show evidence of pattern-welding and sophisticated decorative techniques. Beautiful brooches, like the tortoise brooch found at Fetlar by Time Team, were evidence of the fine skills used for personal ornaments and in the later Viking period metalworkers developed the technique of inlaying to produce swords and axes inlaid with silver.

Although the Viking boat that Time Team found at Fetlar was small, it exhibited many of the features that were to help the Vikings dominate the seas and spread their culture to Britain's shores. According to Time Team's wood technology expert Damian Goodburn, it is clear that features such as the framing systems used in later medieval clinker-built ships and boats were strongly influenced by Viking ways of doing things. This influence still shows in the work of twentieth-century traditional wooden boat builders. The Viking clinker boat buried at Fetlar is very much the 'ancient ancestor' of the small clinker fishing boats of that region built into the

last century. The Viking planked boats and ships were made in the 'clinker' style which developed in the Iron Age and could be from 6m (20ft) to 30m (100ft) long. A backbone or keel was joined to end posts then a light shell of partly overlapping planking was added, held together with iron rivets. Surprisingly the strengthening curved rib timbers were added afterwards, further braced with integral cross beams. The seams were waterproofed with tarred hair or wool. Whether the ships were long narrow warships or wider cargo vessels the hulls were light, supple, but strong structures, slightly like early aircraft! Supple strength was increased by the use of planks, which were made by splitting out along the grain and trimming with axes rather than by sawing. Viking shipwrights or 'stemsmiths' could build state-of-the-art raiding craft capable of crossing the North Sea and also burdensome cargo ships which could trade to Greenland.

The ships were propelled with oars and a single square sail of woven and felted wool, which enabled them to sail into the wind with the help of a deep side rudder. The decoration and finish of Viking vessels shows that they were much loved by their owners, users and builders. The waterlogged remains of the larger rowed vessels found in burial mounds show both an appreciation of style and the power of kings and chieftains to control people and materials. Experimental archaeology, mainly at the Roskilde Viking Ship Museum in Denmark, has shown the high levels of labour, skill and fine materials that went into building such vessels.

It is worth remembering that these ships enabled the Vikings to make some of the longest voyages of their time. From their homeland they not only raided the coast of Britain but ventured far into the centre of Europe using the river system, and also made the first crossing of the Atlantic.

9 NORMAN

THE NORMAN PERIOD covers the reign of four kings, stretching from William the Conqueror in 1066 through to the end of Stephen's reign in 1154. It lasted less than 90 years, but it was a period when the landscape of Britain changed dramatically. The Bayeux tapestry (see page 185) records the events which ushered in Norman rule in Britain, and our greatest national treasure, Domesday Book (see page 186), records the degree to which new Norman landowners took over throughout the country afterwards. However, it was William's policy of castle-building and severe reprisals against local uprisings that had the greatest immediate impact on the country.

We dug one of William the Conqueror's constructions at Alderton, near Northampton in 2001. A local man, Derek Batten, had purchased an overgrown 'castle' and asked Time Team to find out more about it for him. It turned out to be an early Norman ringwork – a flattened mound surrounded by bank and ditch – and one of the many strategic castles William threw up across the country after the Battle of Hastings to secure his newly-conquered country. Alderton was also refortified at the end of the Norman period, during the civil war between Stephen and Matilda, a reminder of how violent and conflict-ridden the politics of the time were.

This was also clear when we dug at Bridgnorth Castle later in the same series. Constructed by the deeply unpleasant Earl of Shrewsbury, Robert of Belleme, in 1101, Henry I laid siege to it and confiscated it from him a year later to end his treasonous plotting. It was a very different Norman castle to Alderton, one which went on to be a major stone fortification until it was blown

up in the civil war. The dig produced lots of new information about the castle, but I have to say my lasting memory of this programme is Phil conducting an experiment in Norman warfare, and using a siege catapult to hurl flaming grapefruits around the public park in Bridgnorth – truly terrifying!

As Mick is always reminding us, however, the Norman period isn't just about castles, and on Time Team we've dug quite a few of the religious sites that he loves so much. The Normans brought new types of monasteries and church architecture to Britain, and for many people, these new-style stone buildings and their inhabitants would have been as solid a reminder of Norman rule as the castles were. The most spectacular surviving Norman church is probably Durham Cathedral (see page 184), but we came face to face with this kind of architecture ourselves when we set out to locate the plan of Coventry's lost cathedral. The pier bases Phil discovered were an impressive 4m (13ft) across, and gave a real insight into the impact which these innovative and massive buildings must have had on local communities.

For me though, the most striking thing we've discovered over the years is how often these new Norman buildings were sited at important Saxon locations. For our second live programme we dug at Bawsey in Norfolk. Today, a ruined Norman church stands on its own in the middle of a cornfield, but our excavations revealed a long and complex history stretching over hundreds of years. The church was placed at the heart of a large Saxon enclosure, which probably contained a monastery or palace, where the inhabitants used high-status items like tweezers and coins, and the

site continued in use into the medieval period. Both Athelney Abbey in Somerset and Thetford in Norfolk told the same story of continuity – of Saxon churches and monasteries replaced by Norman institutions.

Everyday life

For ordinary people, it can often be hard to judge how much the Norman conquest changed their lives. Unless you're dealing with a monument like a castle or church, short historical periods like the Normans don't always show up very well in archaeology. Instead, what you see are settlements with long occupation histories like the one we dug at High Worsall, a deserted medieval village in North Yorkshire. Starting with impressive 'lumps and bumps' revealed by aerial photographs, Stewart was able to unravel the layout of the vanished village, and our trenches revealed how it had grown from a small Saxon hamlet into

a planned village after the Conquest, with streets and rows of houses and plots.

Archaeological work at places like High Worsall has shown that after the Conquest, many settlements do appear to have changed from irregular groups of houses to deliberately laid-out villages, perhaps stimulated by the new Norman landowners. High Worsall was abandoned in the fourteenth century, but many of our towns and villages today have medieval and probably

Norman origins. For me, our programme at Plympton in Devon probably sums up the Norman impact on Britain the best. Plympton's main street is lined with post-medieval façades, but Time Team spent several enjoyable days knocking on residents' doors and investigating their houses to show that the street had been laid out in the medieval period, probably to go with the fine Norman motte and bailey castle that still stands in the local park.

Previous spread: Durham Cathedral at sunset. The Normans embarked on a passionate quest to build churches and cathedrals, their architecture one of their greatest legacies.

Above left: Tony Robinson getting to grips with Norman stonework.

Above: The dramatic ringwork earthworks of Beaudesert Castle in Warwickshire. A formidable obstacle for any determined attacker.

THE NORMANS IN DETAIL

THE NORMANS WERE an incredibly powerful and wealthy people that stemmed from the Viking, or Norse, invaders of France. They were given their own domain in the northern borders of the country back in the late ninth century, a region that became known as Normandy.

The original Viking leader, King Rollo, became a Christian and allied himself with neighbouring kingdoms. His son, William Longsword, inherited Normandy in 931, and the rest of the tenth century saw the gradual break with the Viking ancestors and the development of a feudal system with the ruling Duchy the most powerful centre of the state.

By the end of the tenth century, Richard II, Duke of Normandy, remained in power as a direct descendent of Rollo. When he died in 1026, his brother Robert took the Duchy. He took leave for a long pilgrimage to Jerusalem which left home affairs unattended, and on return to France he died. With his absence and death in 1035 without an heir, the Norman kingdom fell into the boiling pot of internal power struggles. At around eight years old, the bastard son of Duke Richard I was the only rightful candidate. He had a name that would rock Britain in three decades' time – William.

The Norman hierarchy

The intricacies of the Norman invasion of Britain will be discussed later, but what followed was an impact on society which ended the Anglo-Saxon period and took us through to the Middle Ages. The Normans brought a new royal house and a structured hierarchical society, a different culture of art and a revived church. Norman style can clearly be seen in the typical architecture of period churches, and in one of their most dramatic and domineering creations, the castle.

The feudal system that permeates the Norman period was a dynamic, security-enhancing concept. Acting as both a social and legal framework for society, it worked by giving land to people under

the 'protection' of a lord in return for their labour and, at times, their lives when called to arms. William the Conqueror, as king, ultimately owned everything, and though lands were gifted to barons and dukes, and smaller manors to knights, they all were in essence tenants subject to the king's will.

Norman architecture and art

One of the classic elements of Norman occupation was castle building and their associated parishes. Not since the Romans had we witnessed such widespread construction of defensive sites. Often acting as centres of control and administration for local lords, castles were commonly situated on natural defensive positions in areas of likely trouble. Like the Romans with their lines of forts, the Normans developed a system of strongholds which controlled the surrounding countryside. They were first built as motte and bailey bases; the motte (or hill) topped by a timber tower or small fort, while the bailey acted as a defended terrace or courtyard enclosing the mound. By the twelfth century many castles were rebuilt in stone and most featured additional defences which made them formidable obstacles. Many castles were either built in towns, where substantial demolition took place to accommodate them, or developed their own surrounding settlements. A typically Norman town plan can be seen at Devizes in Wiltshire, where the streets of the settlement mimic the curving defences of the Norman castle.

The art and architecture of the Normans is easily recognisable. The most famous art piece, which is also a most remarkable document of the invasion of Britain, is the Bayeux Tapestry. This linen embroidery, some 70m (230ft) long, depicts the events of William's encounters with Britain and the invasion, in a detailed 'movie storyboard' featuring nearly 2000 elements, each carefully stitched in woollen thread. A Latin narration runs through the central area which shows the key events and depicts in detail the weapons, buildings, ships and characters of the time.

Architecturally, the distinctive features of Norman buildings are like a trademark, with the signature heavy, solid walls and grand roof spans with substantial arched doorways and windows, often decorated with a distinctive dog-tooth geometric pattern commonly known as Romanesque.

Law and administration

Although the Normans effectively wiped out much of the Anglo-Saxon high society, they kept many aspects of the robust Anglo-Saxon law system. Shires may well have been renamed as counties, and lords replaced thanes with the feudal system, but the delegation of regional responsibilities to local centres of power remained. Exceptions introduced by the new administration included trial by combat, when disputes were settled by fighting, and Forest Law, an incredibly harsh set of laws constructed by William relating to Royal Forests, which eventually covered much of the country. The penalty for poaching or openly hunting on the king's land was draconian, with the punishment for killing one of the king's deer being the loss of your sight.

The Normans ruthlessly imposed their power, particularly with a campaign of savage retribution against revolt in the north. Time Team came across evidence of this campaign, known as the 'Harrying of the North', at Skipsea, Yorkshire, where they found one of the villages which had been devastated by William's forces. The harrying is recorded in our first census of property, the Domesday Book. Essentially a survey to quantify what had been conquered, and register who owned what, the Domesday survey of England is held in two books, Great Domesday and Little Domesday (the latter actually the larger volume), which survive to this day. Commissioned by William in 1085, it was finished just two years later by the king's commissioners who travelled the land recording every estate, house, mill and tenant. As a document it makes fascinating reading.

William the Conqueror died in 1087 near Rouen while fighting the French King, Philip I. While Normandy was left to his eldest son, Robert, England was inherited by his unpopular second son, William Rufus, who died while hunting in the New Forest in 1100. William the Conqueror's youngest son, Henry I, took the throne and led for 35 years until his succession by Stephen and a general fall into anarchy. By 1154 Stephen was dead and the line from William was broken. However, in less than 100 years, the Normans had made an impression on Britain which remains to this day.

Above: *A section of the Bayeux Tapestry, showing a cavalry charge. Note the fallen under the hooves of Norman horses.*

Norman Chronology

This timeline gives you a quick, at-a-glance guide to what happened in Britain when in the Norman era, helping you to understand the order of events. We've also included, in pink type, some key events that happened elsewhere in the world.

Battle of Hastings (see page 182)	**1066**
World event: *Chinese astronomers recorded Halley's comet*	1066
English rebellions	**1067–1070**
The harrying of the North	**1069–1070**
Tower of London built	**1075**
Bayeux Tapestry (see page 185)	**1085**
Domesday Book (see page 186)	**1086**
Death of William I and accession of William II Rufus	**1087**
Robert pawns Normandy to Rufus	**1096**
Civil War (see page 187)	**1090**
World event: *The People's Crusade*	1099
World event: *Crusaders took Jerusalem by storm and massacred almost all inhabitants*	1099
Death of William Rufus and accession of Henry I	**1100**
Henry I takes Normandy	**1106**
Sinking of the White Ship (see page 187)	**1120**
Death of Henry I	**1135**
Matilda and Stephen fight for the throne	**1135–1148**
Matilda retires to Normandy	**1148**
Henry II succeeds	**1154**

World event: The People's Crusade
Also called the 'Peasants' Crusade', this was linked to the First Crusade. The Pope sanctioned the crusade for August 1096 but peasants, affected by drought, plague and starvation, organised a migration of 100,000 unskilled fighters in April 1096, led by Peter the Hermit of Amiens, a charismatic monk and supporter of the crusade. They were joined by a large German contingent. However, a few thousand French crusaders led by Walter Sans-Avoir, a former knight, marched on ahead. In Semlin, Hungary, 16 of Walter's men were stripped of their armour after robbing a market. The armour was hung from the castle walls. When Peter's crusaders saw this, it led to an assault on Semlin with 4000 Hungarians killed. The crusaders fled to Belgrade where they burned the city. Eventually, Peter's crusaders met with Walter's at Constantinople. They were escorted into Turkey by Byzantine troops, who warned them not to engage the Turks. However, inner turmoil split the crusade and the crusaders pillaged Turkish suburbs, leading to the Turks sending an army that slaughtered and enslaved their attackers. Just 3000 individuals survived the People's Crusade.

World event: Crusaders took Jerusalem by storm and massacred almost all inhabitants
The Crusades took place between 1096 and 1291, with Christian Europeans seeking to attain control of Palestine from the Muslims in the Middle East. The Pope granted sanction for the crusades, based on a desire for land and wealth and to spread Christianity to the holy lands. Factors that encouraged the First Crusade were reports that the Fatimid Caliph Al-Hakim bi-Amr Allah of Egypt had ordered the destruction of all churches and synagogues in Jerusalem, and rumours that Christian pilgrims suffered cruelty at the hands of Muslim rulers. Thus, Christian soldiers marched from Europe in August 1096, reaching Jerusalem in June 1099. An arduous siege lasted for one month with soldiers and horses perishing from thirst and starvation until the Crusaders finally broke through on 15 July. The slaughter that followed invoked reports that men waded knee-deep in the blood of the dead as the majority of Jerusalem's population was massacred indiscriminately. Following its capture, Jerusalem became the capital of the Kingdom of Jerusalem, a feudal state that lasted until 1291.

THE NORMAN STONE ARCH

EARLY NORMAN BUILDINGS in England were built in the Romanesque style favoured in Normandy and derived from the architecture of Lombardy in Italy. Superseding the earlier Saxon architecture, the development of this style in England was confined to the period from 1066 to 1154, a time of tremendous building activity.

The early Romanesque buildings constructed by the Normans in England were massive because, fearful of collapse, masons built walls up to 7.3m (24ft) thick at the base to provide support for these tall buildings. In general, they overestimated the thickness necessary for safety, although, since this work had wide joints and the mortar was poor, the collapse of towers and roofs was not unknown. Windows were small and arched, partly in order not to weaken the walls and partly for defensive reasons, such as in castles where the lowest row of windows was at first-floor level.

Churches, abbeys and castles were the principal buildings constructed by the Normans and initially they had sparsely adorned masonry, plainer than their Romanesque counterparts in southern Europe. The Romanesque arch was the main form of decoration, varying in form from the semi-circular shape, which was the most usual, and where the centre was on the diameter line, to the segmental, with a centre above diameter level, and the stilted, where it was below. Since Norman walling was thick, there was considerable depth between the inner and outer faces of the arch. In early work, the arch was not recessed; the edges were square in section and not ornamented. Later work was moulded

Right: A classic signature Norman arched doorway. This one is on the western façade of Iffley church in Oxfordshire. Visitors can see fine examples of typical round-topped windows here too.

in deep rolls and rounds and often enriched with chevron or zigzag, nail-head, billet, lozenge, cable or houndstooth decoration.

These Norman arches were often used in arcading, where a row of columns or piers supported the arches. Sometimes the arcades were used for decorative purpose only, known as 'blind arcading', standing in front of a plain wall surface and frequently interlaced with one another, as can be seen in the interiors of many early churches and the cloisters of abbeys. After the 1150s the Romanesque style was gradually replaced by the newer Gothic style with its telltale pointed arches and flying buttresses that can still be seen adorning many famous cathedrals today.

THE HARRYING OF THE NORTH

After the victory at Hastings, William the Conqueror still faced a population that hated his presence, and from 1066 to 1070 his troops conducted a merciless campaign of terror and repression aimed at rubbing out any revolt. The north of Britain suffered badly and this picture captures such a moment. In the background there is a typical motte and bailey settlement at an early stage of what would often later become stone castles. These provided a base from which the Norman soldiers could impose their control. They made particularly effective use of soldiers on horseback and their use of mail and relatively sophisticated armour gave them a great advantage over their foe.

In 1072 William carried out an invasion of Scotland and followed this up with attacks on Wales in 1081. The picture conveys a time when many ordinary Britons suffered great hardship at the hands of an invading force.

William the Conqueror and the Battle of Hastings

THE BATTLE OF Hastings signalled the end of the Anglo-Saxon period and is held in legend as the iconic death of the last Anglo-Saxon king, fighting to save England from French invasion. However, the picture is more complicated than a simple defence against a bullying invader. The key lies in the intriguing build-up which sees the King of England offering his country to another, individuals fighting for succession, and a feud between brothers which affected our history.

Above: *A section of the Bayeux Tapestry recording the Norman invasion of England. Note the Saxon long-handled battle axes, and the Norman cavalryman with his feet out of stirrups. The Saxon's shield is filled with arrows from an arrow storm and further archers are depicted on the border.*

Edward the Confessor had an interesting life which saw him the son of an English king and a Norman aristocrat (Ethelred the Unready and Emma), exiled to Normandy for years, struggling with diplomacy in the face of commanding families in the regions of England, constructing one of the greatest buildings of the period (Westminster Abbey), and dying without a blood heir. In England his reign was dominated by the Godwin family of Wessex, the most potent earldom in the land. Harold and Tostig Godwin held the power in court, yet after an acrimonious falling out Tostig was exiled to Norway. Harold became an almost *de facto* king, running much of England for Edward, yet in a shrewd political move, Edward regularly entertained his Norman friends and installed some in lucrative positions, perhaps as a check against Godwin power. This was a dangerous game to play for a man who had no blood relative as heir to his throne.

No records survive of the actual agreements, but as Edward breathed his last words in 1066, supposedly stating that Harold should be king, William, Duke of Normandy, was under the impression that Edward had gifted England to him in gratitude for protecting him during his exile. The two men were set to collide, yet Harold also had to contend with the return of Tostig.

A moment in time: the death of Harold

As Edward was buried, Harold was crowned king and William set about building his invasion fleet. In the aftermath of assuming the throne, Harold started building alliances with the English earls to consolidate his position. On hearing that Edward had died, the Viking king, Harald Hardrada, in cahoots with Tostig, set sail for England. In a year unlike any other, the new king Harold was going to have to be something akin to a superman to survive.

By September 1066 William had called in favours from Normans all over his domain from northern France to Italy and gathered forces estimated at over 7000 fighters. The Duke waited for his moment. As Hardrada and Tostig landed with Viking forces in the Humber Estuary and fought their way to York, Harold was forced to move his army in a desperate march of nearly 200 miles, from positions protecting the south coast to rescuing the English army of the north. In a remarkable effort Harold arrived to the surprise of the Vikings and in an episode of severe fighting and bitter slaughter, the Saxons destroyed the Viking army, including Tostig and Hardrada, at Stamford Bridge.

Unfortunately for Harold, William launched his invasion with perfect timing and on 28 September the Normans stormed the beaches of Pevensey in Sussex. Harold about-turned his victorious yet exhausted army and marched another 200 miles south to combat his second invasion of the year. After pausing to collect more troops Harold made for Battle Hill (known to the Saxons as Senlac) near Hastings with an army of similar size to William.

By the end of the second week in October both sides faced each other. Harold held the high ground and assembled his warriors along the top with their traditional shield wall – an almost impregnable formation of interlocking shields backed by archers and axemen, the front bristling with spears and pikes. William's cavalry charged but each time the thunderous onslaught was repelled by the impenetrable wall. Norman archers whittled away at the wall but amid terrible showers of arrows Harold's reinforcements withheld attacks.

As evening approached the Normans employed a false retreat/counter-attack tactic. As the Saxons saw the Normans pulling back they broke the wall line and pursued, only to be cut down by ruthless cavalry counterattacks. The Saxon wall was now weakened and Harold may have already been wounded by the famous arrow to the eye. William finally committed his whole force and as the Saxons collapsed, Harold was surrounded by a pack of knights and killed.

The archaeological and historical story

At Battle Abbey, built by William the Conqueror, the visitor can get a good impression of the site. After Hastings the remaining Saxon leaders struggled to accept defeat. William was forced to bring more troops to England and set about a campaign of violence to instil his authority. On Christmas Day 1066 he was crowned in Westminster Abbey, the church so lovingly built by Edward the Confessor before the trouble began. King William set about stabilising his new kingdom in a way that saw the Saxon aristocracy virtually eliminated. In the space of a year England had witnessed three kings and from now on, nothing would be the same.

PALAEOLITHIC

MESOLITHIC

NEOLITHIC

BRONZE AGE

IRON AGE

ROMAN

ANGLO-SAXON

VIKING

NORMAN 1066–1154

William the Conqueror and the Battle of Hastings 1066

MIDDLE AGES

TUDOR

STUART

GEORGIAN

VICTORIAN

MODERN

The Building of Durham Cathedral

DURHAM CATHEDRAL IS the most complete surviving example of Norman architecture in Britain, and considered to be one of the finest in Europe. It is a dramatic symbol of the huge ecclesiastical and architectural changes that swept the country in the aftermath of the Norman Conquest.

William's accession brought alterations to the English Church, just as it did to the secular world. The incoming Norman landowners granted a substantial amount of their new English property to the Church; a shrewd political move as well as a pious gesture. Having loyal religious institutions holding large estates in key areas throughout the country was a valuable tool in securing the country. Some landowners gifted lands to French institutions, others established new monasteries here, following William himself who founded Battle Abbey to celebrate his victory at Hastings. These new institutions were often daughter-houses of monasteries in Normandy, and brought Norman ideas about religious life and practice to Britain.

There was already an influential Saxon ecclesiastical network of bishoprics and monasteries in the country at the time of the conquest, and William made many key personnel changes, designed to ensure their loyalty. Durham Cathedral was one of 60 or so Saxon religious institutions, and its history in the decades following the conquest is a classic example of the merging of Saxon and Norman political and religious ideas. It had long been famed as the shrine of the Northumbrian saint Cuthbert, whose bones had been brought there to save them from the Viking raids on Lindisfarne. In 1083, a group of Benedictine monks re-established Durham as a Benedictine Cathedral Priory, creating an institution which revered Saxon heritage but which was also in line with Norman religious ideas.

Ten years later a massive programme of rebuilding began at Durham, which continued for 40 years. Indeed, throughout the country, huge architectural changes were taking place. Large numbers of new monasteries and churches required construction, but it appears that the Normans also found the Saxon ecclesiastical building stock unsatisfactory, and the vast majority of existing institutions were also rebuilt. A new Romanesque style of architecture from Europe characterised this widespread reconstruction. It used round-headed arches and is often associated with distinctive carved chevron patterns around doors and windows.

Durham Cathedral is the definitive example of this early Norman architecture, relatively untouched by later alterations. It is a massive building, 130m (435ft) long, with huge twin towers at the west end and another over the crossing. Internally, its most striking features are the rows of pillars which support the round-headed arcading in the nave. At over 9m (30ft) high and 2m (6ft) wide, they give the cathedral the massive, solid feeling that distinguishes Romanesque from later Gothic architecture, and are incised with dramatic chevron, spiral and other geometric designs. However, Durham Cathedral was also an innovative structure, containing a very early example of pointed arched vaulting which is widely regarded as a precursor of the Gothic style which later developed in France.

Standing high on a bluff above the River Wear, Durham Cathedral was, and still is, a powerful reminder that Norman political dominance dramatically changed religious and architectural life in Britain as well.

The Bayeux Tapestry

THE CONQUEST OF England by William the Conqueror in 1066 is one of the most significant dates in British history and is often referred to as the last time that England was successfully invaded. The images borne out of the Battle of Hastings are imbedded in our minds due to the recording of the events leading up to and including the conflict itself on the Bayeux Tapestry. The tapestry is actually an embroidery and not a tapestry in the true sense of the word but, nevertheless, it is perhaps one of the most important relics to survive from medieval history. The detail in this work of art is historical evidence, which gives us an insight into a key event in British history.

It is widely believed that William the Conqueror's half-brother, Bishop Odo of Bayeux, commissioned the work but, depending on your nationality, there is some dispute as to the exact location of the tapestry's construction. There is a notion in France that the tapestry was embroidered on their own soil by none other than William's wife, Queen Matilda, since it is often referred to there as the *Tapisserie de la reine Mathilde* (Queen Matilda's Tapestry). However, the credibility of this can be discounted because, as both Queen of England and Duchess of Normandy, her royal duties would not have afforded her the time to do it all alone.

Perhaps more realistic is the theory that, having been declared Earl of Kent shortly after the battle in 1066, Bishop Odo recognised that there existed a centre of excellence for embroidery in Canterbury and had the tapestry constructed by experts.

The origin of the tapestry's design also instigates a measure of debate. Given that there are graphic depictions of gratuitous and grisly combat sequences, it is reasonable to assume that only a male soldier would be aware of such precise details since women would not have been present to witness such vivid acts of tremendous violence. In addition, there are claims that more than one person was involved in the design because it is generally considered that it would have been extremely difficult for one man alone to be responsible for the recording of the tapestry's entire chronology.

The Bayeux Tapestry is a work of at least eight different colours of wool embroidered into a series of linen panels. At its fullest extent, the tapestry measures around 50cm (20in) in width and is 70m (270ft) in length. It is separated into 13 chapters comprising 32 scenes chronicling Duke Harold Godwinson's journey to Normandy, his oath of allegiance to William and his apparent betrayal of the sworn oath, culminating with the Battle of Hastings. The fact that the tapestry ends abruptly with the battle indicates that a significant portion of the tapestry is missing, perhaps a section measuring as much as 8m (26ft).

Since the tapestry gives an account of the events from a Norman perspective, it is difficult to establish a truly independent view due to the fact that, apart from a mention of just one sentence in the *Anglo-Saxon Chronicle*, there is no alternative record of the Norman invasion in existence. Indeed, the fact that the Bayeux Tapestry survives to this day is a remarkable feat in itself. For instance, it was nearly used as a tarpaulin during the French Revolution and had to be hidden from Nazi clutches in the Second World War, as they had a penchant for stealing art treasures. The survival of the tapestry was aided by a restoration project in the mid 1800s, with it being placed under glass for its protection. Today, it is preserved and on display to the general public at Bayeux in Normandy.

The Domesday Book

THE DOMESDAY Book was compiled at the command of William the Conqueror in 1086. It was the most comprehensive survey of England, or any Western European country, and is a unique document. The commissioners visited 13,418 places to determine who was there and what they owned, and it was the thoroughness of the survey which led to its name, a reference to the biblical Day of Judgement.

The 900-year-old Domesday Book is our oldest public record and is housed at the National Archives at Kew. It consists of two volumes – the 'Great', which includes finished returns for 32 counties, and the 'Little', which contains separate returns for Essex, Norfolk and Suffolk. In addition, detailed preparatory survey material survives for some areas, along with the checklist of questions the commissioners used. The final version was written by one scribe in highly abbreviated Latin.

Although a great deal of information about the survey survives, there is one crucial question we don't know the answer to: why did William require such an unprecedented record of the country? The detailed answers in the survey itself provide clues. Returns are arranged geographically by county, and also grouped by major landowners – individuals such as the Count of Mortain, the king's half-brother, or institutions like Glastonbury Abbey. Within this structure, each property or estate has an entry, listing its owners and tenants, annual worth, population and agricultural and natural resources. Most entries value estates before and after the Norman Conquest, and it seems likely that the basis of the survey was the Saxon taxation system which had developed to finance wars in the pre-Conquest period.

Domesday Book can be seen as an attempt by William to assess the wealth and taxable assets of the Saxon country he had acquired. However, the emphasis on valuing the property of major land-owners also suggests it was a way to check tenure and feudal obligations. The Norman Conquest had led to huge changes in landownership, and Domesday Book allowed William to check the position 20 years on, confirm who his tenants-in-chief were and what they owned, so he could assess how much support, in terms of men, arms and revenue, he could extract from them.

Domesday Book was used as an important legal document throughout the Middle Ages, and is still a vital source for historical research today. It is a unique record of the period of profound change, which brings together Saxon and Norman England into one document. In addition to the financial and tenurial detail, the survey supplies an unparalleled wealth of local information about England in a period when reliable documentation is scarce. For many towns and villages, Domesday Book is the first time their existence is recorded.

Above: A copy of Domesday Book, held by the Public Record Office in London. Our first census and a vital legal document throughout the Middle Ages.

The Sinking of the White Ship

SEVENTY YEARS AFTER the Battle of Hastings, the Norman dynasty in England seemed secure. Henry I was a shrewd statesman. His marriage to a queen of English descent had produced a popular heir, William, of mixed Saxon and Norman heritage. However, on 25 November 1120, one single event, perhaps the worst disaster in English political history, changed the Norman monarchy for ever and caused a brutal civil war.

Both Henry and William, then aged 17, were returning separately from a successful campaign waged against French king Louis VI to secure their lands in Normandy. William and his companions, perhaps as many as 300 people, set sail from Barfleur in a state-of-the-art vessel called 'The White Ship'. Contemporary chroniclers suggest that there was much celebratory drinking before the ship set sail which delayed departure. After nightfall, The White Ship struck a rock and sank, and all lives were lost, bar one survivor. The loss of England's only legitimate heir to the throne was a disaster in itself, but a large swathe of the Norman aristocracy was also on board. Other members of the royal family also drowned, including two of William's half-siblings, as well as prominent members of the Church, along with the Earl and Countess of Chester and other nobles. In a single disaster, a significant proportion of England's prominent landowners and political families were lost. The consequences were far reaching.

Henry outlived his son by 15 years, but he was unable to produce another legitimate male heir, so the succession fell to his daughter Matilda. He ensured that oaths of allegiance were sworn to her in his lifetime, but at his death it was his nephew, Stephen of Blois, who was crowned king. Matilda's husband, Geoffrey of Anjou, was unpopular with English nobility, but perhaps more fundamentally, they were unable to accept a woman as monarch.

Above: A sorrowful Henry I contemplates the loss of his son and heir, William, in this 1320s illustration depicting the White Ship disaster.

Stephen couldn't overcome Matilda and her powerful supporters, particularly her uncle, the King of Scotland, and half-brother Robert, Earl of Gloucester. Stephen's reign degenerated into a series of conflicts for almost a decade, which is sometimes known as the Anarchy. The fighting was localised and sporadic, with large swathes of the country probably unaffected, but neither side could achieve decisive victory, leading to general disorder. Matilda did succeed in capturing Stephen in 1141, but was unable to capitalise on her position and was never crowned. After a heavy defeat at Winchester in the same year, she retired to Normandy in 1148. Stephen reigned until 1154, but he died without a male heir, and Matilda's son Henry II succeeded to the throne.

The Cistercians

THE BISHOP OF Winchester established a new monastery on his estates at Waverley in Surrey in 1128. It was the first Cistercian monastery in Britain, and the start of a new wave of religious foundations that would profoundly affect the landscape, economy and spiritual life of the country in the following centuries.

In the eleventh and twelfth centuries, a climate of monastic reform swept Europe. Pioneering holy men and women established new institutions which aimed to achieve a more strict religious life than was practised in contemporary monasteries, which were often very wealthy and perceived as having lost religious ideals such as poverty and simplicity. As these reformed institutions founded daughter-houses across Europe, they became the heads of new families of monasteries, most of which established offshoots in Britain in the twelfth century.

By far the most successful of the new orders were the Cistercians, founded by Robert of Molesme at Citeaux in 1098. The initial English house at Waverley was set up by monks from L'Aumone in France, and in the following two decades, over 40 Cistercian monasteries were founded across the country. The reputation of the order for a strong spiritual life, combined with the patronage of senior clerics and royals ensured their popularity, and by the end of the twelfth century, the number of Cistercian establishments in Britain had risen to over 80.

The Cistercians favoured locations for their monasteries which were as divorced from secular life as possible, and many of them were built in remote areas, or in places where the local population could be removed. Tintern in south Wales, and Fountains and Rievaulx in Yorkshire are some of the greatest Cistercian ruins in this country and their beautiful locations provide evocative examples of the desire to achieve seclusion. However, these massive and elaborate ruins are also a sharp reminder that the Cistercian order became incredibly wealthy, in contrast to the early ideals of poverty and simplicity.

As with the majority of religious houses, Cistercian monasteries were sustained by gifts from wealthy patrons, primarily landed estates, but also other forms of property and financial revenue. However, in their aim to be free of the secular world, the Cistercians developed a new way of managing their property. Wherever possible they created estates free from the feudal relationships that normally tied landownership in the Middle Ages. To do this, they established self-contained grange farms outside the manorial system, sometimes bringing new land into cultivation.

These new methods of farming changed the British landscape, and the order also revolutionised the country's wool industry. Many grange farms were used to run sheep, and the British Cistercian houses became renowned through Europe as major wool-growers. Their contribution was not so much in the quantity of wool they produced, although it was significant, but in the innovative changes they made to the way the wool was grown, sold and traded, which turned the industry into a large-scale enterprise. They became entrepreneurs and international exporters, some Cistercian monasteries even owning their own sea-going ships. By the late twelfth century, wool had become Britain's biggest cash crop, and the monastic order which had begun with such strict religious ideals had achieved a fundamental impact on the country's economy.

CASTLES WERE THE means by which the Normans secured their hold on England after the Conquest and every Norman baron raised one to protect his lands. The earliest ones were temporary shelters, made of wood and earth and were both motte and baileys or ringworks in plan. The motte was the mound on which a wooden tower was constructed and was man-made by digging a huge moat and throwing the spoil into the centre. The bailey was the courtyard at the foot of the mound with living quarters, stables and work-shops, with a palisade protecting the enclosure.

On the top of the motte was a timber tower and this tower and motte formed the strongpoint of the castle; the last defence if attackers overran the bailey. The entrance to the bailey was by means of a strongly defended gate, fronting a bridge over the ditch and access to the motte was by a drawbridge that connected the motte and the bailey. The great advantage of motte and bailey castles was that they were quick and cheap to erect, yet they presented a formidable obstacle to attackers equipped with the weapons of the period.

Mottes ranged from 7.5m (25ft) to over 25m (80ft) in height, with the timber tower giving the defenders a further advantage, and the bailey could cover 1–3 acres in area. It was usually laid out so that any point on its circumference would be within bowshot of the tower. However, they suffered from one major drawback – timber was perishable and vulnerable to fire, so timber defences were gradually replaced by stone, although the layout remained unchanged. The motte was replaced by a stone-built keep that remained the focal point of the castle and was the

strongest part of the defences. It was designed to sustain a long siege, with living and service quarters, storerooms and its own well. It frequently doubled as the residence of the lord and his family.

The keep was usually rectangular with walls 3m (10ft) thick, strengthened with buttresses, which were taken up to form turrets at the corners. It was divided into several storeys with separate rooms. There was only one entrance, usually at second-floor level, and windows were small and restricted to the upper storeys, with loopholes and arrow-slits at the lower levels. The timber stockade of the bailey was also replaced with a stone wall, with battlements like the upper walls of the keep tower, but most of the other buildings remained as timber. The gateway was either enclosed in its own stone tower or had two flanking towers against the outer wall of the bailey.

By the end of the twelfth century, the Norman motte and bailey castle had adopted the form generally recognised as a medieval castle. It was defended by a stone curtain wall bounded by a moat, possessed a keep and a gatehouse, and had all the buildings necessary to support its dual role as residence and fortress.

Right: *Castle Rising, near Kings Lynn in Norfolk. Constructed from 1140, this stronghold of the d'Albini family features a superb keep surrounded by a large stone and earthwork bailey.*

10 MIDDLE AGES

WE'VE DUG A large number of medieval sites on Time Team over the years. They've all been very different, from the live digs in the cities of York and Canterbury to small villages like St Osyth, even a medieval pig factory in 2004, and they really give an idea of what a varied and interesting period of British history this was. I've always particularly liked doing medieval sites on Time Team where we get the chance to look at standing buildings and do some above- as well as below-ground archaeology. Putting the architectural historians and dendrochronologists together with the diggers in the trenches often produces big arguments but always interesting results. We've learnt many times that buildings aren't always what they appear, from the supposedly medieval preceptory at Temple Combe in Somerset that turned out to be much more recent, to the derelict

farm at Aston Eyre in Shropshire that hid an incredible medieval manor house with state-of-the-art plumbing.

At Plympton, near Plymouth, the town was based around a motte and bailey and became a bustling medieval town in the twelfth and thirteenth centuries. The pleasure of Plympton was that a lot of medieval features are still surviving in the houses of today's town. We were able to find medieval cellars and Mick and Stewart were able to work out the medieval street plan and the way the fields were divided. Mick points out that this pattern can often survive, despite the later enclosure process: 'It is important to the understanding of the pattern of today's towns to understand the medieval street and field systems – the field boundaries are particularly important – and in over 60–70 per cent of most English towns

and villages the pattern of the place is based on something laid down in the Middle Ages.'

During the Middle Ages, Britain consisted of the kingdoms of England, Scotland and Wales. Relations between the kingdoms were often strained, as we discovered at the deserted settlement of Roxburgh, once an important Scottish border city that was captured by the English and held for much of the fourteenth century. Our history was also closely tied to that of France for the greater part of the medieval period, with various English monarchs crossing the Channel to enforce their claims to French territories during the Hundred Years' War. Time Team dug Henry V's royal shipyard at Smallhythe in Kent in 1999. Today the shipyards and even the river have largely disappeared, but with Stewart's careful mapping we were able to discover the slipways and rare evidence for medieval shipbuilding. It was an odd sensation removing the topsoil and seeing pristine beach sand and ship debris underneath. In 2005 we got even closer to Henry V's impressive fleet, recovering timbers from the *Grace Dieu*, his royal flagship and the largest medieval ship ever built. Seeing the sophisticated construction techniques on the *Grace Dieu* is a reminder that in the Middle Ages, England was already a powerful maritime nation and sea travel and trade played an important role in our economy.

Some of the most impressive medieval sites we've dug have been Mick's favourites – the monasteries. As he often points out, monasteries probably owned as much as a quarter or third of all land in Britain in the Middle Ages, which made them a very big part of everyone's life.

MIDDLE AGES: THE TIME TEAM OVERVIEW

We've been lucky enough to dig some important and unusual monasteries. At Chicksands in Bedfordshire, we were invited to a high-security military base to locate the missing parts of the Gilbertine priory there. The Gilbertines were the only home-grown English religious order and pursued a strange (and not very successful) religious experiment where monks and nuns lived side by side. There were only eleven priories like Chicksands in Britain, but it wasn't Time Team's most unusual monastery. At Syon House on the River Thames near London, we found the massive church of the only Brigittine nunnery in Britain.

Rural life

Ninety per cent of the medieval population lived in the countryside, in villages, hamlets or farms. Many of these settlements are still with us today, and unravelling their history is a complicated archaeological job. That's why experts like Mick are so interested in deserted medieval settlements, because they allow archaeologists to investigate evidence of medieval life that hasn't been destroyed or altered by more modern development, although it doesn't always prove easy. At Castle Howard, we were looking for the lost medieval village of Henderskelf, but it seems the builders of Castle Howard had demolished it very effectively in the eighteenth century and there was little evidence left to find.

At High Worsall in Yorkshire we were more successful. These kinds of villages are fascinating to Mick – 'I find the contact with ordinary people and their lives really interesting. High Worsall was well preserved with all the key features – houses, crofts, roads and lanes, church and a manor house. Where they survive, these kinds of sites are important because many have been destroyed by ploughing.' We traced the development of the village from Saxon through to the medieval period, watching it grow from a small hamlet to a

thriving planned village. However, the settlement came to an abrupt end in 1354, when it too was cleared. It seems likely that the inhabitants of the village fell victim to the destructive power of the Black Death, and the local landowner took advantage of the depopulation to make way for a deer park.

In the popular imagination the main cause for deserted medieval villages is often the plague or Black Death but as Mick points out, although this was the case sometimes, a lot of the time it was just the final straw in a series of economic and social developments that saw people moving out of the country and into the towns.

Finding evidence of diseases like the plague has always been difficult but Time Team has come across evidence of that other scourge associated with the Middle Ages – leprosy. All over Britain, hidden away in deserted corners are 'Lazar Homes' or hospitals and settlements dedicated to caring for leprosy victims. St Lazarus was the patron saint of lepers and in the thirteenth century over 200 settlements existed to provide areas where the victims could be quarantined away from the rest of society. Leprosy at that time was incurable, and it left signs of damage particularly to the facial bones that our osteo-archaeologist could detect (typical damage included the erosion of the nose

bridge with the top lip bone destroyed, often producing a hare-lip effect).

Without a doubt though, Mick feels we learnt most from our Time Team dig at the leper hospital in Winchester. Although leprosy was a common disease and there were a very large number of these hospitals, very few have ever been excavated properly, and Mick was delighted to get the chance to reveal its layout.

Previous spread: *Wharram Percy, the site of a deserted medieval village in North Yorkshire which has been extensively excavated and analysed.*

Above: *Ian Powlesland, regular Time Team digger, standing amid the remains of a medieval wall.*

MIDDLE AGES IN DETAIL

THE TERM MIDDLE AGES is used in the history of many nations in western Europe and, as a result, it can be confusing trying to tie down specific dates. The very fact that during this period many of the European monarchies, and therefore the histories of their countries, became interrelated through a succession of alliances and pact-making marriages makes the task of clarifying the Middle Ages harder.

For some people, the period is from the end of the Roman empire in the fifth century to the Renaissance, for others it means from the Crusades to the later fourteenth century. For us, the Middle Ages covers all things medieval, which for this book is essentially from the first Plantagenets (sometimes called Angevins), or the dynasty which followed from the end of William the Conqueror's blood line in 1154, to the end of the house of York and the beginning of the Tudor period in 1485.

The Middle Ages in Britain were a hard and often unforgiving time with savage wars and epidemics of hideous disease, yet they also gave birth to the age of chivalry, a blossoming of the arts and learning, and breakthrough technologies in crafts from metalworking to the development of printing. In an age which observed some fourteen kings and numerous wars, the power of the church, castles, knights and barons ruled the day.

The power of the Church

The Church was immensely influential in the lives of common people and the aristocracy. During the medieval period, the Crusades became an important mark of passage for many. These were military campaigns by European Christians which forged into the Middle East in successive attempts to reclaim the Holy Land from Arab occupation, following a call from Pope Urban II to liberate the land of Christ. Knights and foot soldiers, wearing the sign of the cross emblazoned on their tunics, fought savage battles and sieges against the Saracens who stood with their great general, Saladin, as head of the Muslim domains.

The costly Crusades took their toll, both in financial terms and in the politics of Europe, with many influential leaders away from their home countries for long periods. Though they ultimately failed, they did give rise to the most famous order of knights – the Knights Templar. Originally basing themselves in Jerusalem, the Templars later went on to become the medieval equivalent of the World Bank through the lucrative loaning of money. They became hugely powerful and benefited from protection against prosecution by any state because they were only answerable to the Pope.

Problems at home

Fighting in the Middle East wasn't the only conflict. In Britain the Middle Ages witnessed both Wales and Scotland at war with England (in a series of battles which essentially set the borders we have today), internal civil wars amongst the barons and kings of England, an ongoing struggle to conquer Ireland, a peasants' revolt, and a drawn-out series of wars with France which became known as the Hundred Years' War.

As if the fighting was not enough to make life miserable, in 1348 an outbreak of disease occurred in Weymouth which saw victims covered in seeping boils. At the time it wasn't known that squalor, rats and fleas were contributing factors. There was no understanding of germs or good hygiene and streets ran free with sewage, which weakened the general health of the population. In this environment the disease spread until almost half of the population died. This was the first occurrence of the Black Death, a scourge which was to haunt the Middle Ages.

Highlights of the period

As with most times of war, the upheaval also brought great invention. Through the medieval period we see amazing advances made in the armourer's art. Hammer welding, sheet metal work and the jointing of hardened plate armour came of age. By the later Middle Ages fully-closed suits, or harnesses, were being made which we all recognise as the iconic knight in shining armour. In fact NASA scientists studied medieval armour joints when designing their space suits for the 1969 moon landing because they worked so well. The period also brought us the widespread use of gunpowder, an element which soon ended the armourer's advantage and made many castle walls less effective.

Advances weren't only made with war in mind, and culturally it wasn't all doom and gloom. This was the age of founding universities and of the poet Geoffrey Chaucer, who composed pieces for Richard II and became very popular. His most famous work is *The Canterbury Tales* which tell a selection of stories belonging to pilgrims heading for Thomas à Becket's shrine.

The education of broader society also benefited greatly from the development of the printing press by William Caxton in the later 1400s (see page 209). Prior to this nearly all books were written by hand in monasteries, yet Caxton, with his common language of the press, opened the written word and the English language for many.

One of the highlights of the Middle Ages was the establishment of the Great Charter, or Magna Carta. A ruthless campaign against the Church and his own barons set King John on a collision course with his subjects in the early 1200s. After being backed into a corner by rebellion, the king had no choice but to sign a binding document which set out the rights of the aristocracy and the Church (these were the only people who counted at the time). Key among these was the decree that none will be denied the right of justice. This effectively made nobody above the law (including the king) and laid the foundations for Parliament.

The Middle Ages was a period of incredible artistic and architectural achievement, which have left us with an impressive physical legacy. Perhaps the finest examples of these achievements are the medieval Gothic cathedrals and churches which still dominate British cities. These soaring buildings, such as Salisbury Cathedral, Westminster Abbey and King's College Cambridge, represent the peak of medieval engineering, skilled craftsmanship and art. Indeed, the vast majority of art in the Middle Ages was religious, with rich patrons commissioning works from highly-skilled guilds of specialised artists and craftsmen to celebrate their devotion, or monasteries and churches creating their own masterpieces.

Much medieval art has been lost to us, but enough survives to demonstrate what visually rich and sophisticated artistic traditions the period produced, from dramatic wall-paintings and sculptures in churches, to breathtaking gold vessels and textiles, to illuminated manuscripts and the entirely new art form of engraving and woodblock printing.

Middle Ages Chronology

This timeline gives you a quick, at-a-glance guide to what happened when in Britain in the Middle Ages era, helping you to understand the order of events. We've also included, in red type, some key events that happened elsewhere in the world.

Henry II and Anjou (see page 200)	**1154**
Becket appointed Archbishop of Canterbury	**1162**
World event: Genghis Khan	1167–1227
English conquest of Ireland begins	**1169–72**
Murder of Becket	**1170**
Richard and the Crusades (see page 202)	**1189**
Field systems and feudalism (see page 203)	**1190**
King John and Magna Carta (see page 204)	**1199–1216**
King John loses Normandy to King of France	**1204**
Robert the Bruce	**1306**
Scottish victory at Bannockburn	**1314**
The Hundred Years' War begins	**1337**
The Black Death (see page 205)	**1348**
World event: The Great Wall of China	1368–1644
Bible translated into English	**1369**
The Canterbury Tales published	**1387**
Rebellion of Owain Glyndwr	**1400-10**
Battle of Agincourt (see page 206)	**1415**
Wars of the Roses (see page 208)	**1455**
Caxton prints first book in English (see page 209)	**1477**

World event: Genghis Khan

Born in Mongolia between 1155 and 1167 and originally named Temujin, Genghis Khan became perhaps the most successful conqueror in history. His ascent to power began after he married into the Konkirat tribe, with their leader adopting him as heir following campaigns against a rival tribe. Through his charisma and strong will, Temujin united the Mongol tribes – a remarkable feat after their long history of internal strife and economic struggle. A council of Mongol chiefs recognised Temujin as first true 'Khan' (or emperor) and he was bestowed with the title of Genghis, meaning 'true' or 'just'. Genghis Khan created strict laws to organise his people and embarked on a campaign to establish the largest unified empire in history. He was a wise ruler, but a ferocious, merciless fighter. His military tactics overwhelmed the empires of northern China, Khwarazm and northern India between 1211 and 1221. His strategy was based on fear as he invoked destruction and slaughtered entire populations to the point where he radically altered the demography of Asia. It is estimated that millions died during Genghis Khan's campaign. When he died in 1227, his empire stretched from the Black Sea to the Yellow Sea.

World event: The Great Wall of China

The Great Wall of China is one of the most astonishing constructions ever completed by human hands and is regarded as one of the seven wonders of the world in terms of its history, scale and unique architectural style. Much of the present remains were built during the Ming dynasty (1368–1644) but its actual construction began over 2000 years ago. Prior to the unification of China in 214BC by Emperor Qin Shi Huang, military fortifications had been built on the borders of several northern Chinese states. The Emperor ordered that the sections of wall be connected to serve as a defensive barrier and to emphasise the power of the Qin dynasty. Construction took about ten years but on completion it spanned 5000km (3000 miles) across mountains from east to west. Under the Ming dynasty the wall was renovated and a further 1000km (620 miles) added. Averaging 10m (32ft) in height and 5m (16ft) in width, the wall was dotted with watchtowers, beacon towers and garrison posts.

MEDIEVAL ARMOUR

THE USE OF body armour can be traced back at least 5000 years – at first tanned skins and then leather as used by the Ancient Egyptians, and finally metals, as used by the Ancient Greeks. In the Middle Ages the earliest armour was the 'coat of mail', made of conjoined iron rings, which followed the movements of the body. At the back of this chainmail a hood was attached, known as the 'camail', to protect the head, and this armour was padded underneath, which helped to soften blows received. A large shield and a helmet worn during battle completed the mail coat. The helmet had no visor and was fitted with an extension that covered the nose and another broader plate to protect the nape of the neck.

Later, trousers made of metal links came into use and consequently mail coats were shortened. The mail coat was an effective means of protection against direct thrusts and sweeping strokes, but far less effective in safeguarding against blows from blunt weapons.

This shortcoming was eventually overcome by using sheet metal overplates fastened by leather thongs to the outer side of the mail coat. During the fourteenth century steel plates were coming into greater use, especially to cover the limbs, and by the fifteenth century chainmail had given way to suits of armour made entirely of articulated steel plates.

This new plate armour had elegant lines and it covered the entire body from head to foot, and was first developed in Europe. The parts were perfectly co-ordinated, and the steel was tempered to give maximum resistance to penetration. This was necessary due to the growing use of the longbow in warfare, especially by the English during the Hundred Years' War.

Except for jousting tournaments, the older, massive helmet was replaced by a lighter one, modelled to the shape of the head, and fitted with a movable visor that enabled the combatant to see clearly. However, with the invention of accurate and powerful firearms during the sixteenth century, the days of armour were soon numbered and it had virtually disappeared by the mid seventeenth century.

Above: A marvellous full suit of armour in the Italian style. Though heavy, the weight was distributed all over the body and the suits were remarkably easy to move in. The biggest threat to the knight was heat exhaustion.

MEDIEVAL YORK

The three characters in the foreground may appear familiar to you and were drawn by Victor during our live programme in York in 1999. They are making their way to a medieval hospital which would have been part of an Abbey site.

This connection between medical care and religion was one of the distinctive aspects of medieval life and it's clear that these three are in dire need of attention. The buildings are typical wooden structures with wattle and daub panels and Victor's drawing captures the busy and lively atmosphere of a town that was of major importance in the medieval period due to its monastic connections.

The medieval city was dominated by York Minster and protected by city walls which can still be seen today. It's likely that our trio were heading for St Leonards, which was one of the biggest hospitals in Britain at the time.

The Angevin Empire

WHEN HENRY I died in 1135 he left no male heir to the throne. This led to a period of civil war, often referred to as the 'Anarchy'. Henry's daughter, Matilda, fought hard for the throne against her cousin, Stephen of Blois, the other contender. Stephen gradually gained the upper hand but, as he had no heir, it was Matilda's son Henry who secured the throne on Stephen's death in 1154, becoming Henry II of England.

Above: *The murder of Thomas à Becket by knights of Henry II in Canterbury Cathedral, strikingly portrayed in stained glass.*

Henry was known as a Plantagenet (*planta genista*, Latin for a broom-like plant) because of the sprig of broom that the Angevin family used for their symbol. Through a shrewd marriage he found himself the king of a massive empire which stretched right from the Scottish borders down to southern France and across to the Holy Roman Empire. Henry spent most of his time in France, leaving the governance of England to such loyal and able supporters as Thomas Becket. It's with this first of the Plantagenet rulers that we truly enter the Middle Ages.

A moment in time: Thomas à Becket

With his huge empire Henry II was one of the most powerful men in the world. Through the control of a vast economy he became extremely rich, while diplomatically he successfully stabilised the post-Stephen-and-Matilda England and comfortably ruled his empire in a comprehensive and most confident way. At the height of his powers, Henry commanded an empire that stretched from the Pyrenees to Scotland. However, his friendship with a priest called Thomas Becket was to change his life.

Thomas Becket was already a close friend of Henry's when he became king. On his succession Henry II appointed this merchant's son his Chancellor as a mark of their friendship and trust, and while Henry enjoyed great power, Thomas also grew in influence as the controller of the royal purse. In 1162 Henry made Thomas Archbishop of Canterbury, with a mind to the fact that with his best friend as the highest power in the Church Henry would have greater control over such a troublesome independent institution. Cue the grand falling out as Becket resigned his Chancellorship and fought for all he was worth to keep the Church independent of the state. Becket went into exile in France in 1164, yet returned in 1170 to take up the Archbishop of Canterbury seat once again, worried he would lose power following Henry losing patience and delegating important church responsibilities to other bishops.

Almost at once, the theatrical Becket resumed his position as a thorn in Henry's side by publicly discrediting him and admonished the other bishops for carrying out the king's commands. A corner had been turned and following Henry's outrage at court, four knights decided to travel to Canterbury to arrest Becket. On entering the cathedral the knights found Becket in a confrontational mood and, after heated arguments at the altar, the situation erupted into violence. Becket was struck twice about the head by the knights' swords and fell to his knees where a final, horrific slash took off the top of his head.

The archaeological and historical story

The murder of an archbishop certainly rocked the Church, but it was not the end of Henry II. While Becket became a saint and also grew into a folk hero as Thomas à Becket – he who fought against oppression – Henry concentrated on his legacy and how he would leave his empire to his sons. In time-honoured fashion it would be the infighting of his wealthy and fortunate family which would be Henry's, and ultimately his Angevin empire's, downfall.

Archaeologically this is a time when we see many of the castles and churches of England, and in the Marches of Wales and Scotland, becoming enhanced with additional buildings and fine architectural stonework. This was a boom time for the economy and the wealthy let it show. In a quirk of fate, excavations in the grounds of Oxford's Institute of Archaeology, in advance of a building project, may well have discovered the remains of the lost Beaumont Palace, a favourite home of Henry and the birthplace of two of his sons.

Though the legacy of Henry II is inextricably tied to the infamous Thomas Becket affair, and also the invasion of Ireland (an act which would spark troubles between the two nations for hundreds of years), he should also be remembered as a great reformer who established our system of judges and courts, who made peace with Wales and Scotland, and who ruled successfully for some 34 years following the turmoil of the Stephen and Matilda conflicts.

PALAEOLITHIC

MESOLITHIC

NEOLITHIC

BRONZE AGE

IRON AGE

ROMAN

ANGLO-SAXON

VIKING

NORMAN

MIDDLE AGES 1154–1485

The Angevin Empire 1154

TUDOR

STUART

GEORGIAN

VICTORIAN

MODERN

DURING THE ELEVENTH century all of Europe was caught up in a variety of independent feudal skirmishes, battles and wars between countries, principalities and neighbouring families. This general unrest was often a result of not-so-chivalrous knights and powerful personalities who challenged and wagered each other as a matter of course. Pope Urban II recognised both the futility of these actions and the opportunity to turn the attitudes and nature of medieval society to his advantage. The need was for a common enemy for the Church and aristocracy to unite against and this was found in the lands of the Levant; essentially the eastern shores of the Mediterranean Sea. Modern-day Israel and Syria, together with Turkey, all came under the Levant, and at the heart of this Holy Land was Jerusalem.

As reports reached Pope Urban II that pilgrims to the Holy Land were being attacked by hordes of Muslim warriors, he made his 1095 declaration that all Christians were to unite together against such a threat, and in a motion which was to cost countless lives, he asked for a crusade to reclaim the Holy Lands. By 1096 the first crusade was underway following in the path of warrior monks who had set off previously and had already caused untold damage with a brutal campaign against non-Christians. In all, some eight major crusades were launched over the next 180 years.

Britain's most famous crusader was Richard I, or Richard the Lionheart. The first two crusades had a limited success and even established a royal foundation with a succession of Kings of Jerusalem, but invading Turkish forces under the great general Saladin had reclaimed the city by 1187 and soundly beaten the Europeans. Two years later (93 years after the first crusade) the third crusade began with the

Above: *A depiction from the Luttrell Psalter from around 1340 showing Richard I charging on his horse wearing a great helmet, with banner raised and lance in the offensive position.*

new English king, resplendent in his cross-marked tabard, leading a massive British and French army with Philip of France to liberate the land of Christ. Though their campaign did not reach the city, they showed enough force to settle terms with Saladin and guarantee the safe passage of pilgrims through the Levant.

In reality, the Crusades were a bitter and elongated struggle between the two main religious ideologies of Christianity and Islam, with Judaism caught up in the middle. Ultimately unsuccessful throughout their attempts, the Christian Crusaders found that the assumed honour and glory of fighting for their cause became an integral part of living in the Middle Ages for those of pious or landed gentry origins, ultimately draining resources and men from their homelands for generations.

The Feudal System

FEUDALISM WAS THE structure by which medieval society functioned. With the organised central government of the Romans long forgotten, the Saxons developed their own society based on regional kings and their supporting cast of landowners. Following the invasion of 1066 the Normans introduced their own brand of governing, which essentially removed the old Saxon kings and imposed a system of organised domains which were each under the control of lords or barons, all ultimately accountable to a single overruling king. This feudal system worked by a clear definition of loyalties and sworn allegiances.

A lord who swore allegiance to the king would be provided with an estate and granted the honour of being able to build a manor or castle from which to run his administration. In turn, the people on his lands would swear allegiance to their lord. This meant that they could live and work on his lands in return for payment of taxes and tithes and the acceptance that they may be called to arms to fight for their master. These serfs, or peasants, made up the majority of the rural population and were valuable to the lord as his profit-providing workforce.

The economy of the rural peasant was based on agriculture, with local specialists in wood and metalworking and travelling craftsmen covering other trades. A typical medieval village would contain a parish church and manor house. Peasant housing would range along a main street with each house allotted a strip of land to cultivate. Further larger fields, or furlongs, would have been divided up in a similar way with strips allocated to different families in a manner which allowed people to equally benefit, or share the burden, of the varying quality of land.

These medieval patterns of field systems can still be clearly seen on many modern street plans or maps showing village field boundaries. The tell-tale linear humps and troughs of ridge and furrow medieval ploughing also remain as a common sight for those who take a walk in the countryside or gaze from a train carriage window. It was common practice to rotate the plots between crops and animals to maintain the fertility of the soil, and these methods remained successful until the fifteenth and sixteenth centuries when the trend towards enclosure, or the seizing of individual plots of land by the lords, irreversibly changed the way our villages looked and developed.

Right: A further depiction from the Luttrell Psalter from the fourteenth century showing details of an archer stringing his bow and a crossbowman setting his weapon.

Monarchy and Magna Carta

WHEN HENRY II died in 1189, he left a huge territory, the Angevin Empire, of which the English crown was just one part. It comprised a huge swathe of western France, some of which was held from the French king, other parts independently. Two of Henry's sons succeeded him as lord of this empire – first Richard, the Lionheart of legend, and on his death, John. For both, juggling the demands of the English crown and the Angevin Empire was a difficult business.

By the time he became king in 1189, Richard the Lionheart was a talented warrior and military strategist, and it is his prowess on the battlefield for which he is chiefly remembered. Within six months of his coronation, he set off for the Holy Land to fight in the third crusade, where he was very successful, taking the crucial port of Acre, in modern Syria, and negotiating access for Christian pilgrims to Jerusalem with the Turk leader Saladin.

However, Richard's qualities as king are more questionable – he was a far less successful monarch than legend might suggest. The government of England in the Middle Ages relied on co-operation between the monarch and the land-owning aristocracy who held strong political power throughout the regions. Richard's long absence on crusade, and subsequent fighting to retain his lands in France, ensured his fame, but was politically problematic, as were the huge financial demands his military exploits placed on the country. John proved a dangerous rival for the throne, although an able administrator capable of collecting the taxes the absentee king required to fund his wars. Richard died in 1199 from an arrow to the shoulder, received whilst besieging the French castle of Chaluz, and John succeeded him.

In many ways, it was John's legacy as the 'tax collector' which made him an unpopular king. His reign demonstrates the complex political balance all medieval monarchs needed to keep power. His Angevin lands were under constant pressure from the King of France, whilst in England, his attempts to raise money to defend them were unpopular, as was his ultimate failure to retain the lands. At the same time, John was engaged in political and military conflict with the Welsh princes, and struggled to achieve a strong royal control over his English nobles. A dispute with the papacy led to the excommunication of the entire country, and combined with an unfavourable treaty with the King of France, the English barons rebelled against John in 1215, taking London by force.

The result was Magna Carta, one of the most important documents in English history. John was forced to put his seal to the charter, prepared by the barons, which confirmed their traditional rights in relation to the monarch, and essentially declared the rule of law was supreme, and that both king and subjects were bound by it. John very rapidly rescinded his agreement, and civil war followed, but this did nothing to detract from the significance of Magna Carta. It represents nothing less than the beginning of the development of constitutional law, and assumed a central role throughout English legal history.

Above: The Great Seal of King John. This stamp assured the legal standing of the Magna Carta, or Articles of the Barons, when drawn up in 1215.

THE BLACK DEATH epidemic was the most dramatic and horrific event of the Middle Ages, killing a third or even half of the population of Europe. Contemporary chroniclers record that the disease arrived in Britain in 1348 on ships from Europe which docked in Melcombe Regis, in Weymouth. Its spread across the country can be traced in medieval accounts, and in parish registers and other local documents which record individual deaths. For months, it raged across southern Britain, reaching London in September 1348, and from there moving on to East Anglia, Wales, the Midlands and north to Scotland and across to Ireland, coming to an end in 1350.

High mortality rates were a familiar part of life in medieval Britain. Sanitary conditions, particularly in towns, were poor, and episodes of disease and starvation not uncommon. However, the rapid spread and huge death count of this plague were unprecedented, and accounts give a vivid idea of the widespread panic it engendered: 'the plague raged to such a degree that the living were scarce able to bury the dead…'. The epidemic is widely believed to have been caused by three forms of bacterial plague, *Yersinia pestis*. Bubonic plague, which causes inflamed glands, nausea and fever, is carried by rat fleas and lasts for several days, often causing death. However, in its more severe pneumonic and septicaemic forms, it affects respiratory and blood systems, causing distinctive black discolouration of the skin, and can be caught from saliva. Septicaemic plague has a 100 per cent mortality rate, most victims dying within hours.

In recent years, some scientists have raised doubts about whether the Black Death was caused by *Yersinia pestis*. They question whether the characteristics of the epidemic, as recorded by eyewitnesses, match those of modern *Yersinia pestis* or whether another organism might be to blame. The only way to solve the debate will be to identify bacteria in the skeletal remains of someone who died of the Black Death. Although the number of Black Death burials was huge, the number of excavated cemeteries that can be firmly linked to the disease is small. There were three established for London outside the city walls, and the first at East Smithfield was excavated in the 1980s. It provides a gruesome picture of the epidemic, containing nearly 600 bodies, half of them in a mass trench, packed five deep. However, none has yet yielded evidence for the plague bacteria.

Whatever organism caused the Black Death, its effect was unequivocal. The disease returned several times over the next 300 years, although in less virulent form. The agriculture, economy and social life of Britain were fundamentally altered by the huge decline in the population. Many medieval settlements disappeared in this period altogether, changing the landscape of Britain for ever.

Right: An illustration from an Italian manuscript dating to the fourteenth century clearly showing the horrors of the plague, a disease which swept all of Europe.

THE BATTLE OF Agincourt is one of the great legendary victories of English history, immortalised in Shakespeare's play *Henry V*. It was the most famous episode in the Hundred Years' War, a series of conflicts between England and France which lasted from 1337 to 1453. The origin of the wars dated to the twelfth century when the Angevin king Henry II controlled a large swathe of France. Despite the loss of most of this empire, English territorial claims remained and in 1337 Edward III, taking advantage of a problem with the French succession, declared himself king of France. There ensued many decades of largely inconclusive warfare, mostly fought in France, although there were some raids along the English coast.

With the accession of Henry V, the Hundred Years' War picked up momentum. Henry was a charismatic war leader, experienced in conflict with the Welsh, and with far-reaching military aspirations. Enforcing the English claim to the French throne would bring him important new lands and wealth, and acquire prestige for the Lancastrian royal dynasty in the face of Yorkist rivals. He thus set sail from Southampton in 1415 with a force of several thousand men, and after a month-long siege, took the port of Harfleur.

This campaign left Henry with pressing problems. Winter was approaching, and his force was becoming severely weakened by dysentery and lack of food. He mounted a march to the English stronghold at Calais, but was intercepted by French forces, intent upon defeating his army before they could gather new supplies. The two sides met at Agincourt on 25 October 1415, about 30 miles south of Calais. Estimates of the numbers on both sides vary, but the French outnumbered the English, possibly by as many as five times. Despite this, Henry won a decisive victory, with several thousand French deaths to only hundreds of English. Henry used topography to prevent the French deploying their greater numbers, and his technology was famously superior, with a large number of English and Welsh longbowmen. Perhaps most critical was the fact that the English were less heavily armoured than the French,

Right: This illustration from a French fifteenth-century manuscript by Froissart shows the forces of King Henry V facing up to the French army of Charles d'Albret.

especially the archers who wore little at all and relied on rows of stakes to protect them from charging cavalry. The battle took place on a ploughed field after days of heavy rain, and under these circumstances, the less encumbered men had a distinct advantage. The battle turned into a mudbath and massacre, contemporary accounts describing men and horses sunk to the waist: many fatalities were caused by drowning.

Through victory at Agincourt, Henry V achieved an unprecedented position in Europe. He married Catherine of Valois, daughter of the French monarch, and was declared his heir. However, he died seven years later, too soon to realise his dream of becoming king of England and France. Within a few years, the French had revolutionised their armies, and in 1453, all English possessions in France, with the exception of Calais, had been lost.

Wars of the Roses

THE 'WARS OF the Roses' is a romantic title for a brutal episode of dynastic quarrelling and civil disorder which lasted for much of the second half of the fifteenth century. The strife stemmed from a political struggle which saw the houses of York and Lancaster vying for the English throne. Both were descended from Edward III, the Lancaster branch including Henrys IV, V and VI; the Yorkists comprising Edwards IV and V, and Richard III.

In the fifteenth century, political power in Britain rested with ancient aristocratic families, many controlling enormous territories, wealth, private armies and large numbers of peasants who owed them feudal obligations. Political and family allegiances created a network of power at the heart of which was the monarchy, surrounded by rival factions. In 1451, a disastrous loss to the French left the Lancastrian king Henry VI in a weak position, and Richard, Duke of York attempted to seize the throne. He failed, but in the ensuing years, political struggles between some of the most powerful English lords escalated into bloody episodes of civil war between Yorkist and Lancastrian kings and their rival supporters.

The first real conflict of the Wars of the Roses is reckoned to be the Battle of St Albans on 22 May 1455. Richard of York led about 3000 men on a march to London but was intercepted at St Albans by Henry VI's army. The royal army was defeated, but it was only the first of many engagements in which both sides suffered defeats and casualties.

The years 1459 to 1461 saw the heaviest fighting, with eight battles culminating in the Battle of Towton, in Yorkshire, in March 1461. It is considered the bloodiest conflict in all English history, with intense fighting in driving snow. The casualties and loss of life were huge – perhaps as many as 28,000 men – and it brought a temporary halt to the wars, with a decisive victory for the Yorkists. As a result, Henry VI fled to Scotland, and Yorkist Edward IV was crowned king.

Towton is also famous as the site of one of the key finds in battlefield archaeology. In 1996, workmen unearthed a burial pit containing 43 male skeletons. The bodies were stripped and jumbled together, but the remains tell a horrific story of the battle. Many of the dead men already had healed wounds, some severe, when they died, suggesting that they were experienced fighters. The injuries which killed them were equally harsh, and confirm accounts that describe Towton as a violent, intense conflict. Most had sustained massive trauma to the head and arms, and less to the body, suggesting they were wearing armour, but possibly that they were attacked from above, perhaps by horsemen.

The Wars of the Roses continued until the Battle of Tewkesbury in 1471 saw Edward IV able to rule in relative peace. However, it was only with the Battle of Bosworth and the accession of Tudor king Henry VII that they truly came to an end.

Left: *A nineteenth-century print depicting Lord Stanley handing the crown of Richard III, who had fallen in battle, to the new king, Henry Tudor.*

THE ADVENT OF PRINTING

ALTHOUGH JOHANNES Gutenberg invented the printing press around 1450, it only reached England in 1476, and by 1500 there were still only five printers working in England, all in London and all foreigners. However, the man who introduced printing to England was William Caxton. Born in Kent in the early 1420s, he had a good education, and was apprenticed in 1438 to one of the most important merchants in London.

In 1441, he went to the Low Countries, settling in Bruges in 1446, the centre of the wool trade, where he became an important member of the merchant community. By 1463, he was acting as governor of the merchant adventurers, but he gave up this post to enter the service of Margaret, the Duchess of Burgundy and Edward IV's sister. After learning to print at Cologne in 1471–72, Caxton set up a press at Bruges around 1474. His first book, *The Recuyell of the Historyes of Troye*, was his own translation from the French and its production was the reason why this semi-retired merchant gentleman took to printing at the age of 50. He then returned to England to set up a press in London with the encouragement of Edward IV.

Caxton is also important because he published in English instead of Latin and so helped to shape the English language. He determined the diction, spelling and usage of the language for the books he printed, gaining much credit for standardising the language. Of the approximately 100 books he printed, 74 were in English, of which 22 were his own translations. In 1477 he published the first English book in England, *Dictes or Sayengis of the Philosophres*. He was famous for two editions of Chaucer's *Canterbury Tales*, Gower's *Confessio Amantis* and Malory's *Morte d'Arthur*.

His assistant, Wynkyn de Worde of Alsace, continued Caxton's work. A shrewd businessman, he relied less on producing expensive books and

Above: A 1478 print of the opening page of The Canterbury Tales *by Chaucer. This remarkable birth of a new print media was led in Britain by William Caxton.*

more on a variety of religious books, grammars, schoolbooks, and collections of popular tales. He published more than 700 titles, and continued Caxton's standardisation of the language. With the advent of printing, books eventually became cheap and available for all levels of society.

Type was still largely imported from Europe until about 1567, and paper until about 1589. By an Act of 1484 to restrict foreigners engaging in trade in England, Richard III exempted those in the book trade to encourage its development. In the following year, Henry VII appointed a foreigner, Peter Actors of Savoy, as royal stationer, with freedom to import books. Henry VIII imposed regulations on foreign craftsmen and finally prohibited the free importation of books.

11 **TUDOR**

TIME TEAM HAS had a number of excavations on sites that have an interesting connection with key aspects of the Tudor period, from churches and monasteries devastated by the Reformation, like Syon Park in London and St Mary's in Coventry, to Armada wrecks and some of the great houses and palaces that became important seats of power during this time.

Whenever we have dug on a site that was deliberately destroyed during the Reformation we have always been amazed at how efficient the process has been. If Henry VIII wanted no trace left of a structure that represented an institution that stood in his way, he carried out the process with brutal efficiency. We have often been left with rubbed-out foundations as the only reminder of what was once a magnificent building. We are familiar with the religious changes that the

Reformation brought about, but it also destroyed a large proportion of the beautiful artistic and architectural legacy of the Middle Ages. As Mick says, 'It's a sobering thought that it took Henry just four short years to destroy a way of life and much of its artistic legacy, that had been followed in a bewildering variety of forms for over a thousand years'. It is difficult to draw any modern cultural parallels with this, but one could perhaps suggest that the Cultural Revolution in China and the actions of the Taliban in Afghanistan carried elements that are not so very far removed from the destruction brought about by Henry's gangs of zealous demolition teams during the Reformation.

At the start of his reign, Henry began a new phase of building that introduced new forms of architecture often with European and Renaissance influences. Whilst grand domestic buildings had

existed in the medieval period, it is only in the Tudor period that we see the survival of the great country houses or palaces, the most familiar example of which is Hampton Court. The king extended Hampton Court, after taking it over from Cardinal Wolsey. It's worth remembering that this was the first time such vast structures were being built of brick since the Roman period.

The business of measuring bricks to see if they are the 20 x 5cm (8 x 2in) of a typical Tudor example has become a regular event on many Time Team programmes looking at sites from this time. In 2001 we were excavating at Rycote in Oxfordshire where Henry VIII came in 1540 for his honeymoon with his fifth wife, Catherine Howard. Elizabeth I also visited Rycote.

Geophysics surveys of these kind of sites are often helped by the tendency towards a symmetrical layout, so if main entrances and one wing can be located it often gives a clue to the other half of the building. These large houses had vast numbers of bedrooms, as they were intended to accommodate the king and all his retinue as he travelled around the country. The joy of a royal visit, which might lead to advancement at court, was often tempered by the fact that a visit from the monarch could bankrupt a family.

All over Britain at this time, great houses were springing up, many with royal connections, and European craftsmen would be brought in. For Sutton Place in Surrey, Henry used Italian craftsmen and on many such sites excavation has revealed fascinating details and motifs that show their owners keen to adopt continental influences. In the Elizabethan period, palaces like Burghley, Longleat and Hardwick Hall continued the tradition. These were often families representing a spreading of wealth beyond the court but as we have said, opening your doors to visiting royalty could involve vast expense.

In 1530 Henry visited Chenies Manor in Buckinghamshire, and it was here that Time Team excavated early in 2004. The king's visit required a major upgrade of the site and we had a 1585 inventory that described a whole new set of buildings. These would have to have accommodated an extra 750–2000 people. For two days we struggled to find any trace of what should have been substantial buildings, but finally solved the mystery when Stewart's work on the orientation of the manor house made us realise that at the time of Henry's visit the main house and new extensions would have been located to take advantage of the views over the landscape – a direction that had subsequently been disregarded by later buildings.

Naval power and armoury

Time Team programmes that looked at the late medieval shipbuilding industry revealed that Britain had already begun to improve the navy and that ships from places like Smallhythe had been used to ferry troops across to France. At the start of his reign Henry was not only keen to improve his fleet, but also to improve the guns and armour. At Greenwich Palace in London he wanted to create a new centre for armour and it was here that we excavated in 2003. The analysis of early documents became crucial to locating the site which, as in many cases in London, had been repeatedly developed. The programme included the memorable sight of Phil in Tudor armour complete with magnificent codpiece!

In 2000 we excavated an Armada-period wreck in north-east Scotland at Kinlochbervie. Dating from 1588, the wreck contained an amazing treasure trove of Italian Renaissance pottery. This was potentially either a gift from a wealthy Spaniard to a Scottish sympathiser, or the tableware of a Spanish nobleman, so confident of victory that he decided to bring his best china along with the Armada. The excavation was an interesting reminder that not all of Britain's subjects would have been disappointed if the invasion had succeeded, but also that the Spanish had a well-founded confidence in their success. If it hadn't been for the weather and a few brave Elizabethan sea captains, it might have been a close run thing.

The final days

It is interesting to note that in two Time Team programmes from the Tudor period we have come close to the final days of both Henry VIII and Elizabeth. At Syon Park we excavated near the chapel where Henry's body was temporarily laid on its journey up the Thames. Syon had been one of the palaces his men had so efficiently destroyed, a centre of ecclesiastical power, run by an order of Brigittine nuns, with a church larger than Westminster Abbey. It seemed fitting that the gruesome prediction that Henry would eventually be 'eaten by dogs' came to pass at Syon, when the local hounds took advantage of his decomposing corpse.

It was at Richmond that we excavated a great house begun by Henry VII and expanded by Henry VIII. Looking in the trenches at the huge foundations made us realise how impressive and structurally strong building in brick could be, and at Richmond we also found evidence of the more traditional beautifully carved stonework that decorated the upper storeys. It was here that Elizabeth had finally died, and it was moving to see in the documents the description of her last hours, as she refused to lie down, and the courtiers followed her for days on end, placing pillows on the floor to cushion her fall.

Previous spread: A view of Hampton Court Palace, which was extended during the reign of Henry VIII.

Left : Phil resplendent in a Tudor suit of armour.

Below: Greenwich Palace and grounds, photographed from the Time Team helicopter.

THE FIFTEENTH CENTURY was a time of great conflict which swept back and forth across the country. There was a time-honoured struggle between influential families as to who would rule, and the main protagonists, the Lancastrians and the Yorkists, fought under the respective banners of their associated flower emblems – the white rose of York and the red rose of Lancaster. These Wars of the Roses dominated the end of the Middle Ages.

Richard III, who famously 'lost' the young Edward V and his brother Richard in the Tower of London (neither were ever seen again), was the last of the Yorkist kings. He was defeated at the Battle of Bosworth in 1485 by a Lancastrian heir to the throne who effectively ended the Middle Ages and heralded a new era, the Tudors. The Tudor dynasty takes us into and through the sixteenth century where reform and enlightenment take the place of the ancient feudal ways.

The Tudor dynasty

Henry Tudor became Henry VII and set about clearing up the mess of the wars by disposing of enemies and providing some security for the nation. He had ongoing troubles with Richard's sister, Margaret, who put forward a number of impostors, or pretenders, to the throne acting as the missing princes, but Henry did much to calm the waters by marrying Elizabeth, a Yorkist princess. In the new enlightened age of discovery, Henry literally 'missed the boat' when he declined a plea by Christopher Columbus to sponsor his quest for the New World, but he did back John Cabot, who sailed the *Matthew* from Bristol in 1497 and discovered Newfoundland.

When Henry VII died in 1509, he handed a wealthy and stable dynasty to his strapping 17-year-old son, a young man of wit, accomplished sporting achievements and bursting with confidence, Henry VIII. With many wives, barrelling weight gain and the ruthless dissolution of the monasteries, Henry VIII has a reputation as a bombastic and headstrong king, yet he was also a highly educated and cultured man who led much of the new Renaissance movement in Britain with a great love of the arts and literature. On Henry's death in 1547 the Duke of Somerset sat as protector to the nine-year-old King Edward VI. This was a period of great reform in the Church, following the previous break with the Church of Rome. A German style of worship (originally designed in protest at what were considered Catholic indulgences) was adopted. This Protestant faith was widely accepted and by the mid sixteenth century a common book of prayer was in print which became the standard service text of the religion.

Left: The Drake Cup, gifted to the executor of Francis Drake's will, the cup depicts a map of the known world in 1587 and is made from silver and gold.

A short reign by Mary I, daughter of Henry VIII and Catherine of Aragon, started in 1553 and this upset the status quo as she tried to reinstate the Catholic Church in England. A sombre woman, who looks woefully downbeat in most of her portraits, Mary died in 1558, making way for one of the most powerful and successful rulers the monarchy has ever known, Elizabeth. Elizabeth, who we'll investigate more closely later in this chapter, ruled unmarried for an amazing 45 years and her death in 1603 ended the Tudor Age and heralded the beginning of the Stuart period.

Life in Tudor times

Apart from two particularly lengthy reigns (Henry VIII also ruled for an expansive 36 years), over a century of the Tudors provided England with a great strength in European terms. The population grew and as a result so did the economy, trade and settlements of the nation. Research by Wrigley and Schofield, authors of *Population History of England*, suggests that the population almost doubled to over four million through the Tudor period. Outside of the royal dramas, the Tudor world thrived with new thinking and adventures in the arts and the blossoming disciplines of science.

This was the age of William Shakespeare, the English actor, poet and playwright who is widely regarded as a genius, a writer who could produce works of both comedy and tragedy with equal skill. Born in 1564, Shakespeare was the son of an alderman, a kind of civic councillor, and probably attended a grammar school. He married Anne Hathaway in 1582 and had three children. By the late 1580s he was churning out works and gaining a fine reputation as an actor, one which enabled him to live a most comfortable life. By his death in 1616 aged 52, Shakespeare had created over 50 plays and poems (not to mention countless lost works) and in doing so has left us many phrases commonly used in the English language. The pace and flow of Shakespearian theatrical language also gives us an insight to how people talked in the Tudor Age; rather like a sound recording device today, Shakespeare's grammar was recorded in his text and the marvel of the printing press has preserved the work. Using the plays, actors today can bring the sounds of the Tudor Age to life, almost like musicians using sheet music.

Tudor exploration

In the age of exploration the New World, with its unsuspecting native populations and untapped resources of gold, silver, potatoes, tomatoes and tobacco, was discovered by the Europeans. The global map was developed with greater accuracy as explorers proved the world was not flat, while astronomers looked to the stars for answers to heavenly questions; an occupation which saw many run into trouble with the Church.

The Tudor Age was a time of free thinking and challenges to traditional beliefs. Discoveries made by scientists across Europe were quickly published in both books and on paper newsletters (the first newspapers) which could be read in the latest places to be seen – coffee houses. The boom in publishing led to some fascinating works arriving in Britain, such as those of the Polish astronomer Nicolaus Copernicus who developed his heliocentric theory which placed the sun, rather than the earth, at the centre of our solar system, in his 1543 book, *On the Revolutions of Heavenly Spheres*. The world was certainly a changing place for those who lived in Tudor times and the medieval period was well and truly over.

Tudor Chronology

This timeline gives you a quick, at-a-glance guide to what happened when in Britain in the Tudor era, helping you to understand the order of events. We've also included, in orange type, some key events that happened elsewhere in the world.

Richard III dies at Battle of Bosworth	**1485**
World event: Spanish Inquisition	1478–1843
World event: While trying to find a new trade route to India, Columbus discovers America	1492
Henry VIII and Naval Power (see page 220)	**1509**
War with France and Scotland	**1512**
Battle of Flodden; English victory over Scotland	**1513**
Act of Supremacy	**1534**
Dissolution of monasteries (see page 222)	**1536–1540**
Welsh Rebellion and Act of Union (see page 224)	**1536**
Tudor Palaces – Henry and Elizabeth (see page 225)	**c1540**
Mary, Queen of Scots (see page 228)	**1542–1587**
First Book of Common Prayer	**1549**
Elizabeth I (see page 226)	**1558–1603**
Shakespeare – Rose/Globe Theatre (see page 229)	**1564–1616**
Spanish Armada – Drake/Raleigh (see page 230)	**1588**
Death of Elizabeth; accession of James VI of Scotland as James I of England	**1603**

World event: *Spanish Inquisition*
The Inquisition was organised by the Roman Catholic Church in 1233 to subdue heresy in Italy, France and Spain. Designed to uncover any non-believers, the Spanish Inquisition was notorious as it was used for political and religious reasons. As a nation, Spain was born out of conflict between religions, including Catholicism, Protestantism, Islam and Judaism. After the Christian Spaniards won back Spain following the Crusades, the Spanish monarchy chose Catholicism to unite the country and was granted permission by the Pope in 1478 to commence with the Inquisition to purify their subjects. Non-Catholics were the first to suffer and, with the appointment of Tomas de Torquemada as inquisitor-general in 1483, the Inquisition gathered momentum. During his 15-year tenure, Torquemada executed about 2000 Spaniards. Those accused of heresy against the Catholic Church were given the chance to admit their crime and indict others in exchange for release or imprisonment. Failure led to incarceration or public execution. Torture and execution were so common that the Pope attempted to intervene. However, Spanish rulers used the Inquisition as a political tool for several centuries.

World event: *Columbus discovers America*
Christopher Columbus was born in Italy in 1451. At the age of 14 he went to sea and travelled extensively before settling in Portugal, from where he made voyages to lands such as Iceland and Guinea. Columbus was keen to find a westward route to Asia but extensive funding was required. When King John of Portugal denied his request, Columbus moved to Spain to receive sponsorship from Queen Isabel and King Fernando. Columbus and 90 crewmen set sail in August 1492, and on 12 October 1492 he first set eyes on the 'New World'. Columbus understood that the world was round but since he first believed he had landed in the East Indies, off south-east Asia, he seriously underestimated the size of our globe. After landing in the Bahamas, Columbus later set sail for Cuba and Hispaniola (Haiti). He made several more voyages to the New World, discovering the South American mainland and helping to colonise discovered islands, much to the chagrin of the indigenous population who were subjected to slavery. Contrary to popular belief, Columbus never set eyes on the North American mainland, but his voyages are highly significant, as they linked Europe to the Americas for the first time.

THE GALLEON

THE MARY ROSE was not only Henry VIII's greatest warship, but it also became an astonishing archaeological exhibit after it was raised from Portsmouth Harbour in 1982. The remains of the hull have become a long-term fascinating study of the difficulty of preserving wooden remains. The whole vessel has had to be kept saturated with chemical agents in order to stop the wood from drying out and turning to powder. The superb collection of artefacts, including longbows, cannons and tools, and the details of the ship's interior were all preserved due to the speed with which it sank and the inundation of mud and silt which created anaerobic conditions.

Mary Rose is a marvellous time capsule of Tudor life. Small items, like the personal possessions of the crew, including clothes, games and cutlery, and complete groups of artefacts, such as the well-preserved rather gruesome set of tools available to the barber-surgeon, enable us to imagine life on board.

Mary Rose was built between 1509 and 1511. On the Time Team dig at Smallhythe, we had seen Damian Goodburn constructing a small section of ship using clinker-built planking. *Mary Rose* used the very latest technology and was built with a smooth carvel construction, which may have helped in installing more gun ports on the lower decks. She may have been one of the first ships to fire a broadside and it is clear that cannons were increasingly added to her throughout her life. Technically she is described as a fighting carrick – a type of ship that had a distinctive raised platform at the stern which acted rather like a sea-going castle, and it was here that the many cannons were placed. She was richly decorated and, in addition to her fighting role, acted as a place for Henry to display his wealth and power. It was in ships such as these that Henry went to meet the king of France in 1520.

It has been estimated that when she sank, she would have been carrying nearly 200 crew and a similar number of soldiers and gunners. There were some 140 cannons and it is possible that the added weight of the cannons and the relatively recent innovation of gun ports almost at sea level contributed to her loss.

Above: *A remarkable contemporary image of the* Mary Rose *from a charter recording the vessels of the navy drawn up around 1536. Laden with cannons and banners, she looks every bit the flagship she was meant to be.*

THE TUDOR FLEET

Victor's drawing shows Tudor noblemen and women, possibly on their way to view the fleet in the area of Portsmouth. The galleon in the background represents the Tudor concern for the Navy. Henry VIII had inherited many ships from his father and from the start of his reign he began to build new ships, including the *Mary Rose* in 1510, which tragically sank while getting ready to oppose the French in 1545.

It's likely that this grand party would have been on their way to spend the night at one of the magnificent palaces that were being built at the time. Much of the Tudor world was obsessed with displaying both their wealth and power and their familiarity with some of the new ideas being introduced by the Renaissance, and the grand palaces and country houses were ideal for doing this.

It's worth remembering that shortly after Elizabeth had taken the throne, ships like the one seen here would have seen action against the Spanish Armada and to a great extent it was Henry's development of the Navy that enabled Elizabeth to defend her shores.

Henry VIII

HENRY VIII WAS king of England for 38 years, from 1509–1547. He was the first English monarch to express the independence of his power from any external authority, either temporal or spiritual. The son of the Lancastrian Henry VII and Elizabeth of York, Henry came to the throne uncontested. His birth marked the true end of the Wars of The Roses (see page 208) and assured the continuation of the Tudor line.

Henry VIII is famous for being a strong and wilful leader. When the Pope would not allow him to annul his marriage to his first wife, Catherine of Aragon, Henry divorced her anyway and had himself declared in Parliament 'the only supreme head of the Church of England'. Henry had sought an annulment because Catherine could not bear him a male heir. His split with the Catholic Church marked the beginning of the Reformation in England. Henry VIII went on to have a total of six wives who bore him three future English monarchs, two of whom ironically were female, the most famous being Elizabeth I (the daughter of Henry's second wife, Anne Boleyn).

In his youth Henry was an energetic lover of sports, including 'real tennis', wrestling and jousting, but he is perhaps most well known now as the enormous red-bearded king of the Holbein portrait (painted late in Henry's reign, c1536). He inherited a relatively stable and prosperous kingdom from his prudent father and early on in his reign embarked on an ambitious military and political programme of expansion. Henry invested substantial funds to enlarge the size of his navy – increasing its size from five to 53 ships – a decision which was to prove fundamental to the emergence of Britain as a major naval power over the next 400 years.

Although several of his French military campaigns were not particularly successful, Henry managed to secure significant victories at home. The Scots had been subdued at Flodden Field in 1513, the Act of Union with Wales was passed in 1536 and Henry was accorded the title of 'King of Ireland' in 1541. His use of Parliament, too, was unique in the history of England up until his time. Due to the harmony of interests between the king and Parliament after separation from the Catholic Church, Parliament was involved to a greater degree than ever before in policy making for the realm. This was in effect the beginning of the modern parliamentary system – as members were allowed to form political alliances and associate more freely as independent members.

By the end of his reign, however, Henry VIII had managed to drain much of his earlier inherited riches. Despite transferring vast funds from religious houses to the crown during his suppression of the monastries (see page 222), a second war with France and the necessity of paying back forced loans with a depreciated currency had severely depleted his treasury. Due to several bad sporting injuries received while jousting and hunting, Henry, unable to exercise, had become increasing overweight and irascible in temperament. He had, however, laid the foundations for the development of a new kind of parliamentary monarchy which was separate from Rome, Protestant and independent in mind and increasingly strong in arms. By taking over the roles of both head of Church and head of State, he had greatly enhanced the prestige of English kingship. In a Europe torn apart by constant wars and in-fighting, Henry VIII had thus laid the foundations for the golden age of Elizabeth.

Right: *The famous sixteenth-century Holbein portrait of a robust and slowly expanding Henry VIII, a formidable character both in personality and physical presence.*

Henry VIII and the Dissolution of the Monasteries

THE YOUNG HENRY was supremely confident with no reason to doubt his natural position of power, yet it was this inborn arrogance which was to lead him on a collision course with the Church in Rome.

Above: *Vicar-General Thomas Cromwell, the powerful and influential director of the Dissolution of the Monasteries programme for Henry VIII.*

The roots of Henry's disputes with the Church revolved around his marriage to his first wife, Catherine of Aragon. Catherine was the Spanish widow of Henry's brother, Arthur, and their arranged marriage was set in place to continue an alliance with Spain. It was critical for the king and for his country to produce heirs to ensure a stable succession. After 18 years without producing a male heir, Henry decided to annul his marriage to Catherine, but had to ask permission of the Pope. He sent his papal legate, Cardinal Wolsey, to Rome but was denied. In a rage Henry set about removing the authority of the Pope over the Church in England and, as Church governor, granted himself his own divorce.

A moment in time: the end of the monasteries

Tudor England had more than 800 monasteries across the land. Many of these had been set up as small independent concerns by sponsoring knights and barons back in the medieval period as signs of their wealth and insurances against their souls. Others were colossal and grandiose complexes, which owned large tracts of land, produced and manufactured all manner of things from meat and crops, to metalwork and beer, and were extremely rich.

The idea of suppressing a monastery, where the king would take ownership of the property and close down the monastic settlement completely, actually came about before Henry had his big falling out with the Church. In the early 1500s Henry obtained permission from the Pope to close some 40 small monasteries which were badly run and, some believe, centres of corruption. Though from one side this cleared some unwanted, regionally influential institutions from the country, it also had a second beneficial side effect – the property of the monks was sold or leased by the king to the local aristocracy and as a result added a small fortune to the royal coffers.

By 1536 Henry had revived the idea with a vengeance. The concept of the Reformation was taking hold, where it was believed that every person could have a direct relationship with God, and not need the trappings of Catholic priests and religious ceremony to do so. The Reformation certainly helped in the general acceptance of dissolving monasteries, but at the same time Henry didn't need the acceptance of his subjects – he just did what he wanted. The programme of the dissolution wasn't a particularly religious affair; it was all about power and money. Henry sent inspectors, under the guidance of his Vicar-General Thomas Cromwell, to the religious houses to discover what corruption and depravity existed and it was on this 'evidence' that he acted.

In less than ten years Henry would wipe out monastic life in England. It started with only monasteries which were valued at less than £200 a year being closed (about 240 houses) and some of the larger houses paying fines. The monks or nuns were either pensioned off or billeted into other monasteries. Those who resisted were arrested or, in one or two extreme cases, executed. The lands were claimed, buildings either demolished for their stone or altered for secular use, while sometimes the monastic churches were converted for parish use. In 1539 the big monastic houses were forced to surrender to the commissioners and this phase of the dissolution was accompanied by more violence for those who did not submit. In less than a decade the landscape of England and its management changed. Though Henry now had undisputed power over the people and the Church in England, the sick and poor, who took refuge in the care offered by monastic settlements and their valuable outreach work, would sorely miss their pious friends.

The archaeological and historical story

The legacy of the dissolution can be seen in the hundreds of monastic ruins which are spread across our landscape today. As Mick Aston points out in his book, *Monasteries in the Landscape*, it was often a matter of the closing contract that the roofs of monastic buildings were to be destroyed or walls demolished so that a later reversal of the policy would be impossible. Some of the finest examples which can be visited today include Fountains Abbey in Yorkshire and Tintern Abbey in Monmouthshire, both sites which clearly illustrate the power and wealth of the once mighty large monasteries.

Though Henry was ultimately not adversely affected by his actions and went on to even greater strengths for which he is also renowned, such as the building of a great navy, epitomised by the *Mary Rose* warship which can be seen in Portsmouth, he never found long-lasting happiness in marriage as the well-known stories of his six wives testify.

PALAEOLITHIC

MESOLITHIC

NEOLITHIC

BRONZE AGE

IRON AGE

ROMAN

ANGLO-SAXON

VIKING

NORMAN

MIDDLE AGES

TUDOR 1485–1603

Dissolution of the Monasteries 1536–1540

STUART

GEORGIAN

VICTORIAN

MODERN

Welsh Rebellion and the Act of Union

THE TRADITIONAL AND often vehement rivalry expressed by the Welsh towards the English can perhaps be traced to the last notable act of rebellion in the Principality and an inaugural piece of legislation, which sought to 'absorb' Wales into the realm of England's administration. Schism between the English and Welsh originated prior to any sense of identification of a nationality, with Celtic tribes often having to stave off invasion attempts by England's Anglo-Saxons. At this time, Wales was an assemblage of minor parochial kingdoms that often competed with each other but were bound by a common language and culture.

Wales became dependent on English protection following an alliance formed by several Welsh noblemen with England's King Alfred in the ninth century. Throughout subsequent centuries Welsh leaders attempted the unification of the country by military conquest, with Llewellyn ap Gruffudd, the so-called last true Welsh monarch, proving to be the most successful. However, his success was short-lived with Wales becoming subjugated by Edward I in 1283. Consequently, restrictions were enforced limiting the rights of the Welsh whilst large numbers of English settlers moved in.

A last attempt for Welsh independence was made at the beginning of the fifteenth century when Owain Glyndwr (or Owain Glyndyfrdwy) led a revolt against English rule following the seizure of the English throne by Henry IV from his predecessor, Richard II. Much of the Welsh gentry were allied to Richard II and their allegiance to the crown became considerably weakened with Henry IV's usurpation of the throne. As such, Henry had problems imposing his authority, which led to his unwillingness to mediate fairly in a dispute between Owain and a neighbouring marcher lord.

Owain's chagrin at being rebuffed led him to revolt. His followers proclaimed him Prince of Wales at Glyndyfrdwy on 16 September and embarked on a guerrilla campaign of attacking English settlements before disappearing to hide out in the mountains. Fervour to support Owain's campaign grew following the occupation of Conwy Castle in 1401 by his allies, the Tudor family of Anglesey. Owain later captured Aberystwyth and Harlech castles and became allied with the Scottish and the French at a time when virtually the whole of Wales acknowledged his authority.

However, Owain was soon abandoned by his allies and lost his grip on his acquisitions due to Henry IV's son (later to become Henry V) employing superior military tactics. Having been defeated, Owain fled to the mountains where he remained as a fugitive until his death. The outcome of the revolt paved the way for annexation with England mainly due to the Welsh gentry believing that their prosperity would only thrive under English authority. Thus the first Act of Union was passed in 1536 with Wales becoming wholly assimilated into the English governmental system.

Wales' county boundaries were redrawn and the counties and boroughs of Wales were granted representation in the English Parliament. Unfortunately, this came at a price. Certainly from a Welsh perspective, the most debated and reviled aspect of this act was the banning of the Welsh language in all matters pertaining to official business, politics and law. Wales' ruling classes became divorced from the Welsh language, which became the common tongue of the working and lower middle classes. Use of the Welsh language gradually declined over the centuries but, in 1993, the Welsh Language Act was passed which formally repealed the 1536 legislation, over 450 years after its introduction.

Tudor Architecture

WHEN TIME TEAM digs at a Tudor site, we always expect the unexpected, because Tudor architecture offers a wonderfully weird mixture of influences. The finds trays might include glazed floor tiles decorated with camels, a fragment of classical terracotta or maybe a spiral-cut brick once belonging to an exotic chimney.

What does Tudor architecture mean? Depending on your perspective, this era could be the end of the Middle Ages or the beginning of the Renaissance in Britain. The 1530s saw the sudden and massive, if not quite decisive, change. Henry VIII passed the Act of Supremacy in 1534 to place him above the papacy, which severed a thousand-year tradition of Roman Catholicism in England. The dissolution of the monasteries beginning three years later smashed the legacy of that tradition: whereas Henry maintained Catholicism privately, the destruction of medieval church furnishings and art continued under his Protestant son Edward VI (1547–1553).

The new spirit of the sixteenth century was characterised by classical decoration and planning, inspired by experience of Italy, France, or the new technology of illustrated books. Ironically, the pre-Reformation bishops and cardinals had been the earliest importers of Roman Renaissance culture into Britain, whilst Protestant nobles and monarchs enjoyed parading their learning through classical motifs. Gothic and Renaissance styles can be found combined on a single building.

In Britain, there's another likely factor which makes our Renaissance architecture unlike any other country. Because most of western Europe was once part of the Roman Empire, classical remains offered a means of reassessing the origins of a nation's civilisation. But we often mistook our medieval buildings for classical ones, incorporating Norman features into the Renaissance style. The Tower of London was once thought to have been built by Julius Caesar, as were many other castle keeps. Dover Castle was attributed to King Arthur. Stirling Castle was assigned to both Arthur and the Roman Governor Agricola for good measure, whilst nearby Arthur's O'on – a genuine Roman temple – was mistaken for a work of King Arthur.

Nostalgia for a pre-dissolution age of 'merry England' further complicated our approach to building by encouraging retro-medieval qualities. At William Cecil's Burghley House near Stamford (c1565–88), the arched roof and bay window of the great hall are archaic in comparison with the French-classical courtyard and staircase, but the hall was the last part of the construction. On any Tudor dig, the only safe bet is that the archaeology will continue to surprise and intrigue us.

Above: *The striking architecture of Hampton Court Palace, a grand royal residence but only one of a succession of great houses constructed with no expense spared by the Tudors.*

The Reign of Elizabeth I

ELIZABETH I WAS a clever and talented woman who took the male chauvinist Tudor world and turned it on its head. With great artistic and sporting ability, her sprightly personality was fortified with the diplomatic and political skill to rival her most earnest counterparts. Though many say she inherited the age of culture and development, the truth is that Elizabeth was undoubtedly a tour de force; a phenomenon of her age.

Elizabeth was the daughter of Henry VIII and his second wife, Anne Boleyn, a former lady of the court. An initially ecstatic Henry was completely demoralised when he found that his pregnant new queen had given birth to a daughter and as such he largely ignored her existence. A second pregnancy miscarried and subsequently Henry had Elizabeth's mother put to death on trumped-up charges of adultery. While Elizabeth spent her youth outside the royal circle, she retained her Tudor spirit and was renowned as both headstrong and tough. After Mary's short Catholic reign ended in 1558, Elizabeth found herself the next in line, and as a reformer, she immediately set about returning the Church to the status it had once enjoyed under her father as a developing Church of England.

Above: A portrait of Queen Elizabeth which was painted around 1590. Holding the trappings of power, she is dressed in her coronation robes.

A moment in time: heart and stomach of a king

After the persecution of Protestant churchmen by Mary, the diplomacy of Elizabeth did much to restore some stability to religious society. In a series of carefully chosen arrangements she constructed an atmosphere of passive acceptance between the different Christian factions which resulted in some security at home. Yet on the world stage she stood steadfast against Catholicism and supported the Dutch Protestant campaigns against the Spanish – a move which would finally break any remaining old alliances made by her father's marriage to Catherine of Aragon, and ultimately lead to war.

Elizabeth received several marriage proposals during her lifetime but she declined them all. Though she was known to flirt with several prominent members of her court, she was reluctant to be drawn into the political wranglings of European monarchy intermarriage and was famously known for saying that she was 'already married, to the kingdom of England'. Her spinster existence, though affairs are often debated, gave rise to her name as the Virgin Queen, or Gloriana as she was known in court. But Elizabeth was more than a gentle art-loving reformer; she was also ruthless in her rule with any who crossed her and handed out imprisonments and death sentences without compassion, only troubled by those which included her immediate family or old friends.

Her robust leadership and undying love for her country are shown no more clearly than in her speech to the army during the attempted invasion by the Spanish Armada. In 1588, when over 130 heavily laden Spanish warships crossed the Channel and clashed with the Royal Navy in a battle that would see the Spanish chased out into the North Sea, Elizabeth faced the English army and gave them one of the greatest pep talks of all time: 'I know I have the body of a weak and feeble woman, but I have the heart and stomach of a king, and a king of England too.' She goes on to state that a great victory awaits over the enemies of her God, kingdom and people. One can imagine hardly a dry eye in the house.

The archaeological and historical story

As Elizabeth aged and slowly declined, she tried to retain her youthful looks with a copious use of (at the time innocently applied) poisonous make-up and extravagant wigs. The last 20 years of her reign were a mixed bag of victories and great wealth from the Americas, coffer-sapping unproductive wars with France and Spain, and the drama of dealing with her cousin, Mary, Queen of Scots.

The great explorers of the age – Grenville, Drake and Raleigh – took advantage of the Spanish situation (and were in part responsible for it) by acting as pirates in the Atlantic, seizing slow-moving Spanish galleons loaded with treasures. This made them very rich but they also paid their dues to their monarch. In England the growing use of the addictive but 'medicinal' tobacco leaf took hold. Anybody digging their garden today is likely to find the small white snaps of broken clay pipes – a sign of the drug's increased use. When first introduced, tobacco was very expensive and as a result the early clay pipes have very small (sometimes pea-sized) bowls, but as the lucrative business of growing and selling tobacco developed, so did the size of the pipes. The main centre of tobacco production was even named after the Queen as Virginia.

When Elizabeth finally died in 1603, she left her beloved kingdom to the son of her natural enemy, Mary, Queen of Scots, but the country James I inherited was one that had flourished under Elizabeth's strong and uncompromising rule.

PALAEOLITHIC

MESOLITHIC

NEOLITHIC

BRONZE AGE

IRON AGE

ROMAN

ANGLO-SAXON

VIKING

NORMAN

MIDDLE AGES

TUDOR 1485–1603

The Reign of
Elizabeth I 1558–1603

STUART

GEORGIAN

VICTORIAN

MODERN

Mary, Queen of Scots

MARY STUART WAS born in 1542, the daughter of King James IV of Scotland and his French wife, Mary of Guise. Her life is symbolic of the fractious sixteenth-century European monarchies. Catholic supporters considered her to have a better claim to the English throne than Elizabeth, since she was the great-granddaughter of Henry VII, whereas Elizabeth was the daughter of divorcee Henry VIII.

At just six days old, Mary became Queen of Scotland when her father was slain at the battle of Flodden Field. Her mother wanted the child to grow up Catholic and favoured alliance with the French whilst the Scottish nobility, wanting peace with England, arranged that Mary should marry Henry VIII's son, Edward VI. However, Mary was sent to France and the marriage contract with Edward broken. Instead, Mary was betrothed to the Dauphin Francis, the heir of King Henri II of France. When the Dauphin succeeded in 1559, Mary became queen of both France and Scotland.

On her husband's death in 1560, Mary returned to Scotland and petitioned Elizabeth to grant her succession to the English throne as well as attempting a Catholic marriage for herself with Don Carlos, son of Phillip II of Spain. Phillip, however, was opposed to Mary's succession to the English throne given her French allegiances, and Elizabeth knew that to acknowledge Mary's right would encourage Catholic conspiracies. Instead, Mary married her cousin Lord Darnley, in 1565. He was Catholic and a descendant of Henry VII (re-inforcing Mary's claims to the English crown). Darnley soon became envious of Mary's intimacy with her secretary David Rizzio and with a group of conspirators, Darnley had Rizzio murdered in front of Mary at Holyrood Palace in 1566. Despite the birth of their son James (the future King James I of England and VI of Scotland), the marriage degenerated until Darnley was murdered in 1567

Above: *Mary, Queen of Scots with her Catholic husband Lord Darnley. A jealous Darnley had Mary's male friend killed while she most likely had him killed later on.*

and Mary was suspected of involvement. Worse still, only months after his death, Mary married the Earl of Bothwell, thought to be Darnley's murderer.

This was the final straw for Scottish nobility and the Earl of Murray led a rebellion, defeating Mary's forces at Carberry Hill. She was taken prisoner and forced to abdicate in favour of her son. Escaping from Lochleven Castle in 1568, Mary raised another army, to be defeated at the Battle of Langside. This time Mary fled to England, hoping Elizabeth would offer her support, but Elizabeth had her imprisoned. Mary was held in captivity for 19 years, during which time a series of unsuccessful plots were hatched to free her and restore the Catholic religion. After a brief trial she was executed on 8 February 1587. Mary's tempestuous life nonetheless resulted in the birth of James I and the 111-year succession through him of the Stuart line.

William Shakespeare

WILLIAM SHAKESPEARE WAS the greatest English dramatist of his age and one of the most admired of any time. Born in Stratford in April 1564, Shakespeare was educated at the local grammar school. Moving to London, perhaps around the late 1580s, he began to write plays for the thriving London theatres. However, his first known authenticated publications are not plays, but the two long narrative poems *Venus and Adonis* and *The Rape of Lucrece*, printed by the Stratford printer Richard Field in 1593 and 1594 respectively. *Venus and Adonis* went through 16 editions before 1640 and was Shakespeare's most reprinted work during his lifetime.

It is difficult to ascertain which was his first play, as many early works were anonymous and it is thought that many of his earliest efforts may have been in collaboration with playwrights, such as George Peele and Thomas Kyd. Records show that in 1594 he received payment for performing with the leading acting company The Lord Chamberlain's Men, at the Royal Palace in Greenwich. The play performed was probably his early farce, *The Comedy of Errors*.

In the 1590s theatres were the hub of London's cultural life. Leading playhouses such as Phillip Henslowe's Rose (where Marlowe's plays were first performed) and later the Globe (which Shakespeare helped build), saw the works of all the leading playwrights of the day staged. Shakespeare became the principal writer for the Chamberlain's Men, and his plays were watched in the Globe by a broad spectrum of London society.

As early as 1598, a contemporary playgoer, Francis Meres, noted that Shakespeare was 'the best for Comedy and Tragedy… among ye English'.

Right: A seventeenth- (possibly even sixteenth-) century picture by Dutch artist Visscher depicting Shakespeare's Globe Theatre in London.

Written with an assured metrical competence and displaying an exuberant interest in language, plot and characterisation, Shakespeare's plays moved English drama away from the simpler traditions of religious mummers' plays and formulaic masques which had previously dominated drama.

Shakespeare was renowned as a poet and his 'sugared sonnets' won the critical acclaim of his contemporaries, but he was also the first playwright to be an actor, shareholder and playwright in the same company. While many actors lived hand to mouth, Shakespeare was a successful businessman as well as a prolific artist. Between 1598 and 1601 alone, Shakespeare wrote some of his greatest plays, including *Hamlet*, *Julius Caesar* and *Henry V*.

The Spanish Armada

THE SPANISH ARMADA is the name given to the fleet of ships assembled by Phillip II of Spain to invade England in 1588. It consisted of up to 130 warships (including Mediterranean-style galleons), with almost 30,000 soldiers. The purpose of this force must be seen in the context of the growing Anglo-Spanish war of 1585–1604.

In 1570 Elizabeth I was excommunicated by the Pope and her Protestant monarchy began to align itself against the Catholic interests of Phillip's Spain. English aid was given to Protestant rebels on the continent, in particular in the Netherlands, where Protestants had revolted against Spanish rule. At the same time, English merchant shipping interests began to clash with those of the Spanish. The English privateers bypassed Spanish taxes on slave trading and quickly became profitable.

Francis Drake, who in 1580 had become the first Englishman to sail around the world, also plundered the Spanish treasure ships sailing from the New World, and raided Spanish coastal towns. Things came to a head when Elizabeth, fearing Catholic conspiracy, executed the last possible Catholic heir to the English throne, Mary Queen of Scots, in 1587. Phillip thus formulated the invasion to put a stop to the English privateers, end English financial and military aid to Dutch and French rebels, and replace Elizabeth with a Catholic.

Phillip's ambitious plan was to have the Armada meet up with the troops of his general in the Netherlands, the Duke of Parma. The two armies would meet in the English Channel and then sail across to subdue their foes on English soil. It is not clear how the Spanish fleet, under the command of Medina Sidonia, was to encounter the Duke's men. Communications were slow and weather conditions could hugely change the fleet's manoeuvrability. Furthermore, the Duke's fleet needed a large harbour in which to meet up with the Spanish, making it vulnerable to attack. The British fleet, lead by Drake and Lord Howard of Effingham, numbered perhaps as many as 200 smaller, more manoeuvrable craft, equipped with rapid-firing, long-range canons and crews familiar with the conditions in the Channel.

After two inconclusive battles with the English fleet in mid-July 1588, the Armada anchored off Calais to await the Duke, but the English sent fire-ships (old hulks packed with gunpowder, canons, pitch and tar) into the tightly grouped Spanish fleet. The Spanish slipped their anchors and drifted out to sea, where strong winds almost beached them on the French shoreline. The next day, the English attacked off Gravelines, avoiding close battle by firing from a distance, using their manoeuvrability to great effect. The battle was inconclusive, but its outcome proved fatal to the Spanish cause. Though only eleven Spanish ships were lost or damaged, the British had used up much of their shot. Unaware of the depleted English weaponry, and with strong winds rendering return home via the Channel impossible, Medina Sidonia tried to reach Spain by sailing around Scotland. However, a storm ripped into the depleted Armada off the Irish coast, sinking over half the fleet and resulting in the loss of 15–20,000 Spanish lives. The loss of Spanish lives, ships and prestige was a huge boost to English propaganda, but Spain was to retain much of its command of the ocean for many years. It was this lasting sense of English national pride, however, which made the wreck of the Armada a landmark in European history. Spain, the greatest maritime nation at that time, had failed to subdue its feisty adversary and the English victory would serve as an inspiration to future sea-faring heroes such as Admiral Lord Nelson. The development of Britain as the greatest of world maritime powers had begun.

HENRY VIII FOUNDED the nucleus of the modern navy by constructing purpose-built warships, building the first dry-dock at Portsmouth and encouraging the expansion of the merchant fleet. He was the first to create a standing navy by building almost 50 new vessels during his reign, and experimenting with new ship designs and types of guns. At the start of the sixteenth century the principal vessel for both trade and war was the carrack, and warships were merchantmen equipped with guns. They differed from merchant ships only in that they had very high castles to house guns.

The power of weapons increased dramatically during this period, but the newer heavy, iron cannons could not be placed in the castles as they affected stability. Holes were therefore cut in the main hull below the weather deck, so the guns could be mounted as close as possible to the waterline. This improved stability and made the guns easier to aim. These gun ports could only be mounted in the skeleton-framed hulls of the new galleons, not in the traditional clinker hulls of the carracks. From these new galleon designs came the genesis of the purpose-built Tudor warship.

Naval tactics had previously depended on engaging the enemy at close quarters and fighting across decks, but the adoption of cannon firing at long range changed that. As the quality of cannon improved, naval battles could be undertaken by artillery exchanges without the need to come alongside. These changes revealed the drawbacks of the carrack. In addition to the target they presented, the castles made it difficult to sail in a straight line (essential if the guns were to be accurate) and the tendency of carracks to roll displaced the guns.

The ability to sail in a straight line and to hold the guns level became a prime design objective. Furthermore, it was sensible to design ships which rode low in the water and thus presented a less

Above: The cast seal of a Tudor Rose emblazoned on one of the 'bastard culverin' guns of the HMS Mary Rose.

obvious target. Unlike Henry VIII's navy, which never ventured far from shore, the Elizabethan fleet sailed the world as the queen encouraged private trade and privateering expeditions, which could be taxed. Her goals were profit, the expansion of overseas trade, exploration and the pursuit of political aims that the under-developed Tudor army could not achieve in continental politics.

When Sir John Hawkins became treasurer of the navy in 1577, he initiated a naval building programme, constructing almost 20 new galleons. His use of progressive ship designs and innovative gunnery made the English fleet of the 1580s more manoeuvrable and better armed than any other navy of the time, and the ships which fought at Trafalgar (see page 270) were direct descendants of the ships introduced in the sixteenth century.

12 STUART

TIME TEAM'S DIG at Richmond Castle on the Thames was actually on the site where it could be said the Stuart period began. Elizabeth died here on 24 March 1603 and it was from here that her ring was taken to the eldest son of her cousin, Mary Queen of Scots, to begin the Stuart dynasty. It lasted just over a hundred years, but saw a number of events which have made a considerable impact on our history including the bloodiest civil war, the public execution of a king – Charles I – and the beginning of the colonisation of America. On the wider political front we saw the beginnings of a system of democratic government allied to but not dictated by a monarchy that would become the envy of Europe and the basis for many of our political structures today.

In 2000 Time Team worked on the site of High Ercall in Shropshire. On the final day Stewart

Ainsworth had begun to examine the structures that were still standing, including a local church, and discovered evidence of small pits created by musket balls. Here in the middle of the peaceful English countryside, in an area nowhere near any great centre of power, in the walls of an ordinary English great house, was evidence of a ferocious battle that had been fought between Royalists and Roundheads. The Civil War had set family against family, village against village and in a series of bloody skirmishes and battles vast numbers of ordinary British people had been killed. The height of the Civil War came in 1655 and the defences and strategic location of High Ercall had provided a rallying point for Royalist forces. After two final sieges, the Parliamentary troops surrounded the property once again and built siege works, including small mounds for their cannons, and

poured merciless fire into the building. The foot soldiers on both sides would have been equipped with matchlocks and, as part of our reconstruction cameo, we had seen the power of small artillery fire as it smashed into the stonework.

High Ercall was like a small snapshot of battles that took place all over Britain. It was a grim struggle which initially saw the Royalist Cavaliers achieving some success. Over 900 troops and 40 dragoons under Sir William Vaughan attacked the besieging forces, leaving 500 Roundheads dead. These kinds of losses were repeated throughout the country on both sides and it is important to remember that some estimates put the number of Civil War dead as greater than those lost in the Second World War. In our excavation we find evidence of cannon shot and musket balls all over the site, some flattened by contact with

buildings or bodies. In 1646, the Royalists were finally defeated after a nine-hour bombardment destroying complete sections of the house, evidence of which we found in our trench. Over 1000 people died in this quiet, rural part of England and it is disturbing to think of a time when civil war was as rife in Britain as it is in some other parts of the world today.

One of the main causes of the conflict was a struggle between a monarchy that claimed to rule by divine right and a Parliament representing the people who wanted power independent of the crown. When Charles I became king in 1625 he became ruler of a country split by religious factions. Anti-Catholic feelings after the Armada and the gunpowder plot were rampant. Charles finally went too far in 1642 when he attempted to enter the House of Commons and arrest some of its members. War became inevitable and the first battle of the Civil War took place at Edgehill in Warwickshire. Oliver Cromwell's military skills and his ability to create a deadly and efficient fighting force, called the New Model Army, was vital to the Parliamentarians' success.

When Time Team excavated at Basing House Hampshire – a moated manor and site of another brutal Civil War battle – we were joined by members of the English Civil War Society. We were able to see details of the dress and equipment of the New Model Army in action. They had styled their uniforms on the Fairfax Battalions, a troop that had taken part in the siege of Basing, and it was fascinating to wander through the camp watching them prepare meals and ready weapons in an authentic manner and see the preparation of musket shot. Watching a matchlock fire one of the huge lumps of lead was a frightening experience

and although it was slightly less frightening seeing Phil re-enact the role of a 'pike man', one could see that here was the basis of a 'professional' army. Cromwell himself came to take charge of the Basing siege and a report of the battle in a contemporary news sheets gives some idea of feelings associated with the civil war – 'the dispute was long and sharp, the enemy deserved no quarter and I believe that they deserved what little was offered to them. They were most of them Papists, therefore our muskets and swords did show but little compassion.' Not only soldiers but many civilians died at Basing, including women and, memorably for us, an actor player called Mr Robinson, who had come from Drury Lane and was shot on the battlements when he made the mistake of taunting Parliamentarians and was killed by long-range musket shot!

Basing was civil war at its bloodiest, driven by religious differences and a battle for supreme power in the land. The British people were soon to find that a country run by zealous Christian Parliamentarians was little better than Monarchists believing in divine right, and eventually the monarchy would be returned but importantly with curtailed powers. The bloody battles of the Civil War helped to create a balance between king and state, between monarchy and Parliament, that is one of our most valuable constitutional elements, but Time Team has never dug on a Civil War site without feeling the horror of it and feeling thankful that we do not have to live in such circumstances today.

Previous spread: *The statue of Oliver Cromwell outside the Houses of Parliament in London – an institution he felt passionate about.*

Left: *Time Team diggers at Basing House record some architectural masonry from the Stuart period.*

Right: *The formidable earthworks and defences of Basing House in Hampshire still survive to a fair height. The further 'lumps and bumps' relate to Civil War defences.*

STUART IN DETAIL

WHEN THE SCOTTISH royal family of Stuart inherited the crown of England in 1603, and thus united Britain under one rule for the first time, it took over a pair of kingdoms with chronic political, social and economic problems. When the last Stuart monarch died in 1714, Britain had for the first time been turned into an entity of amazing dynamism, strength and security.

The most important aspect of this achievement, perhaps, was the conquest of famine and plague. In 1603 every bad harvest was followed by widespread death from starvation. Likewise, people remained apparently helpless in the face of repeated epidemics of bubonic plague, carried by fleas on rats, which came once or twice in each generation and removed up to a quarter of the population of individual communities within a few months. By 1714 a mixture of improved food production and marketing, better controls on population size, better care for the poor, and the arrival of new crops, had ended the threat of famine for the first time in British history. At the same time, apparently due to improved systems of quarantine, plague had been reduced to a few stray cases, and it has never yet returned. People still did not understand what caused it, but they no longer feared it. These great processes of release must have done much to make the British, from the top to bottom of society, more at ease with their environment and more confident of their ability to take on the world and improve it according to their own desires.

One factor in the eradication of famine was the installation of the best system of poor relief in Europe. For centuries the old, sick and unemployed had been left to the mercy of fortune, their relatives and their richer neighbours. Under the Stuarts a state-imposed system was installed that meant that every propertied person in a parish had to contribute money regularly to assist those who could not support themselves: it is the direct ancestor of the modern welfare state. At the same time the British began to lose their fear of magic. In 1603 people were still being put to death for the alleged crime of witchcraft. By 1714, it was accepted that nobody could be successfully prosecuted for it in England and Wales, and educated opinion was starting to turn against it in Scotland as well.

The later Stuart period saw huge leaps forward in science and mathematics, in large part due to the work of Sir Isaac Newton. In 1687, the Cambridge scholar published the book widely regarded as the greatest scientific text ever written, called *Philosophiae naturalis principia mathematica*, defining new ideas about physics and astronomy, which revolutionised understanding of the forces at work in the natural world, and laid the foundations of modern science.

The beginning of the Empire

The same period saw the foundation of the British Empire. In 1603 England had virtually no colonies at all. By 1714 it owned a huge swathe of the North American seaboard, several rich West Indian islands, and bases in Africa, Asia and the Mediterranean. The tremendous opportunities for trade provided by this expansion enhanced an economic boom that set in during the second half of the period.

Having only intermittently been able to feed themselves, the British turned into exporters of foodstuffs to Europe, and developed metal- and textile-working industries that diversified and improved what they could sell to the world. With wealth came sophistication: for the first time the

British were turned in the eyes of Europe from semi-barbarous peoples on the edge of the world to a source of interesting, important ideas and products.

The Stuart monarchs

Much of the reputation of the age, however, relates to its spectacularly colourful political and religious history, in which England and Scotland turned, successively, from two of the most ramshackle states in Europe, into two of the most terrifyingly unstable, and finally into one of the strongest and most successful. The period started with the two kingdoms still separated by mutual suspicion and antagonism, afflicted by their own severe internal weaknesses. Scotland was divided between Highlander and Lowlander, and between Protestant and Catholic, and had one of the poorest economies and governments in Europe. England was much stronger, but had a seriously run-down system of taxation that was driving its monarchs close to financial collapse, and the worst-defined, and most deeply divided, national church in the world.

The response of the first Stuart king of England, James I (1603–25), was to try compromises and short-term solutions, which only made the tensions worse. Despite these pressures, he found time to support the James I edition of the Bible which had a great influence on British religion and culture. His son, Charles I (1625–49), accordingly attempted to remodel both kingdoms to make them more like each other and more subservient to his own royal will. As a result, both had exploded by 1642 into civil wars and wars with each other that became the bloodiest conflicts that either has ever known, including the World Wars of the twentieth century. When these ended in 1653, England had undergone a revolution that had swept away the monarchy and the House of Lords and produced a republic ruled by radical Protestants from outside the traditional ruling class, which had conquered the entire British Isles. The republic, however, collapsed in 1660 because of its own internal divisions, and the monarchy, aristocracy and independence of the two kingdoms were all restored together.

Under Charles II (1660–85) and James II (1685–88), both realms remained badly divided and turbulent, while the monarchy's power increased to the point at which it seemed that the democratic element in government might disappear. This was averted by the revolution of 1688, which overthrew James, and under the last three Stuart monarchs, William III, Mary II and Anne, England and Scotland were united into a single kingdom, with a government of mixed monarchy, aristocracy and democracy in which ultimate power lay with the people and freedom of worship was given to all religions. This new model of government proved so strong that ever since any alterations to it have been made within the same framework and by consensus. The bloodshed and insecurity of the Stuart age have never returned, and the British have continued to enjoy the stability and unity which was achieved as the reward of its suffering.

Above: *A copy of a Van Dyke portrait of Charles I. The interesting composition shows the king from three angles.*

TIMELINE

This timeline gives you a quick, at-a-glance guide to what happened when in Britain in the Stuart era, helping you to understand the order of events. We've also included, in red type, some key events that happened elsewhere in the world.

Gunpowder Plot and religious division (see page 242)	**1605**
King James' Bible	**1611**
World event: Romanov family comes to power in Russia and will rule for 300 years	1613
Pilgrims to America (see page 243)	**1620**
Charles I dissolves Parliament	**1629**
Colonial settlement of St Mary's, USA (see page 244)	**1634**
Oliver Cromwell and Civil War (see page 246)	**1642**
World event: The Sun King of France	1643
Trial and execution of Charles I	**1649**
Cromwell conquers Ireland and Scotland	**1649–52**
Cromwell becomes Lord Protector	**1653**
Charles II restored	**1660**
Great Fire of London/Great Plague (see page 248)	**1666**
The first reflecting telescope built by Newton	**1668**
The Glorious Revolution (see page 250)	**1688**
Bill of Rights	**1689**
Bank of England founded	**1694**

World event: Romanovs come to power

The Romanov family became absolute rulers of Russia in 1613 when Mikhail Romanov was elected tsar and imposed autocratic rule. This was a government of one, meaning the tsar did not seek advice from an elected parliament but appointed a ten-man ministerial council to assist in running the country. Internal strife, the threat of foreign invasion and the prospect of financial collapse hampered the first tsars, until the reign of Peter the Great transformed the country. Peter became enamoured with warfare and travelled throughout Europe to learn of western culture and military strategies, particularly naval combat. He strengthened his army, established a navy and westernised Russia's culture. The rule of the tsar gave an unprecedented solidity to its foundation, with Peter expanding Russia's borders to create an empire, making it a true European power. The Romanov dynasty improved education and medical conditions and even defeated Napoleon in 1812, but conflict between workers and the wealthy led to the revolt of the workers in 1917. The Romanov reign ended when Nicholas II and his family were executed in 1918.

World event: The Sun King

Louis XIV of France, known as the Sun King, became monarch in 1643 at the age of 5. His mother ruled for him until 1651. His energies were poured into controlling France and expanding its territories. His palace at Versailles was built on a grand scale over 47 years, and 5000 courtiers lived in extravagant style at court. Court routines were carefully regulated and theatrical, even his rising in the morning and going to bed at night were elaborate ceremonies attended by noblemen. His famous mistress, Madame de Pompadour, was a power at court for 20 years. Louis built up France's wealth and power by encouraging agriculture and industry, developing the navy, shipping and trading and by increasing his markets and colonies overseas. France became the cultural and intellectual leader of Europe in the mid seventeenth century with dramatists such as Racine and Molière. The French Academy was founded to dictate literary style and guard the French language.

THE ROUNDHEAD HELMET

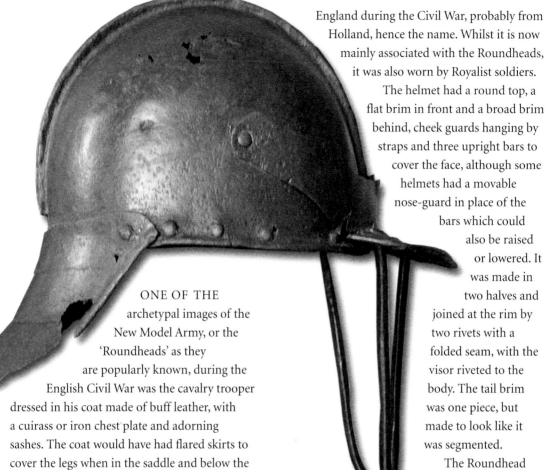

ONE OF THE archetypal images of the New Model Army, or the 'Roundheads' as they are popularly known, during the English Civil War was the cavalry trooper dressed in his coat made of buff leather, with a cuirass or iron chest plate and adorning sashes. The coat would have had flared skirts to cover the legs when in the saddle and below the coat, his legs would be enclosed by 'bucket-top' boots, which could be fashionably rolled down. He was armed with a sword and, suspended from the buff leather shoulder belt, a carbine or short musket. A gentleman could also wear a pair of pistols, which were often carried on the belt.

The most distinctive part of his uniform was his helmet, known at the time as a 'lobster pot' or 'lobster tail' helmet because of its shape. This type of helmet, sometimes also referred to as a 'Dutch pot', is more correctly termed a *Zischägge*. It was a popular style of helmet, widely used throughout Europe during the middle of the seventeenth century, and was imported into England during the Civil War, probably from Holland, hence the name. Whilst it is now mainly associated with the Roundheads, it was also worn by Royalist soldiers. The helmet had a round top, a flat brim in front and a broad brim behind, cheek guards hanging by straps and three upright bars to cover the face, although some helmets had a movable nose-guard in place of the bars which could also be raised or lowered. It was made in two halves and joined at the rim by two rivets with a folded seam, with the visor riveted to the body. The tail brim was one piece, but made to look like it was segmented.

The Roundhead General Monck described the helmet as 'a headpiece with three small iron bars to defend the face… often pistol proof'. The contract books of the New Model Army quoted the cost of such helmets as 8 shillings each and the total cost of equipping a trooper was about £4 10s.

Above: A wonderful example of a Roundhead 'lobster pot' helmet. Highly fashionable among swish officers of the day, the lobster tail protected the back of the neck, while the face grate ensured limited protection against sword blows.

THE BATTLE AT BASING HOUSE

This drawing is based on Time Team's work at Basing House and features a dramatic moment when the attacking forces set fire to one of the towers. The fury of the battle illustrates the vicious nature of civil war and just below where this attack took place we found large numbers of lead shot, many flattened by contact with bodies or armour. The two opposing sides are typically dressed and the Parliamentarian forces include soldiers wearing the distinctive 'lobster-tail' helmet.

The occupiers of Basing had survived a two-year siege until Cromwell and over 7000 Parliamentary forces joined the attack. In the excavations we found evidence of the tower on the right having been burnt down and we know that the attackers used burning straw combined with sulphur and brimstone. Accounts of the battle included details of ladders being used to scale the tower. The attack was fuelled by religious bigotry and those involved showed little compassion to either side.

The Gunpowder Plot

THE GUNPOWDER PLOT, officially revealed on 5 November 1605, was the greatest act of terrorism ever planned against the English state, a forerunner of events that we have become all too familiar with today. Had it succeeded, it would have killed the monarch, his two nearest heirs, most of the aristocracy, and hundreds of the leading men of every county and major town. This was intended to be achieved by blowing them up with gunpowder when all were gathered in one room for the official opening of Parliament.

This was the first employment of the new-style technology of explosives for an act of large-scale murder. It resulted from the persecution of Roman Catholics, imposed by the regime of Elizabeth I from the 1580s, as the Protestant Church of England which Elizabeth had established turned with increasing savagery against those who remained loyal to the old religion, fining them for not attending the national church and killing their priests. The new king, James I, who came down from Scotland to inherit the English throne when Elizabeth died in 1603, had previously made informal promises to Catholics to end their suffering. He soon found that such a policy of tolerance would be unpopular in England, and broke his word. As

a result, a dozen reckless young Catholic gentry formed the plot, aiming to destroy the whole regime and to capture the king's daughter Elizabeth and put her on the throne instead, as their puppet. Their leader was Robert Catesby, but the person best remembered among them was a professional soldier who became their explosives expert, and who was actually captured when waiting to set fire to the gunpowder, Guy Fawkes.

The plot failed because it was betrayed – we do not know by whom – and the plotters were all killed, either resisting arrest or executed afterwards, leaving a long legacy of bitterness on both sides. Protestants believed that it revealed how dangerous Catholics were, and justified suppression of them, and the date of its discovery became a national holiday, with widespread burning of images of the Pope on bonfires: the most popular English Protestant seasonal festival. Catholics felt with equal justice that the government had used the actions of a few fanatics, of which the bulk of their co-religionists heartily disapproved, to encourage a worse persecution in which innocent people were put to death. Some have argued that James's advisers themselves invented the whole plot, and it does seem as if they knew about it at least some weeks before they pounced on the plotters, but let it ripen in order to secure maximum dramatic effect. Religious rivalries have now ebbed, and the national holiday was abolished in 1858, but the bonfires and fireworks remain every 5 November, to provide the English with some joy at the opening of the darkest season of the year.

Left: *An engraving of 1605 showing the main conspirators in the doomed Gunpowder Plot. Guy 'Guido' Fawkes is third from the right.*

The Pilgrim Fathers

THE PILGRIM FATHERS are perhaps the true founders of modern America. They were a group of 102 would-be immigrants who sailed from Plymouth, England to the 'New World' in 1620 on a small ship called the *Mayflower*. Though they were neither the first settlers from England (the first successful English colony had been planted in Virginia in 1607) nor a homogenous religious group (only 35 were Puritans), the success of their settlement was influential on the development of the New World colonies, and led to other Puritan settlements across the region. By 1700, there were over 100,000 Puritans living in New England.

The Puritans were passionate Calvinist-Christians who believed the New World was the place to found their 'New Jerusalem'. In 1620 they negotiated to use a charter for settlement in Virginia owned by a group of London merchants. The merchants expected to share any income made by the settlers over the next seven years and insisted that the Puritans take with them other colonists and hired help, including a soldier, carpenter and cooper. However, arguments arose over the nature of the charter and the Pilgrims set sail without having reached a final agreement.

When the *Mayflower*'s passengers first sighted land in November 1620 (in what was to become Provincetown), they were worried. Miles from Virginia and with no legitimate charter to settle where they stood, the Puritans feared the other passengers would reject their authority. And so the Mayflower Compact was signed by the 41 male passengers. It stated in the name of God and King James I, that the group would 'combine and covenant' themselves together in a 'civill Body Politick' for their 'better Ordering and Preservation' under 'just and equall Laws'. This became the basis of government for the colony, now based in Plymouth, Massachusetts. The egalitarian spirit of

Above: *The modern replica of the* Mayflower, *vessel of the Pilgrim Fathers who established a successful settlement now known as Plymouth, Massachusetts.*

the compact became central to the development of the US constitution and the rise of America as an independent, democratic nation.

The new colony was by no means secure and the colonists struggled to survive. In the first year more than half of them died, suffering from malnutrition and the harsh winter, and they also faced many battles with unfriendly natives. It is doubtful whether the colony would have survived without local Native Americans (the Wampanoag), who taught the settlers to trap, hunt and fish, as well as grow maize and tobacco. Tradition has it that in 1621 the Puritans held a thanksgiving feast to celebrate their first harvest. This has become the annual feast day in the United States to give thanks for the foundation and prosperity of America.

Colonial Settlement

THE COLONISATION OF the North American continent began in earnest during the early seventeenth century when the British established settlements along the eastern coastal borders from Newfoundland down to Florida. The earliest colonies were made up of farmers and merchants, together with foreign hired hands utilised for labour duties. The colonists were of a varied social, political and religious background, from which stem the possible reasons why they left Britain to make a home in these new territories. The dense populations of British towns and cities coupled with a desire to escape persecution for their beliefs and seek religious freedom motivated many to cross the Atlantic.

The first successful British colony was Jamestown, which was founded in 1607 and was financed by the London Virginia Company, a wealthy stock company. They sent jewellers, goldsmiths and aristocrats in the hope of finding gold but the lack of a social bond caused by a male-dominated community prospecting for individual wealth threatened the community. However, the search for gold was a futile one, so the colonists turned to the cultivation of tobacco, which yielded massive profits. Subsequent colonies were populated by men and women escaping religious oppression at home, with the Pilgrim fathers that founded Plymouth, Massachusetts the most famous example (see page 243).

The origins of one other early colonial settlement began when around 200 migrants sailed across the Atlantic from the Isle of Wight on 22 November 1633 aboard two small vessels, the *Ark* and the *Dove*. The colonists landed on 25 March 1634 and soon purchased part of a Native American village named Yaocomico, which the settlers later renamed St Mary's City, a title that many believed to be named after Jesus Christ's mother, Mary. It is easy to accept the religious connotation of this assumption since religion played an important role in establishing the community. The majority of the colonists were Catholics escaping religious persecution in England. Several Jesuits and Protestants accompanied them but all were seeking an existence whereby they could co-habit with each other regardless of their respective faiths and belief systems.

By searching for religious freedom the colonists became renowned for religious tolerance and for encouraging people to worship the faith of their choice. This was taken to such an extent that the settlers made freedom of religion law in St Mary's City during the 1640s. Unfortunately, this religious tolerance did not last. In a bitter twist of irony, the religious freedom promoted by the colonists saw them extend invitations for Puritans to settle amongst their diverse society. The Puritans soon overthrew the existing government and began persecuting the Catholics and Anglicans alike.

During this period of persecution the Puritans burned down all of the original Catholic churches and their reign continued until the Catholics regained control in 1658. However, Maryland's Protestant community expressed resentment of the Catholic dominance in St Mary's City. Therefore, when the Protestant monarchs William and Mary succeeded the Catholic James II, a rebellion stirred in Maryland, which culminated in the naming of the Church of England as the official religion of the province. St Mary's City was abandoned soon after with the provincial capital being shifted to the Protestant-led Anne Arundel Town, now known as Annapolis. St Mary's City was excavated by Time Team in 1996.

Right: *Maryland, home to settlers who under George Calvert, the Baron Baltimore, applied to King Charles I to grant this their own recognised province.*

The Civil War

FOR JUST OVER a decade in the seventeenth century, Britain became embroiled in a devastating crisis which destroyed hundreds of thousands of lives, almost bankrupted the state and wreaked havoc through countless cities, towns and villages. In a clash of egos and ideologies, the royal house went to war with Parliament. The result was a ruthless split between countrymen which witnessed brothers fighting brothers and fathers fighting sons.

Above: The death warrant of Charles I who was sentenced to death in 1649 for being a tyrant and a public enemy of the people.

The battle was over who would rule the kingdom. King Charles I, backed by Royalist Cavaliers, believed he had a divine right to rule the people directly, and that as a representative of God he was above the law. Meanwhile, the well-to-do members of Parliament (who were not elected by the public at the time) believed they should represent and govern through the House of Commons. Their army of the people became known as the Roundheads – a force which developed into the disciplined Puritan New Model Army.

As an event in history the Civil War represents some striking aspects of our nation. Not only does it show how the veneer of civilised society could so easily break down to reveal hideous and gruesome rivalries, but it also highlights the power of people, and ultimately Parliament, who fought for an early form of democracy, and were willing to put their own king to death to achieve it.

A moment in time: the execution of Charles I

Commonly known as the English Civil War, the event had an impact on Ireland and Scotland too. From 1629 Charles I had wrangled power from Parliament and ruled as an individual, but his Anglican beliefs and heavy taxes drove what remained of the influential Puritan House of Commons to despair. While Puritan members put together a list of complaints against the king, moderate members sided more closely with the royal house, outraged at any slight against the monarchy. Events came to a head in 1642 when Charles drew up charges of treason against the House and in August of that same year he declared war on Parliament. The next nine years saw some of the bloodiest battles on British soil, resulting in a death toll of over 250,000.

Charles' nemesis was Oliver Cromwell, renowned for both his fiery temper, and later his outstanding abilities as a general. The Civil War battles ring out like a roll call of familiar names. October 1642 witnessed the first major encounter at the Battle of Edgehill which effectively ended in a draw. For the next two years Charles and his Cavaliers had the upper hand, winning battles at Lansdown Hill (1643), Roundway Down (1643), Bristol (1643), Beacon Hill (1644), Castle Dore (1644) and Inverlochy (1645). As for the Roundheads, they won the day at Newbury (1643) and Marston Moor (1644), and drew at the second battle of Newbury (1644). Throughout this series of battles marching armies of tens of thousands were moving across the land, destroying villages and towns while the agricultural rural economy fell to ruin. Bitter fighting erupted between the Scottish clans with the Covenanters invading England on the side of Parliament, while in Ireland the Confederates rallied to the Royalist cause. Amid the turmoil Cromwell developed his militia into the Puritan force of the New Model Army, and in June 1645 the tables turned when they decimated the Cavaliers at the Battle of Naseby. The surrender of Bristol followed and in May 1646 King Charles surrendered to the Scots.

From this point Charles endeavoured to make several concessions to Parliament, but a Royalist rebellion in 1648 in Kent, followed by a Royalist Scottish 'Engagers' uprising the same year, brought the royal house to the brink. While Charles tried to make peace and treaty with the moderate Parliamentarians, Cromwell struck with a purge of the Commons and Charles was brought to justice for being a public enemy of the nation and a tyrant. In 1649 Charles was sentenced to death and beheaded at Whitehall in London.

The historical and archaeological story

The death of Charles I didn't mean the end of the Civil War. A lobbying group called the Levellers, who first made demands for the free vote of every man in England in 1647, had gained support within the army and an outbreak of democracy fever in May 1649 was crushed by Cromwell, who was less keen on handing too much power to the people. The next two years were used by Cromwell for a campaign of clearing up trouble spots and changing legislation. He fought a ruthless campaign in Dublin to quell the Confederates and then took action against Scotland which culminated in the defeat of the Cavaliers and Scots in 1651 in the Battle of Worcester. The Civil War was effectively over.

Though the Puritans abolished the Anglican laws of compulsory church attendance, they tried to keep the populace in check with laws against incest, fornication, adultery and blasphemous opinions. This was a regime that was disliked for its repressiveness and caused many to wish for a return to a monarchy. By 1653 a 'nominated' Parliament made Cromwell Lord Protector of England, ruling England until his death by malaria in 1658, after which the Restoration of the Royal House began, leading to Charles II being crowned. The people may not have mourned the death of the pious Cromwell, but they did recognise the price that had been paid to lay the foundations of democracy.

PALAEOLITHIC

MESOLITHIC

NEOLITHIC

BRONZE AGE

IRON AGE

ROMAN

ANGLO-SAXON

VIKING

NORMAN

MIDDLE AGES

TUDOR

STUART 1603–1714

The Civil War 1642

GEORGIAN

VICTORIAN

MODERN

The Great Fire of London

THE MOST DESTRUCTIVE fire that the British Isles have ever known began in the early hours of 2 September 1666, when an oven overheated at a bakery in Pudding Lane, near the eastern edge of the City of London. It was not unusual for accidental blazes to level an entire country town about once every decade during the period. Most buildings were still built wholly or partly of timber, and heated and lit by naked flames, while fire-fighting equipment consisted only of leather water-buckets and hooks to pull down blazing thatch. In that sense, a fire that would burn down most of London – by that date one of the biggest cities in the world – was always a risk. For this very reason, its fire-fighting teams were unusually efficient for the time, and a very remarkable combination of circumstances was needed to foil them. These were provided when the flames in the bakery spread from Pudding Lane to a range of nearby warehouses full of tallow fat, oil and hemp – perfect combustible materials – at the end of a long period of dry weather and with an easterly gale striking the city.

The resulting blaze lasted for three days and nights, roaring westward to destroy St Paul's Cathedral (at that time probably the largest church in Europe), 87 parish churches, 13,200 houses, three national markets, the financial centre of England, half of the country's greatest port, many valuable historical records and the accumulated landmarks of 700 years of the capital's history. Estimates of the total cost of the damage ranged from seven to eleven million pounds (in the values of the time), though remarkably only six lives were lost as most people had time to flee. No blaze on this scale had been seen in Europe since the Great Fire of Rome in the first century, and none was to be seen again until the bombing raids of the Second World War. It was stopped only when the

wind dropped at noon on 6 September, allowing fire-fighters time to pull down houses in the path of the flames and thus clear a barrier of bare land in which they could find no more fuel.

The immediate result was to halt a hitherto successful naval war with the Dutch. The loss of the national financial centre, compounded by other difficulties, left the government of Charles II unable to afford another year of fighting and force it to make a humiliating peace. The rebuilding of

the city took more than 40 years, but advantage was taken of the opportunity for a radical improvement in its physical environment. Houses were often rebuilt in brick rather than wood, making them both healthier and more fireproof. Over half of the parish churches were replaced, to radical designs, proposed by Sir Christopher Wren, which introduced the new-style classical forms, modelled on Greek and Roman temples, to English religious architecture. Wren's masterpiece,

the new St Paul's, consisted of a huge dome erected over the centre of a cross-shaped church to create one of the enduring wonders of the world. Neither accident nor war have ever damaged London as severely since, and so it has been able to preserve the advances made, however reluctantly, as a result of the Great Fire.

Above: *An oil painting of the Great Fire of London depicting black skies and the city in flames. The artist is unknown, but the painting is believed to date close to 1666.*

The Glorious Revolution

FOLLOWING THE YEARS of Parliamentary rule after the Civil War, troubled wranglings continued as different cells of power vied for control. Cromwell's son Richard briefly took the reigns after his father's death, but was found unsuitable, while the old Parliament proved equally disorganised. The people were calling for open elections and unrest waited in the wings.

Above: A 1689 engraving of William and Mary, joint rulers after 1688 when King James was exiled to France.

An astute diplomat called George Monck, who was general of the English army in Scotland, took his chance and made for London. Monck arrived to settle the crisis and became the ruler of England, but he also understood the precarious situation of an England without a monarch and prepared the ground to restore Charles II to the throne. What he didn't seem to appreciate, however, was that he was cementing the foundations for continued religious fighting.

Charles had entered into secret negotiations with the French Catholic King Louis XIV, and although Charles kept his Catholic sympathies well hidden, the Protestant powermongers in Parliament remained suspicious.

The Restoration period found Charles' brother James succeeding to the throne in 1685 and as King James II he openly flaunted his Catholic faith. Parliament held fast in the knowledge that James' marriage to his second wife, Mary of Modena, was barren and that his two daughters from his first marriage, Anne and Mary, who were both Protestants, were almost guaranteed the succession. However, in 1688 a 'miracle' birth found Mary of Modena providing the ageing James II with a Catholic son. The powerhouses of London were thrown into a state of panic.

A moment in time: William and Mary

The fallout of Civil War and the Restoration politics may well have been played out in London but an event was about to unfold which would eventually affect everyone in the country – the Glorious Revolution. James'

Protestant daughter, Mary, was married to the influential Dutch Protestant, William of Orange, who was engaged in wars with Catholic France. In a bid to secure the future monarchy, Parliament sent for William and requested that he come to England to petition the king on his intentions and verify the legitimacy of his new son, whom they believed to be an impostor. In an aside, they also suggested that he bring a security force, essentially inviting him to invade.

William duly arrived with 20,000 men, but in an astute manoeuvre he managed to avoid fighting with the king's standing army. If he was to take the crown successfully, William needed to balance carefully his handling of the English army, a decisive component in keeping the peace. With increasing bad health, James fled from the West Country to London where he was captured, but wanting to avoid killing the king, William turned a blind eye and let him escape. Unfortunately he was captured again on the Thames, but once more William let him run until eventually he made exile in France. Now Parliament was presented with their goal. As far as they were concerned, James had left his responsibilities and in 1688 William and Mary were jointly handed the throne.

The archaeological and historical story

From this episode a number of important changes took place, many of which remain to this day. A series of decrees settled the status quo between king and Parliament and laid the path for the democracy we enjoy today. The monarchy managed to keep many of the privileges of state, such as the right to appoint judges and councillors, and the power to veto Parliamentary bills if they did not like them (as the monarch still can today), but other fundamental powers were reduced. The king could no longer set his own taxes or draw his own revenue; these powers now belonged to the government, though a comfortable retinue was provided by Parliament in its place.

While the ever-present threat of invasion from France and the exiled James II kept the royal family in position, the burden of running the country became more widely spread. The Privy Council, who had once bullied the government on behalf of the king, lost much of its power and in its place Parliament found its feet. The central control of England became dispersed to the provinces with a gradual devolution of power to the counties, where individual thinking parties evolved with representation in Parliament.

In many ways this 'Bill of Rights' was the birth of our liberal democracy, a kind of free voice for the people which was first called for way back in the 1647 demands of the Levellers. Though around this time we see a ruthless campaign and great troubles in Ireland, we also see the grounds of our political system establishing themselves, and shortly (in 1694) the Triennial Act, which limits the duration of government between elections, offering the opportunity for change.

PALAEOLITHIC

MESOLITHIC

NEOLITHIC

BRONZE AGE

IRON AGE

ROMAN

ANGLO-SAXON

VIKING

NORMAN

MIDDLE AGES

TUDOR

STUART 1603–1714

The Glorious Revolution 1688

GEORGIAN

VICTORIAN

MODERN

DURING THE SEVENTEENTH century hand-held firearms and iron cannons became an integral part of the battlefield, replacing older weapons, such as bows and spears, which had been used for hundreds of years. Firearms went through many different changes in design and firing mechanisms, but by the seventeenth century the most common form was the flintlock, invented about 1620, replacing the cruder matchlock that had used a glowing taper to fire the musket.

The flintlock musket was a hefty piece of equipment requiring many accessories, including a ramrod to pack the bullet and powder into the barrel and a powder pouch to ensure an ample supply of powder and shot. As it was large and heavy, the musketeer would need a musket rest, a pole that supported the barrel while he was shooting. Flintlock pistols were secondary weapons and their length varied, the average being about 37cm (14½in). They were single-shot weapons, specifically designed for personal protection and close combat. They were often carried by gentlemen and saw extensive use by the Royalist and Parliamentarian cavalry during the English Civil War.

The smooth-bore cannon first appeared in the early fourteenth century in Europe and had assumed its characteristic shape, tapering from base to mouth, by the beginning of the seventeenth century. In 1543 an English parson working for Henry VIII perfected a reasonably safe and effective method of casting iron cannons. They were significantly heavier and bulkier than bronze cannons, prone to corrosion and burst into fragments when they failed, but they possessed the overwhelming advantage of costing only about one-third of the price of a bronze cannon to produce. This gave the English, who

alone mastered the process until well into the seventeenth century, a significant advantage in naval warfare.

Cast-iron cannons added a new branch to the army, and artillery joined the cavalry and infantry as an integral part of any contemporary army. It was a shock weapon, most effectively used in mass, and its placement was critical. It had to be protected from assault, while its field of fire had to be as open and level as possible. One good volley across the front of a cavalry or infantry charge would lead to incredible destruction. The ammunition could be the solid ball, a bag of grapeshot or even scrap metal, used for maximum casualties at close range. A different tactic was the artillery duel, or counter-battery fire, where the muzzles would be elevated for long range, and the fire directed on an enemy battery.

The advancements in firearm technology made during the seventeenth century, especially by the English, changed the face of warfare for ever. Gone were the massed ranks of archers so famed at Agincourt, made redundant by the advent of the flintlock musket and the cast-iron cannon. Fast disappearing were hand-to-hand battles with pike and sword, now replaced by muskets and cannons and naval warfare was transformed from capturing ships by boarding them to sinking them with long-range cannon fire.

Whenever Time Team have involved re-enactors in firing of muskets, it has been obvious how difficult it is to fire them accurately. However, just the effect of large lumps of lead heading in the enemy's direction would have provided sufficient threat to deter attackers.

Right: Royalist musketeer re-enactors unleash a volley of shot. The seventeenth century witnessed a rapid decline in the use of armour after firearms became widespread in warfare.

13 GEORGIAN

DURING THE GEORGIAN period there seems to have been an upsurge in scientific inventions and developments, which in many cases were linked to the mass production of consumer goods in small-scale industrial units (the first factories). Men like James Watt, Matthew Boulton and Josiah Wedgwood combined scientific genius with commercial acumen in a way that was to become one of the main features of the period. In addition, improvements in agriculture produced food surpluses which enabled the new industrial urban workers to be fed. Towns expanded and in places like Birmingham the landscape began to change. Sites with good supplies of water and access to raw materials became the focus for the new 'manufactories' – the factories began to produce large amounts of goods in numbers unimaginable in previous periods.

When Time Team excavated a site in Soho in Birmingham, we found evidence of a mint powered by steam that could produce 40,000 coins an hour! In a way, Soho was typical of the new factories that were springing up all over the country. Matthew Boulton created what was probably one of the world's first factories in Soho, making buckles, buttons and coins, initially using water power. In 1774 he was joined by James Watt who created an advanced form of steam engine which provided power to a variety of stamping machines (see page 266).

The steam engine developed at Soho and first seen working in public in 1776 was an advanced machine which used a condenser to cool the steam and provide additional power to the system. Watt had worked for over ten years on his engine, initially inspired by a steam engine created by

the Cornishman Thomas Newcomen in 1705. Watt's realisation that condensing steam created a vacuum that could provide additional motive power to engines was critical. When Watt's inventive genius was combined with Boulton's entrepreneurial skills, the result was not only the spread of factories but of the system of power to drive them. Boulton and Watt steam engines were exported in large quantities and by the time Watt died in 1819, these engines were at work throughout the world.

In Coalbrookdale in Shropshire, another genius was working away, looking to improve the production of iron. Abraham Darby and his family were to revolutionise the business of casting iron. The grandfather of the builder of the Iron Bridge first smelted iron in 1709 and it was in the same area that the first cast-iron cylinders for steam

engines would be produced and the first cast-iron rails. In 1779 the world's first iron bridge was regarded as a miracle of modern invention. Never before had such huge spans of iron been created.

The combination of advanced steam power and cheap cast iron that could be moulded into a range of shapes vastly increased the production of iron and objects made from it. By the middle of the nineteenth century, over 50 per cent of the world's iron was being produced in Britain.

Cast iron was the first new material to be created since iron's first discovery in the Iron Age. Abraham Darby's invention of a process that made iron flow into moulds made it a uniquely adaptable material and the ability to create complex shapes fired a whole new range of inventions. Iron components were key to some of the machines and objects which formed the basis of our modern world. Stephenson's Rocket was the world's first steam-powered train capable of 50km (30 miles) per hour – running on iron rails and steam power, it was the fastest machine in the world in 1829.

The industrial pioneers

In Lancashire, mills run on water and steam power produced vast amounts of material at a fraction of the price and in a fraction of the time of the earlier handmade processes. During the filming of Time Team in Soho we were able to see a Boulton and Watt steam engine in action and it was an astonishing and magical process. Here was a power vastly superior in strength to the horse power or the wind and water power that it would replace. It must have taken a tremendous imaginative leap of faith and genius to harness the forces in a way that seems beyond the ordinary human scale.

Developments were made which resulted in the accurate measurement of time. This was essential for the advances of science, exploration and the control of people in factories.

Josiah Wedgwood was another pioneer of the Industrial Revolution and in 1999 Time Team excavated one of his potteries at Burslem. By around 1850, there were over 130 potteries in this area, employing nearly 20,000 people. Pottery from Stoke on Trent was exported throughout the world and it was fascinating that we found a large range of Wedgwood pottery when we excavated on the Caribbean island of Nevis in 1998. Wedgwood made many advances in the industrialisation of pottery production, creating some of the world's first production lines. The large bottle kilns we were excavating were kept lit almost permanently and added to the image of

these industrial areas as red glowing smoke-filled hell-holes – a landscape that had never been seen before in Britain. Wedgwood was for his time an enlightened factory owner who took care of his workers. He also kept meticulous records of his output and these records have provided a useful archive for archaeologists needing to date sites where fragments of Wedgwood pottery have been found, which seem to be just about everywhere Time Team digs!

Agricultural advances

While the industrial process in Britain advanced, it's worthwhile emphasising that the agricultural revolution helped to sustain it. As Francis is keen to point out, all this industrial activity could not have taken place without an improvement in the efficiency of farming and food production, enabling large numbers of agricultural workers to leave the land and move into the cities to work in new factories. New crops and new developments in breeding produced more food per acre of land. Farmers began to understand the improvement of soil and mechanical aids like seed drills and hoes made working the land easier.

One of the main changes in the landscape, which we can still see today, was the process known as enclosure. Most of the medieval English landscape was made up of small fields, which were in many cases 'common' land and open to use by the community in general. In the 1750s Parliament passed many 'enclosure' acts which made field sizes larger – more regular and more easily controlled by the government and landowners. Time Team has often come across the difference between the earlier, more irregular landscape of medieval fields and

the straight lines and square shapes of the enclosed fields. In the Highlands of Scotland, a similar but more draconian process got underway in the late eighteenth century with the Highland clearances, fuelled by landowner greed for more land.

Many of the developments in the Georgian period would lay the basis for the industrial and agricultural revolutions that would expand into the next period.

Britain's place in the world

This was also the period that saw Britain's expansion into the world and the setting up of new colonies in the Caribbean at places like Nevis, and in America. In 1996 Time Team excavated one of the earliest American colonial sites at St Mary's City which, although it belongs to the end of the previous period, was typical of the colonisation that took place in the Georgian era. Countries across the globe would not only provide a new market for the consumer goods produced in the new factories, but in return Britain would be able to import raw materials. Cotton and tea from India, sugar and tobacco from the Caribbean and the huge resources of North American colonies provided rich materials for Britain's trade. One of the strongest archaeological images for this trade was the vast range of pottery, glass and metal work all created in English factories that we found in the trenches in Nevis. Nevis is also a reminder that the wealth of that period was being underwritten by the slave trade – a growing horror that essentially provided free labour for the production of raw materials in many of Britain's colonies and enabled vast profits to be made at home at the cost of millions of lives.

Previous spread: *The iron bridge at Ironbridge in Shropshire. A majestic symbol of Georgian industrial power and engineering.*

Above: *Time Team excavating a pottery kiln at Burslem.*

Left: *A typical example of the famous white on pale blue works by Wedgwood.*

GEORGIAN IN DETAIL

HISTORIANS AGREE that the Georgian age was hugely important in British history, but there are many opinions over how long it actually lasted; for the purposes of this book, it is treated as including what is commonly called the 'Regency' period as well, to give it the years between 1714 and 1837.

This was the time in which Britain became both the greatest military power in the world, and its greatest economic powerhouse. It saw the beginning of our connection with German-born monarchs and gave us a range of civilising influences, including the neo-classical architecture of towns like Bath, which add to our sense of what 'Georgian' means.

The monarchs certainly contributed to this, although none of them were very popular or had anything remotely resembling charisma. George I (1714–27) was mean and bossy; George II (1727–60) was like a bad-tempered sergeant-major; George III (1760–1820) was dull, plodding and eventually went insane; George IV (1820–30) behaved like an overgrown spoiled child; and William IV (1830–37) resembled a decent but not very bright country gent. What they all had in common was their willingness to listen to the views of their people and to obey the rules of the constitution; and this was enough to give the increasing strength of the British the chance to achieve its full potential.

One result was an improvement in farming processes, both of grain and livestock, known as the Agricultural Revolution. This increased productivity to the point at which, combined with improvements in trade and transport (especially through better roads and canals), for the first time in history the population could grow enormously without fear of starvation. This supplied a huge new labour force for what has been commonly called the Industrial Revolution: an expansion in the production of wool, cotton, coal, iron, steel,

copper and tin, which made Britain the only nation to provide all at once. Each of these processes needed technological inventions – such as the safety-lamp for miners, spinning and weaving machines, sowing and reaping engines, pumps for mines, improved furnaces – which were made and tested in this period. By its end, factories, blast-furnaces and mines were taking over large areas of the British landscape.

Politics at home and abroad

Political stability and economic dynamism combined to produce military power, and this was the period in which the British Royal Navy became the supreme force on the world's oceans, capable of defeating the warships of all other nations put together if necessary. This seaborne strength turned the British into the leading power in world trade and in the planting of overseas colonies. Between 1763 and 1775, it looked as if Britain was destined to take over the whole of North America, but this was prevented by the rebellion of most of the colonies there in 1776, which broke away to form the United States of America.

The speed with which Britain recovered from this disaster surprised everyone: within 20 years its volume of trade with its former colonies was greater than it had been before independence, and the good diplomatic relations formed with them by the end of the period was a lasting source of strength. Furthermore, having lost one empire, the British set about gaining another. They hung onto Canada and several rich Caribbean islands, and expanded into India, settled Australia and New Zealand, and gained footholds in Africa. By the end of the period they had regained their position of 1775, as the world's leading colonial power.

The increasing respect in which the British were held by other Europeans was not simply a result of military might and wealth, but also of the remarkable stability of government. The mixture of monarchy, aristocracy and democracy that had been achieved at the end of the Stuart age proved capable of surviving the strains and expense of regular prolonged war, the loss of the American colonies, and the social and economic changes produced by industrialisation. The final ingredient to its success was developed in the 1730s: a parliamentary system in which parties competed for power, and in which those defeated in each general election had a right to monitor the performance of the government. One consequence of this was a degree of free speech remarkable in the world at that time, which in turn encouraged the vitality of English literature and other arts. Handel came to Britain and although Britain had not quite matched continental Europe in music and fine arts, in the printed word, including works of fiction and scholarship, it had come to lead it.

Furthermore, the political system proved capable of reforming itself. During the years 1829-37 it relaxed the qualifications for holding public office, to admit newly-enriched industrial and commercial middle classes, and Christians outside

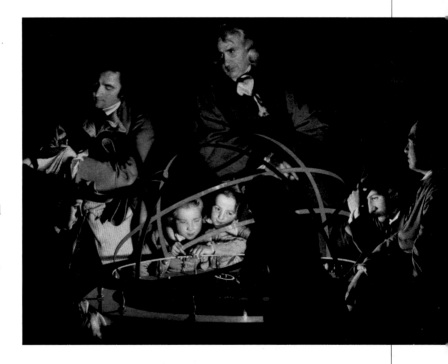

the national Church. A new sense of humanity accompanied these changes, and the British led the world in abolishing slavery, preventing cruelty to animals, and according kinder treatment to convicts and the insane. It is true that the total Georgian achievement was only made by inflicting great suffering on many different people, such as natives of the areas drawn into the overseas empire, the Irish, the Scottish Highlanders, and workers exploited by new industry. In some respects the mental scars left in each case have not quite healed, even today. Against this, it can be said that the British behaved no worse than other people of their time; and that they began to regret their misdeeds rather earlier. The true tragedy is that the regret often came too late.

Above: *A painting of an orrery by Joseph Wright. Essentially a mechanism for explaining the stars and the movement of planets – a hot topic in the Age of Enlightenment.*

Georgian Chronology

This timeline gives you a quick, at-a-glance guide to what happened when in Britain in the Georgian era, helping you to understand the order of events. We've also included, in green type, some key events that happened elsewhere in the world.

Age of Enlightenment	**1700–1789**
Union of England and Scotland	**1707**
Thomas Newcomen devises the first practical application of the steam engine	**c1712**
Reigns of Georges I, II and III	**1714–1820**
Jonathan Swift's *Gulliver's Travels* published	**1726**
Wesley's conversion and the start of Methodism	**1738**
Battle of Culloden (see page 265)	**1746**
Adoption of Gregorian Calendar	**1752**
James Watt's steam engine patented (see page 261)	**1769**
American War of Independence (see page 268)	**1775–1783**
British penal colony established in Australia	**1786**
World event: Signing of US Constitution	**1787**
World event: French Revolution	**1789–1799**
Vaccination against smallpox introduced	**1796**
Union of Britain and Ireland (see page 272)	**1801**
Battle of Trafalgar (see page 270)	**1805**
Slave trade abolished (see page 273)	**1807**
Battle of Waterloo (see page 274)	**1815**

World event: *Signing of US Constitution*

The US Constitution was drafted in May 1787 and is considered one of the most durable and influential legal documents in history. Prior to this, the 13 British colonies that had declared themselves the United States of America were each self-governed under the Articles of Confederation and Perpetual Union. Tenuous links existed between the states, meaning that the federal government had limited influence when it came to defence, public finance and trade. These circumstances led to the drafting of the constitution. The main objective of the constitution was to represent the will of the people although several obstacles needed to be addressed, such as cultural and religious diversities. Thus, in building for the future of the country as a whole, the constitution was written with provisions for its amendment if certain social, economic or political conditions required it. Following its ratification in 1788, a strong centralised government was established. George Washington was elected as the first President of the United States in 1789 and began presiding over a constitution that has only had 27 amendments since its inauguration over 200 years ago.

World event: *French Revolution*

In 1789, France experienced the most defining aspect in its history when the French Revolution impacted. France was in financial turmoil due to the Seven Years' War and the US Wars of Independence. Bankruptcy threatened to strangle the country and pressure mounted on Louis XVI to recognise a single national assembly. The king's resistance and the poverty permeating French society led angry mobs of Parisians to attack the city gates and storm the Bastille prison on 14 July 1789. The uprising spread across France, forcing the aristocracy to flee as the mobs focused their disdain on the wealthy. The king was forced to accept his new position within a constitutional monarchy, which reduced his political status. Many French émigrés settled in Prussia or Austria and won their hosts' support in fighting the revolution. However, in 1792 the King was captured and on 21 September 1792 a National Convention was elected and the monarchy abolished. Louis XVI was executed for treason in 1793 but extremists took control and a 'Reign of Terror' followed until Napoleon Bonaparte seized power in 1799.

BOULTON AND WATT STEAM ENGINE

DESPITE THE FOLK story of James Watt watching a kettle boil on the kitchen range and noticing how the steam raised the lid, he did not invent the steam engine. Engines using steam power were running long before Watt was born. His real claim to fame is based on the radical improvements he made to Newcomen's atmospheric engine, which enabled steam power to fuel the Industrial Revolution. The major problem with the Newcomen engine was that three-quarters of the steam was wasted in heating

permanently cold, a large saving in energy was obtained. With the commercial and financial backing of a Birmingham industrialist, Matthew Boulton, this idea was converted into commercial success. Between 1775 and 1800, the period over which Watt's patents were extended, the Boulton and Watt partnership produced some 500 engines, despite them being more expensive than the Newcomen engine. They were extensively used by the tin-mining industry in Cornwall and in the new textile factories that required an economic and reliable source of energy.

During this period Boulton and Watt exercised a virtual monopoly over the manufacture of steam engines and they introduced many refinements. The most important of these improvements was the use of steam to push the piston against a vacuum in two directions, rather than just one, thus increasing power. Watt also developed new methods of transmitting power from the pistons into rotary motion and ways to control the engine. This rotary action engine was quickly adopted by British textile manufacturer Sir Richard Arkwright for use in a cotton mill. Many other industries followed in exploring the possibilities of

the cold cylinder to 100 degrees before the steam stopped condensing and started generating power.

To overcome this, Watt patented a condenser in 1769, which separated the two actions of heating the cylinder and cooling it to condense the steam for every stroke of the engine. By keeping the cylinder permanently hot and the condenser

steam power, and it soon became the main source of energy within the emerging industrial heartlands of Britain.

Above: An early model of a steam engine. A remarkable piece of engineering, and incredibly efficient by design, steam engines revolutionised industry.

GEORGIAN INDUSTRY

Here we see some of the key features of the Georgian period, including the kilns for pottery production, canals which carried much of the raw material of the Georgian period, and a water-powered mill. This was the period of the beginning of the industrial revolution.

In 1758 Josiah Wedgwood set up his factories in Burslem, Stoke on Trent, where we excavated in 1999. We managed to find the base of some of these kilns in our excavations. The bottle kilns, which Victor has shown on the left of the picture, were incredibly smoky and contributed to the unhealthy environment which began to develop in the new industrial towns of this time. These towns often developed in locations where water power and raw materials like coal and iron were readily available. Leading the search for new improvements in production were groups of Georgian entrepreneurs, one of whom can be seen standing on the right with his family.

Canal building expanded so quickly in the second half of the eighteenth century that it was often referred to as 'canal mania'. Individual companies and investors would often construct short lengths of canal for their own purposes, and many would go out of use in the Victorian period.

King George I, II and III

THE GEORGIAN PERIOD is one of the most momentous periods in British history, quite simply because so much happened during the reigns of George I, II and III. Britain changed radically on the domestic, international and industrial fronts as she leapt to an unprecedented status of prestige. Conflicts at home and abroad were ever present in the Georgian era, whilst technical innovations and developments were to add much might to British industrial output.

George I was a controversial monarch as he spent much of his reign residing in Hanover. Ascending the throne after the death of Queen Anne, he quelled the first Jacobite rebellions of 1715 and 1719, but faced political opposition to his dubious dealings with the South Sea Company. Many people lost vast amounts of money as a result of inflated and unsustainable share prices and George I was saved by the interference of Sir Robert Walpole and Viscount Townshend, both powerful Commons figures. George I decided to leave Britain's affairs to these administrators but his unpopularity permeated throughout society, mainly due to his inability to speak English.

His death in 1727 led to the accession of his son, George II, whose lack of confidence ensured that he too would rely heavily on his ministers. The first few years of his reign saw Britain go to war against Spain (allied with France) who was irate at British trade expansion. In 1743, George II became the last British king to command armed forces during the War of the Austrian Succession at the Battle of Dettingen, whilst in 1745–46 his reign subdued the second Jacobite rebellion led by Bonnie Prince Charlie. His reign saw advances in the textile industry, improved roads and canals, the establishment of the British Museum (1753) and the beginning of the Industrial Revolution. George II died in 1760 during the Seven Years' War

Above: *George I sounding in the Georgian era in suitable pose. Though great innovation and cultural advances were made at this time, George I was quite unpopular because he didn't speak English.*

(1756–63) and was succeeded by his grandson George III. He is remembered as the monarch who lost the American colonies following the War of Independence (1775–83) but Britain's emergence as a serious world power occurred during his reign. The voyages of James Cook ensured British colonisation of Australia and New Zealand (1788), the first £1 notes were issued in 1797 and the first British census was taken in 1801. The French Revolution paved the way for the Napoleonic Wars (1803–15) with the Battle of Trafalgar (1805), emphasising British naval superiority, proving to be one of the decisive battles during this conflict, which ended with devastating finality at the Battle of Waterloo in 1815. Several years prior to this, George III was diagnosed with mental illness and the Prince of Wales was appointed Regent (1811) until his death in 1820.

The Battle of Culloden

CULLODEN IS THE name of a gentleman's country house that stood in the early eighteenth century beside a wide expanse of boggy open ground, a few miles east of Inverness in north-eastern Scotland. Upon that open ground, on 16 April 1746, occurred the last full-scale battle to take place on British soil. It was fought between the supporters of two rival kings: the reigning one, George II, of the German Hanoverian family, and an exiled one, calling himself James III, leader of the Scottish Stuart royal house, which had been thrown out of Britain by a revolution in 1688.

One army, about 5000 strong, was led by the heir of James, Charles Edward Stuart, better known as Bonnie Prince Charlie. Facing him was a younger son of George, William Augustus, the Duke of Cumberland, with about 9000 men. It was also, however, fought between two different cultures: that of England, Wales and Lowland Scotland, and that of the Scottish Highlands, which had a different language (Gaelic), costume (shirt and plaid shawl) and social system, based on clans loyal to their hereditary chiefs.

Charlie declared war on George on 19 August 1745, having landed in Scotland with help from the French, King George's main European enemies. He took George's government by surprise, and was able to win control of Scotland and then invade England, getting within 120 miles of London before retreating ahead of gathering government forces. Charlie's men were slowly pushed back into the Scottish Highlands, where they turned on Cumberland's pursuing army at Culloden. Against the advice of his generals, Charlie launched his smaller force into an attack across the open moor, where it was shot to pieces by the superior enemy firepower. Up to 1600 were killed, and after fleeing the field Charlie gave up further hope of resistance and returned to France.

Historians differ over whether his rebellion ever had a chance of succeeding, but agree that his inept leadership at Culloden brought it to a premature end, and with it the last chance for his family to rule again in Britain. It also brought about the end of Highland culture, as a vengeful British Parliament abolished the traditional costume and the whole clan system, even though no more than a fifth of the clans had supported Charlie. These acts broke the bond between the former clan chiefs and their people, and over the next hundred years many ordinary Highlanders were evicted from their land to clear it for sheep-farming. Most settled far away in the British overseas colonies.

There is no doubt that the defeat of the Stuart threat and the clearing of the Highlands contributed to the subsequent stability of British politics, which is part of the reason why there have been no battles since Culloden. This peace was, however, bought by losing a proud, colourful and valuable part of our national heritage.

Right: A clan burial stone at Culloden, site of slaughter and fierce fighting in 1746 when supporters of James III and George II went head to head.

The Industrial Revolution

THE EIGHTEENTH AND nineteenth centuries were a period of dramatic change, which saw the British economy alter from one predominantly based on agriculture, to one driven by mechanised industry. Technological innovation in the 1700s brought new machinery, water and steam power to the two industries which dominated the revolution – textiles and iron. Related activities such as mining boomed, and Britain's transport system was revolutionised, first by canals, then railways. By the nineteenth century, individual discoveries and localised production had given way to huge mass production, and Britain had become the leading industrialised nation in Europe, exporting manufactured goods across the world.

Above: *An icon of the Industrial Revolution, George Stephenson's* Rocket *locomotive. Built in 1829, the* Rocket, *with its tubular boiler, was at the height of technological advances.*

The newly unemployed from the rural regions moved to the cities where the factories were based and, as a result of the incoming workforce, massive areas of cheap housing were developed. These slums existed in terrible conditions and the new working class found themselves at the mercy of the factories which owned their homes, livelihoods and even their local shops and pubs. In many cases workers were part-paid with factory tokens which could only be spent in factory-owned places. From as young as four or five years, until an early grave from appalling working and living conditions, the workers were effectively owned by the company.

Whilst the effects of the Industrial Revolution were often appalling on the workers, for the rest of society it was a marvel. It would provide them with unparalleled freedom, quality mass-produced goods, and lucrative returns for those who could afford to invest.

A moment in time: power in the second phase

The most amazing advances had been made at the start of the Industrial Revolution with pioneers such as Abraham Darby experimenting with coke-fired ironworks at Coalbrookdale, Shropshire, in 1709, and with the development of steam power for use in stationary engines by James Watt in the 1780s, but it was to be the second phase of the Industrial Revolution in the 1800s which really heralded the changes. The key was power – the power of steam, harnessed and advanced to such a degree that the lives of everybody would be affected. Steam-powered factories were hungry for resources and their demand and output was channelled along the growing network of canals. Machines were used to make machine tools, so that even more machines could be quickly built. Then in 1821, George Stephenson started work on the Stockton to Darlington Railway, a scheme to create a special transport line running on rails over 40km (25 miles) long which could haul coal from the collieries around Darlington to Stockton for loading onto ships. Opened in 1825 and with cargoes pulled by Stephenson's steam engine *Locomotion*, the line was a great success and put many horse-drawn hauliers out of work.

The railway success was extended and in 1830 both the Liverpool to Manchester and Canterbury to Whitstable railways were open. Fast and (at that time anyway) cheap transport had arrived and this led to a dramatic social change as people discovered a new efficient mobility and also benefited from cheaper goods in towns associated with the railways. The canals slowly declined as the railways grew, but steam wasn't the only power to emerge at this exciting time. In 1831 Michael Faraday was experimenting with electric power, while in the later nineteenth century the telephone, lightbulb, radio and petrol-driven car were all taken advantage of, following invention overseas. The Industrial Revolution had set the path towards our modern age.

The archaeological and historical story

The Museum of Science and Industry in Manchester has some fantastic displays which outline the development of one of our first industrial cities, while numerous historic industrial sites also have their own museums and information centres. The Energy Hall at the Science Museum in London is also well worth a visit as it displays many of the machines and engines which revolutionised our world. While acts of Parliament changed the way children were used in the workplace, and revised the terrible working and living conditions of the people who drove the revolution forward, some surviving examples of slums, such as the National Trust's preserved 'back-to-back' housing in Birmingham, serve as sobering reminders that, although we profited and learned from the breakthroughs in science and manufacturing, these benefits were carried on the shoulders of a hard and poor labour force.

Some refer to the post-Second World War nuclear age as the third phase of the Industrial Revolution, the invention of labour-saving devices from automatic washing machines to microwaves, and the increased use and reliability on the micro-processor representing our next step in advancement. Only time will tell as retrospect is needed to understand historic periods, though it is interesting to reflect that the labour-saving devices promoted to us since the 1950s no longer mean that we have more leisure time, they just mean we have more time to work.

PALAEOLITHIC

MESOLITHIC

NEOLITHIC

BRONZE AGE

IRON AGE

ROMAN

ANGLO-SAXON

VIKING

NORMAN

MIDDLE AGES

TUDOR

STUART

GEORGIAN 1714–1837

Industrial Revolution c1750

VICTORIAN

MODERN

The American War of Independence

THE SEEDS FOR the War of Independence were first sown following the conclusion of the Seven Years' War, fought between the British and the French, and the signing of the Treaty of Paris in 1763. The Seven Years' War pulled several countries into the conflict with North America, providing manpower and funding to aid the British war effort in particular. The cessation of hostilities saw the French handing over their North American territories to the British and, at this time, Britain and the American colonies enjoyed firm cultural and political relations.

This did not last. Relations rapidly deteriorated when Britain tried to impose policies implemented in Parliament on colonies over 3000 miles away. In 1763, the British budget deficit stood at a staggering £122 million. It was decided that, since Americans enjoyed the protection of the British army and navy, it would be logical to have them contribute to the defence of the colonies. The Stamp Act of 1765 was a piece of legislation that sought to reach as many Americans as possible. It was also designed to remind the colonists that Britain remained their political sovereign.

Americans were vociferous in their opposition towards this act, arguing that they should not have to contribute to their own defence due to having assisted the British in the recent war by providing men, money and supplies. Violent opposition to this unpopular tax erupted in Boston and the Stamp Act was repealed in 1766. The British tried other methods of raising revenue through America but all were met with protest. Indeed, the infamous 'Boston Tea Party' of 1773 saw protesters destroying £10,000 of tea in response to tea duty. The British saw fit to place the colony of Massachusetts under military rule in 1774.

Increased resistance to British policies gave way to the inevitable and war commenced

between Britain and her colonists in 1775. As the conflict spread, George Washington was appointed commander-in-chief of the American military forces to fight the British and their loyalist supporters. Washington forced the British to retreat from Boston and, in 1776, the Americans declared their independence. In 1777, the defeat of the British at Saratoga improved Washington's fortunes, as it prompted the French – still smarting from their defeat by the British – to enter the war allied to the Americans. Spain (1779) and

the Netherlands (1780) followed suit. Britain's civil conflict had become (technically) a world war.

Crushing defeat for the British at Chesapeake Bay in 1781 led to their surrender at Yorktown. With war being fought on several fronts, the cost was escalating, thus prompting Parliament to surrender. The Treaty of Versailles was signed in 1783 and the United States of America formally recognised. It could be argued that Britain lost the colonies when Parliament sought to impress its sovereignty by force in the face of opposition to

Above: A dramatic depiction of George Washington, the first President of the United States, crossing the Delaware River.

draconian British taxation policies. Consequently, colonial loyalty and tradition were compromised with war the only solution. Even if Britain had won, they probably would have had to subjugate the colonies. Lessons were learned and the British refrained from directly imposing taxes on their colonies, which ensured a flourishing Empire.

Nelson and Trafalgar

THROUGHOUT THE YEARS of the French Revolution (1789–99), which saw the old monarchy and church of France overturned and replaced by a people's republic, the repercussions echoed through other European states. As a republican general, Napoleon Bonaparte won great respect and a wider reputation as a fine military commander, one who had the vision to lead huge campaigns and control strategy on a continental scale.

By 1804, through a shrewd political nature, Napoleon was made Emperor of France. By this time he had conquered massive swathes of Europe and had even briefly held great influence in Egypt and Syria. In fact, it was during Napoleon's Egyptian campaign that the Rosetta Stone was discovered, the key to interpreting ancient hieroglyphics.

Back in the revolutionary years, under a cloud of revolutionary anxiety, France declared war in 1793. As an island on his western front, Britain was a constant thorn in Napoleon's side and the only answer was to invade. During the later 1790s several attempts were made with French raiders attacking via Ireland and Wales, but Napoleon understood that only a full-scale invasion would work. As the French planned, the British built their army and in 1799 a new income tax was introduced to fund the war effort. One result of this tax was a massive refurbishment of the Royal Navy, which was to save the day under the leadership of one of our greatest national heroes, Admiral Horatio Nelson.

Napoleon knew he had to destroy the Royal Navy before he could invade Britain and so he entrusted one of his greatest commanders, Admiral Villeneuve, to muster a combined fleet of French and Spanish warships for the task while the French Grand Army assembled at Calais. At the time the Royal Navy was successfully blockading enemy ships in harbours all along the coast of France and Spain. After a breakout which saw Villeneuve racing across the Atlantic in March 1805 to harry the West Indies, and a series of encounters, the French Admiral found himself with 33 warships at Cadiz in southern Spain, blockaded once more in the port overlooking the Gibraltar Straits. Out in the Bay of Trafalgar, Nelson and 29 warships of the Royal Navy waited.

As Villeneuve set sail with his combined fleet to break out of Cadiz, he headed south in an elongated line with his own ship in the centre. On spotting the Royal Navy they about-turned and tried to reach the safety of Cadiz once more. In a wonderful tactical move Nelson led a two-pronged attack at ninety degrees to the line. The plan was to split the enemy line in half and also attack the rear. By the time the front half of the enemy line had turned and repositioned, their support elements would have been destroyed.

Though the tactical skill of war at sea does resemble a grandmasters' chess game, the reality of fighting is one of speed, daring and absolute brute force. The race to position correctly and outmanoeuvre the enemy takes the vessels to a tactical brink until the moment arrives to unleash the full force of their armaments. Cannons would fire solid shot up to 14kg (30lb) in weight to smash the solid oak sides of a ship, hailing those inside with lethal splinters. Chain and bar shot (two cannon balls linked together) were used to destroy masts and rigging. In close quarters the dreadful broadside was the most feared. Two ships would draw up side by side and fire all their cannons directly into the gun decks of each other, causing colossal damage and hideous injury.

On 21 October Nelson sent his famous signal to the fleet – 'England expects that every man will

do his duty' – which was later followed by 'Engage the enemy more closely'. Nelson, aboard HMS *Victory*, cut into the French fleet as planned and drew along the rear of the *Bucentaure*. *Victory*'s massive carronade, or heavy cannon, was loaded with 30kg (68lb) of solid shot and a keg of musket balls and fired directly through the cabins and along the enemy gun deck. *Victory* was then rammed alongside by the next enemy ship in the line, *Redoubtable*, both ships locking together and unleashing broadsides into each other. Amid the horror Nelson was shot and taken to his cabin where he died at 4.30pm after hearing the day had been won.

The bloody terror aboard *Victory* was repeated on the other 61 ships engaged in the action. It has been estimated that the British lost nearly 2000 men, killed or wounded, while the French lost nearly 7000. The prize was the virtual destruction of the powerful combined French fleet, securing the Royal Navy as the rulers of the waves for decades, and ultimately Britain was saved from almost certain invasion by the French Grand Army. The silts and sediments at the bottom of the Bay of Trafalgar encase the remains of over a dozen warships, resting from their dreadful fate, while HMS *Victory* continues to this day, based at Portsmouth, as the oldest commissioned battleship in the world.

Above: An 1805 oil painting of the British ships at Trafalgar. The Flagship, HMS Victory, *can still be seen today at Portsmouth harbour.*

Union of Britain and Ireland

THE RELATIONSHIP between Britain and Ireland has endured a chequered history over the centuries. Politicians in London had long regarded Ireland as a back door into England and thus, at times of conflict, deemed it to be of significant strategic importance. This became evident when France declared war on Britain in 1793 with the ideals of liberty, equality and fraternity promoted by the French Revolution attracting Irish sentiment. Moreover, the religious common ground that both countries shared was favoured by the Irish, who aspired to the abolition of religious inequality enjoyed by France and their establishment of a democratic government.

However, many Irish politicians believed that Ireland should maintain its links with Britain and show support during the crisis. Furthermore, the same politicians sought Catholic emancipation and parliamentary reform in Ireland. Contrary to these views, a group of politicians shared a more extreme perspective and formed the United Irishmen in 1792, which aimed to sever Ireland's connection with Britain entirely, establish full independence and unite the Irish people.

The United Irishmen found that their plans to unite Dissenters and Catholics against Anglican rule were swiftly finding favour amongst the populace. Britain's Prime Minister, William Pitt, reacted by persuading the Irish Parliament to pass the Catholic Relief Act in 1793. This legislation gave Catholics the right to vote but, although they were allowed to stand as parliamentary candidates, Catholics were not permitted to possess a seat in Parliament. In truth, the Act enabled Catholics to vote solely for candidates belonging to the Protestant faith ensuring that this was merely a short-term solution to the existing problem.

Ireland's Catholics were given false hope in 1795 when Earl Fitzwilliam was made Lord Lieutenant of Ireland. He announced a policy based on his belief that all Catholics should enjoy political equality but, no sooner than this was announced, George III recalled Fitzwilliam and stripped him of his title. Seeing their hopes vanish, Catholic Irishmen engaged increasingly in acts of sectarian violence. The United Irishmen sought to enlist the aid of France in their struggle to overcome English control and, in response, the Irish Protestants formed the Orange Order to protect their own interests. This served only to spark escalation of the number of violent clashes.

Pitt was troubled by the ongoing problem in Ireland and staunchly opposed to an independent Irish Parliament, as he was concerned that Britain's enemies could establish a base there to launch attacks. Pitt therefore formulated an Act of Union to unite the Kingdom of Great Britain with the Kingdom of Ireland. The Act was passed in 1801 and Pitt had plans to follow up with more far-reaching reforms, which included Catholic emancipation. George III refused to allow this so Pitt felt compelled to resign. The unification presented by the 1801 Act was symbolised by the assimilation of Ireland's St Patrick's cross flag with that of Britain's Grand Union flag to form the Union Jack, which has been the national British emblem ever since.

As it turned out, the Act did not solve any of the existing problems and merely served to tighten Britain's grip on Ireland following the abolition of the Irish Parliament. Political representation would be at Westminster, the Anglican Church became the official Church of Ireland and Catholics could not hold positions in public office. This led to decades of strife between Britain and Ireland until the 1922 War of Independence resulted in 26 southern Irish counties seceding from Britain to form an Irish Free State with Northern Ireland remaining within the UK.

Abolition of the Slave Trade

ALTHOUGH THE PRACTICE of using slaves can be dated back to Ancient Egyptian times, it did not become a lucrative trade on a world scale until its exploitation by European countries in the fifteenth century with the discovery of the New World. Slaves were transported to these new colonies and it did not take Britain long to cash in on the slave trade. By the mid eighteenth century it has been estimated that Britain was transporting 50,000 slaves per year from Africa across the Atlantic to be sold to plantation owners in the West Indies and southern American colonies. Britain made a huge profit out of slave-produced goods and there was much opposition to slave trade abolition from plantation owners. Ironically, the staunchest opposition to the slave trade eventually emanated from Britain.

In 1772 a law was passed making it illegal for an individual to be recognised as a slave in Britain. However, Britain still held an overwhelming dominance over international slave trade in the late eighteenth century. It is estimated that Britain traded in over one million slaves between 1782 and 1807. The anti-slavery movement began when the Quakers petitioned Parliament in 1783, but did not begin in earnest until the formation of the Society for the Abolition of the Slave Trade in 1787.

The public remained indifferent towards the slave trade until they discovered the horrendous conditions the slaves had to endure and anti-slavery sentiment quickly progressed to become one of the most significant reform movements. The Society presented to Parliament two nationwide petitions attacking the slave trade, with William Wilberforce leading the campaign. He nearly succeeded in 1792 until the French Revolution and subsequent war with France halted its progress. However, with a twist of irony, the war in Europe became an unexpected ally. The established plantation owners found themselves facing greater competition when new territories in the West Indies were acquired. These planters surrendered their anti-abolitionist stance and the campaign began again in 1804. A bill abolishing the slave trade was passed in 1805, with the outlawing of the British Atlantic slave trade in 1806. By 1807 slave trade in the British Empire was banned altogether and it became illegal to carry slaves on British ships. However, it remained legal to own slaves until 1833. This led to a renewed campaign to abolish it completely and the passing of one of the most important pieces of legislation in British history – the Abolition of Slavery Act.

Right: A broadside news sheet of the Printers' Picture Gallery press campaigning for the abolition of slavery.

The Battle of Waterloo

KEY EVENT 1815

ON 18 JUNE 1815 an astounding battle took place – the culmination of a campaign involving French troops under Napoleon fighting British, Dutch, Belgian, Austrian, Russian and Prussian armies. In a remarkable comeback from exile, the French emperor gathered his old army of 73,000 men as he marched on Paris. As Louis XVIII fled, the old enemies of Napoleon prepared to challenge their nemesis. The chosen battleground was Belgium, around the village of Waterloo.

The allied forces were arranged in two great armies. The British Duke of Wellington commanded the Anglo-Allied troops, numbering around 67,000, while the Prussians acted under their own general, Gebhard von Blücher, with a strength of approximately 60,000. As Napoleon moved into Belgium, he knew that his only hope was to cut the allied armies in half and defeat Wellington and Blücher separately. Napoleon split his own army into two forces. On 16 June, the first two battles took place. Blücher was beaten back at Ligny, but Wellington managed to hold fast at Quatre Bras. Wellington then withdrew his troops to his headquarters at Waterloo while the Prussians consolidated themselves.

Seeing his chance to crush the allies, Napoleon moved his forces to the field at Waterloo, but heavy rainfall made the logistics of moving over 300 cannon and thousands of cavalry and infantry across country difficult. Meanwhile Wellington dispersed his armies across high ground and a number of strategic farmstead locations in the vicinity. On 18 June battle was joined. Without full knowledge of the location of the Prussian forces, Napoleon was forced to act quickly. While the French closed action against Hougomont Farm

on the right flank and drew fire by a central assault and bombardment of the high ground, the Prussians unexpectedly joined the field. Ney, one of Napoleon's generals, used up valuable cavalry resources by repeatedly charging Wellington's high ridge, while Napoleon was forced to commit his reserves to quell the Prussian threat. With actions on both flanks and a failing central assault, Napoleon was forced to use his own personal guard, the highly trained Imperial Guard, on the centre. They bravely fought up the ridge but were eventually forced to retreat (for the first time ever in their history) by a counter-attack of the British Guards. Their finest troops in disarray caused the beginnings of a rout, and it was here at Waterloo that the death knoll sounded for the Napoleonic Wars. Taking flight for a short time, Napoleon eventually gave himself up to the British and was exiled to the island of Saint Helena in the South Atlantic where he died in 1821.

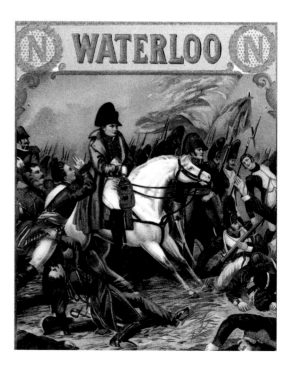

Right: A magazine illustration of unknown date depicting Napoleon Bonaparte at the Battle of Waterloo in 1815. An historic victory for the British and Napoleon's downfall.

THE RAPIDLY EXPANDING population of the new industrial towns was fed largely by home production. In 1750 the English population was 5.7 million, but by 1850 it reached 16.6 million and agricultural output increased to cope with this. Although each agricultural worker produced more food, the actual proportion of the workforce involved in agriculture fell, so only improved agricultural production could make this possible. It was a revolution that received support from Georgian royalty, notably George III.

The new farming systems involved crop rotation with fallow crops, such as turnips, to aid land recovery and allow more food to be produced from one area. The mix of arable crops changed, with higher yielding types such as wheat replacing low-yielding ones, such as rye. This brought about changes in livestock farming. Most cattle and sheep used to be slaughtered before winter, as there was no food to feed them, but harvesting turnips meant that livestock could be fed throughout the winter. This increased the number of animals available to provide manure, which could be fed back into the soil to improve crop yields.

Livestock farmers, such as Robert Bakewell and Thomas Coke, introduced selective breeding programmes to improve the quality of animals. Bakewell crossed different breeds of sheep to select their best characteristics, known at the time as 'breeding in and in'. Bakewell separated male from female, only allowing mating between animals whose traits he felt to be desirable.

Bakewell's experiments in selective breeding produced the Dishley or New Leicester breed in 1755. These sheep were big and delicately boned, had long, coarse wool and produced a high yield of meat. He also began the practice of hiring out his prize rams to farmers so they could improve their own stock.

Bakewell was one of the first to breed cattle and sheep for their meat value. Before his breeding programme, these animals were kept for wool and milk production or for working on the farm. Selective breeding produced livestock with more market value in the towns. Bakewell's work was in

Above: *A typical Georgian oil painting of a country scene, this one depicts Thomas Coke inspecting his crossbreed sheep.*

response to a general requirement for stock that would fatten to greater weights at an earlier age and at less cost, to cope with the demands of the growing population.

Andrew Meikle, a Scottish millwright, made the breakthrough in mechanising the threshing of cereal grains. In 1786 he built a machine using a strong revolving drum and fixed beater bars. At first animals on treadmills supplied the power for these new threshing machines, but in time the portable steam engine was used. The modern combine harvester uses the principles that Meikle introduced and is merely an improved model of it.

14 VICTORIAN

THE PROCESS OF change that we call the Industrial Revolution, which began in the Georgian period, increased massively in the Victorian era. It was as though all the processes we had seen on sites like the Soho Mint with the use of steam power (see page 254), the beginning of factories and the production-line technology were accelerated. The inventions of people such as Watt and Boulton (see page 261) were replicated by a new breed of engineers and scientists led by characters like Brunel.

A perfect illustration of this was in steel production, which Time Team featured in a special documentary filmed in Sheffield in 2004. The invention of crucible steel by Benjamin Huntsman made Britain the first country to produce cast steel bars. It has been estimated that before this invention only around 200 tons of steel were produced per annum. In the early years of Victoria's reign this increased to 20,000 tons – nearly half of all the steel production in Europe. Steel not only provided an improved material for manufacturing boats, trains and machinery, it also helped to supply the growing domestic market with everything from knives and tableware to sewing machines and guns.

In Sheffield we followed the work of a group of archaeologists who had been excavating in the city for over six years, looking for the remains of the city's past. The invention of crucible steel and later the famous Sheffield Plate (a thin layer of silver fused onto copper) came together with the use of steam power in factories. By the end of the eighteenth century there were already nearly a hundred water-powered mills in the city. The local river supplied power and the hills around

provided coal, iron, millstone grit and charcoal. In the nineteenth century steel production caused a massive increase in the population of the city, rising to nearly 500,000 in the first decade, making it the fourth biggest city in Britain. This expansion took place with little care for health and safety or the rights of the workers. Accidents were a regular occurrence, culminating in over 250 people being killed when a dam burst in 1864. The urban poor whose treatment was to give Victorian England its dark reputation were housed in squalid conditions. When George Orwell visited the town he commented on the foul stench from the factories and the terrible state of housing. On a number of Time Team sites, including York and Castleford, we have had to excavate through some of these dwellings. The cramped conditions and tiny living spaces revealed in the trenches made us

aware that this was a new kind of living space that people were forced to inhabit. This was probably one of the greatest concentrations of people into a small area that had been seen in Britain's history. Sheffield became one of the centres for trade unions in Britain, but this was only to make a difference later in the Victorian period.

All over Britain new towns sprang up to supply labour for a vast increase in consumer products. The Stoke-on-Trent potteries that we had excavated at Burslem boomed in the Victorian period and one of their most popular lines was blue and white wares, usually based on Chinese patterns, that turn up on almost every archaeological site.

As well as the larger factories, smaller centres were set up to supply the new demand for consumer goods, sold in the new stores like

277

Boots, Liptons, and Freeman, Hardy and Willis, some of which are still household names.

In 2002, Time Team excavated the Merton Abbey Mills site in south-west London, which supplied fabrics for the Liberty shops. Liberty supplied beautiful materials for dresses and decorating the house, but in quantities and at a price that made them available to the wider general public. A process that began with hand-made materials and then water-powered machines became increasingly industrialised, although ironically the Merton works were also connected with William Morris who was a key figure in the Arts and Crafts Movement that flourished in the late Victorian period.

Crime and punishment

At Appleby in 2003 we saw the remains of a police station, one of the key elements of society that were aimed at keeping these new urban poor in their place. The police and other elements of Victorian society were intent on keeping the working classes under control, and law and order were often enforced with brutality. New legislation introduced from the eighteenth century onwards was aimed at improving prison conditions – women and men were separated and cells were introduced, to an extent reducing crowding, but there was the application of mindless tasks and a severe physical regime that included treadmills that made the prisoners' lives even worse than in earlier centuries.

At Appleby we saw the way such regimes were enforced and it was a grim reminder that beneath all the progress and empire building there was a darker side to Victorian society.

Previous spread: *Bliss Valley Tweed Mill at Chipping Norton in Oxfordshire. Factories like this became the powerhouse to fuel the empire.*

Right: *An 1880 photograph of a slum street in Newcastle. Note the heavy smog in the air. Thousands of people lived in terrible conditions in an age without any welfare and only charity support for the poor and infirm.*

Below: *Excavating in an urban environment can present many challenges.*

THE VICTORIAN AGE lasted for just one lifetime, covering the reign of Queen Victoria between 1837 and 1901, but it was the longest reign of any monarch in British history, and the period in which Britain achieved the summit of its power, almost certainly for all time. That is why it is so important, and has such a hold on the historical memory.

Victoria herself deserves some credit for the achievement. Her long life, added to her devoted sense of duty and high moral standards, gave the British political system a fundamental stability. It helped also that she had a conspicuously happy marriage to her German husband Albert, and produced a large number of children to secure the succession and provide useful marriage alliances with foreign royal families. Her own heir, Edward, Prince of Wales, had a boisterous love of fun which eventually made an effective balance to his mother's high seriousness.

The Victorian achievement really consisted of making full profit from all the advantages left to Britain by the Georgian age. Victoria inherited the largest colonial empire of the time, and under her rule it almost doubled in size, particularly by taking over huge areas of Africa, to leave her ruling over one quarter of the entire human race. British explorers mapped out many of the remaining parts of the earth unknown to Europeans, and made contact with their peoples. Ways were found of giving home rule to the main areas settled by the British – Canada, Australia and New Zealand – that kept them loyal to the motherland.

Contact with so many other parts of the earth inevitably enriched British culture and scholarship, giving birth to the science of anthropology: the systematic study of the way in which humans of all kinds behave. Britain's dominance of the oceans was increased to the extent that by 1860 about half of all the ships in the world had British owners. This in turn enabled investors from Britain to develop large areas of the world – especially in Latin America – that were not under direct British rule. Careful diplomacy kept the peace with other European powers, so that for only two years in Victoria's huge reign was she ever at war with any of them: with Russia in the Crimea, 1855–6.

The home economy

Peace and colonial expansion powered surges of economic growth at home, allowing Britain to consolidate its position as the world's leading commercial and industrial nation. This in turn made it the first urban superpower. When Victoria began to rule, three-quarters of her people still lived in villages and were concerned with farming; by the time of her death, four-fifths lived in towns or cities and were involved in buying, selling and manufacturing. The huge new, overcrowded urban centres brought great health hazards, and so further inventions were produced to meet this challenge.

The typical town became a place with metalled roads, pavements, running water and street-lighting. Doctors developed anaesthetics and antiseptics, and microscopes that could for the first time in history discover the true causes of disease. The expanding coal industry provided cheap fuel and gas with which the expanding population could heat and light its homes, and cook more effectively without destroying the island's remaining trees. To connect the new urban and industrial centres, railways were laid across the nation, speeding up the movement of people and goods to an unprecedented extent and bringing the component regions of the nation into regular, easy contact for the first time. With them also came new possibilities for leisure, and the seaside holiday and the tourist resort both appeared.

The growth of knowledge

As the geographical horizons of the British expanded, so did their mental horizons. Scholars pioneered the scientific disciplines of geology (study of rocks) and palaeontology (study of fossils found in those rocks): in 1844 British scientist Richard Owen invented the word 'dinosaur'. The discovery of the vast age of the earth, and of the huge number of vanished species that had lived in the successive epochs since it was formed, demanded a new sense of the place of humanity in it. This was provided in the 1860s, as Charles Darwin's new theory of evolution won acceptance and it became realised that humans had evolved from apes, as part of a tremendous chain of existence by which all living things were interconnected.

These discoveries meant that, for the first time in history, science replaced religion as the main source of knowledge about the nature of the world. In Europe, this meant that the authority of the Bible no longer dominated issues of how humans had come to be and what their place was on earth. To help to fill the gap, another discipline, archaeology, developed to dig up the human past systematically. The new science could not answer the great questions of the meaning of death, and of the purpose of human life, and so the Victorian age remained one of dynamic Christian piety, especially among new chapel-based Protestant sects. Religion separated from politics and scholarship more than ever, and for the first time Jews and atheists were allowed to participate in public life.

With this expansion and discovery came a great deal of anxiety. The most serious failure of

Victoria's Empire came closest to home, in Ireland, where her ministers failed to integrate the Roman Catholic inhabitants into the new United Kingdom. The bitterness left by three centuries in which they had been treated as a conquered people was reinforced in 1846 when the potato crop failed and about two million either died of hunger or fled abroad. With some justice, the survivors blamed the British government for negligence, and from that time a movement built up for Ireland to take its independence.

In Britain the newly enriched upper and middle classes feared the impoverished new industrial working class. Increasingly, as the other European powers developed industrial economies and colonial empires, it seemed likely that Britain's dominance in both would be overtaken. By the time Victoria died, many of her subjects thought that the British state might collapse in revolution or military defeat. The fact that they were wrong makes their successes seem still more impressive.

Above: *A commemorative plate issued to celebrate Queen Victoria's Golden Jubilee. It features a world map clearly showing the massive expanse of the British Empire.*

Victorian Chronology

This timeline gives you a quick, at-a-glance guide to what happened when in Britain in the Victorian era, helping you to understand the order of events. We've also included, in green type, some key events that happened elsewhere in the world.

Victoria (see page 280)	**1819–1901**
Charles Darwin – 1859 Origin of Species	**1809–1882**
World event: 1800s – Native American Wars	**1800s**
Catholic emancipation	**1829**
Liverpool and Manchester Railway opens	**1830**
Factory Act limiting child labour	**1833**
Tolpuddle Martyrs	**1834**
Charles Dickens publishes *The Pickwick Papers*	**1837**
Naval Power – Spithead Review (see page 288)	**1840**
Penny Post	**1840**
Potato famine begins in Ireland	**1844–45**
World event: Communist Manifesto published	**1848**
Victorian Industrial and Scientific Revolution (see page 290)	**c1850**
The Great Exhibition	**1851**
Crimean War – Florence Nightingale (see page 292)	**1854**
Death of Albert – Prince consort	**1861**
Towns and the urban poor (see page 293)	**1870**
Boer War (see page 294)	**1899**
Death of Victoria	**1901**

World event: *1800s – Native American Wars*
During the nineteenth century, white settlers in North America encroached onto Native American land, while the discovery of gold in California in 1848 pushed the frontier further westward. Skirmishes involving the US Army with the Sioux and Cheyenne occurred with savagery on both sides. One of the most renowned was the Battle of Little Big Horn in 1876. General Custer led 225 men to confront the Sioux and Cheyenne after they resisted white prospectors on their lands in North Dakota. The general underestimated the strength of the Native Americans led by Chiefs Sitting Bull and Crazy Horse. Custer's unit was overcome and all were killed. The Battle of Little Big Horn was the last major Indian victory of the Indian Wars, which came to an horrific conclusion at Wounded Knee Creek in 1890. To quell activism on the reservations, white officials called in troops. The Indians offered no resistance and were taken to Wounded Knee Creek. The next day, soldiers demanded all firearms be surrendered. A struggle ensued and the military opened fire, killing at least 150, making Wounded Knee Massacre a poignant symbol of the demise of the American frontier.

World event: *Communist Manifesto published*
Authored in 1848 by Karl Marx and Friedrich Engels while members of the Communist League in London, the Manifesto of the Communist Party advocated a revolutionary theory that human society should abandon capitalism and proceed to communism. Marx believed that the progress of society was stunted by capitalism and that a socialist society, based on a dictatorship of the working class, should replace it. Marx and Engels professed that the Manifesto was linked to the struggle of the working classes, stating that they had a role to play in the overthrow of capitalism. Ahead of their time, Marx and Engels professed that global capitalism was responsible for wars, the downfall of nations and the poverty of millions. The Manifesto explains that there is constant 'class struggle' between the oppressors and the oppressed. Marx and Engels divided a capitalist society into the proletariat (working class) and the bourgeoisie (capitalist class). The former represents those who work to provide and maintain the wealth, control and ownership of production for the latter. Communist ideals became firmly entrenched following the Russian Revolution in 1917 where the working classes rose to claim ownership of land and production.

ENFIELD RIFLE

THE VICTORIAN PERIOD was one of huge invention and technological development, but few nineteenth-century objects have achieved such iconic status as the Enfield Rifle.

Until the mid nineteenth century, infantry soldiers were generally armed with muskets – long, muzzle-loaded guns with a smooth bore, which fired lead balls. They were notoriously unreliable weapons to load and fire, and woefully inaccurate over most distances. The American War of Independence (see page 268) demonstrated on a large scale how inefficient these British Army muskets were, and throughout the following decades, the search for a more effective weapon gathered pace.

It had long been known that 'rifling' or grooving a gun barrel to spin the projectile created a more accurate weapon, but early rifles, such as those used in the Napoleonic Wars, were very difficult to load in combat. All that changed in 1853, when the Pattern 53 Enfield Rifle was introduced, named for the Royal Small Arms Factory at Enfield in Middlesex where it was first manufactured. It was the most effective firearm ever issued to the British army up to that time, capable of hitting a target at over 600m (650 yards) and reloading three times a minute.

However, its most immediate impact was not positive. The new rifle became a trigger for the 1857 Mutiny when it was issued to British troops serving in India. To load the rifle, a greased paper cartridge containing the bullet and charge was inserted into the barrel, and the soldiers were instructed to tear the cartridge between their teeth to expose the powder. However, they were greased with pork and beef fat, something totally unacceptable to the Muslim and Hindu troops who made up much of the British force. Their objection to the cartridges escalated to wider issues and months of warfare and huge loss of life ensued.

Despite this inauspicious start, the Enfield rifle was hugely influential in following decades. It became the first in a family of rifles which changed warfare across the world for ever. The Enfield itself was the second most common weapon in the American Civil War, with British companies exporting an estimated 900,000 firearms to both sides during the conflict, whilst the famous Lee-Enfield rifles became the major weapons of the First and Second World Wars.

The increased range, accuracy and firepower that the Enfield rifles provided put an end to the slow-moving, massed ranks of infantry of traditional warfare, and were a key factor in creating the more flexible, small unit and camouflaged approach to combat that we are familiar with today.

Below: *An Enfield percussion cap rifle.*

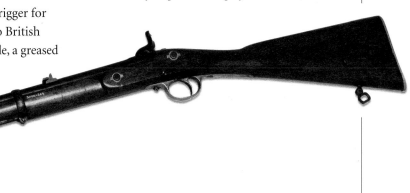

VICTORIAN TOWNS

This drawing is based on Victor's research into Sheffield for the Time Team special we filmed there, and gives a wonderful idea of the combination of industry and pollution that typically characterised many Victorian towns. We see here pottery works and mills and a combination of housing styles, including the back-to-backs that at the height of industrialisation would have even had people living in the cellars.

We see also the different elements of society – some who are clearly doing well from the expansions of factories and some who are not. The soldiers, armed with Enfield rifles, are there as a reminder that the military were on hand to quell any industrial strife. Although in the later Victorian period the canals would become uneconomic, at this stage they provided the main means of getting raw materials and finished products in and out of towns.

The British Empire

THE BRITISH EMPIRE was a phenomenal institution which, at its height, controlled over a third of the Earth's landmass and embraced hundreds of millions of subjects. It remains as the most colossal empire the world has ever seen and was famously quoted as the 'Empire on which the sun never sets' with concerns dotted across the globe.

Above: *A group of Maharajas taking tea in 1875. India supplied a huge amount of resources to the Empire. The Indian continent also provided fiercely patriotic troops in support of the First World War, a debt only recently recognised by historians.*

The Empire had its roots in the Tudor period, where the age of exploration, early colonisation and the results of wars left Britain with substantial interests abroad. The loss of America in the later eighteenth century following the Wars of Independence caused some upset, but it was also found that by planning and implementing strict trade agreements even greater profits could be realised without the need to actually govern regions directly.

Rather than employing a costly and difficult invasion policy, the British notion was one of breaking into new markets and undeveloped countries, mostly with military backing, and building them up under the 'guidance' of a British model of living. Christianity and British rule were inflicted on unsuspecting countries which had little capacity to resist. The Industrial Revolution added to the momentum as Britain became the world's largest producer of manufactured goods, and as Victoria enjoyed her reign through the nineteenth century, a revival in colonisation and the development of massive global conglomerates reached an all-time high.

A moment in time: the race for Africa

The eighteenth century witnessed a campaign by the British East India Company to secure much of Asia, while the Opium Wars in the Far East tied the lucrative trades of China into the Empire. But during the next century Britain's prominent position came under threat as other European nations became more industrialised. Under Queen Victoria and the Conservative Prime Minister, Benjamin Disraeli, a new ideology gained ground: Imperialism. As competition picked up between Britain and the emerging empires of countries such as Germany, America, France and Holland, colonial expansion became the buzz-word. Trade empires were simply no longer enough. In what many refer to as the 'scramble', a race for unclaimed territory took place in Africa under the shamefully racist policy of assuming that many ethnic groups were uneducated savages incapable of governing themselves.

The imperialist expansion was enforced with a tough military edge. Egypt and the Sudan were occupied by force, while South Africa came under the Empire at the end of the nineteenth century. In all, Britain fought off native populations and European powers to gain over twenty African countries and 30 per cent of the continent's population. A 'divide and rule' policy was used where native groups were deliberately set against each other, or existing divisions taken advantage of, to stop populations uniting in a common cause. Governor-Generals sat as direct representatives of the crown and as such oversaw the dealing out of British law, language and church. In return Britain enjoyed practically inexhaustible resources for her industry, and by sheer volume of people, a position of power unequalled elsewhere in the world.

The archaeological and historical story

The battlefield sites of South Africa, in the KwaZulu-Natal region, are a stark reminder of the brutal conflicts between British troops and their unwilling subjects. The most famous site is Rorkes Drift, a farmstead used as a supply base. A resting station for sick and injured soldiers with a complement of some 110 men, Rorkes Drift came under attack from over 4000 Zulus in 1879. In a desperate battle which lasted over 12 hours, the small garrison prevailed, with the men earning an astonishing 11 Victoria Crosses.

Though Empire had its benefits for Britain, colonisation had its price. In an attempt to lose some of the financial burden, a number of Dominion states were permitted to rule themselves under strict controls from Britain. Yet by the onset of the twentieth century many of the smaller nations had also realised their own nationalist movements which threatened imperial control. The onset of the First World War was the death knell for the Empire. A venture of such astronomical cost in lives and material, the war meant that Britain was struggling to cope with the administrative and financial cost of maintaining her empire. Though further expansion took place after the war (with the annexation of Iraq and Palestine), the inter-war years were witness to an increase in Dominion states and the building of a Commonwealth, or club of ex-Empire acquisitions. With the near bankrupting of Britain following the Second World War, the Empire was rapidly deconstructed in the 1950s and 60s as much of Asia and Africa was given independence.

Though expanded with the ignorant attitudes of the time, often ruthlessly applied, the British Empire stands in our history as the most powerful moment of our nation on the world stage, no more so than during the Victorian period. The multi-culture of the independent Commonwealth nations is rightfully celebrated today, a culture that we share through history.

PALAEOLITHIC

MESOLITHIC

NEOLITHIC

BRONZE AGE

IRON AGE

ROMAN

ANGLO-SAXON

VIKING

NORMAN

MIDDLE AGES

TUDOR

STUART

GEORGIAN

VICTORIAN 1837–1901

The British Empire c1848

MODERN

Spithead Reviews and *Turbinia*

NAVAL REVIEWS HAVE been popular, extravagant events for centuries. The Tudors, from Henry VII to Elizabeth I, were great proponents of reviews as stages upon which the world could gaze at the power and might of England. Henry VIII had a great passion for the navy when he became king in 1509, and soon set about turning the superb natural harbour of Portsmouth into a Royal Dockyard. From that point on, the Spithead Reviews became something of a national institution, building to an all-time high during the reign of Queen Victoria, and featuring again most recently in 2005 during the events hosted to commemorate the 200th anniversary of the Battle of Trafalgar.

Spithead itself is the waters immediately outside Portsmouth, butting the Solent to the west, the Isle of Wight to the south and the open English Channel to the east. During her reign Victoria held no fewer than 17 reviews of the navy, marking occasions from state visits to celebrations of new technologies, such as the 1853 steamship review. One of the largest and grandest Spithead reviews was held in June 1897 to celebrate the Queen's Diamond Jubilee. Over 160 ships of the Royal Navy were drawn up in lines stretching for miles. Battleships, cruisers and gunboats stood proud in the water as a firm reminder to the invited foreign dignitaries of the power of the British Empire, yet a surprise was waiting.

Three years earlier, in 1894, the inventor and engineer Sir Charles Parsons had sunk a fortune of his own money into a business created to develop his new idea: The Steam Turbine Company. Up to this point few people were interested in his wild ideas of using steam jets to directly power a turbo fan, creating an incredibly powerful yet efficient engine. As far as the movers and shakers of the industry were concerned, all paddle steamers and screw-driven ships of the day used traditional mechanical steam engines and they chugged along quite nicely thank you.

Parsons worked incredibly hard to perfect his idea using model boats and prototype engines so highly engineered that they almost drove his company to financial ruin. Finally, by 1897, he had created the perfect design of steam turbine and he built a speedy ship called the *Turbinia* around it. Where better to show his pride and joy to the world than at Victoria's Spithead Review? The crowd were awestruck as the 30m (100ft) *Turbinia* mustered over 900 horsepower and shot through the water at nearly 35 knots, racing past the assembled ships and VIPs. The steam turbine was here and within a few years Parsons' engines were powering the navy's vessels and the new power stations across the Empire, and were shortly adopted by the rest of the world.

Above: *It was estimated that over 50km (30 miles) of ships were present at the Spithead review in 1897.*

Advances in Industry and Transport

INDUSTRIAL GROWTH ACCELERATED in the Victorian Age, powered by new inventions and the commercial acumen and genius of people like Isambard Kingdom Brunel. Transport was improved too, with heavy goods moving along both canal network and the new railways that criss-crossed the land.

New roads and railways

New railway links and roads also revolutionised the way we travelled and the time it took. The long-distance stage coaches were gradually replaced by trains and new developments in steam engines meant that by the late nineteenth century, just 25 years after Stephenson's *Rocket* (see page 266), trains were travelling at over 50 mph and pulling vast loads.

The first steamships

Ordinary people could experience more of the countryside and coast and popular tourism expanded. If Britain had become a country that could be more easily explored, so had the world beyond and critical to this process were the steam-driven ships that no longer depended on wind and tide. Steam for propulsion of ships was tried with varying success in many countries during the late eighteenth and early nineteenth centuries. All early steamships were paddle-driven and were small vessels because it was believed they would require too much fuel to undertake a long journey. Further

Left: A strangely workmanlike image of the Victorian engineer and inventor, Isambard Kingdom Brunel, standing before the massive chains of The Great Eastern, *a ship he designed with John Scott Russell.*

development was thus delayed until the 1830s, when Brunel turned to steamship construction. His three iconic steamships – *The Great Western*, *The Great Britain* and *The Great Eastern* – each marked a significant step forward in technology.

The Great Western, launched in 1837, was the first steamship built specifically for ocean service in the North Atlantic, and showed that the proportion of space required for fuel decreased as the volume of the ship increased. *The Great Britain* was originally conceived as a paddle steamer, but Brunel quickly recognised the advantages that screw propulsion could give the vessel, and converted the ship to power a 5m (16ft) iron propeller. At the time of her launch in 1843, she was the largest ship in the world, over 30m (100ft) longer than her nearest rivals, and the first screw-propelled, ocean-going, wrought-iron ship.

Designed initially for the transatlantic luxury passenger trade, she could carry 252 passengers and 130 crew. *The Great Eastern*, launched in 1858 with a total displacement of 18,918 tons, was the largest ship ever built in the nineteenth century. With a double iron hull and two sets of engines driving both a propeller and paddles, she was never an economic success, but fully demonstrated the technical possibilities of the iron steamship.

The new warships

As far as warships were concerned, the development of larger guns with explosive shells made armour plating imperative. The development of the screw propeller allowed the application of steam power to the warship and the first steam ironclad, HMS *Agamemnon*, was ordered in 1849. The Crimean War of 1854–56 proved the value of iron armour and France hoped to gain an advantage over Britain by putting armour on her new wooden ships of the line. In response, in 1861 Britain built HMS *Warrior*, the first all iron-hulled, seagoing, armoured man-of-war. She displaced 9,210 tons, mounted 28 breech-loading 18cm (7in) shell guns, carried sails, and had a speed of 14.5 knots. It was quickly decided to replace all wooden ships with ironclads.

As armour got thicker and guns bigger, smaller quantities of guns were carried and the bigger guns were mounted in revolving turrets. It was difficult to combine these turrets with the sails that were required due to uneconomical steam engines. By the 1890s, steel was used for warship construction, and sails were abandoned because of advances that had been made in engine design. The term 'ironclad' was replaced by 'dreadnought'. A dreadnought usually had two turreted guns at each end and a battery of quick-firing ones along the sides. By the end of the century, iron warships had replaced wooden ones and were displacing the sailing ship as the principal means of sea transport around the world.

PALAEOLITHIC

MESOLITHIC

NEOLITHIC

BRONZE AGE

IRON AGE

ROMAN

ANGLO-SAXON

VIKING

NORMAN

MIDDLE AGES

TUDOR

STUART

GEORGIAN

VICTORIAN 1837–1901
Advances in Industry and Transport 1837–1901

MODERN

The Crimean War

THE CRIMEAN WAR of the mid 1800s was the result of conflicts between Orthodox and Catholic Christian beliefs and the chest-beating displays of swaggering European superpowers. The arguments centred around Palestine, where the ownership of the churches of the Holy Sepulchre and Nativity, which sat within the Ottoman Empire, were disputed between the European Catholics and Russian Orthodox monks. After months of debate, conflict ensued and the Sultan of the Ottoman Empire attacked Russian forces near the Danube in 1853. In return the Russians destroyed the Ottoman navy and landed in Turkey, and in the following year France and the United Kingdom declared war on Russia to protect their Ottoman interests.

To close down the powerful Russian Black Sea fleet and stop further Russian actions into the Mediterranean, the British and French laid siege to the city of Sevastopol in the Crimea. By 1855 the Russian fleet had been destroyed and the city taken. War raged for another year until peace terms were finally reached with the Paris Treaty of 1856.

Though relatively short, the war is often perceived as one of extreme violence, but as one of the first wars to be regularly reported on in the press, its particularly harsh reputation could be a result of how it was publicised. In a time of warfare when the wounded were often left where they fell, as soldiers marched forward against cannons and cavalry in disciplined block formations, the sensitive reading public became horrified. Fighting actions included the Charge of the Light Brigade, which Tennyson brings to life with his poem about the shocking waste of sending lightly armed cavalry against cannons: 'Theirs was not to make reply. Theirs was not to reason why. Theirs was but to do and die. Into the valley of death rode the six hundred.'

Yet changes were in the making. Modern nursing techniques and field hospitals became accepted as generals realised they could actually save brigades rather than write them off. Florence Nightingale, also known as the Lady with the Lamp, cleared the disgusting squalor from the military 'butcher's shop' at Scutari and pioneered nursing techniques which incorporated hygiene and genuine care of the sick in proper hospitals. Meanwhile the almost-forgotten character of Mary Jane Seacole, a Jamaican who travelled to the Crimea on her own after being turned down by the military because of her ethnicity, worked tirelessly on the front lines herself, often retrieving the wounded while under fire. From the pomp of the military and the horror of the war came these two brave women who offered comfort and care to a generation of young soldiers.

Above: A painting depicting the Scots Guards, resplendent in their red tunics, saving the colour at Alma during the Crimean War.

Towns and Urban Working People

MODERN ARCHAEOLOGY BEGAN as a study of the ancient past, but since 1960 industrial archaeology has been recognised as an important branch of the subject, especially in Britain where the Industrial Revolution can be said to have started. Inevitably the archaeology of the Industrial Revolution has tended to concentrate on machines, mills, mines and factories at the expense of the towns and houses where the workforce actually lived. In the 1960s, for example, huge areas of working-class housing were demolished in Bath. Such wholesale demolition would never have happened in the smarter areas of grand Georgian houses where the gentry stayed while visiting the baths. These beautiful buildings still survive, but we now know little or nothing about the lives of the ordinary people who serviced, maintained and supplied them.

The growth of the urban population in Britain during the sixteenth and seventeenth centuries was not necessarily accompanied by the expansion of the towns. This was because many late medieval towns were actually quite thinly populated. After the population decline that followed upon the Black Death of 1348, waves of plague kept the numbers of people low and many towns had open areas among the housing. These areas – what today we would call 'brown-field sites' – were developed first.

It was not until the eighteenth and nineteenth centuries that most towns began to acquire new suburbs around their original, medieval core-areas. The houses of working people continued to be built much as they had always been well into the seventeenth century, with each building constructed for a particular family and using traditional materials. However, from the eighteenth century we see a new approach to the construction of urban housing. Newer,

mass-produced materials, such as brick, began to be employed. Towards the top end of the housing market, landowners began to impose building standards, which resulted in some superb urban architecture, at places like Bath, the Duke of Bedford's estates in London and the magnificent New Town of Edinburgh, which was begun in 1750. But despite these improvements at one end of the market, the housing provided for early Victorian working people in the new industrial towns of the Midlands and north was rarely properly planned. The main aim of all but the most enlightened landowners was to pack as many people as possible into a given area of land. This was a very dark period in the history of housing in Britain.

Before the advent of mass transport by rail, housing for the early Victorian workforce was arranged close by the mill or factory where people worked. This housing was usually built by the employers. It was in their interests to keep building costs down, but on the other hand it was not in their interests to provide accommodation that was so poor and unhygienic that disease could take hold and spread. But soon it did, and there were a series of severe cholera outbreaks in London in the mid-nineteenth century which led directly to improved sewage systems, and the provision of other services such as cleaner water and gas for heat and light.

Slowly these changes resulted in better and less crowded housing. The new streets were wider and parks or other open areas were provided. From about 1850 mass transport became more popular and large areas of new working-class housing could be constructed in healthier locations around the periphery of the towns. Some of this housing was both well-built and well-planned – and is still in use today.

The Boer War

THE BOER WAR covers two major phases of conflict between Britain and the other European settlers of South Africa – Holland, France and Germany. The first phase is often referred to as the Transvaal War as it took place in the Transvaal valley, an area settled by the Dutch (known as Boer) people who had their capital at Pretoria.

In a typical example of imperial expansion, Britain annexed the Transvaal in 1877, with an eye to the abundance of mineral deposits in the region. Further colonial settlement followed, which pushed the patience and resources of the Boers to the limit and in 1880 they revolted with the famous action at Bronkhorstpruit, where a convoy of the British army was destroyed. Attempts by the army to beat the Boer farmers were thwarted with embarrassing defeats where the tried-and-tested method of artillery bombardment, cavalry charges and infantry attacks were beaten back. After further skirmishes the British settled for a truce in 1881; a few mineral deposits weren't worth losing an army over.

Everything changed when the Boers discovered gold in the Transvaal south of Pretoria in 1887. Gold diggers arrived in a veritable gold rush, including thousands of British fortune seekers. During the 1890s Johannesburg developed out of the miners' camp and the Boers controlled the region, exercising a restrictive administration over the miners who toiled over a gold reserve estimated at over £500 million. In 1895 a British-backed coup failed and, as pressure mounted, the British army gathered on the borders. In 1899 an ultimatum was issued by the British government for equal rights for British settlers, while the Boers released their own demands for British troops to leave the borders. In October 1899 war started.

Initially the Boers fared well by placing towns under siege and their developed tactic of trench

Above: *A large artillery detachment lay a piece of heavy artillery during the siege of Ladysmith during the Boer War.*

warfare, backed by mercenary forces of Britain's imperial enemies, once again took its toll on the British army. However, with reinforcements and a new commander arriving at Cape Town, British fortunes changed and in 1900 both Bloemfontein and Pretoria (capitals of the Orange Free State and Transvaal respectively) were captured.

From this point on the Boers started a guerrilla campaign which caused immeasurable problems for the British. The answer was the development of concentration camps in 1901 which forced Boers to live in sheds within compounds, a concept taken to further terrible extremes 40 years later by the Nazis. Over 200,000 Boers and black African men, women and children were forced into the camps as their farms were burned to starve out the guerrillas hiding in the landscape. Thousands died of disease and starvation, while thousands more were sent into exile. By 1902 the Boers could no longer fight and so signed the Treaty of Vereeniging, effectively signing over their lands to the British Empire.

THE FACTORY SYSTEM

THROUGHOUT THE eighteenth and nineteenth centuries Britain was transformed from a predominantly agricultural society into a manufacturing one, during a period that has become known as the Industrial Revolution. Rapid scientific, technological and commercial innovations, a rising population, improved transportation and expanding markets combined to provide the context for this development. During the early/mid nineteenth century British-manufactured goods dominated world trade, being produced more efficiently and competitively than anywhere else. In some industries, most notably textiles, massive changes took place in technology and production methods that led to dramatic productivity growth.

New and faster steam engines were more economically operated within factories employing large workforces, replacing the old cottage industries. New methods of labour organisation were employed, heralding the division of labour and new relationships between employer and employee. As Adam Smith, the Scottish economist and philosopher, said, a single worker 'could scarce, perhaps with his utmost industry, make one pin in a day, and certainly could not make 20'. These new methods enabled a pin factory to turn out as many as 4800 pins a day. In addition, transport systems were revolutionised by canals, railways and better roads, enabling the manufactured goods to be moved to their markets quickly and cheaply.

The textile industry was the first to be transformed by these new technologies. Innovations such as the 'Flying Shuttle', the 'Spinning Jenny' and the 'Spinning Mule' meant that by the beginning of Victoria's reign in 1837, factories were preparing raw cotton, spinning it into yarn and weaving finished cloth. By the early 1850s, almost all the weavers had been brought into the factories and 20 years later, only a handful of handlooms still operated. The textile factory system was complete and had successfully cornered the world market in cloth production.

New processes of iron manufacturing led to expanded steel production and the development of electrical and internal combustion engines improved the transmission of power. In most industries these technological innovations reduced human skill requirements and greatly increased per capita production within factories, as opposed to the older workshops.

These changes made possible the mass production of goods available at affordable prices to millions of ordinary people who had not been able to buy them before, but at a cost. It also led to political changes as wealth moved away from the landed aristocracy and towards the new manufacturing middle classes. There were massive social changes brought about by internal migration, a rising population, and the growth of factory towns (see page 293). Mills, factories and workshops were constructed within these expanding towns and terraces of cheap housing were put up for the workers and their families.

This in turn created slum conditions with the attendant health problems and increased mortality, which was only counteracted by the flood of people from the countryside to the towns. Manchester, the first city of the Industrial Revolution, experienced this type of phenomenal growth – its population of 89,000 in 1801 grew to more than half a million by 1891. It was the advances in technology that made the Industrial Revolution possible, and thus transformed the social and economic life of Britain for ever.

15 MODERN

IT IS PERHAPS a sad reflection of one of the key elements of the modern era that most of the sites Time Team has excavated from this modern period have been related to war. This is obviously a reflection of our archaeological focus, but the planes we have excavated involve the combination of high technology, advanced science and production line skills, allied to the cause of warfare, that many people think of as the distinctive characteristic of our time. Two of the planes can be regarded as almost iconic representations of the twentieth century's ongoing relationship with warfare.

In 2000 we excavated a Spitfire that had been shot down in France in May 1940. The Battle of Britain, which can probably join the list of battles which secured the country, was fought with planes like these, piloted by heroic men and reliant on

technology made by companies whose names are still familiar to us today, like Dunlop and Rolls-Royce. At a time when British forces were being evacuated from Dunkirk, planes were sent from Britain to attack the advancing German tanks. At the end of the dig, with the Spitfire exposed, one of the few remaining flying planes flew overhead to honour just one of the over 1500 pilots who had given their lives.

Both Mick and Phil were keen to stress that our excavations on modern sites have followed the same route as our work on the more distant past. We still carefully dig down layer by layer and attempt to work out the sequence of events from the stratigraphy.

At Reedham Marshes in Norfolk, where Time Team excavated in 1999, we were looking for the remains of a B17. This was one of the most

advanced aircraft of its time and the wartime development of the plane by Boeing led to advances in aircraft design that would create the passenger airlines of today. The B17 represented the relationship with America that has become such an important alliance in our modern history. It is a sobering thought that the B17 that we excavated at Reedham would be one of the forerunners of the plane that dropped the atomic bomb on Hiroshima, a bomb that partly came into being through the work of British scientists.

Over 50,000 American pilots and aircrew died or were missing in action during the war, with over 1000 aeroplanes coming out of the Boeing factories being involved in the conflicts. Factories were a key element of the battle for victory and one of the main targets for the bombers who

flew into Germany. The production lines of the industrial revolution, that had led the way to mass production, were now in their twentieth-century form, producing engines, ball bearings and munitions in vast amounts. America's ability to keep supplying Britain with the essentials of a war-time economy was critical to Britain's survival.

The Second World War also saw the arrival of what could be called the first computer, a new breed of machines that could be the defining discovery of the future.

For those of us working on the Time Team programmes, the modern world represents some strange paradoxes, but from the archaeological perspective it has some distinctive qualities. There is an exponential expansion of consumer objects, many of which are made of material that does not rot – plastic. Despite this massive increase in possessions, in general we still go into our graves in a Christian fashion with no grave-goods. The records of our events are copious and in their digital form will create a vast, if potentially vulnerable archive for the future. The modern world's ability to replicate means that information can be stored several thousand times over in a digital form, but much of that evidence lacks the tactile quality of the majority of the archaeological records.

Our monuments and buildings have become less substantial in general – an Englishman's home is no longer his castle but his semi, and when you look at the photo on page 297 with the 'Gherkin' building in the background and the Tower of London in the foreground, it is somehow pleasing to think that the Norman structure is still likely to outlast its modern neighbour. Like castles, we no longer construct cathedrals and the work of Henry VIII at the dissolution has been followed to an extent by a modern intellectual dissolution from religion itself.

What will the archaeologists of the future be excavating, or will they cease to have a job and be replaced by digital researchers in the archives, virtual reality? Where will we look to tell the story of our time in a form that cannot be re-written for political purpose or 'spun' for some future expedient? Well, it's nice to be around at a time when the story of our period, from, say, the Palaeolithic Elvedon hand axes to the Wierre Effroy Spitfire, poses plenty of questions that can only be uncovered by archaeology and many of these concern the basic nature of ourselves as human beings that was created in a period vastly longer than our current historical blink of an eye!

In terms of the artefactual evidence we are now a multi-cultural country, importing goods from all over the world. Evidence in the trenches of the future would be from a bewildering number of sources.

It was an interesting moment in Soho in Birmingham when we were showing the archaeology to local West Indians and Indians who were British born, the children and grandchildren of people who had come from countries that had received floods of exports from Birmingham factories and had been part of the Empire that had now all but disappeared.

We will also be unlikely to excavate quite so many factories as in the past – Britain has completed the process of de-industrialisation. The car factories and other production lines have become less visible in the landscape.

One of the fascinating changes that has taken place in recent times has been an appreciation of archaeology from the more recent past. Archaeological features from the First and Second World Wars, including those related to the defence of Britain such as bunkers, radar sites and other structures, have now attracted the attention of archaeologists. There has been a realisation as well that some of the archaeology from the post-1900 industrial areas may be under greater threat than the more ancient monuments. In general this has contributed to an appreciation that archaeology can look at the most recent past and that an awareness that some of our most familiar objects and buildings may leave very little evidence for the future. Given a choice between the 'Gherkin' and the Tower of London, which do you think is most likely to survive into the future?

Previous spread: *The Swiss Re Tower, otherwise known as the 'Gherkin', pokes its nose out from behind the more ancient Tower of London in the foreground.*

Right: *The Time Team excavation site of a Spitfire shot down in 1940 is overflown by one of the few Spitfires still flying.*

THE MODERN AGE IN DETAIL

ARE WE STILL modern? Many intellectuals think not, believing that at some point in the recent past the human race moved into a new age, so different from the preceding parts of the twentieth century that another descriptive term, such as 'post-modern', is needed to describe it. They seem unable, however, to agree on just when that new age began, or exactly of what it consists.

This being so, it seems wisest to regard ourselves as still being in a modern period which began, for the British, with the death of Victoria, but which has indeed changed its nature in important respects during the past couple of decades.

The twentieth century at war

The clearest defining characteristic of modernity has been the pace and impact of technological change, and the most terrifying aspect of that has been its application to warfare, first in the form of barbed wire, machine guns, tanks and planes, and then as nuclear weapons. The first development resulted in European states triggering the two largest wars in world history (1914–18 and 1939–45), and the second in the long Cold War between the Warsaw Pact and North Atlantic alliances (1948–89), with its constant threat of mutual annihilation by atomic warheads.

Britain has suffered from all three, sustaining its greatest ever loss of men to foreign enemies in the First World War, and having many of its cities bombed into ruins in the Second World War, while it remained a prime target for the nuclear warheads kept ready all through the Cold War.

Nonetheless, compared to the rest of Europe it escaped lightly. Between 1914 and 1968 most of the other nations in Europe experienced devastating invasions by foreign enemies, bloody revolutions and civil wars, and rule by repressive regimes that executed or starved large numbers

of their own subjects. Britain evaded all of these horrors, for three reasons: its own accumulated military and economic strength, its geographical position as an island guarded by a powerful navy, and its long-established friendship with the rising superpower of the United States, which came to its rescue in both world wars and supported it all through the Cold War.

The end of the Empire

Britain still, however, paid a heavy price. Its Victorian strength had been accumulated because of the absence of war in Europe, and, once that peace ended, was rapidly bled away. The Suez crisis of 1956 proved that it was no longer able even to punish a weak Middle Eastern state that had seized control of one of its main naval highways, unless America gave permission. In view of this change, it is remarkable how rapidly, and successfully, it adapted. In both world wars it continued to fight, and emerged eventually on the winning side, when at times defeat seemed inevitable.

Between 1947 and 1968 Britain gave independence to almost all of its colonial empire – the largest that the world had ever known – with the minimum of violence and disruption. This great achievement was marred by the fact that the worst and most protracted violence happened right next door, in Ireland. In 1922, after a hundred years of agitation for independence, the island was divided between a mostly Catholic free state and six counties in the north-eastern corner that remained mostly Protestant. This compromise broke down in 1969, ushering in decades of civil war and repression in the British province which are only now apparently coming to an end.

In the later twentieth century Britain's economy gradually moved from dependence on heavy industry to a range of light manufacturing and service industries based on smaller and more flexible units. From 1971 onward it moved into an ever closer association with other European states, first in a common market and then in a limited constitutional union, while maintaining its role as the closest ally of the United States. As a result, although long fallen from its position as the world's greatest power, it remains one of the four strongest military states on the planet and one of the eight richest countries. Along with the USA (and controversially), it is currently one of the two nations most active in the policing of the world.

Benefits of the modern age

Because of its wealth, Britain has also been able to reap most of the positive rewards of modern technology, which means that in the course of the twentieth century its inhabitants achieved collectively a comfort and prosperity of living hitherto possible only to aristocrats. Food is available in an unprecedented quantity, variety and state of cleanliness.

Many traditional diseases have been brought under control or almost eradicated, epidemics have ceased to devastate entire communities, and parents no longer expect to lose at least some of their children to sickness. The British invention of antibiotics, in particular, has greatly reduced the danger from bacteria. Homes are warmer, cleaner and more solidly built than

ever before. The ordinary people of Britain now live on average for 20 more years than they did at the beginning of the twentieth century, reach puberty four years earlier, and have three times as much leisure. Improvements in contraception make reliable family planning possible. The provision of old-age pensions, unemployment benefit and state-funded medicine have combined to add to the security and comfort of each part of the life cycle.

Modernity is also characterised by speed, mobility and communication, and the successive inventions of motor vehicles, aircraft, the telephone, the typewriter, the photocopier, the radio, cinema, television and the new, microchip-based computer technology have tremendously expanded the horizons of ordinary people and their knowledge of the world. This has combined with the end of mass warfare in Europe and the new health and security of lifestyle to allow an unprecedented freedom to individual people to choose their own identities and form their own attitudes, unregulated by the influence of family and community.

This achievement of a virtually free market in lifestyle as well as in the economy is the latest aspect of modernism, which some think heralds a new age altogether. Shadows still hang over it: the loss of the old-style bonds of family, locality and community brings insecurity as well as liberation, and technology now threatens mass destruction through pollution and climate change as well as nuclear war.

On a day-to-day basis, however, the British have currently achieved a material comfort and prosperity, and an individual freedom of action and belief, of which their ancestors could only dream, equivalent to that of the fairy folk or gods of old mythologies.

Modern Chronology

This timeline gives you a quick, at-a-glance guide to what happened when in Britain in the Modern era, helping you to understand the order of events. We've also included, in purple type, some key events that happened elsewhere in the world.

Britain	Year	World
Parliament Act curtails power of House of Lords and establishes five-yearly elections	**1911**	
Titanic sinks	**1912**	
First World War (see page 306)	**1914–1918**	
World event: Russian Revolution	1917	
Treaty of Versailles establishes peace in Europe	**1919**	
General Strike (see page 307)	**1926**	
World event: US stock market crash/Great Depression	1929	
Second World War (see page 308)	**1939–1945**	
World event: Hiroshima bomb dropped	1945	
Decline of Empire – Indian Independence (see page 310)	**1945–1950**	
Post-war Labour government welfare state	**1946**	
NATO founded	**1949**	
Immigration and the multi-cultural society (see page 314)	**c1950**	
Popular culture and broadcast communications (see page 312)	**1960s**	
Britain enters European Common Market	**1973**	
Terrorist attacks on New York	**2001**	
Queen Elizabeth II's Golden Jubilee	**2002**	

World event: Russian Revolution

The Russian Revolution involved two main episodes. The first took place in February 1917 and ended the 300-year rule of the Romanov dynasty. The second occurred in October 1917 and established communism and the formation of the Union of Soviet Socialist Republics. The February Revolution was a result of tsarist repression, food and fuel shortages, and the ineptitude of the Russian First World War campaign. Riots in St Petersburg led to the abdication of Tsar Nicholas II and a provisional, ineffective government was formed. Events took a new turn when Lenin returned from exile (caused by the failed 1905 revolution) as head of the Bolsheviks. The October Revolution saw the Bolsheviks effect a coup on 25–26 October 1917. Lenin announced an immediate cessation to their involvement in the war and pledged that land be returned to the peasantry. Workers were given control of factories, banks were nationalised and a secret police force (Cheka) was formed. However, Communist control was not completed until after the 1918–22 Russian civil war when Trotsky's Red Army defeated the tsarist White Army.

World event: Hiroshima bomb dropped

Although the Second World War in Europe ended with the Allies' defeat of Nazi Germany in May 1945, hostilities against Japan continued until one of the most devastating events in military and world history in August 1945. Japanese resistance crumbled when the Americans dropped an atomic bomb on Hiroshima (6 August) and on Nagasaki (9 August). Research into nuclear weaponry began in the UK in 1940 but was handed to the USA after they entered the war in 1941. The American physicist J. Robert Oppenheimer oversaw the 'Manhattan Project' in New Mexico, which effectively changed the world. Following a successful test explosion, the go-ahead was given to drop atomic bombs on Japan. In 1945, Hiroshima was the seventh largest city in Japan but became a scene of devastation. Over four square miles were completely annihilated with further heavy damage outside the blast area. Over 78,000 people died on the day, but by 1995 the death toll was estimated to be around 192,000 due to radiation-induced illness. The bombings inaugurated the 'nuclear age' and instilled a concern of nuclear warfare in the global public psyche.

THE SPITFIRE PROPELLER

AN AIRCRAFT PROPELLER consists of two or more blades connected together by a hub, which attaches the blades to the engine shaft. These are made in the shape of an aerofoil, like the wing of an aircraft. When the engine rotates the propeller blades, they produce thrust and lift, which moves the aircraft forward. While the propeller is rotating in flight, each section of the blade has a motion that combines the forward motion of the aircraft with circular movement of the propeller. The slower the speed, the steeper the angle of attack of the propeller edge must be to generate lift. Therefore, the shape of the propeller's cross section must change from the centre to the tips. This results in the characteristic twisting shape of the propeller.

The Vickers Armstrong Supermarine Spitfire, which during the Battle of Britain in 1940 became the symbol of Britain's defiance against Germany, was first introduced by the RAF in 1938. The Mk I Spitfire had a Watts wooden fixed-pitch two-blade propeller, a Rolls-Royce Merlin engine and a top speed of 583kph (362mph). Later a De Havilland three-blade, two-position metal propeller was adopted after trials on the first prototype. This could have its pitch changed from one position to another angle by the pilot while in flight. The new propeller provided a 8kph (5mph) increase in speed. In 1940 a De Havilland three-blade constant-speed metal propeller was introduced. It is termed constant-speed because, during operation, the propeller would automatically change its blade angle to maintain a constant engine speed.

As the war progressed, urgent solutions were sought to increase the speed/altitude performance of the Spitfire, which was inferior to that of the German Messerschmitt Bf 109 and the Focke Wulf 190s. This called for two principal modifications to aircraft – the introduction of a pressurised cabin and the use of an engine suitably rated for higher altitude. The Spitfire Mk VI was introduced in 1942 and was fitted with a Rolls-Royce Merlin 47 engine using a four-blade Rotol propeller. The propeller of the Spitfire evolved from four to five blades in 1944 with the introduction of the Mk XIV, which came with a new Rolls-Royce Griffon engine and a top speed of 448mph. By the end of the war the Mk 22 or Seafire had a six–blade contra-rotating propeller and a speed of 726kph (451mph), making it one of the fastest fighters of the Second World War.

Above: *Propeller and nose cone of a Supermarine Spitfire, one of the most beautiful and deadly aircraft created and soon adopted by the British people as an icon of the Second World War.*

THE NORMANDY LANDINGS

This drawing is based on the work we did when filming a Time Team special on the Normandy Landings. Many of the troops we were investigating were members of the Dorset regiment and, unknown to them, they faced formidable concrete and steel fortifications, some of which included 88mm guns. The fortifications and the hidden bunkers turned the whole area of the beach into a killing zone. Once the soldiers had managed to get off the beach, they faced fire from the machine guns in the bunkers, and it was one of these bunkers that we were able to excavate. We were all surprised by the depth and relative sophistication of the structures that were involved.

The Dorsets landed on Gold Beach at around 7.25am on 6 June 1944. It is likely that the attack at some stage was supported by Spitfires, one of which is shown here. The markings are taken from the records of those planes which flew in support of the landings. As well as the British troops here, elsewhere on the Normandy coastline American and Canadian forces were facing similar problems. One of the strongest memories Time Team had of these excavations was the large numbers of spent shells from standard issue British weapons found around German gun positions. These indicated the desperate close-quarters fighting that had gone on to secure these areas.

The First World War

AS AN ASSASSIN'S shots rang out on 28 June 1914, cutting down the Austrian Archduke Franz Ferdinand and his wife on a state visit to the recently annexed Bosnian town of Sarajevo, nobody understood that one of the most sickening and costly conflicts of our time was about to start. With the egos of powerful European imperial powers already precariously balanced, what began as a minor news story became the catalyst for a war that was to involve the world; a war of such violence and despair that a generation was consumed with a death toll of astronomical proportions.

As Austria declared war on Serbia in what they considered a local affair, the Russians came to the aid of their Slav cousins. On 1 August Austria's German allies (known as the central powers) declared war on Russia and in return Russia's ally France took up arms. The Germans quickly declared war on France on 3 August. The next day, Germany invaded Belgium with its sweeping Schlieffen Plan, designed to reach the coast and then turn left and drive through northern France. With no reply from Britain's demands that Germany withdraw, we declared war on Germany the same day.

What started out as a mobile war found opposing forces grinding to a halt as they met at the Battle of the Marne. As each tried to leapfrog and outflank the other, a frontline became established from the English Channel to the Swiss border. With nowhere to go, the armies dug in and the horrific reality of trench warfare came of age. The next four years witnessed a practical stalemate and the front became the cauldron that consumed millions of lives. The battle conditions and statistics of the First World War are almost impossible to fathom. As millions volunteered to go to the front with a patriotic fever and the innocence of those who have never been under fire, the massed artillery and machine guns devoured them as quickly as they arrived. The 1915 winter campaign in Verdun cost the lives of 500,000 French casualties alone, while in just one day in the 1916 Battle of the Somme, British forces suffered 60,000 casualties – as many as would fill the Millennium Stadium in Cardiff today.

The First World War ended at 11 o'clock on the 11 November 1918 (the eleventh hour of the eleventh day of the eleventh month – Remembrance Day) after a series of events, including American engagement, the Russian Revolution, and the invention of the tank, altered the deadlocked status of the war and defeated the central powers. The sorry legacy of this 'war to end all wars' lies with the combined death toll of a lost generation. In four years over 25 million men were killed or wounded.

Left: A shell-filling factory in the First World War. Millions of shells were fired during a war where static artillery ruled the stagnant trench lines.

The General Strike

IN MANY WAYS the First World War led to the General Strike in May 1926. Following the war, the embedded forelock-tugging subservience of the working classes towards their middle-class managers and the aristocracy, so heavily instilled since Victorian times, was vividly called into question. The end of the war also allowed thousands of tons of free German coal to be exploited as the fallen German Empire was milked by the victors. The result was an environment where workers became stronger and united under a combination of trade unions (the Trades Union Congress), while businesses struggled to compete in a chaotic market pushed off balance by external influences.

In an effort to keep profits alive, the mine owners decided to increase the hours miners worked by an hour a day, while at the same time cutting their wages. The workers now used their powerful union as a voice and stood their ground. Sensing trouble, the Conservative government stepped in and subsidised the mines to enable a status quo to continue. However, although the unions gained confidence from their victory, a line had been crossed and both sides knew that the situation could not continue.

The Government set up a commission under Sir Herbert Samuel which recommended that the mining industry should be restructured to make it more efficient, yet stopped short of the union's hopes of nationalisation. With the commission's backing, the mine owners once again pushed for their demands and so the union played its trump card – a general strike would be called where not only the miners, but other unionised trades such as steel workers, printers and transport workers would all down tools and walk out in sympathy with their 'brothers'.

Using the militant elements of the trade union movement to their advantage, the Government launched a widespread publicity campaign warning the population about the rise of socialism, at the same time calling in the army to run essential services. After ten days, which saw the country slowly grind to a halt, and the families of workers who lived a hand-to-mouth existence going hungry, the TUC was drawn into negotiations with the Government. They agreed to end the strike but

Above: *A scene from the streets of Crewe where workers demonstrated in favour of the General Strike in 1926.*

a split occurred when their terms were rejected by the Miners' Federation (the miners' own union). Though many services returned to work after their display of union power, many miners continued to strike until long after the ten days. On reflection, the strike was a disaster; the workers ultimately lost and the miners had to accept poorer terms. It illustrated that the working class now had some teeth and that social attitudes had changed, but it also showed that the Government would not fold under people-power and that no revolution, real or imagined, was going to take place in Britain.

The Second World War

THE SECOND WORLD War has been described as the largest event in world history. It resulted in the conservatively estimated loss of over 50 million lives and drew almost every continent into conflict. The reasons for the war are varied but can be traced back to the end of the First World War (1914–18), which ended with an armistice, not a surrender. Though Germany lost the war, many of the soldiers who returned home felt they had been betrayed by the high command and politicians who had folded to the allied pressure.

Above: December 1940, a dark hour for Britain as this ghostly image encapsulates so well. The dome of St Paul's Cathedral reaches out from a mass of smoke and fire.

As Germany was bankrupted and pulled apart by the victors, a small group of extreme right-wing national socialists, the Nazis, gained popularity and through a carefully planned propaganda campaign slowly gained power under the leadership of one of those returning soldiers, Adolf Hitler.

Hitler's driven campaigning was set at one ultimate goal – the recreation and expansion of the German Empire, or the building of a Third Reich, at any cost. The Versailles Treaty, signed after the First World War, forbade Germany raising any army over 100,000 strong, but secretly the Nazis built a new military force. New mechanised units would race into battle with the support of aircraft, in far-reaching penetrations of enemy lines known as Blitzkrieg. After annexing states in eastern Europe, the West became distinctly worried about the surprise possibility of a new war. Then on 1 September 1939 Germany invaded Poland.

A moment in time: the Battle of Britain

With an Anglo-French treaty to protect Poland's interests, Britain declared war on Germany on the 3 September. As Russia started actions to claim parts of eastern Europe, Hitler turned his war machine west and quickly invaded Denmark and Norway (April 1940), Holland and Belgium (both in May), and completed a lightning conquest of France by June. With Germany holding pacts with Spain and Italy, Britain stood alone in western Europe against this new German army which appeared unstoppable.

With his extraordinary delusions of racial purity, Hitler didn't perceive the Anglo-Saxon British as his enemy, yet preparations were made (Operation Sealion) to invade a defiant United Kingdom, and in the summer of 1940 the Battle of Britain was set to be fought. The opening phases of the German invasion plan were dedicated to gaining air superiority. This decisive factor was fortunate for Britain, as much of our professional land army was in disarray after unsuccessful fighting in France, ending in the retreat from Dunkirk. The defence of Britain would rest almost solely on the shoulders of the Royal Air Force, and the summer and autumn of 1940 would become the defining moment for action.

In early July the German Luftwaffe started to attack British shipping convoys in the Channel with their screaming JU87 Stuka bombers backed up by Messerschmitt fighters. As the RAF sent up their Spitfire and Hurricane fighters to intercept, the steady war of attrition began. Up against what appeared to be a limitless Luftwaffe, every single aircraft of the RAF fighter wings was absolutely vital. Losses in aircraft mounted every day as dogfights filled the skies of southern and eastern Britain, leaving tangles of vapour trails in the summer sky, while bombers also attacked airfields destroying aircraft on the ground. August witnessed the change from convoy and airfield targets to include the early-warning radar stations and it's at this point that we reached our darkest hour.

With fighters running almost continuously and training squadrons forced into early action, pilots were drawn from exiles and all over the Commonwealth. By the beginning of September we were on our last reserves and facing defeat. However, following the actions of Britain's Bomber Command, who bombed Berlin in late August, the Germans switched targets to the bombing of cities. This gave the RAF and their long-suffering airfields vital breathing space as they were about to take their last gasp. The 'Blitz' may well have begun, but the RAF had held out for long enough to survive and for Hitler to put Operation Sealion on permanent hold, his thoughts now lying elsewhere in the planning of his fateful invasion of Russia.

The archaeological and historical story

With an event as colossal as the Second World War, it's hard to choose a particular moment in time, but the Battle of Britain stands as a milestone; when we stood alone at the edge of the abyss and fought for our very soil. Other events of the war which particularly stand out for Britain are numerous – D-Day, North Africa, Monte Cassino and Market Garden among others, but they would be another book in themselves.

The Second World War ultimately ended in September 1945 after the atomic bombs were dropped on the Far Eastern cities of Hiroshima and Nagasaki, nearly four months after the end of war in Europe. A titanic battle had been fought across the world which destroyed millions of lives, yet also led to a surge in invention and in many ways shaped much of the modern world that we know today. The remains of this conflict can still be seen today in the museums, lives and landscapes of people and cities around the globe.

PALAEOLITHIC

MESOLITHIC

NEOLITHIC

BRONZE AGE

IRON AGE

ROMAN

ANGLO-SAXON

VIKING

NORMAN

MIDDLE AGES

TUDOR

STUART

GEORGIAN

VICTORIAN

MODERN 1901–present

Second World War 1939–1945

The Decline of the Empire

AT THE PINNACLE of its powers, the British Empire was the largest and most dominant global force in history. It influenced the culture and economics of countries far removed from the British Isles. The vast scale of the British Empire cannot be understated. It covered approximately 33 per cent of the world's surface, which is roughly 15 million square miles. The Empire matured and expanded at a phenomenal rate, but it would have been far bigger had it not been for the success of the American colonies in winning their independence.

Historically, the traditional height of the British Empire consisted of over 80 territories throughout Africa, the Americas and Atlantic, Antarctica, Asia, Europe and the Pacific. By 1921 the Empire governed a population of around 470–570 million people, which was about a quarter of the world's population. Interestingly, the success of the Empire became the notable envy of Adolf Hitler, who used his own insidious methods to create an empire in his own vision.

But how did such a small country like Britain become the ruler of so much territory? Britain was a very powerful country in its own right, boasting great wealth together with superior military might that was utilised to defeat any opponent and conquer territories. The Empire relied on the local populace of their territories to ensure that the complex network of people and nations remained linked via trade and political systems, although force was necessary on occasion to keep order.

There is no easy answer as to why the Empire declined. British territorial dominance brought innovations in areas such as medicine, education and transport to many countries but for many, the Empire symbolised loss of land, prejudice and inequality. If the symbolic beginning of the Empire was the colonisation of Newfoundland in 1497,

Above: *President Jomo Kenyatta inspects a Kenyan Guard of Honour in 1963, the year of Kenya's independence from the British Empire.*

then its end would be marked by the handover of Hong Kong to China in 1997. The Empire lasted over 500 years and, in this context, its decline was sudden and rapid. The years after the First World War witnessed the final expansion of the British Empire but the impact of the Second World War left Britain in a weakened state. The heavy cost of the war effort and its aftermath undermined the capacity for Britain to maintain its vast Empire.

De-colonisation by a series of territories was a regular occurrence over the remaining twentieth century. The rise of nationalistic fervour and a desire for independence became commonplace throughout the Empire's colonies but almost all former British colonies joined the Commonwealth of Nations, which replaced the notion of an 'empire'. Once described as 'the Empire on which the sun never sets' the handing over of the only remaining significant colony of Hong Kong in 1997 consigned the British Empire to history.

Welfare State

MOST OF OUR events through time are connected with remarkable discoveries, fascinating characters or filled with drama, yet one of the more recent important moments in time is connected with the world of politics and the changing social values of our society. During the Second World War we witnessed the Conservative government of Neville Chamberlain, which then changed into a coalition war government under Winston Churchill. Chamberlain resigned after a vote of no confidence following his unfortunate handling of foreign policy as the Nazis came to power in Germany. The multi-party government proved successful in the war years and, as ministers looked into how we could restructure our society ready for a new and better world, many liberal attitudes came to the fore.

A special report by economist Sir William Beverage, entitled *Social Insurance and Allied Services,* was published in 1942 and this outlined some important concepts for the long-term care of the state and its population. The idea revolved around citizens paying a small subsidy for the benefit of their state – a National Insurance. The funds raised would pay for state pensions to provide security for the old, benefits to help the unemployed, and a national health service which would provide free services for the sick.

Though Churchill backed the Beverage report, the tough and unsubtle Conservative prime minister of the war didn't appear to have the more sympathetic ear of the public when compared with his Deputy Prime Minister, the Labour leader Clement Attlee. In July 1945 Attlee won a landslide election victory for Labour on the back of change and the new concepts of a welfare state. From 1945 to 1951 Attlee and his government introduced the National Insurance Act (1946) and developed the National Health Service Act (1948) which introduced maternity, sickness and unemployment benefits, free dental care, eye tests and glasses, and the free treatment of the poorly. The catchphrase of the day was that you would be looked after 'from the cradle to the grave'.

The 1970s and 80s of the Thatcher years started to cut back on the state services. The welfare state, which guaranteed a quality standard of living, was expensive to run. Today people live longer, creating a greater burden on the state, and as a modern government would say, also require more 'choice'. The fact is that the marvellous idea of the welfare state, which was once truly workable, struggles in our modern capitalist society. As more private funding is sought to cover the government's spending, we find companies and trusts running many hospitals and private dental care and ophthalmic treatment the norm. Welfare may well be in a state of flux today, but it started as a grand and brave political move which has benefited the lives of thousands.

Right: A nurse in a National Health hospital weighs a baby for a mother. In 1948 the NHS was a groundbreaking phenomenon.

Popular Culture and Communication

The broadcast culture that we now take so much for granted in the modern world has created a system of global interconnections that have revolutionised our culture. Britain is now part of a global village where films, magazines, music and other arts are shared within a short time of their creation. Our knowledge of world events is immediate and all this information is available to all members of society through relatively cheap and widely available technology.

Above: *The famous Cavern Club in Liverpool. A regular venue for the Beatles and other groundbreaking artists of the 1960s, such as Cilla Black.*

Marconi had been a pioneer in long-distance wireless telegraphy, a forerunner of all the communications systems that would enable the exchange of information worldwide. His first signals crossed the Atlantic from Cornwall to Newfoundland in 1901. The British science fiction writer, Arthur C Clarke, writing in 1945, had first raised the idea that satellites could be used to send messages and with the successful launching of *Sputnik 1* in 1957, the necessary technology and the first communication became available using Telstar took place in 1962.

John Logie Baird, a Scotsman, is credited with the first invention that led to television and in using Baird's system the BBC began broadcasting prior to the Second World War, but it wasn't until the post-war period that broadcast television reached mass audiences.

Television became the main way of communicating popular entertainment and with the growth of independent television beginning in 1955, and colour television being launched in the 1970s, by the last quarter of the twentieth century 95 per cent of homes in Britain had a TV set. Radio expanded in the 1960s to provide a medium for popular music. The birth of Radio 1, and the rise of the DJ, or 'Disc Jockey', provided for a new generation who had cast off the austerity of post-war years, and in music found a voice for a new outlook.

Popular music

Young people chose to follow the likes of the Beatles, Rolling Stones, Hendrix and Dylan with their groundbreaking music. Scores of youths chose the path of the 'Rocker' or the 'Mod' (a new generation fighting on the beaches), or became involved in the peace-loving hippie movement. Women found new freedoms with the advent of convenient birth control and a changing perspective saw new liberal attitudes being pursued by women in the workplace and at home. The media-driven pop culture stylisation adorned everything from logos on canned beverages and magazine layouts to home decor and clothing. Fuelled by Britain's fervent youth, many elements of the culture, emphasised by a 'swinging' London, would raise many aspects to an iconic status, such as the Union Jack-decorated Mini car still sold today.

As the youth matured and produced their own offspring, the 1970s moved into an interesting era of progressive rock music and sugary pop. The fun-loving disco scene was in stark contrast to the anarchy of punk rock, but the impact of these movements encouraged those untrained in musical arts to create new kinds of music. The development of electronic music gave rise to movements such as new wave, new romantics and the gothic scene.

The 1980s saw pop culture become commercialised into a massive money-spinning industry, whilst the import of American pop culture in the 90s has brought with it a vibrant music scene, extreme sports and American sports clothing. The movement of popular culture, instigated by mass media and marketing campaigns, has provided generations with their own unique identities mostly emphasised by adolescents and the twenty- and thirty-somethings. The global village of our world provides access to a wealth of diverse cultural phenomena that makes your youth and the age you live in a unique experience.

Global broadcasting

With the birth of the World Wide Web (an invention developed by an English academic, Sir Tim Berners-Lee), the global communications industry joined to satellite broadcasting. With the advent of 24-hour news channels like CNN this has combined to create a world in which, for better or worse, a Western perspective and the English language is dominant. This may alter with the growing strength of the Far East and China, but the broadcast systems that developed in post-war Britain and America have become one of the defining technologies of the modern world.

PALAEOLITHIC

MESOLITHIC

NEOLITHIC

BRONZE AGE

IRON AGE

ROMAN

ANGLO-SAXON

VIKING

NORMAN

MIDDLE AGES

TUDOR

STUART

GEORGIAN

VICTORIAN

MODERN 1901–present

Popular Culture and Communication 1950s

Immigration

IMMIGRATION IS NO new phenomenon to Britain. The Iron Age witnessed migrations of Celtic peoples from northern Europe, the Romans brought Syrian soldiers, Saxons from Germany and Vikings from Scandinavia followed, and the Normans brought their own Gallic influence. By the eleventh century our 'Britishness' was already a concoction of influences gained from over 1000 years of foreign settlers. The sixteenth century saw small numbers of the first Africans arriving in Britain and the seventeenth century heralded large-scale Jewish settlement, yet it was eighteenth-century slave trade which led to the biggest influx of African peoples. Expansion of the Empire at this time also witnessed the first Chinese immigrants, while the abolition of the slave trade in 1833 brought some freedom for those who lived within its borders.

Though racial tensions continued to exist, the Empire drew on its colonial 'resources' during the First World War. Over a million Indian soldiers were drafted into service and their fighting prowess has only recently been given full credit. The Second World War found even more Commonwealth countries fighting for Britain. After the war, opportunities arose for workers in Britain and a gradual influx of Commonwealth immigrants, many of whom had served the Empire in its forces, settled in the UK. Many were attracted by the expectation of better employment prospects and living conditions in the 'Mother Country'.

The new arrivals received a cautious welcome in bombed-out post-war Britain and, with housing at a premium, immigrants found themselves facing growing resentment. Having been invited to Britain and then treated with disdain, the increasing tension eventually exploded into periodic violence. Recent examples include a race riot which erupted during the 1958 Notting Hill Carnival, whilst Enoch Powell's infamous 'rivers of blood' speech ignited further schism during the 1960s. It wasn't until the Race Relations Act in the 1970s that the government dealt with the issue in earnest and it is clear that elements of British society still harbour racist attitudes.

Subsequent generations of British-born ethnic minorities struggled for racial equality in a society itself struggling to come to terms with its own multi-cultural development. Thirty years on and black, eastern and Asian cultures have become well grounded as integral parts of British society, yet immigration remains a highly topical issue. Today over 100,000 foreign nationals settle in Britain each year, and asylum seekers are rarely out of the popular press, yet our ever-evolving rich culture has been indisputably influenced by immigration for over 2000 years.

Right: On the steps of the Empire Windrush, *a vessel which brought many immigrants to Britain, these Jamaican boxers, accompanied by their manager, are hoping for a new life.*

THE DEVELOPMENT OF FLIGHT

ON 17 DECEMBER 1903 Orville and Wilbur Wright's 'Flyer' took its first flight covering a distance of 35m (120ft) and, later the same day, 263m (862ft). Man was airborne in a powered heavier-than-air machine for the very first time. By the end of 1908 Wilbur Wright had made a flight lasting 2 hours 20 minutes, during which time he covered a distance of 124km (77 miles), setting a world record. On 25 July 1909 Frenchman Louis Bleriot landed a monoplane close to Dover Castle, having just completed the first crossing of the English Channel by a heavier-than-air machine, taking 37 minutes to make the journey.

The First World War accelerated the development of aeroplanes and engines. Skirmishes between observation aircraft using rifles eventually led to the development of more sophisticated gun technology and fighter planes were created and bombing was adopted to a limited extent. After the war, in 1919, a converted Vickers Vimy bomber, flown by Alcock and Brown, made the first non-stop crossing of the Atlantic. This encouraged the design of larger twin-engined aircraft, which provided the basis for the first post-war airliners.

The Schneider Trophy, introduced in 1912, led to a series of ever faster and sleeker monoplane designs culminating in the Supermarine S.6B, the forerunner of the Spitfire. Aircraft went from being constructed mainly from wood and canvas to being almost entirely made of aluminium. Engine development moved from in-line water-cooled petrol engines to rotary air-cooled engines, with an appreciable increase in power.

In the 1930s the USA made great strides in airliner development as fast, all-metal monoplanes were developed by several manufacturers. Significant advances included the development of wing flaps, variable pitch propellers and retractable undercarriages.

In 1939, war again accelerated technological advance in aircraft in not only their size and range but also in engines, their power and efficiency. The most important development towards the end of the war was the jet engine. In June 1944 Germany launched pilotless, explosive-carrying jet planes against Britain, the V-1, or 'Doodle Bug' and later the V-2 rocket. The first British jet fighter, the Gloster Meteor, entered service one month later. The jet engine with its higher speeds and power-to-weight ratio was to power both military and civilian aircraft of the post-war era.

During the 1960s the British and French governments funded a joint project which produced the supersonic Concorde, introduced into service in 1976. It could fly at twice the speed of sound, but was used only by British Airways and Air France because of its high operating costs. In the USA Boeing started planning for an entirely different approach: a huge airliner with 400 seats. The resulting 747 jumbo jet was introduced in 1969, making international travel an almost commonplace experience.

In 1961, the manned space age began as the Russian, Yuri Gagarin, orbited the planet in 108 minutes. This accelerated the space race that had started in 1957 with the revolutionary launch of Sputnik 1 by the Soviet Union. The United States responded to the challenge by launching Alan Shepard into space on a sub-orbital flight in a Mercury space capsule. Both superpowers used the experience of German rocket designers captured at the end of the war to develop their space programmes. The space race ultimately led to the present pinnacle of manned flight, the landing of Neil Armstrong and Buzz Aldrin on the moon in 1969.

Author's Acknowledgements

I'd like to thank the many people who made this book possible. Francis Pryor played a crucial role writing key sections and being a source of support and intelligent analysis and, as usual, Mick Aston contributed his invaluable advice. Matthew Reynolds did much of the original work on the 'in detail' sections, and Jenni Butterworth provided an excellent editorial eye on the archaeological content as well as contributing additional material. Guy de La Bédoyère, Helen Geake, Phil Harding and Ronald Hutton were invaluable with advice and content in their core subject areas. All the writers listed on page 320 enthusiastically contributed, and without the dedication of all those individuals we would not have been able to get such a bold enterprise onto the bookshelves. Special thanks to Victor Ambrus, whose pictures have been such an inspiration to us all.

Co-ordinating the project was an essential task and Jackie Stinchcombe and Jo Pye played key roles, Jinx Newley kept a close eye on educational content and key chronology dates, and Andrew Stinchcombe provided the computer design element in producing the 'What Happened When' circle on page 2.

Finally, a big thank you to the team at Transworld – Sarah Emsley, Phil Lord, Doug Young, Gillian Haslam, Bobby Birchall and Louise Thomas – who coped with the whole process of producing a book with a group of people who were also making Time Team programmes, with professionalism and good humour!

TIM TAYLOR

Picture Credits

Text Contributors

Guy de La Bédoyère: pages 112–115, 127.

Steve Bumford: pages 16, 38, 58, 78, 98, 118, 138, 158, 178,
196, 216, 224, 238, 244, 260, 264, 268, 272, 273, 282, 302, 310.

Jenni Butterworth: pages 139, 148, 150, 164–165, 168, 169,
170, 172–175, 184, 186, 187, 188, 190–193, 204, 205, 206, 208,
209, 283.

Marcus Dahl: pages 220, 228, 229, 230, 243.

Jonathan Foyle: page 225.

Helen Geake: pages 132–135, 144, 145, 152–155.

Damian Goodburn: pages 159, 171.

Phil Harding: pages 17, 59.

Ronald Hutton: pages 236–237, 242, 248–249, 258–259, 265,
280–281, 300–301.

Ian Powlesland: pages 44, 50, 90, 125, 126, 131, 151, 179, 189,
197, 209, 231, 239, 252, 261, 275, 295, 303, 315.

Francis Pryor: pages 23, 24, 28–29, 30, 39, 45, 51, 52–55,
64–71, 72–75, 82, 83, 88, 91, 92–95, 104, 105, 106, 108, 109, 110,
111, 293.

Matthew Reynolds: pages 14–15, 20, 22, 26, 36–37, 42–43,
46–47, 48–49, 56–57, 62–63, 76–77, 79, 84–85, 86–87, 96–97,
99, 103–103, 116–117, 122–123, 128–129, 136–137, 142–143,
146–147, 156–157 162–163, 166–167, 176–177, 182–183,
200–201, 202, 203, 214–215, 222–223, 226–227, 246–247,
250–251, 266–267, 270–271, 274, 286–287, 288, 290–291, 292,
294, 306, 307, 308–309, 311, 312–313, 314.

Jackie Stinchcombe: pages 16, 38, 58, 78, 98, 118, 138, 158,
178, 196, 216, 238, 260, 282, 302.

Tim Taylor: pages 6–9, 10–13, 32–35, 52–55, 72–75, 92–95,
112–115, 119, 124, 130, 132–135, 152–155, 159, 171, 210–213,
217, 232–235, 254–257, 276–279, 296–299, 312–313.

TRANSWORLD PUBLISHERS
61–63 Uxbridge Road, London W5 5SA
A Random House Group Company
www.rbooks.co.uk

This book is published to accompany the Time
Team television series produced by Videotext
Communications in association with Picture House

The Time Team Guide to What Happened When
first published in Great Britain in 2006 by Channel 4 Books
an imprint of Transworld Publishers

This trade paperback reissue published in Great Britain
in 2010 by Channel 4 Books
an imprint of Transworld Publishers

A CIP catalogue record for this book
is available from the British Library.

ISBN 9781905026708

Addresses for Random House Group Ltd companies outside the
UK can be found at: www.randomhouse.co.uk
The Random House Group Ltd Reg. No. 954009

The Random House Group Limited supports the Forest
Stewardship Council (FSC), the leading international forest-
certification organization. All our titles that are printed on
Greenpeace-approved FSC-certified paper carry the FSC logo.
Our paper procurement policy can be found at
www.rbooks.co.uk/environment

Typeset in Minion and Frutiger
Printed by Firmengruppe APPL, aprinta druck, Wemding,
Germany

2 4 6 8 10 9 7 5 3 1

Editor: Gillian Haslam
Designer: Bobby Birchall, DW Design
Picture researcher: Louise Thomas
Illustrator: Victor Ambrus